**Social Studies
for
Children
in a
Democracy**

FOURTH EDITION

JOHN U. MICHAELIS

Professor in the School of Education, University of California, Berkeley

PRENTICE-HALL, INC., *Englewood Cliffs, New Jersey*

Social Studies
for
Children
in a
Democracy

Recent Trends and Developments

Social Studies for Children in a Democracy

Recent Trends and Developments

FOURTH EDITION John U. Michaelis

Current printing (last digit):
10 9 8 7 6 5 4 3 2

Library of Congress Catalog Card No.: 68-11342
Printed in the United States of America

PRENTICE-HALL INTERNATIONAL, INC., London
PRENTICE-HALL OF AUSTRALIA, PTY. LTD., Sydney
PRENTICE-HALL OF CANADA, LTD., Toronto
PRENTICE-HALL OF INDIA (PRIVATE) LTD., New Delhi
PRENTICE-HALL OF JAPAN, INC., Tokyo

To Elizabeth Ann Michaelis, John Barry Michaelis, and Susan Ann Michaelis

Foreword

This revised edition has been prepared to reflect significant changes that are directly related to the work of classroom teachers. New material has been included on foundations of the social studies, the structure of disciplines, methods of inquiry, valuing, cognitive processes, objectives of instruction, structure of the curriculum, teaching strategies, instructional media, basic skills, and evaluation. Several chapters have been revised to highlight principles and strategies that are essential to individual and group inquiry in the social studies. Material not directly related to the most promising new directions in the social studies and to the tasks of teachers has been eliminated to make room for new developments of greatest use in improving instruction. New visual material has been included to provide practical examples of new trends and developments.

The central theme of this book is that the social studies should be grounded in history and the social sciences. Components of structure of foundation disciplines are presented and illustrated. Related thinking skills and cognitive processes are outlined along with strategies for using them in classroom instruction. Attention is given to ways in which units of instruction and instructional media can be used to contribute to insight into concepts and methods of inquiry drawn from history and the social sciences.

The order of presentation is designed to facilitate instructional planning. Chapters 1–4 set the stage for the entire book. The first chapter includes objectives of new social studies programs, examples of behavioral objectives in the cognitive and affective domains, a summary of major trends, and characteristics of new programs, and is followed by three chapters that deal with the foundations of the social studies—social, disciplinary, and psychological. New material is presented on strategies for dealing with values, cognitive processes that underlie inquiry, and key elements in the structure of disciplines. The structure of selected disciplines is outlined in terms of concepts, concept clusters, and generalizations. Specific attention is given to models and methods of inquiry that are most useful in the social studies.

Chapters 5–7 deal with the structure of the curriculum, current affairs, and unit planning. New ways of organizing the curriculum are presented along with examples of concepts and main ideas that are used as strands in planning. The role of current affairs is reviewed and specific guidelines for teaching contemporary affairs are included. The planning of units of instruction is considered in detail in Chapter 7.

Chapters 8 and 9 deal in depth with individual and group inquiry in the social studies. Teaching strategies and specific techniques are presented and illustrated.

The next six chapters include teaching strategies and guidelines related to instructional media and basic skills that are used extensively in the social studies. Criteria for selection, steps in planning, uses of media to further inquiry, and techniques of utilization are treated in detail.

Chapter 16 includes teaching strategies and guidelines for developing expressive experiences in the social studies. The presentation includes dramatic, literary, musical, artistic, and construction activities.

The final chapter deals with principles and techniques of evaluation. Special attention is given to ways of evaluating children's learning in the social studies. Concrete examples of charts, checklists, questions, and test items are presented. Assessment of both cognitive and affective outcomes is considered, and examples of specific procedures are included.

A critical selection has been made of related readings, project materials, and teaching guides for the reader who wishes to go beyond ideas presented in the text.

Acknowledgment is made to the following individuals who contributed ideas, photographs, charts, and suggestions that have been included in this edition: Val Arnsdorf, Ruth H. Goodman, Ruth H. Grossman, Larry Hill, Robert Kresse, Susan Olson, Helen M. O'Neill, F. Edward Peacock, Ward Phillips, Haig Rushdoony, Priscilla C. Smith, Fred Wilson, and Helen Cowan Wood. Specific acknowledgment is made in the text to school systems, publishers, and others for the use of photographs, quotations, and other material.

JOHN U. MICHAELIS

Contents

Social Studies
for
Children
in a
Democracy

Definition, Objectives, Trends

The American people have shown unparalleled interest in their schools during recent years. Much of this interest has been focused on a searching examination of the curriculum. Special curriculum projects and centers for studying, developing, and disseminating new materials have been established. Local and state groups have launched programs of curriculum revision and in-service education with the assistance of Federal and foundation support. A variety of innovations and new curriculum materials are under study. Opportunities for the improvement of instruction have never been greater, nor have they been so diverse and ably supported.

A variety of current trends and new developments may be noted in social studies instruction. The most promising new directions are presented in this chapter as a background for viewing proposed changes and new developments in later chapters. The assumption is made that teachers and other school personnel should be grounded in the directions that social studies instructional planning is moving so that they can participate effectively in decision-making at the local level. Such a background is essential to the continuing evaluation and improvement of instruction which is the direct responsibility of teachers and other school personnel in communities and states throughout the nation.

Attention is first directed to definition of the social studies as an area of the curriculum. This is followed by a consideration of contributions of the social studies to primary goals of education and objectives of the social studies so that they can be used as reference points for later sections and chapters. Attention is next given to an overview of major trends in various facets of the social studies program. The final section includes a summary of characteristics of new programs of instruction which can be used to plan and assess the social studies curriculum.

Definition of the Social Studies

The social studies curriculum encompasses those aspects of history and the social sciences that are believed to be of greatest value for the general education of students in elementary and secondary schools. Primary attention is given to the study of man's social, economic, and political activities of the past, present, and emerging future in places near at hand and far away. Instruction is focused on the variety and change in human behavior in groups, and the interaction of people with their human and physical environment. Human relationships are emphasized in the study of interaction among people, between people and institutions, between people and the earth, and between people and value systems. The purposes of individuals and groups are studied along with the processes used to achieve them, problems that have emerged, material and nonmaterial products of human efforts, and prospects for the future. Man's cultural heritage and its dynamic ongoing characteristics are of central concern. Chart 1 highlights the relationships in this definition.

Educators in some schools refer to the social studies as *social science education*, as *history and the social sciences*, as *history, geography, and the social sciences*, or as *citizenship education*. A primary reason for the change is dissatisfaction with *social studies*, which has been interpreted by some individuals to mean a mish-mash of socially oriented material that lacks structure and is not rooted in basic disciplines. At the present time, however, *social studies* is used most widely throughout the country by school personnel and by scholars at work in curriculum projects. No particular pattern or organization or point of view is implied. In a curricular sense *social studies* as a title is similar to *the language arts, science education*, and *humanities education* in that each denotes a broad area of the curriculum based on several disciplines. Because *social studies* is most widely used by both scholars and school personnel, it will be used in this volume.

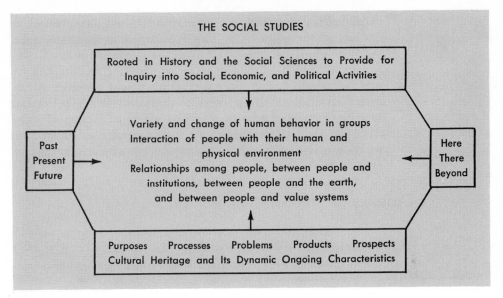

THE SOCIAL STUDIES

Rooted in History and the Social Sciences to Provide for Inquiry into Social, Economic, and Political Activities

Past Present Future

Variety and change of human behavior in groups
Interaction of people with their human and physical environment
Relationships among people, between people and institutions, between people and the earth, and between people and value systems

Here There Beyond

Purposes   Processes   Problems   Products   Prospects
Cultural Heritage and Its Dynamic Ongoing Characteristics

Chart 1

The term *social studies* should not, however, be confused with the following closely related terms which are much broader in meaning:

Social competence—one's ability to engage in group enterprises, both in and out of school.

Social learning—all experiences that help one to become oriented in society.

Social education—all school activities designed to promote social learning and to improve social competence.

Social living—processes involved in daily interaction with others; refers, in a few schools, to the social studies and other school activities provided to develop social competence.

Social learning takes place in all situations in which children interact with others—the community, the playground, the lunchroom, the social studies class, and so on. In all school situations, attention should be given to effective group processes, cooperation, responsibility, and other aspects of desirable behavior. Children's social attitudes, ideals, and concepts grow and develop as a result of many experiences, not just those in the social studies. This fact is recognized in better school systems where many parts of the educational program contribute to social learning.

But the social studies go far beyond children's own experiences to explore the world and its people. Social living and social learning throughout the school day may make contributions to the social studies, but they are not viewed as taking the place of instruction in the social studies. Children's social experiences are drawn on and utilized if they are pertinent, but they are not substitutes for planned areas of study in the basic program. The social studies program includes subject matter and planned experiences designed to achieve primary goals, as noted in the following section.

Contributions of the Social Studies to the Goals of Education

The objectives of each area of the curriculum should be related to the primary goals of education. When this is done, one may identify unique contributions of each area of the curriculum, and maintain a unifying sense of direction. In this section, therefore, primary goals are noted and examples are given of direct contributions that the social studies can make to their attainment.

The central purpose of American education has been defined by the Educational Policies Commission [1] as the development of the rational powers of the human mind, that is, the ability to think. The Commission points out that this is not the only purpose of education, but that it is essential to the achievement of other purposes. The schools must keep it in central focus, and all areas of the curriculum should contribute to its attainment.

Intimately associated with the development of thinking ability are key values of science or rational inquiry.[2] In fact, the development of one's rational powers is in large part dependent on the extent to which these key values are made a part of ongoing processes of thinking: longing to know and understand, questioning of all things, searching for data and their meaning, insisting on verification, respecting logical thought, considering premises or assumptions, and considering consequences. Values such as these are given high priority in new programs of instruction, as we will see in later sections.

Although the development of thinking ability is central to the achievement of other educational goals, one cannot assume that other goals will be achieved incidentally. Too much is at stake to use incidental approaches to the attainment of other educational

[1] *The Central Purpose of American Education* (Washington, D.C.: National Education Association, 1961).

[2] Educational Policy Commission, *The Spirit of Science* (Washington, D.C.: National Education Association, 1966).

goals in a democratic society because both individual and group needs must be met and a delicate balance between them must be maintained. Thus, in addition to thinking ability, attention must be given to self-realization, human relationships, economic efficiency, and civic responsibility. Also important is learning how to learn, a goal that is stressed in many areas of the curriculum. The following paragraphs give examples of ways in which the social studies contribute to all six of these primary goals.

THINKING ABILITY

The social studies make many direct contributions to the development of thinking abilities as problem solving, critical thinking, and creative thinking processes are put to use in units of instruction. In each unit of instruction, for example, many opportunities exist to define problems and issues, raise questions, search for and select related information, organize and reorganize ideas, propose and test hypotheses, express thoughts and feelings in original ways, and make critical appraisals of proposals, procedures, and plans of action. The social studies make other significant contributions to the development of thinking abilities as basic concepts and generalizations are developed, and as reading, study, and other basic skills are brought to ever higher levels of development. Not to be overlooked are the many ways in which open-mindedness, objectivity in the study of issues and problems, respect for the views of others, and other scientific attitudes are nurtured in the social studies.

SELF-REALIZATION

The social studies contribute to self-realization by providing experiences that foster maximum growth of each individual's potentialities. The capabilities of gifted, average, and less able children may be increased by the use of varied approaches to the study of topics, problems, and issues. Individual study, group work, reading, listening, and other skills are put to use and refined so that children become increasingly self-directive as they progress from level to level. Creativeness, responsibleness, and inquisitiveness may be nurtured while children undertake studies of people at home and in other lands. Concepts and understandings related to family and community activities are developed, thus helping each child to increase his personal effectiveness in living and working with others.

HUMAN RELATIONSHIPS

Of basic importance is the development of concepts and generalizations essential to an understanding of human relationships, such as interdependence, cooperation, and impact of culture on ways of thinking, believing, and acting. Cross-cultural understandings and appreciations are nurtured by considering the needs, problems, and points of view of others. Concern for others and open-mindedness are stressed when differences in ways of living and the contributions of various individuals and diverse groups to human welfare are studied. Appreciations of the vital functions of the home, school, church, and other basic institutions are also nurtured.

ECONOMIC EFFICIENCY

The social studies contribute to this goal by providing experiences that develop concepts, skills, and attitudes related to man's use of limited resources to meet his needs and his unlimited wants. Illustrative concepts are specialization to increase production, operation of supply and demand in the market, use of land, labor, and capital to produce goods and services, contributions of different workers, and wise use of resources. Skills and attitudes essential to good workmanship are highlighted as children learn about the work of others and as they carry out their own responsibilities. Also emphasized is the development of an appreciation of the economic opportunities in a free society that enable people to choose occupations, buy and sell, and move without being hampered by the restrictions that exist in a totalitarian society.

CIVIC RESPONSIBILITY

Civic responsibility is given direct attention in the social studies. The acceptance and discharge of responsibilities by the children themselves at home, in school, and in the community are first considerations. Also basic are concepts, generalizations, and appreciations related to the contributions of others, respect for constituted authority, the role of government, the operation of civic institutions, and an awareness of the responsibilities each individual must assume to preserve freedom for himself and others. School and community service projects give children opportunities to participate in civic activities. Loyalty to American ideals, values, and ways of living may be developed while children study the growth of their community, state, and nation. As issues and problems are studied, children can put basic thinking, reading, and study skills to use and gain increasing appreciation of the importance of skills in carrying out civic responsibilities.

LEARNING HOW TO LEARN

Related to all of the broad goals noted above and emphasized in new materials is learning how to learn. Effective thinking is characterized by the ability to learn on one's own, to find new solutions to problems, to employ processes of inquiry independently. Self-realization, human relationships, economic efficiency, and civic responsibility call for competence in exploring and handling problems and issues independently and require cooperation with others. The accelerating explosion of knowledge characteristic of our times has given new importance to the need to view life-long learning as both a personal and a social responsibility. Learning how to learn, therefore, is being given high priority in new programs of instruction. Models and techniques of inquiry, skills for independent study, techniques for using a variety of instructional media, and self-evaluation as a means of continuing self-improvement are among the current emphases related to this basic outcome. The social studies, along with other areas of curriculum, contribute directly to making the ideal of life-long learning a reality in the lives of American citizens.

In summary, the social studies curriculum abounds with opportunities to contribute to the broad goals of education at all levels of instruction. The next section further illustrates contributions that can be made.

Objectives of the Social Studies

Several trends are evident in statements of objectives of the social studies. Knowledge outcomes are being defined in terms of concepts, themes, and generalizations as they are structured and used in history and the social sciences. Processes of inquiry are being emphasized along with the related skills that are needed to use the variety of sources of data contained in instructional media. Attitudes and values associated with rational inquiry are being stressed along with societal values that underlie democratic ways of living. Objectives are being defined in behavioral terms in order to facilitate instructional planning, selection of materials, and evaluation.

New statements of objectives are better balanced than those of the past. Both cognitive (content and process) and affective (attitudes and values) outcomes are stressed. The outcomes to be derived from the study of history and the social sciences are included along with related qualities of citizenship. Recognition is given to the importance of societal values and changes, the nature of children, and the nature of knowledge derived from the disciplines. Thus, none of the foundations of the social studies is neglected.

The following summary of basic objectives drawn from new curriculum guides, units of instruction, and social studies project materials for Grades K–XII is illustrative of current trends. Notice that intellectual power is emphasized in attaining both humanistic and scientific outcomes essential to effective citizenship. Bear in mind also that although many relationships exist among the objectives, they have of necessity been listed in four categories in order to highlight the primary emphasis given to each one.

OBJECTIVES IN NEW SOCIAL STUDIES PROGRAMS

Knowledge Objectives

To develop understanding of data, concepts, themes, and generalizations related to the:

Interaction of social, economic, political, geographic, and historical factors in human affairs

Impact of science, technology, education, and interaction with others on ways of living

Influences of values, traditions, innovations, and other aspects of culture on ways of living in our society and in others

Similarities and differences in meeting basic human needs here and now and in other times and places

Operation of systems of human activities common to all societies such as transportation, communication, government, education, production, distribution and consumption of goods and services, conservation, and esthetic and religious expression

Social forces that give shape to contemporary life now and in the past

Various groups that give the individual a sense of self-understanding, insight into his potentialities, and conceptions of his roles

Contributions of individuals and groups to man's changing cultural heritage

History, geography, and contemporary ways of living in America

Conceptual backgrounds of democratic beliefs essential to our way of life, including:

Respect for the human dignity and worth of each individual

Responsibility for maintaining rights and freedoms under law

Freedom of speech, religion, press, assembly, and inquiry

Equality of justice, security, and opportunity for all

Faith in the ability of men to govern themselves

Use of intelligence to solve human problems

Government by consent of the governed

Majority rule with minority respect and protection

Cooperative action for the common good

Separation of church and state

Cooperation with others to secure world peace

Processes of social interaction and decision making in social, economic, and political institutions

Conceptual, inquiry, and value components of the structure of history and the social sciences

Affective Objectives

To develop attitudes, values, and appreciations characteristic of individuals who:

Place high premium on objectivity, thoughtful skepticism, longing to know, respect for logical thinking, consideration of premises and consequences, search for data and their meaning, and other values of rational inquiry

Recognize personal feelings and opinion as possible sources of error and bias that influence interpretations and points of view

Consider multiple causes of events, evidence that is contrary to personal views, and the limitations of generalizations

Search for new perspectives, creative ideas, divergent views, and new ways of dealing with issues and problems

Are sensitive to the influences of moral, ethical, and spiritual values in human affairs

Value democratic beliefs, human freedom, civic responsibilities, enlightened loyalty, and other aspects of our American heritage

Value the contributions of individuals and groups to our cultural heritage, including contributions to knowledge made by historians and social scientists

Respect duly constituted authority, due process of law, and procedures for making changes

Have self-respect and show respect for others regardless of race, creed, social and economic status, and national origin

Examine critically the actions of those entrusted with the general welfare of individuals and groups

Evaluate their own actions and the efforts of others to implement democratic beliefs

Are open-minded, responsible, cooperative, and creative, and show concern for others in group endeavors

Inquiry Objectives

To develop the ability to inquire by means of processes that unite concepts, values, and methods of inquiry in cognitive forms that enable students to:

Analyze topics and problems, weigh alternatives, consider consequences of alternatives, and make decisions

Formulate criteria and use them to make judgments

Use models of inquiry flexibly, adapting them to different topics and problems

Use such techniques of inquiry as systematic observation, the planned interview, critical reading of source materials, role-playing, field trips, and interpretation of graphic materials

Use geographic methods of inquiry to derive space-bound generalizations, such as: Our state has a variety of productive resources.

Use historical methods of inquiry to derive time-bound generalizations, such as: The idea of self-government was evident in early America.

Use methods of inquiry from the social sciences to derive generalizations of wide applicability, such as: Families around the world differ in size and composition.

Use a variety of methods of inquiry in area studies and in studies of such topics and problems as the growth of urban centers, Japanese culture, and contributions of minority groups

Use cognitive processes involved in defining, classifying, applying, analyzing, synthesizing, evaluating, hypothesizing, inferring, interpreting, and generalizing

Sharpen the thinking abilities that underlie all forms of inquiry, including perceptual, associative, conceptual, critical, creative, and problem-solving abilities

Build cognitive structures that include concepts, values, and processes of widespread use in studying human relationships

Skill Objectives

To develop competence in skills essential to the attainment of other objectives and to life-long learning, including the ability to:

Use a variety of sources of data including primary and secondary materials, textbooks, library materials, current periodicals, community resources, and audio-visual materials

Locate, gather, appraise, summarize, and report information

Read social studies material critically, listen critically, and study independently

Interpret and make maps, graphs, tables, time lines, and other graphic materials

Interpret sequences of events, time periods, chronology, and trends

Organize material from several sources and present it in pictorial, oral, written, and graphic form

Distinguish facts from opinions, relevant from irrelevant information, means from ends, primary from secondary sources, and conclusions from supporting evidence

Detect errors of thinking, unstated assumptions, unwarranted assertions, and the use of propaganda techniques

Work as a member of groups, participating in decision-making, carrying out plans, adhering to group standards, and evaluating individual and group efforts

Stating Objectives in Behavioral Terms

Interest has been renewed in stating objectives in terms of observable behavior. Objectives stated in behavioral terms range from manifestation of basic values to overt evidence of specific skills. Wide use is made of verbs such as demonstrate, describe, distinguish, identify, state, interpret, and apply. Such terms are more definite than the general terms know, understand, and appreciate. The advantages of more specific behavioral statements include clearer direction in planning, individualizing, and evaluating learning experiences.

Until an objective is stated in behavioral terms, planning for its development and evaluating growth toward its attainment are difficult. For example, the purpose *to develop open-mindedness* may be defined behaviorally as an individual who:

> Identifies points on all sides of an issue
> Distinguishes facts from opinions
> Considers and uses ideas of others as well as his own
> Gathers information to settle disputes

With such observable objectives in mind, one can make effective plans for experiences in which students are confronted with differing viewpoints, facts and opinions, and information related to issues and problems. Learning experiences can be individualized for those children who need to grow in particular aspects of open-mindedness. In addition, evaluation can be improved when observable aspects of behavior are made the focus of both informal and formal means of appraisal.

Helpful suggestions for formulating goals in behavioral terms and for designing related evaluation materials are contained in *Taxonomies of Educational Objectives*.[3] The suggestions are especially useful in formulating cognitive and affective objectives for units of instruction and lesson plans. The cognitive objectives are arranged according to level of complexity. The affective objectives are arranged according to degree of internalization. The categories included in each domain of objectives and specific examples of objectives in each category are presented below. Notice that each example is stated in terms of behavior that can be observed.

Cognitive domain

> *Knowledge:* Of terms, facts, trends, concepts, generalizations, and the like.
>> *Example:* The student identifies goods and services produced at home.

---

[3] Benjamin Bloom, ed., *Taxonomy of Educational Objectives: Cognitive Domain* (New York: David McKay Co., Inc., 1956), and David R. Krathwohl, *et al.*, *Taxonomy of Educational Objectives: Affective Domain* (New York: David McKay Co., Inc., 1964).

Comprehension: Translation of material into another form; interpretation by relating parts, making qualifications, recording ideas, and recognizing essential elements; extension of ideas to past and future situations, and the like.

Example: The student distinguishes facts from opinions.

Application: Of concepts, generalizations, criteria, models, and so forth.

Example: The student uses concepts of fair-play and equal rights in discussion.

Analysis: Of elements, relationships, principles of organization, and so forth.

Example: The student identifies instances in which equal rights were and were not observed.

Synthesis: Of ideas in an original communication, a plan, a generalization, an hypothesis, and the like.

Example: The student states a question or hypothesis based on related aspects of equal rights, such as: "Equal rights seem to be denied to minority groups of various types."

Evaluation: Making judgments in terms of internal evidence, external criteria, and the like.

Example: The student uses criteria to judge the effectiveness of maps he has made.

AFFECTIVE DOMAIN

Receiving (Attending): Awareness, willingness to receive, attention, and the like.

Example: The student recognizes incidents involving fair-play.

Responding: Compliance, willingness to respond, satisfaction in responding, and so forth.

Example: The student discusses fair-play and seeks ways of extending it.

Valuing: Acceptance, preference, commitment, and the like.

Example: The student practices and defends freedom of speech.

Organization: Conceptualization of a value, organization of a value system, and the like (a life-long task).

Example: The student defends assumptions underlying freedom of speech.

Characterization by a Value or Value Complex: Generalized set, internalized value system, and so forth (attained by mature adults).

Example: The individual makes judgments on the basis of principles inherent in a consistent philosophy of life.

All of the categories in the cognitive domain are relevant to social studies instruction in the elementary school. Knowledge, comprehension, and application are prerequisite to analysis, synthesis, and evaluation. If students do not understand and cannot apply key learnings, they cannot attain the more complex levels of analysis, synthesis, and evaluation. On the other hand, instruction should move from merely knowing and comprehending to higher levels of cognition. Beginning in the early grades children should have opportunities to bring ideas together into a chart or plan (synthesis), to evaluate how well they are working, and to engage in other activities related to the more complex objectives. Contrary to the belief of a few, analysis, synthesis, and evaluation are not reserved for emphasis in secondary schools and colleges.

The first three categories in the affective domain are most relevant to instruction in elementary schools. A big job for the teacher is to develop children's awareness of values and attitudes as they are expressed in social studies materials as well as in daily activities. The responding and valuing levels call for a variety of experiences in cross-cultural studies as well as in-depth studies of people and events in communities, states, and regions of the United States. Such values and attitudes as respect for the views of others, freedom of speech, fair-play, and equal rights for all take on dimensions of meaning and feeling in unit after unit, year after year, and in both school and out-of-school experiences. A prime function of social studies instruction is to ground such values in events and situations that make sense to children and enable them to develop deeper dimensions of meaning and feeling as they progress through school. The two top levels of the affective domain are life-long tasks fully attained by few adults. The quality of instruction related to preceding levels should be such that far more adults attain the last two.

Major Trends in the Social Studies

A concise summary of dominant trends is given in this section as background for new developments presented in later chapters. Such a perspective is helpful in relating various elements of the social studies program and in interpreting recent changes. We assume here that those concerned with the improvement of the social studies make the greatest progress when they are alert to the directions in which thinking and practice are moving.

FOUNDATIONS OF THE SOCIAL STUDIES

The core foundation of the social studies is made up of material drawn from history and the social sciences. The accelerating volume of knowledge requires that study focus on structures of fundamental ideas identified by scholars in history, cultural geography, economics, political science, anthropology, sociology, psychology, and law. From these and related disciplines are drawn the content and methods of inquiry that are used to build units of instruction, teaching guides, and instructional media. The attainment of the objectives of the social studies is promoted when the core foundation is kept in central focus and the other foundations are viewed in a conditioning or facilitating role.

The other two foundations, fundamental to all areas of the curriculum, are the social and psychological foundations. The social studies program is greatly influenced or conditioned by the values, goals, and changing conditions of the democratic society in which we live. And the program of instruction is facilitated when it is attuned to the stages of cognitive development, ways of learning, and developmental characteristics of children.

The trend is toward a balanced emphasis on the three foundations. Educators recognize that fundamental ideas in history and the social sciences must be identified before such questions as how to teach and when to teach selected material can be answered intelligently. Also recognized is that basic material related to societal values and changing conditions is to be found in basic disciplines. Thus the core foundation is kept in central focus as efforts are made to devise programs that are geared to both the needs of society and children.

EMPHASIS ON STRUCTURE

As in other areas of the curriculum, the trend in the social studies is to focus instruction on the structure of key ideas—the concepts, generalizations, and methods of inquiry that have been identified by scholars in their special fields of study. Geographers, economists, and other social scientists have prepared statements of the fundamental ideas that they believe should be included in the social studies. For example, the following concept clusters and related generalizations may be made a part of units at various levels of instruction:

Markets: Goods, services, buyers, sellers, supply, demand, price, money. Buyers pay money for goods and services offered by sellers. The price is set by supply and demand in an open market.

Resources: Water, soil, plants, animals, minerals. People use natural resources to meet basic needs.

Cultural Change: Invention, discovery, diffusion, adaptation. Changes occur as people invent, borrow, and adapt ideas.

Conceptual outcomes such as these grow out of a series of learning experiences in which pertinent information is studied, organized, summarized, and interpreted by children. Direct attention must be given to vocabulary and concept development and to the grouping of concepts into clusters and generalizations. Detailed suggestions for accomplishing this task are presented in later chapters, and they should be read with the following definitions in mind.

Words are arbitrary associations—the names given to objects, events, qualities, or processes, such as *lake, election, red,* or *transportation.* Such terms are taught through meaningful association and practice so that children can use them accurately and quickly. Various word lists have been prepared, but the most helpful sources of information on vocabulary development are the lists in units of instruction, courses of study, manuals for instructional materials, and children's textbooks. Included in such lists are the actual terms that children will use as they study various topics in the social studies.

Concepts involve broader meanings than do arbitrary associations and may be defined as abstractions that apply to a class or group of objects or activities that have certain qualities in common. Thus *lake* as a concept refers to a general class of objects and not to a particular object. Through instruction in the social studies, children learn the names of various items, discriminate similarities and differences among them, and abstract common elements within a given class or group of items. This process of discriminating and abstracting common elements leads to concept attainment and enables children to use such terms as *lake, election,* and *transportation* to refer to a general class or group of items rather than to a particular item.

Concept clusters are sets of related concepts that are subsumed under a major concept. Clusters of concepts are widely used in basic disciplines and may be found throughout the social studies. For example, geographers inevitably cluster the concepts *plains, hills, plateaus,* and *mountains* around the key concept *major landforms.* Other examples of key concepts and related clusters are: *factors of production*—land, labor, capital, management; *cultural change*—invention, discovery, diffusion, adaptation; and *processes of social interaction*—cooperation, competition, conflict, assimilation, accommodation. Students discover and use concept clusters as specific concepts are developed and brought together into larger and more inclusive concepts. The teacher's task is to guide students so that they group related concepts into clusters and use them to locate and organize data, pose questions, and formulate generalizations. Students with only two of the concepts in the cluster *major landforms*, for example, need to develop the other two if they are not to be cognitively crippled in studying and comparing landforms here and in other places.

Generalizations are on a still higher level than are concepts. They may be defined as statements of broad applicability that indicate the relationships between concepts. Generalizations may be stated as principles, laws, rules, and conclusions. Children develop and extend generalizations as they engage in problem-solving experiences, discover the relationships between concepts, and express the relationships in general statements. As new problems or situations are met and similar relationships between concepts are discovered, children develop greater depth and breadth of understanding of generalizations and can state them with greater precision and clarity.

EMPHASIS ON INQUIRY

The current emphasis on inquiry is based on the assumption that maximum learning takes place when students are actively involved in the teaching-learning situation. The student's stance should be that of the searcher and investigator who is actively involved in learning. He should view textbooks, films, maps, presentations by the teacher, and other "packages of information" as sources of data that can be used to answer questions, test hypotheses, check conclusions, extend or delimit generalizations. The student's searching, questing, and investigating should be guided by questions or hypotheses, all of which he understands and some of which he has formulated himself.

Confusion arises when inquiry approaches are interpreted to mean that the student must discover everything. What is needed is sufficient discovery learning to enable students to obtain a feeling for the excitement and lure of discovery and insight into productive ways of solving problems. Also needed is meaningful verbal learning in which direct instruction is provided to develop concepts, build related vocabulary, and develop skills which are productive of a wider range of discoveries and open new horizons of learning to the student. To be limited to one's own discoveries would greatly narrow the range of learning and future discovery.

In new programs of instruction both discovery learning and meaningful verbal learning are included. Conceptual tools and methods of investigation developed by means of direct instruction are brought to bear upon a variety of problems in which students discover relationships and formulate generalizations. Learning experiences are provided to develop such concepts as factors of production and resources so that students can use them in investigating economic activities at home and in other lands. Map-reading and map-making skills are taught systematically so that students can use them in their own inquiries.

The teacher's role varies from that of director of instruction to arranger of opportunities for independent investigation on the part of students. At times the teacher directs inquiry and provides instruction that leads to the development of needed concepts, skills, and attitudes. At other times the teacher and the students may plan, carry out, and evaluate learning activities that might be classified as group inquiry. At still other times the students themselves may define problems, raise questions, or pose hypotheses and proceed to investigate them with little or no direction from the teacher. What is essential to growth in the ability to inquire is that the student be actively involved in the search for new ideas and new ways of investigating problems, whether the teacher is directing the learning experiences or students are working independently.

Inductive teaching strategies are recommended in new teaching guides so that children themselves can discover ideas, analyze instructional media, find answers to key questions, and formulate generalizations. The trend is definitely away from expository teaching in which the teacher presents facts and conclusions to be mastered by students. Rather, students themselves take an active role in learning that the teacher guides in a search for data relevant to topics under study.

ASSISTANCE OF SCHOLARS

Curriculum planning in the social studies calls for the assistance of experts in foundation disciplines. Among the factors involved in this trend are the great advances in human knowledge, the diversity of content in the social sciences, and the interest of scholars in improving the curriculum. Organized groups in history, geography, economics, and other social sciences have proposed content, outlined concepts and generalizations, and prepared materials designed to improve the social studies program. A major task of curriculum workers and teachers is to organize, adapt, and consolidate these contributions for use in the instructional program. A list of twenty-five social studies projects is included at the end of this chapter.

Difficulties inevitably arise when experts in the different social sciences become involved in curriculum making. Differing schools of thought in the social sciences, varying interpretations of trends and movements, and particular points of view held by individual scholars are certain to be debated. Depth of learning in specific disciplines may be stressed in a collegiate, academic sense without full awareness of the general education values for pupils. Some individuals may insist that their field of study needs main emphasis; most will want a large block of time for their speciality. Some may point out that curriculum workers are too ambitious and want to include too much in the program; others will urge that the children be introduced to more topics at an earlier age. A few may try to impose a particular educational point of view.

Such difficulties and problems should be discussed and resolved in ways that are conducive to the development of the best possible program. In the long run, better programs will be developed and a better understanding of the importance of the social studies will be achieved. Because of the increasing complexity of knowledge in the social sciences, the need is greater than ever before for the assistance of scholars in curriculum planning.

EDUCATION FOR CITIZENSHIP

An effective citizen is a thinking individual who has the depth of understanding, the loyalties to democratic ideals, the attitudes, and the skills needed to assume the responsibilities that accompany the rights and privileges of democratic citizenship. Citizenship education continues to be stressed with special emphasis on the teaching of fundamental concepts and generalizations essential to effective citizenship, the study of current affairs, and participation in carefully selected civic activities that children can understand.

The following generalizations are examples of current trends in thought on citizenship as proposed by a group of political scientists:

The well-being of the state is dependent upon educating its citizens for participation in life's activities.

The citizen has civic responsibilities as well as rights.

A citizen can do his part in making democracy work only if he has the information essential to intelligent reflection on the issues of the day. Such information can be provided best by a free and responsible press.

A democratic society depends upon citizens who are intellectually and morally fit to conduct their government. Civic responsibility and moral courage are balance wheels for a democracy. To fulfill their obligations of citizenship, individuals must be aware of the quality of service that should come from persons who staff the government and must be willing to participate actively in community

affairs. The capable citizen should use scientific methods in evaluat- ·
ing mass communication media and in making political choices.[4]

CROSS-CULTURAL UNDERSTANDING

Increased interest has been shown in recent years in the development of clearer understandings of other cultures. In the
early grades, a beginning is made by developing understandings
and appreciations of cultural differences in the neighborhood,
the community, and nearby communities. In later grades, attention is given to cultures and subcultures in the state, nation, and
in other lands. Among the basic understandings emphasized at
all levels are these: (1) the values and customs of the society in
which an individual lives are the primary determiners of his behavior; (2) differences in ways of living should be viewed in the
light of the values and customs that underlie them; and (3) institutions such as the family, school, and church in a given society "pass on" beliefs, values, and customs from generation to
generation.

One of the most promising aspects of cross-cultural education
in the social studies is the emphasis on finding out *why* particular ways of living of one group differ from those of another. By
asking *why* questions as well as *what* and *how* questions, teachers can guide children to discover underlying reasons for human
activities in cultures that differ from their own. Thus, when units
on Africa, Asia, and Other Lands are provided, children investigate background reasons, conditions, traditions, and beliefs related to ways of living and move beyond mere descriptions of
what people do.

A variety of strategies are used to develop cross-cultural understanding. One of the most helpful is to provide units of instruction that truly enable children to study selected cultures in
depth; that is, consider historical, geographic, economic, political,
anthropological, and sociological information along with problems, needs, changes, arts, crafts, music, and literature. Special
efforts should be made to view ways of living with an open mind
and to consider local beliefs and customs from the point of view
of the people under study. Changes may be viewed in terms of
the concept cluster *cultural change* (invention, discovery, diffusion, adaptation) as children discover creative ideas of the
people themselves and ideas they have borrowed from others and

[4] John U. Michaelis and A. Montgomery Johnston, *The Social Sciences:
Foundations of the Social Studies* (Boston: Allyn & Bacon, 1965), pp. 318–
19.

adapted to their needs. Other strategies that are used to develop cross-cultural understanding are exchange of letters or other materials through *pen-pal* activities, participation in civic activities of various groups, attending festivals, viewing and discussing selected TV programs, studying current affairs, learning about other cultures through foreign language instruction, planning assemblies and school programs, seeing exhibits, engaging in art and craft activities, learning songs and rhythms, and providing direct contacts with individuals or groups. Such approaches are most helpful when they are made a part of basic units of instruction in which children have opportunities to develop depth of understanding as noted above.

DEPTH STUDIES

In an effort to prevent superficiality of learning, the trend is to provide for the study of selected regions and cultures in depth. The two main purposes are to acquaint children with cultures that characterize different regions of the world, and to develop basic understandings of the values, conditions, and problems that exist in the selected cultures. Illustrative of this trend are the comparative studies of families and communities in Grades I–III, the cross-cultural studies of selected lands in Grade IV, the intensive study of selected countries in Latin America, Europe, the Middle East, Southwest and Southeast Asia, the Far East, and Africa in Grades VI and VII, and the study of major regions and cultures in world geography and world history in Grades IX and X.

A critical curricular issue here is the value of a depth study of selected regions or cultures versus the value of an overall study of regions and cultures through the world. The issue has been resolved in some schools by giving an overview of a large region or area followed by an intensive study of one or more representative cultures or countries within the area. Care must be taken so that pupils do not generalize about all countries within the area on the basis of the study of a single country. Although certain common geographical, economic, political, and cultural characteristics are to be found among countries in the Middle East, in Africa, or in Latin America, specific differences exist that can be grasped only through the study of each country in detail. Hence, when representative countries are studied, the pupils should understand that the purpose is to get a view of certain characteristics that are generally typical of the area, but may be manifested specifically in different ways in other countries in the area. For example, the aspirations to attain democracy, improve standards of living, provide better educational and health services, increase industrial output, and obtain stable government are characteristic of many countries in Africa, but the specific ways and means employed to attain them vary greatly from country to country.

THINKING PROCESSES

Direct attention to the improvement of children's thinking abilities has become a major emphasis in recent years. Both school personnel and scholars agree that effective thinking is basic to living in a democracy. In fact, a basic assumption underlying the democratic idea is that people can and will use their rational powers to solve problems; they do not have to rely on an elite group to solve governmental and other problems for them. Effective thinking is also basic to effective learning in school and throughout life. Defining problems and breaking them down into manageable parts; finding, analyzing, and appraising information; and making, testing, and revising conclusions are skills that enable one to improve and accelerate learning. Concepts and generalizations are learned more effectively when children react thoughtfully to what they learn, discover key ideas, distinguish fact from opinion, relate information to basic questions, consider differing points of view, note similarities and differences, use reflective methods, evaluate ideas, and check conclusions. Thinking skills are also essential to a consideration of issues and problems that arise as a result of rapidly changing conditions that are characteristic of our times.

INDEPENDENT INQUIRY AND STUDY SKILLS

The emphasis on independent inquiry and study skills is evident in a number of ways. Concepts and methods of inquiry from the social sciences are built into units of instruction. Reading-study skills are given direct attention in recognition of the special difficulties and problems that arise in dealing with the terms, meanings, concepts, and relationships in social studies materials. Map-reading concepts and skills, interpretation of graphs and tables, locating and appraising sources of information, pooling ideas from several sources, outlining, summarizing, reporting, home study, and other skills are frequently included in courses of study, children's textbooks, and units of instruction. Functional application and immediate use of basic skills in the social studies are coupled with direct instruction and practice in order to bring skills to higher levels of development in each grade. Relationships to other areas of the curriculum, in which the development of basic skills is emphasized, are kept in mind; instruction in the social studies supplements and reinforces instruction in other areas, and, at times, may even go beyond. Thus the skills involved in using textbooks, atlases, gazeteers, indexes, encyclopedias, and library resources can be brought to high levels in the social studies as children use them to locate and organize ideas related to topics under study.

A STRUCTURED CURRICULUM

With the current emphasis on the social studies as a clearly defined field of study has come a more definite assignment of units of instruction to each grade level. In recently published courses of study, specific topics or units are recommended for each grade; some may include various options from which teachers may make a selection. In the main, however, a sequence of units is proposed to assure depth and breadth and to prevent duplication and repetition of topics. Incidental approaches have been abandoned even though significant events are made a part of the basic program. Adaptation of recommended areas of study in the light of children's backgrounds and community conditions continues to be emphasized. Significant experiences of children are utilized to improve social learning, but they do not take the place of basic areas of study recommended for each grade level. The dominant view is that the objectives of the social studies can best be achieved through a planned program of instruction in which teachers know just what areas of study are included.

EARLIER INTRODUCTION OF TOPICS

Although not so pronounced as in science and mathematics programs, certain topics, concepts, and skills in the social studies are introduced earlier than ever before so as to challenge the capabilities of all children—the gifted, the average, and the less able. Older notions of readiness for learning that placed reliance on waiting for children to mature are being replaced by the belief that effective instruction can begin at an earlier age. Examples in the social studies are the development of basic units on Home, School, and Neighborhood, and Children in Other Lands in Kindergarten, comparative studies of the Neighborhood and Community in Grades I and II, Communities Around the World in Grades II and III, and Area Studies of India, Japan, and other countries in Grades IV–VI. In addition, map-reading concepts and skills, and basic concepts and generalizations involving interdependence, adaptation, and the impact of culture on people's ways of living are given greater attention at all levels. Care is being taken to avoid the development of misconceptions and the trap of thinking that any concept or generalization can be taught once and for all in a particular grade. Appropriate follow-through from grade to grade is provided to extend and deepen concepts and to bring them to higher and higher levels of development.

CURRENT AFFAIRS

Thoughtful attention is being given to the study of current affairs because of the need to keep abreast of change and to understand factors that produce change. The trend is not to replace basic units of instruction but rather to bring instructional media up to date. Significant current affairs are selected and related to topics and problems under study. Care is taken in selecting controversial issues which are significant and appropriate for study in the schools. Current affairs, the basic values held by the people involved in them, and current social trends and possible future developments are considered in the light of their historical development. This emphasis on placing the study of current affairs in an historical setting tends to make them more meaningful and helps pupils to see them in perspective rather than as isolated incidents. Another practice that is contributing to the value of the study of current affairs is the emphasis on critical analysis of issues and problems as a means of sharpening critical thinking. Differing points of view are considered, information is gathered and appraised, and tentative conclusions may or may not be made depending on the adequacy of information. Open-mindedness and reservation of judgment are emphasized. In order to provide guidelines for the study of controversial issues, the trend in many school systems is to prepare policy statements which suggest principles for use in the classroom.

RELATIONSHIPS TO OTHER SUBJECTS

At times, the social studies program has served as a broad, integrative subject in which science, health, safety, art, music, and other areas were included in one way or another. The trend now is to include only that related material which is pertinent to questions and problems under study. Only rarely today can one find efforts being made to use the social studies as an all-inclusive core of learning to which all other subjects are related.

The dominant view is that related subjects should be drawn upon to improve problem solving and critical thinking in the social studies, to develop appropriate relationships, and to enhance understanding and appreciations. The intent is to gather ideas and materials directly related to questions and problems under study as is done at higher levels of learning and investigation. The forced relating of content and materials that are not pertinent is avoided because the inevitable result is shoddy and confused thinking coupled with imbalance among basic areas of the curriculum.

In certain ways, this same trend is evident in courses and textbooks in which separate subjects are emphasized. For example, maps and geographic content, examples of arts and crafts, and literary selections may be found in history units and textbooks; and historical, political, and anthropological content may be found in geography units and texts. This trend is also evident in area studies of Japan, Mexico, Latin America, and the Middle East. Geographic features, historical events, ways of living of the people, social and political problems, economic developments, anthropological discoveries, and related topics are brought together to develop understandings and appreciations of the areas under study.

CRITICAL SELECTION OF INSTRUCTIONAL MEDIA

Instructional media are being selected with greater care. Concern has been expressed about the treatment of minority groups in textbooks and other materials. The educational needs of disadvantaged children have sharpened the focus on individual differences. The emphasis on concepts and methods of inquiry drawn from the social sciences calls for new types of materials. These and related developments have brought a flood of new instructional media that must be appraised critically.

Learning experiences are also being selected with greater care. Study trips, people to interview, basic textbooks, films, television programs, and other resources are checked in terms of such criteria as: Is this a good source of information? Do better ways exist to obtain needed ideas? Is this worth the time, effort, and expense? Committee work, map making, dramatic representation, construction of objects, related art work, and other activities are selected in terms of such criteria as: Will this activity contribute to the achievement of worthwhile purposes? Will it challenge children's best efforts? Are needed materials available? Will the activity lead on to other worthwhile activities? Only those activities that meet such criteria are included in the program, and careful plans are made for their use to achieve clearly defined purposes.

OTHER DEVELOPMENTS

In addition to better selection of content and instructional resources, quality of education has been emphasized in several ways. Individualized instruction is being planned more effectively to achieve excellence of learning for all children—the gifted, the average, and the less able. For example, differentiated reading materials may be provided so that each child can explore topics in depth and breadth according to his ability. On the increase in many school systems are individual and small-group activities that require the use of library resources, interviewing of experts, and systematic organizing and reporting of information. The organization of instructional-materials centers in some school systems has enabled teachers to obtain the materials they need to individualize instruction. The use of the nongraded plan of organization has possibilities for instruction in the social studies that need to be explored in detail. Television teaching and systems of instructional media have also extended horizons of learning.

Team teaching is used in some schools. A team made up of teachers with special preparation in social sciences, science and arithmetic, language arts, and fine arts may be assigned to work with 80–100 children. Under the direction of the team leader, both large and small group activities are planned, and each teacher takes responsibility for instruction in his special area of competence. Relationships among areas of the curriculum, grouping of children for instruction, ways to meet special needs of individuals, and other phases of the program are planned and carried out by the team. An attempt is made to achieve greater depth of learning in each subject and to avoid the pitfalls of extreme departmentalization.

EVALUATION

Three distinct trends are evident. First, increased attention is being given to the evaluation of reading-study skills, map-reading skills, and critical thinking and problem-solving ability. Formal devices such as tests and informal devices such as checklists and rating scales are both being used to evaluate skills in the social studies. Second, increased attention is being given to the appraisal of children's grasp of concepts, relationships, and generalizations.

Teacher-made tests and appraisal of children's understanding as revealed in discussion and other means of expression are being used along with standardized tests. Third, evaluation of the social studies program as an area of the curriculum is being done in terms of carefully formulated statements of the characteristics of an effective social studies program. A recent development has been to include a statement of desirable program characteristics in curriculum guides. The concluding section of this chapter includes a summary of characteristics as reported in recently published guides.

Characteristics of New Programs

A promising practice now occurring in curriculum planning, workshops, and conferences on the social studies, is the consideration given to statements of characteristics of an effective social studies program. Such statements have been found to be helpful in overall planning, in evaluating social studies programs, in providing guidance to curriculum workers, and in interpreting the program to laymen. In a way, a statement of characteristics of an effective program can be viewed as a summary of major trends, for it reflects dominant points of view on basic aspects of the program. The following statement is intended to serve this purpose and to be used as a checklist for appraising basic features of the overall social studies program.

Definition
_____The social studies program is defined to include fundamental ideas from history and the social sciences.
_____The program is focused on group behavior, human interaction, and human relationships.
_____Attention is given to man's changing cultural heritage in the past, present, and emerging future and in places nearby and far away.
Objectives
_____Objectives most essential in our times are defined with reference to the following and their interrelationships:
_____Knowledge. _____Attitudes and Values _____Inquiry
_____Skills
Foundations
_____History and the social sciences are viewed as the core foundation.
_____The program is related to values, needs, and changing conditions of society.
_____The program is planned and developed in accord with the

best available knowledge of the learning-teaching process and child development.

Content

_____Up-to-date content has been selected from basic disciplines and current affairs and has been related to objectives and areas of study included in the program.

_____Content is structured to show how fundamental ideas are related and serve as organizing centers for data.

Organization

_____Continuity of learning is maintained from level to level through an organized program of instruction beginning in the kindergarten and extending through the school system.

_____Depth and breadth of learning are assured and needless repetition is avoided through the assigning of specific areas of emphasis to each grade.

_____Flexibility and adaptability are maintained within the framework of the overall program in order to challenge each child's capabilities and to meet needs and conditions in the community.

_____Instruction in the social studies is related to other areas of the curriculum in ways that contribute to the achievement of definite goals.

_____A curriculum guide and units of instruction which provide guidelines for developing the instructional program are available to teachers, and are designed to stimulate creative approaches to teaching.

Instructional Resources, Methods, and Activities

_____Criteria are used to make a discriminating selection of resources, methods, and activities that may be used to:

_____Achieve basic objectives of the program   _____Meet individual differences of learners and local needs and conditions _____Challenge the capabilities of each child and stimulate creative teaching

Evaluation, Revision, Interpretation

_____Provision is made for the use of a variety of procedures in evaluating children's achievement in terms of basic objectives.

_____Continuing appraisal is made of the effectiveness of the program of instruction.

_____The program is revised in the light of evaluation, new knowledge from the social sciences, changing societal conditions, and new knowledge from studies of child development and learning.

_____Parents and other laymen are kept informed as to the nature of the program, its strengths and weaknesses, and changes that are made to improve it.

Instructional Personnel

_____Teachers have the depth and breadth of preparation that enable them to provide instruction in the areas of study included in the program.

_____Supervisory assistance is provided to help teachers meet instructional problems.

_____In-service education is provided to improve instruction in the social studies.

Questions, Activities, Evaluation

1. Obtain a local curriculum guide and check it for the following:

   a. How are the social studies defined? Does the definition differ from the one given in this chapter? How?

   b. Check the statement of objectives and compare it with those given in this chapter. What basic concepts, generalizations, and methods of inquiry are listed? What skills and abilities? What attitudes, appreciations, and behavior patterns? Are any purposes included that are not listed in the summary of purposes presented in this chapter?

   c. Is citizenship education stressed? How is effective citizenship defined?

   d. Which of the major trends presented in this chapter can you find? Which are not included? How might the lack of attention to certain trends be accounted for?

   e. Is a statement of characteristics of an effective program included? If so, how is it similar to the one presented in this chapter? Are additional characteristics listed?

2. Write in your own words a definition of the social studies that you might use with laymen. Discuss it with fellow students or teachers and obtain any suggestions they have for improving it. Discuss it with laymen and find out if it is clear to them.

3. Prepare a statement of the objectives of the social studies that you believe to be most meaningful in your situation. Discuss your statement with others and see if they agree.

4. Which of the trends presented in this chapter do you believe to be most significant in improving children's learning in the social studies? What might you do as a teacher to implement them in your situation?

5. Prepare a statement of the characteristics of an effective social studies program from the point of view of a teacher. Modify the statement presented in this chapter in order to highlight

aspects that you believe to be most important to teachers in their daily teaching of the social studies.

References

Bloom, Benjamin S., ed., *Taxonomy of Educational Objectives: Cognitive Domain*. New York: David McKay Co., Inc., 1956. Objectives on various levels.

Carpenter, Helen M., "Skills for Democratic Citizenship in the 1960s," *Skill Development in the Social Studies*, 33rd Yearbook. Washington, D.C.: National Council for the Social Studies, 1963. Overview of skills to be developed in the social studies.

Cox, Benjamin C., and Byron G. Massialas, eds., *Social Studies in the United States* (New York: Harcourt, Brace & World, Inc., 1967). An appraisal of elementary and secondary programs.

Educational Policies Commission, *The Central Purpose of American Education*. Washington, D.C.: NEA, 1961.

——, *The Spirit of Science*. Washington, D.C.: NEA, 1966.

Fenton, Edwin, *The New Social Studies*. New York: Holt, Rinehart & Winston, Inc., 1967. Report on new projects.

Fraser, Dorothy, "Social Studies," *Curriculum Handbook for School Administrators*. Washington, D. C.: American Association for School Administrators, 1967. Overview of new developments.

Jarolimek, John, and Humber M. Walsh, *Readings for Social Studies in Elementary Education*. New York: The Macmillan Company, 1965. Articles on role of social studies and objectives.

Krathwohl, David R., Benjamin S. Bloom, and Bertram B. Masia, *Taxonomy of Educational Objectives: Affective Domain*. New York: David McKay Co., Inc. 1964. Objectives on various levels.

Lee, John R., and Jonathon C. McClendon, *Readings on Elementary Social Studies*. Boston: Allyn and Bacon, Inc., 1965. Articles on purposes and trends.

Michaelis, John U., "Social Studies," *New Curriculum Developments*. Washington, D.C.: Association for Supervision and Curriculum Development, 1965. Review of developments in new projects.

——, and A. Montgomery Johnston, *The Social Sciences: Foundations of the Social Studies*. Boston: Allyn & Bacon, 1965. Generalizations from social sciences in Appendix; sections on trends and new developments.

Selected Social Studies Projects

The following list includes projects that have produced or are producing materials for one or more of Grades K through VIII.

Materials now available or materials under development with *completion date of the project* are noted. Interested individuals should write directly to project directors for materials or for information on availability of materials.

Anderson, Wallace, *Intercultural Studies*, State College of Iowa, Cedar Falls, Iowa, 50613. Teachers' and students' materials on non-Western world for K–XVI, 1970.

Arnoff, Melvin, *First Grade Materials on Families of Japan*, Department of Education, Kent State University, Kent, Ohio, 44201. Teaching unit available.

Berlak, Harold, and Timothy R. Tomlinson, *Development of Elementary School Social Studies Curriculum*, Metropolitan St. Louis Social Studies Center, Washington University, MacMillan Hall 303, St. Louis, Missouri, 63130. Teaching units and pupils' materials based on social sciences, 1970.

English, Raymond, *The Greater Cleveland Social Science Program*, Educational Research Council of Greater Cleveland, Rockefeller Building, 614 West Superior Avenue, Cleveland, Ohio, 44113. Teaching guides and pupils' materials now available.

Fox, Robert S., and Ronald Lippitt, *Michigan Social Science Education Project*, Center for Research on Utilization of Scientific Knowledge, University of Michigan, Ann Arbor, Michigan, 48107. Units, teaching guides, pupils' materials, 1968.

Gibson, John S., *The Development of Instructional Materials Dealing with Racial and Cultural Diversity in American Life*, Lincoln Filene Center for Citizenship and Public Affairs, Tufts University, Medford, Massachusetts, 02155. Teaching guides, pupils' materials, 1968.

Gill, Clark C., and William B. Conroy, *Development of Guidelines and Resource Materials on Latin America*, 403 Sutton Hall, University of Texas, Austin, Texas, 78712. Teaching guides, units, bibliographies, 1969.

Halsey, Van R., and Richard H. Brown, *Committee on the Study of History* ("The Amherst Project"), Box 72, Amherst, Massachusetts, 01002. Students' materials for Grade VIII on U.S. history, 1968.

Hennebry, H. M., and K. L. Diem, *Conservation Education Improvement Project*, College of Education, University of Wyoming, Laramie, Wyoming, 82070. Teachers' guides and pupils' materials for I–IX, 1968.

Kresse, Frederick H., *Match Box Project*, Children's Museum, 60 Burroughs Street, Boston, Massachusetts, 02130. Units and kits of materials now available on loan.

Maher, John E., *Developmental Economic Education Program*, Joint Council on Economic Education, 1212 Avenue of the Americas, New York, New York, 10036. Materials for teachers and students now available; write for Joint Council Checklist of Materials.

Michaelis, John U., *Preparation of Teaching Guides and Materials on Asian Countries for Use in Grades 1–12*, Department of Education, University of California, Berkeley, California, 94720. Unit on Japan now available.

Moore, Jerry R., *Foreign Relations Project*, North Central Association, First National Bank Building, Chicago, Ill., 60603. Booklets on various countries for use in Grades VII and up available from Laidlaw, Chicago.

Morison, Elting, A *Program of Curriculum Development in the Social Studies and the Humanities*, Educational Services, 44A Battle Street, Cambridge, Massachusetts, 02183. Anthropological materials under development.

Morrissett, Irving, *Social Science Education Consortium, Inc.*, University of Colorado, Boulder, Colorado, 80302. Teachers' materials now available.

Price, Roy A., and Warren L. Hickman, *Social Studies Curriculum Center*, 409 Maxwell Hall, Syracuse University, Syracuse, New York, 13210. Bulletin on social science concepts now available; units on concepts under development, 1968.

Rader, William D., *Elementary School Economics Program*, Industrial Relations Center, University of Chicago, 1225 E. 60th St., Chicago, Illinois, 60637. Materials for teachers and pupils in IV–VI now available.

Rice, Marion J., and Wilfrid C. Bailey, *Anthropology Curriculum Project* (Development of a Sequential Curriculum in Anthropology for Grades 1–7), University of Georgia, Athens, Georgia, 30602. Teaching guides and pupils' materials now available.

Sanders, Norris M., *Cooperative Curriculum Development Center*, 1402 Manila St., Manitowoc, Wisconsin, 54220. Units, course outlines, pupils' materials for K–XII, 1968.

Senesh, Lawrence, *Elkart Indiana Experiment in Economic Education*, Department of Economics, Purdue University, Lafayette, Indiana, 47907. Materials for teachers and pupils now available from Science Research Associates, Chicago.

Shinn, Ridgway F., *Geography and History as Integrating Disciplines*, Department of History, Rhode Island College, Providence, Rhode Island, 02904. Materials for teachers and pupils.

Taba, Hilda, *Curriculum Development Project*, San Francisco State College, 1600 Holloway Avenue, San Francisco, California, 94122. Materials for teachers I–VIII, 1968.

Toy, Henry, *Civic Education Project*, Council on Civic Education, 300 East 33rd St., New York, New York, 10016. A civics casebook for middle grades by Charles N. Quigley now available from Ginn & Co., Boston, Massachusetts.

Vadnais, Lawrence H., *A Cultural Approach to the Study of History in Grades Seven and Eight*, Green River Road, Williamstown, Massachusetts, 01267. Materials for pupils and teachers, 1968.

West, Edith, *Preparation and Evaluation of Social Studies Curriculum*, College of Education, University of Minnesota, Minneapolis, Minnesota, 55455. Teaching guides, unit plans, materials for students K–XIV, 1968.

Social
Foundations
of the
Social Studies

2

The social studies have three interrelated foundations. The *social* foundations include our democratic heritage of values and processes and major societal changes. The *disciplinary* foundations include the content and values and methods of inquiry drawn from the social sciences. The *psychological and methodological* foundations include material on child development, learning, teaching strategies, and evaluation. These foundations are interrelated in that much of the substance of the social and psychological foundations is drawn from the social sciences. In addition, societal values and changes greatly influence the work of specialists in the other foundations and condition the selection and presentation of the program.

Insight into the foundations of the social studies is useful as background information for teachers. It is essential to an understanding of the objectives of the social studies, why certain topics and methods of inquiry are included, and how various teaching strategies and instructional media are used. In addition, specific implications may be drawn for various aspects of instructional planning.

The focus of this chapter is on the social foundations. The other foundations are treated in the following two chapters.

Of special importance to teachers are those aspects of the social foundations that are directly related to instructional planning.

Democratic values and processes and basic societal changes need to be clarified so that they can be given appropriate attention in units of instruction. Strategies for applying values, developing related behavior, and handling value conflicts are needed to make instruction come alive in the classroom. Because of their all-pervasive importance, attention is given first to values and processes in the context of our democratic heritage.

Our Democratic Heritage

The idea of democracy is one of the most powerful ideas ever conceived by man. The power and greatness of the idea stem from man's desire to govern himself, the responsibilities each individual must assume, the emphasis on cooperation rather than coercion, and the faith in the use of intelligence to solve problems. Assumed here is that the true measure of a way of life is appraised in terms of contributions to human dignity and welfare.

The democratic values and processes that are so important in our lives today constitute one of the richest parts of our cultural heritage. From the first concepts of democracy in the distant past to the great power of the democratic idea in the present, there has been a continuing struggle to win and extend human freedom and equality. If present and future generations are to safeguard and extend democracy, they must have a thorough understanding and appreciation of democratic values and processes.

VALUES AND PROCESSES

Democratic values and processes are given a prominent place in new programs of instruction.[1] A core value in all programs is human dignity and equality which is directly related to the following:

Consent of the governed, equality of justice and opportunity, due process of law, general welfare
Use of intelligence and cooperative action to solve problems
Freedom of speech, press, assembly, religion, and inquiry
Individual rights, responsibility, creativity, and self-direction
Respect for majority rule, minority rights, and property
Faith in man's ability to improve conditions and solve problems

[1] See materials from projects listed at the end of Chapter 1 under English, Morrissett, Price, Toy, West.

Open-mindedness, fair-play, and respect for the views of others irrespective of class, color, and creed

Values such as these are made a part of new units of instruction in the social studies.[2] Such units as Family Life, Community Living, Our State, and The United States include much relevant material, and specific values are treated in depth in units on Our American Heritage, The Constitutions, Bill of Rights, and Local, State, and National Government. The conceptual foundations of values are developed by giving direct attention to the meaning of such concepts as consent of the governed, due process of law, and equality of opportunity. Both contemporary and historical events are used as case studies to highlight the strength and enduring quality of basic values. A fundamental outcome is enlightened loyalty and patriotism based on understanding and appreciation of the power of the democratic idea in both the past and the present. Instruction is pointed toward the development of such generalizations as the following, which have been outlined by a group of political scientists in a social studies guide: [3]

Democracy implies a way of life as well as a form of government.

Democracy is based on certain fundamental assumptions. Among these are the integrity of man, the dignity of the individual, equality of opportunity, man's rationality, man's morality, man's practicality, and man's ability to govern himself and to solve his problems cooperatively.

Man develops his fullest potential in a climate of freedom. Much of civilization's advance can be traced to man's search for a larger measure of freedom.

Civil liberty—freedom of thought, speech, press, worship, petition and association—constitutes the central citadel of human freedom.

Basic to democracy is belief in progress. A free society is hospitable to new ideas and to change and encourages the unfettered search for truth. Peaceful action rather than violence is one of its hallmarks.

Certain factors are necessary for democracy to succeed. These include: (a) an educated citizenry, (b) a common concern for hu-

[2] John U. Michaelis, *Teaching Units Based on the Social Sciences* (Chicago: Rand McNally & Co., 1966).

[3] John U. Michaelis and A. Montgomery Johnston, eds. *The Social Sciences: Foundations of the Social Studies* (Boston: Allyn & Bacon, Inc., 1965), pp. 317–18.

man freedom, (c) communication and mobility, (d) a degree of economic security, (e) a spirit of compromise and mutual trust, (f) respect for the rights of minority groups and the loyal opposition, (g) moral and spiritual values, (h) participation by the citizen in government at all levels.

Opportunity sufficient to allow every individual voluntarily to choose the division of labor in which he will perform is a concept that has flourished under democratic philosophy and practice and the capitalistic system.

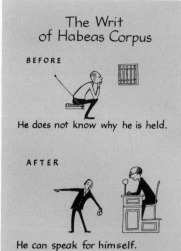

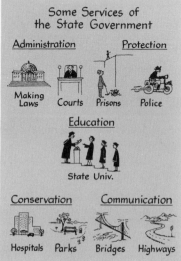

What specific concepts are essential to an understanding of the main ideas summarized in these charts? What basic generalizations about government in a democracy might be formulated? *(San Bernardino County)*

STRATEGIES FOR MAKING APPLICATIONS

In addition to developing generalizations, schools must give practice in utilizing democratic values and processes. Can we expect pupils to accept what is taught if we do not practice what we teach? Is behavior in the classroom consistent with democratic principles? Do children have opportunities to apply what they learn to daily living and to evaluate their progress toward higher levels of democratic behavior?

First of all, any mistaken notions about the meaning of democracy in the classroom should be dispelled, for example, doing and saying as one pleases, failing to consider the rights of others, neglecting individual responsibilities, and exhibiting a lack of discipline. The discipline of democracy is not "soft" or permissive. It calls for self-discipline, individual and group responsibility, concern for others, and adherence to established regulations, laws, and standards. Without these, there can be no progress—only disorder.

Second, the school is a basic institution in a democratic society established by the people to achieve definite goals. Requirements are set in law by the people and in regulations established by representatives of the people. Children should learn early in their lives to understand and to respect the contributions of the school in a democratic society and that the very success of democracy depends upon a well-educated citizenry.

Third, in a classroom atmosphere conducive to effective learning, a teacher can do many things to make democratic values and processes meaningful to children and to provide practice in their use. The following are examples of democratic values followed by specific applications. As you read them, consider other ways in which you can apply each principle in your own teaching.

Government of a group is most effective if there is government by the group. In classrooms where this value is applied, children have opportunities to develop group standards which they can use in planning and working together. Individual and group work are evaluated in such a way that each child grows in responsibility, self-control, and self-direction. Rules and regulations of the school are adhered to, as they must be if the rights and privileges of all are to be respected, and children learn why each has a responsibility to abide by established regulations. When such units as Our Community, Our State, and Our Nation are studied, the class develops specific concepts which relate to government by the group. As children mature, they have opportunities to develop increasing appreciation of their own contributions, as well as those of others, to the improvement of human affairs through government of, by, and for the people.

Each individual is respected and accorded equal justice and opportunity. In classrooms which stress this value, a child's race, status, or group membership neither increase nor decrease his opportunities for learning. A wide range of experiences is provided so that each child has opportunities to develop his capabilities to the maximum. Mutual respect is emphasized and all children in the group are given opportunities to learn the importance of individual effort, fair-play, and integrity in human relations. As units are studied, children, in learning of the great contributions of men and women in the past and present, have opportunities to acquire respect for the individual. As the Constitution and its amendments are studied, emphasis is given to the development of an appreciation and understanding of its historical and present-day significance.

Freedom of inquiry and use of intelligence to solve problems is valued. Freedom of thought, speech, and belief are respected, and emphasis is given to accuracy in reporting information, responsibility in checking its validity, analysis of various sides of issues and problems, and formulation of conclusions after careful study of the facts. The early grades stress issues and problems that are meaningful and significant in the lives of children; attention in later grades is given to current national and international issues and problems of educational value as children develop adequate backgrounds of understanding. The skills involved in critical thinking are put to use in studying issues and problems that arise in daily instruction, in units, and in the study of contemporary affairs. As units are studied, children are guided to discover how men and women have worked to establish and maintain the freedom of inquiry essential to continuing progress.

Democratic Behavior Patterns

Other concrete and meaningful applications can be made by giving attention to the development of democratic behavior patterns. A first step is to clarify what is meant by democratic behavior. Inclusive categories of behavior must be identified that are consistent with the values and processes outlined above. The following are frequently included in courses of study, instructional media, and units of study.

RESPONSIBLENESS

At the very center of the democratic idea is the concept that individuals can and will carry out responsibilities. For every right, privilege, decision, or plan of action, there are related responsibilities that must be discharged. The success of democracy depends on the acceptance of responsibility by the people, both as individuals and as members of various groups.

Responsibleness is developed in the social studies under teacher guidance as children plan, carry out, and evaluate learning activities. Beginning in the early grades with responsibilities such as those related to sharing and discussing ideas, using equipment and materials properly, and carrying out group work standards, the instructional program is extended in later grades to include a wide range of responsibilities related to gathering information, preparing reports, interviewing experts, participating in discussion, analyzing issues and problems, planning programs for parents, and evaluating critically the effectiveness of individual and group work. Children's concepts of responsibleness are extended through direct study of the responsibilities carried out by members of the family, community workers, officials of government, great men and women of the past and present, and people in other lands. Thus, a child's behavior is rooted in a background of meaning and understanding that adds to his ability to accept and carry out responsibilities with increasing effectiveness in an ever-growing number and variety of situations.

CONCERN FOR OTHERS

Individual development and group welfare are nurtured when concern for others is evident in all facets of democratic living. Various aspects of concern for others are reflected in such expressions as "rights for one and for all," "looking out for the other fellow," "lending a helping hand," and "brotherhood among men." Mutual respect, courtesy, tact, and a willingness to help, are evident in the behavior of those who show a concern for others. Concern for others is important in little things as well as in big things, for as Franklin said: "Human felicity is produced not so much by great pieces of good fortune that seldom happen, as by little advantages that occur every day."

Children who are developing concern for others are sensitive to the needs, problems, and interests of others at home, in school, and in the community. They also rely on orderly methods of achieving purposes and consider the rights and responsibilities of others as well as their own. Respect is accorded others when differences in race, religion, status and other factors are discovered; common needs and similarities are recognized and differences are appreciated. There is a growing appreciation of the significance of duly constituted authority in the home, school, and community as a potent factor in the promotion of human welfare. As children mature, they begin to understand that in a democracy authority rests with the people, and that maximum concern for others is secured only when the people give adequate time and thought to problems of government.

OPEN-MINDEDNESS

Clear thinking and problem solving, which are essential in a democracy, call for open-mindedness. Group action is most effective when all points of view are considered in planning and evaluation. Individual study and action can be improved when various ideas are considered and a critical selection is made of those that are most appropriate in a situation. Prejudice and superstition can be rooted out as differing points of view and authenticated facts are considered. As Jefferson put it: "Error of opinion may be tolerated where reason is left free to combat it."

Children who are developing open-mindedness consider and explore the value of the ideas of others as well as the value of their own. They are learning to be impartial, to report facts accurately, to analyze problems, and to appraise the validity of information. They consider facts and opinions in the light of the source from which they were obtained, their relationship to issues and problems, and their usefulness in solving problems. They seek better ways of doing things, establish reasons for making changes in on-going activities, and support what they believe is right with evidence and reason. They are growing in the ability to recognize the impact of feelings on their thinking, and in the ability to curb emotions that lead to bias, prejudice, and erroneous conclusions. They are beginning to recognize the closed mind and the propaganda techniques which are used to instill distorted facts and ideas in the minds of susceptible individuals. As they study basic units of work in the social studies, they discover ways in which open-mindedness on the part of individuals in the community, state, nation, and other lands, is a potent factor in solving problems and making progress. The many advantages of an open society in which issues and problems are examined and discussed become even more evident when an examination is made of the disadvantages of a closed society in which selected doctrines must be followed.

CREATIVENESS

Much of America's greatness has come from the creativeness of her people. Down through the years the people of America have found new ways of doing things as frontier after frontier has been reached and passed and new ones have been opened. The children of America need opportunities to develop creative ways of doing things so that democratic living will be continually improved by a constant flow of new ideas, generation after generation.

Creativeness in children can be viewed as new or original responses made in solving problems, organizing and expressing ideas, using materials, carrying out plans, and making improvements in individual and group work. Children who are growing in creativeness search for and use new ideas to solve problems and to express thoughts and feelings. They are sensitive to originality in others and are growing in their appreciation of creative contributions made by individuals in the past as well as in the present. They are growing in the ability to express ideas clearly in oral and written form, as well as through various art media, and are developing an appreciation of the ability of others to express ideas creatively. As they study various units, they are developing understandings and appreciations of the value and importance of creativeness in the lives of people at home and in other lands.

COOPERATIVENESS

The ability to cooperate is very important in our society. The teamwork required in industry, education, science, government, and other significant activities illustrates this point. From early days when neighbors worked together to raise the walls of a log cabin, or to have a town meeting, to the present time when a crew of workers erects a skyscraper, or a group participates in a meeting of the city council, our progress has virtually depended on our ability to cooperate. And now, cooperation among nations has become necessary for both progress and survival.

Children who are developing cooperative behavior pool ideas, make plans, carry them through to completion, and evaluate the effectiveness of their work. When plans are changed on the basis of group decisions, they continue to work with others to achieve common goals. As they study various topics in the social studies, they discover examples of cooperation in the home, school, community, state, and nation. As they mature and undertake more advanced studies, they gain insight into the need for teamwork in solving international problems, and critically assess the actions of individuals and agencies that are working together to improve human welfare.

Strategies for Developing Democratic Behavior

Each social studies unit should help build the values that are at the base of democratic behavior, and, conversely, each unit should help children to learn and practice the kind of behavior that demonstrates democratic values. Three interrelated strategies may be used. First, plans must be made for specific things that children can *do*, since democratic attitudes and behavior are best learned through active and reflective participation. Second, plans should be made for children to *observe* democratic behavior in action in the school and community. Third, plans must be made for children to *study* and analyze democratic behavior as portrayed in books, films, and other instructional resources. Notice the three levels of abstractness in the suggested planning: *doing*, *observing*, and *studying*. Although actual doing is essential, observing and studying should not be minimized, for they make it possible to extend and enrich the child's concept of democratic behavior. The three examples which follow illustrate the kind of planning that should be undertaken in each unit.

In a Home and Family Living unit, *cooperativeness* may be developed to higher levels through such experiences as the following:

Doing. Planning and arranging a playhouse; sharing tools and materials, working together, and helping each other make furniture, home furnishings, dishes, table settings, dolls and doll clothes, pet cages, and scrapbooks; planning and participating in dramatic representation centered on home activities; making and carrying out standards to use on a study trip to see a home under construction; taking turns and sharing in a group discussion of unit activities.

Observing. Mother, father, brothers, and sisters working together at home; children cooperating at home and at school; monitors and committees at work; men working together to build a house in the neighborhood; ways in which the janitor, teachers, and children in school work together to make the school a happy, clean place in which to work and play.

Studying. Flat pictures, film strips, and films showing members of a family gardening, cleaning the yard, shopping, and having fun together; picture and story books which portray cooperation among children, children and parents, and adults taking part in neighborhood activities; stories and poems that highlight teamwork in home and family living. (Responsibility, creativeness, concern for others, and open-mindedness may be outlined in a similar manner for this unit of instruction.)

Ways in which *responsibleness* may be developed are shown in a Community Living unit.

Doing. Developing and maintaining standards of conduct on a field trip; observing safety regulations in parks and playgrounds and on transportation facilities; using tools and materials properly in making model buildings and other objects; engaging in dramatic play centered on activities of community workers; helping to make picture collections of community workers and activities; carrying out specific responsibilities in making and operating a center of interest such as a post office, airport, or harbor; taking turns and making contributions in discussing, planning, and evaluating activities as the unit develops.

Observing. Responsibilities carried out by children in the classroom at work on murals, layouts, and other activities; the work of policemen, post office employees, and other community workers; duties of nurses, doctors, and other health workers; men at work building a house in the neighborhood; the work of employees in stores, parks, and on playgrounds; and demonstrations put on by individuals from local factories, the airport, or dairy to highlight responsibilities of various workers.

Studying. Film strips on firemen, policemen, and other community workers; films on fire prevention, community health, and safety; current events from newspapers, radio, and television dealing with responsibilities of local citizens; bulletin board arrangements and reading materials which portray responsibilities of both children and adults in community living.

To illustrate ways to develop democratic behavior in upper grades, a Life in Early America unit has been selected. Specific attention is given to ways in which *creativeness* may be developed, recognizing that the other categories of behavior may be analyzed in a similar manner.

Doing. Planning and using a variety of ways to organize information, that is, pictorial summaries, booklets, dioramas, and slides; creating songs and rhythms related to such activities as quilting, husking, hunting, weaving, and churning; make instruments to accompany songs and rhythms; drawing pictures and murals; making candles, dolls with authentic costumes, utensils, and other objects for use in creative dramatics, discussion, and reports.

Observing. Individuals invited to school to demonstrate the use of spinning wheels, looms, and other objects used in early days; models, utensils, quilts, and other objects arranged in an exhibit, or museum, to highlight creative uses of materials in early times; authentic folk dances and songs performed by community or school groups; plays and pageants given to celebrate holidays and events of historical interest; creative contributions made by members of the class as the unit of work develops.

Studying. Pictures, films, books, and other instructional materials which portray creativeness in the use of resources for food,

Materials can be arranged creatively to present and share significant learnings. Why are creative arrangements such as this one effective in developing attitudes and appreciations? *(Alameda County)*

shelter, and clothing; art, music, and literature of early times; contributions of great men and women during the early days of our country; explorers and ways in which they blazed trails and opened up new territories; radio and television programs about people and events in early times.

These examples illustrate practical procedures that teachers have used to develop democratic behavior. The point should be emphasized that examples on the "doing level" can be found in nearly all activities included in the social studies which involve group work; they also can be found in daily living throughout the school program. On the "observing level," children can be guided to notice examples in the classroom, elsewhere in the school, and in the community. As historical units or units on faraway places are developed, plays, festivals, pageants, programs developed by school and community groups, and demonstrations by individuals invited to school may be witnessed by children. On the third level—the "studying level"—books, films, film strips, and other resources offer many good examples of democratic behavior. Television and radio programs should not be overlooked, particularly those related to topics in the social studies. Finally, current events are a good source of examples. Occasionally, a bulletin board of pictures and clippings can be arranged to emphasize concern for others, open-mindedness, or

44

one of the other categories of behavior. By giving systematic attention to the development of democratic behavior in all of these ways, a practical and realistic contribution to democratic citizenship can be made in the elementary school.

Major Societal Changes

The phenomenon of change is an aspect of modern life that touches everyone. The inevitability of change and the need to adapt to change are brought home to us in daily experiences and through television and other mass media. Changes in homes, schools, and communities are observed directly by children and adults throughout the nation. The speed with which various changes take place is a phenomenon that some find alarming, others accept as a condition of life, and still others see as a challenge to improve ways of living for all.

Children in schools today are growing up and living in an age in which such terms as *space flight, urban redevelopment, automation,* and *supersonic airplanes* are commonplace. What may seem like a dramatic change to an older person is just life to-day for a child, and what a child understands and how he feels about changes today becomes his background for dealing with changes in the future. To help students begin to develop insights into the origins and directions of change, and how man attempts to direct and control change, is a challenge that must be faced and met in the social studies.

LONG-TERM CHANGES

A helpful approach is to provide instruction that includes a selection of current and dramatic changes of today and relates them to long-term societal changes. This can be done in the elementary school through the planning of units that include background material on changes in homes, communities, and other places in addition to material on new developments. For example, the development of rapid transit systems, freeways, and other advances in transportation that are considered in commu-nity and city studies should be examined, even though briefly in the primary grades, as an extension of the long-term changes that have taken place in transportation. Similarly, in units that deal with problems of urbanization, conservation of resources, or the population explosion, attention can be given to the back-grounds of development that led to current problems. Such an approach helps to develop perspective and to reveal the continu-ing efforts of mankind to meet change and to deal with it.

The following long-term changes are included in current programs of instruction. A knowledge of them can be used as a frame of reference for planning units of study that include current changes and problems.

The Struggle for Freedom and Equality. Beginning with concepts of democracy in early cultures and moving to revolutions for freedom in the Western world today, we find individuals and groups working to extend equality of opportunity to minority groups and new nations struggling to achieve freedom in a world torn by ideological conflict between democracy and totalitarianism.

Scientific Change. Extending from a few discoveries and inventions that were fundamental to scientific advance is today's explosion of knowledge that has opened new horizons of study in the social as well as the natural sciences.

Technological Change. From a beginning with simple tools that extended and amplified man's use of his hands, today we have a variety of tools and machines that are used extensively in homes and communities of advanced countries. Automation is an extension that further decreases the need for human labor.

Industrialization. The replacement of hand tools by mechanical means of production, which was accelerated by the Industrial Revolution, has now been extended in advanced nations by the use of automated modes of production. Newly developing nations are also putting forth great efforts to secure the benefits of industrialization in order to improve their standards of living.

Transportation. Advancing from reliance on human energy and the forces of nature to transport people and goods, man now uses electricity, petroleum, and other sources of energy to power machines used in networks of transportation that circle the globe. Atomic powered ships, supersonic planes, and space vehicles are extensions of this long-term trend.

Communication. Depending at first on face-to-face exchange of ideas, man greatly extended his means of communication through such inventions as writing, the printing press, the telegraph, the telephone, radio, television, and communication satellites.

Urbanization. With industrialization and improved agricultural production has come a shift of population from rural to urban centers and on to urban sprawl and megalapolis. New and increased needs for housing, education, health services, urban redevelopment, transportation, and recreation have created problems for both governmental and private agencies.

Institutional Changes. Increasing industrialization and urbanization have brought changes in the functions of such institutions as the home and the church. Certain functions of the home have been transferred (in part at least) to the government, for example, formal education of children, health and welfare services, and physical protection. In addition to the expanding role of government, political, economic, and labor organizations have extended their functions to meet problems of living in an increasingly complex society.

Interdependence. From isolated and self-sufficient communities, states, and nations, the trend has been toward increasing interdependence within and among nations.

Population Changes. Technological progress has contributed to longer life spans, decreasing death rates, and a population explosion that has created new problems in many countries throughout the world. Population shifts have occurred as large numbers of people have moved from rural-agricultural areas to urban-industrial areas.

Resource Use. Increasing industrialization, population growth, and rising expectations have resulted in a more rapid exploitation and depletion of natural resources and, of necessity, invention of new synthetic materials, discovery of new sources of energy, and better planning for the use of available resources.

Processes of Interaction. From face-to-face interaction in primary groups, the trend has been toward interaction through organizations that represent the individual. Related changes have occurred in basic processes of social interaction, including greater regulation of competition for increasing use of cooperation or group action to achieve common ends, greater efforts to reconcile group conflicts, and active search for more effective modes of accommodation and more intensive study of the process of cultural assimilation in urban environments.

Expansion of Education. Moving at first from education of an elite group to elementary education for the masses, the trend today to provide increased quality in education extends upwards through secondary schools and higher education. Greater attention is now being paid to the development of individual capacities as well as to the meeting of societal needs. The needs of disadvantaged children are also receiving special attention.

Search for Peace. Man's dream of a peaceful world, as old as the act of war, has led him to develop various alliances and blocs, and to form the United Nations and its different international agencies which are having varying degrees of success in coping with international problems.

Changes and problems such as these have been evident in

varying degrees all over the world. Over the years, industrialized countries have changed more rapidly than have isolated agrarian countries, the changes having been most dramatic and rapid in America and other countries that have led in technological and scientific progress. In new nations and in many older nations that have followed traditional patterns of living, an intense desire exists to move ahead rapidly and catch up with more advanced nations.

Why have some countries advanced more rapidly than others? What factors are involved in change? *(International Society for the Study of Education, Tokyo)*

As interesting as changes and trends are in themselves, attention should also be given to underlying processes of change.

Processes of Change

Social scientists attempt to differentiate social change from cultural change. Social change relates to social interaction, social structure, and social institutions. The ways people interact—competition, cooperation, conflict, accommodation, assimilation—change from time to time because of changes in individual behavior, novelty in new situations, and shifts in roles. Social change refers to a shift in positions of individuals and to change in the positions themselves, for example, changes in the position of minority groups and their leaders. Cultural change, on the other hand, is change in the overall pattern of behavior—values, customs, ideas, and other products of interaction. Cultural changes include new scientific, technological, literary, artistic, educational, and other innovations.

Cultural changes are, in large part, brought about by the diffusion of inventions. The term invention is used to include both material and nonmaterial innovation; for example, the automobile, airplane, and radio are material inventions, and parliamentary government, the Constitution, the United Nations are nonmaterial inventions. Both types of invention are diffused as individuals and groups interact and communicate with one another. Diffusion is most rapid in advanced societies which trade with others, provide a broad base of education, and have highly developed networks of transportation and communication. Material inventions usually achieve faster acceptance than do nonmaterial inventions.

Cultural change may have a number of "chain reaction" or derivative effects. The invention of the radio and television, for example, has led to new industries and governmental regulations, and even to new patterns of family life. Furthermore, as these two mass media have become available to people throughout the country, interaction with others has been greatly extended at least in the sense of getting many new ideas quickly.

Typical patterns of change occur as the impact of cultural innovations strike home. In the case of a technological innovation, for example, first to feel the impact are the economic institutions. Next are the social institutions: the family, church, school, and government. An illustration is the recent change to automation in the production of automobile engines. First, dislocations occurred in employment, and then a search for ways to meet the problem and the planning of education programs to meet related problems. Finally, *social values* that surround social institutions may change, but the change is much slower than is the case with economic institutions. The phenomenon in these examples is known as *cultural lag* because all other changes "run behind" technological change.

Put simply, cultural lag is the disparity in change between two or more related elements, for example, production of automobiles and construction of highways, growth and shifts in population and provision of housing and other facilities and services, decrease in working hours and provision of leisure-time activities, and shortage of resources and conservation practices. Factors in cultural lag are conservatism, resistance to change, and protection of vested interests. Most crucial are deeply held values which change very slowly and are often held long after they no longer apply to existing conditions.

STRATEGIES FOR DEALING WITH CHANGE

In considering changing conditions and related problems, those who guide the learning of children should express themselves positively and constructively. There is no place for attitudes and reactions that contribute to the development of crippling fear, disillusionment, hopelessness, and despair. Rather, teachers must show their belief in progress, courage, integrity, and action to preserve and extend democratic ideals.

Special emphasis should be given to the backgrounds of understanding related to our democratic heritage, for without an understanding and appreciation of historical, geographic, and other pertinent factors, changing conditions and problems cannot be viewed in perspective. Content and materials related to current events should include background information from history, geography, and other areas of study as well as recent information reported in current periodicals for children and adults. The desired outcome is the development of fundamental concepts that can be used to consider a variety of changes as they occur. For example, the concept cluster *cultural change* (invention, discovery, diffusion, adaptation) can be used to analyze information about changes in the home, community, nation, and places around the world. Such an outcome is in sharp contrast to superficial learning related to isolated incidents.

The habits, skills, and abilities involved in critical thinking, problem solving, communicating with others, and individual and group study, merit special emphasis so that each child, to the best of his ability, can develop the competencies needed for learning and living in our times. The skills involved in making choices and decisions are critical because of the many changes and problems characteristic of our times, the need to clarify values as a basis for making choices, the need to sense the consequences of various decisions, and the need to appraise consequences in light of democratic values.

Implications for the design of the social studies curriculum relate to both scope and sequence. The scope of the curriculum should be broad enough to include those goals and changing conditions considered most significant in the lives of children. The sequence or level-by-level gradations of experiences should be planned in terms of their meaningfulness to children, local demands and conditions, and related factors. Balance is needed between stability in providing for fundamental areas of study, and flexibility in providing for new areas of study. Thus continuing review and revision of the social studies program are essential.

Problems beyond the experience and maturity of children should not be included, nor should the study of current events be overemphasized. A general guideline is to set the study of past and present social changes in units of instruction. Thus population growth, conservation of resources, urban changes, and the like are embedded in such units as Cities Around the World, Our State, Regions of the United States, Latin American Countries, and Changing Japan. Contemporary affairs are used to update changes, and basic background material is used to set changes in perspective.

The community can be used as a laboratory for studying changes in the past and present. Discoveries made by students about changes in the community can be used as a basis for comparing changes in other times and places. Aspects of change presented in films, reading materials, and other instructional media usually have their counterparts in the community, and vice versa. The linking of scientific, economic, political, and other developments to changes in community life is without doubt one of the most effective means of making instruction meaningful to children.

A helpful strategy for studying changes that range from those in the home to those at the international level has been outlined in materials from a current social studies project.[4] The

---

[4] Roy A. Price, Warren Hickman, and Gerald Smith, *Major Concepts for Social Studies* (Syracuse: Social Studies Curriculum Center, Syracuse University, 1966).

strategy is based on the following analytical questions which are used to gather data and interpret specific changes: What were the main factors causing the change? What was it that changed? How did it change? What was the direction of change? What was the rate of change? Why did it occur, and why was it possible? What were the effects or consequences?

Teaching results should be judged in terms of attitudes toward change as well as understanding of change. Do students view change as a challenge? What proposals do they make for dealing with change? How do they show concern for the impact of change? Do they understand their own attitudes as well as those that others have regarding change? Do they show an awareness of the need for directing and controlling change? Questions such as these can be used to gather data, which can in turn be applied to the improvement of instruction, so that the ideal of accepting the challenge of change and dealing with change increasingly becomes a reality in the lives of learners.

Developing Competence in Handling Value Conflicts

In our society high premium is placed on the ability to handle value conflicts. Critical analysis of issues and problems and the use of persuasion based on reason help to develop this skill. Children encounter value conflicts in their own experiences and in learning experiences provided in the social studies. A promising new development is to provide instruction designed to develop competence in dealing with value conflicts. Several strategies and a model are presented in this section. They can be put to extensive use as conflicts related to the values, behaviors, and changes presented in preceding sections are considered.

TEACHING STRATEGIES

Early in their lives children encounter situations in which conflict arises between personal desires and group interests, between freedom of the individual and the welfare of others, between expressing one's own view and considering the views of others, and between other common values. As children progress through school, they encounter value conflicts in personal experiences, in incidents they observe, in current events, and in units of study. The increasing attention paid to problems of disadvantaged and minority groups, urban redevelopment, and newly developing nations has given fresh importance to the need to develop competence in analyzing value conflicts. The following strategies are illustrative of promising approaches to instruction in this phase of the social studies program.

Critical Analysis by the Group. A widely used strategy involves group analysis and discussion. Here the class considers fair-play, concern for others, individual rights, or other relevant values in school, community, and elsewhere. The teacher may guide the analysis by such questions as: What is the issue? What are the facts? What do you think should be done? What reasons do you have for your suggestion? What are the alternatives? Would any of them be better in terms of fair-play? Otherwise? What reasons can we give for and against each proposal? Which one seems to be best for everyone concerned? The entire group assumes a reflective and analytic posture and attempts to find a position or solution consistent with the values under consideration.

Defense of a Position. The focus of this strategy is on the defense of a position that a student or committee has taken. Individual students give reasons for their position. The teacher and/ or other students ask questions designed to check the soundness of reasons given for the position, such as: What reasons can you give? What arguments or facts can you give for each reason? Do the facts check with those reported by others? What values are important? Are they applied consistently? Do they apply to everyone? What will the consequences be if your view is adopted? What are the alternatives? Why do you think your position is sounder than that of others?

Identification with Others. This strategy is designed to develop empathy and sympathy as well as understanding. Role-playing may be used to develop sensitivity to the views and feelings of others. Films and other audio-visual media may also be used. Firsthand contacts with others may be provided through field trips or interviews so that students can obtain direct accounts of roles, feelings, and problems. Stories, case studies, or anecdotes may be used to engender empathy for others as well as to provide information about their problems. Debates, committee reports, or discussions may be provided in which certain students "take the other side." In this strategy the focus is on the students' ability to identify themselves as closely as possible with the views, roles, and feelings of others.

A MODEL FOR VALUE ANALYSIS

The common elements present in most strategies can be generalized in the form of a simple model. The model includes the following phases, which may be used in variable order:

Define terms as they are actually used. Meaningful communication is impossible when individuals use the same terms to mean different things. Actual meaning rather than dictionary meaning should be determined by asking such questions as: What does the individual or group mean when they use this term? What do others mean when they use it? What meanings are important in this situation? For example, a primary grade classroom group discovered that some children used *fair-play* to mean, "I get my turn" while others meant, "We stick to the rules." Children in a middle-grade classroom discovered that *individual rights* meant "each person for himself" in some situations and "respect for other people's rights" in other situations.

Collect relevant facts for use in giving reasons for a position. The sharing of uninformed opinion is not the same as making reflective value judgments. Reasons or arguments should be backed by relevant data. The facts in a given situation should be weighed when answering such questions as: What happened? Who was involved? In what way were individual rights or other values overlooked? What facts are reported by both sides? How do the reports differ? Which report seems to be most accurate? Why? For example, in a primary classroom children found that some students had missed turns, some had not followed the rules, and some did not even know the rules. In a middle-grade classroom students found that some individuals did things for personal gain, that respect for individual rights was shown in some situations but not in others, and that minorities in particular have had a rough time in gaining individual rights accorded to others.

Analyze the reasons given for various positions. After facts are gathered, they should be logically related to reasons that are given for a particular position. In addition, attention should be given to premises, assumptions, motives, and claims that may be involved. Illustrative questions are: Have all relevant facts been considered? What reasons are sound? Unsound? Consistent? Inconsistent? Complete? Incomplete? What assumptions or claims are involved? For example, one primary group found that some children were inconsistent, arguing for their turn but not for the turn of others, and wanting others to stick to the rules while they did not. A middle-grade group discovered that some individuals and groups used *individual rights* as an argument for their special interests but did not apply the value consistently when considering the rights of others.

Consider the consequences of various positions. The analysis of consequences that may flow from different positions or solutions forces students to think beyond the immediate situation. Possible questions to raise are: What might be the effects on individuals? Groups? Changes in rules or laws? Who might gain? Who might lose? What might the side effects be for us? For others? For example, a primary group considered such consequences as hurt feelings, missing one's turn, and not learning as much when individuals failed to show concern for others. A middle-grade group considered such consequences as low status, small income, and lack of self-esteem when individual rights of minorities are neglected as against higher status, larger income, and self-respect when equality of rights is emphasized.

Clarify and use value-criteria to make judgments. The emphasis here is on the use of sound criteria in making judgments. Recognition is given to the fact that students do make judgments and that the chances of making sound judgments are greater if meaningful criteria are used. Illustrative questions are: What values are involved? Are certain values in conflict? Which has priority? How shall the criteria be stated? What form is best for making judgments? For example, a primary group decided that "the same rights for all" should be used to make judgments in the situation under consideration. A middle-grade group decided that "individual rights and responsibilities" should be coupled with "concern for others" in making judgments in the situations under consideration.

Consider ways of resolving conflicts. Making value judgments in specific situations is not enough. Attention should also be given to ways of resolving conflicts so that students will develop increasing insights into processes that may be used in a variety of situations. The basic means of settling issues are coercion, compromise, persuasion, and development of a consensus. Coercion or force is used as a last resort in many situations. Compromise and persuasion are widely used. Arriving at a consensus whereby a new plan or solution for resolving a conflict is developed should be the goal even though it is difficult to achieve. Illustrative questions are: How do you think the issue might be settled? By each side giving in on certain points? By finding a new solution? By authorities? Other means? What procedures are available for use in this situation? Which can be used in other situations? For example, a primary group decided conflicts between individual wishes and group welfare could be resolved by "sticking to the rules" in most situations, but appeals should be made to the teacher when individuals could not settle their differences. A middle-grade group decided that a tough-minded policy of resort to law was necessary when other ways of resolving conflicts had not succeeded in extending equal rights to minorities.

A model such as the above can be used to blend together the various aspects of the social foundations considered in this chapter. Values, changes, and democratic behavior can be interrelated as various conflicts are considered. The desired result is for each child to grow in ability to handle the value conflicts characteristic of our times. The beginning that can be made in the elementary school will contribute much to the refinement of the process of valuing in subsequent years.

Questions, Activities, Evaluation

1. Examine one or two social studies textbooks and note examples of each of the following: Democratic values, democratic behavior, societal changes, value conflicts.

2. How are the above presented? How might you guide study and discussion of them? Which of the strategies presented in this chapter might you use? What modifications might you make in the strategies?

3. Examine a course of study and do the same as noted in numbers 1 and 2 above.

4. Examine a unit of instruction and do the same as noted in 1 and 2 above.

5. Critically evaluate the ways in which values, behavior, changes, and conflicts are treated in the above sources? What improvements can you make? Do the same for the suggestions contained in this chapter.

6. Prepare a list of specific ways in which democratic behavior might be developed in a unit you are planning to teach. Make a worksheet as follows for each category of behavior:
Responsibility:
    Doing: _____

_____

    Observing: _____

_____

    Studying: _____

Note specific examples in the appropriate spaces. Share and discuss your examples with others.

7. Make a list of ways in which you can include values, changes, and conflict analysis in a unit you are planning. Seek

an evaluation of how your suggestions might be improved by discussing them with others.

References

California State Department of Education, *Social Studies Framework for the Public Schools of California*. Sacramento: The Department, 1962. Generalizations from eight disciplines.

Fischer, Louis, and Donald R. Thomas, *Social Foundations of Educational Decisions*. Belmont, Calif.: Wadsworth Publishing Co., Inc., 1965. Role of culture, values, and value conflicts in change discussed in first three chapters.

Los Angeles City Schools, *The Teaching of Values*. Los Angeles: City Board of Education, 1966. Identification of key values and presentation of teaching suggestions.

Michaelis, John U., *Teaching Units Based on the Social Sciences*. Chicago: Rand McNally & Co., 1966. Three volumes, one each for Grades K–II, III–IV, V–VI.

Miller, Richard I., *Education in a Changing Society*. Washington, D.C.: National Education Association, 1963. Major societal changes and implications for education.

Morphet, Edgar L., and Charles O. Ryan, *Implications for Education of Prospective Changes in Society*. Denver: Designing Education for the Future: An Eight State Project, 1967. Implications for various aspects of education.

————, *Prospective Changes in Society by 1980*. Denver: Designing Education for the Future: An Eight State Project, 1362 Lincoln St., 1966. Overview of prospective changes in the years ahead.

Price, Roy A., Warren Hickman, and Gerald Smith, *Major Concepts for Social Studies*. Syracuse: Social Studies Curriculum Center, Syracuse University, 1966. Includes a section on value concepts.

Quigley, Charles N., *Your Rights and Responsibilities as an American Citizen*. Boston: Ginn & Company, 1967. Case studies for children.

Raths, Louis E., Merril Harmin, and Sydney B. Simon, *Values and Teaching*. Columbus: Charles E. Merrill Books, Inc., 1966. Concrete suggestions for working with values in the classroom.

Rockefeller Panel Report on American Democracy, *The Power of the Democratic Idea*, VI Report. Garden City, N. Y.: Doubleday & Company, Inc., 1960. A statement of democratic ideals and processes in human affairs.

Shaftel, Fannie R., and George Shaftel, *Role Playing for Social Values*. Englewood Cliffs, N.J.: Prentice-Hall, Inc., 1967. Strategies and episodes for role-playing focused on key values.

"The Elementary School: Focus on Values," *Social Education*, **XXXI**
(January, 1967), 34–48. A collection of articles on values.

Tyler, Ralph W., Chairman, *Social Forces Influencing American
Education*, Sixtieth Yearbook, National Society for the Study of
Education, Part II. Chicago: University of Chicago Press, 1961.
A discussion of the impact of political, economic, demographic,
and other factors on education.

Child Development, Thinking Processes, and Learning

Material drawn from studies of child development, thinking processes, human learning, and classroom instruction provides another foundation of the social studies. Knowledge of developmental growth characteristics is helpful in overall planning and as background for studying a particular group of children. Insight into thinking processes can be used when planning units of instruction so as best to develop those cognitive processes that are essential to effective learning. An understanding of strategies for attitude development can be used in all phases of instruction. Guidelines for the most profitable directions for learning are needed for both long-range and daily instructional planning.

3

Developmental Growth Characteristics

Child development is marked by stages of development and other growth characteristics from which implications for social studies instruction can be drawn. The selected characteristics presented in this section should be viewed as descriptions of development, not as prescriptions of what children can and cannot do. The intent is to illustrate how knowledge of child development is put to use in planning the social studies, and to indicate ways in which teachers can use findings from studies to plan instruction.

PRIMARY LEVEL

When children first enter school, they exhibit a variety of characteristics that they have developed through experiences at home and in the neighborhood. Most children have acquired such physical skills as running, jumping, and using such simple tools as scissors. Language and mental development have grown rapidly and most children have a speaking vocabulary of over 2,500 words and a larger listening vocabulary. Make-believe play is evident, identification with others in group play has begun, and interest is moving from a self-centered basis to concern with what others are doing. A major need of the child is to make the transition from home to school and to find security and affection in the classroom.

Young children need to move around, explore the school environment, engage in physical activity, handle objects and materials, make things, learn to read, listen to stories, show things they have made or brought from home, and take part in individual and group activities. A few have already learned to read at home. Their hands seem to get into everything, and they spend what seems like limitless energy in physical activity, dramatic play, rhythms, talking, experimenting with materials, and making things; yet they tire easily and need frequent periods of rest. Eye-hand coordination is not well developed, large muscles are better developed than small muscles, and far-sightedness is characteristic.

Young children need large manipulative materials, such as blocks, to meet their needs for physical activity. What other materials might be used? (San Diego City Schools)

The intellectual development of children beginning school is characterized by great curiosity, inquisitiveness, and a short attention span. Young children's interests tend to focus on immediate ends, the here and now, and on matters related to their own problems. They ask many questions. *What* questions are most frequent, and the number of *why* and *how* questions increases later as they gain insight into causal relationships. Their concepts of time, space, and distance are limited, and they have many misconceptions regarding home and community life, property rights, and when and how events took place. Fact and fancy may be mixed, imagination is evident in speaking and other activities, and spontaneity of expression is characteristic of typical children.

Piaget's studies [1] indicate that children from the ages of around two to seven are in a preoperational stage; they do not carry on such internalized mental operations as joining objects in a class, putting items in a series, or reversing or retracing various processes. Rather they manipulate objects, move them around, arrange them in various ways, and base conclusions on superficial impressions.

A steady growth occurs in group problem-solving skills throughout the primary grades. Group planning, discussion, action, and evaluation become more effective and to the point. Discussion periods increase in length, and group evaluation is better focused in terms of "things to do" to complete different tasks. Yet, periods of concentrated discussion or planning still rarely exceed ten to fifteen minutes. Growth in reading ability and experiences with television extend children's intellectual horizons and make possible the study of topics beyond their immediate environment.

As children progress to Grade III, their individual differences increase, attention spans lengthen, eye-hand coordination improves, far-sightedness decreases, their ability to carry out tasks over longer periods of time improves, and more detail is evident in their construction and art work. Other growth trends include clearer differentiation between reality and fantasy, extension of interests beyond the community, less dependence on adults, rapid growth in reading ability, and more effective recall and use of past experience.

Attitudes are developing toward authority, officials, and other aspects of political culture as well as toward children and adults in groups and social classes different from the child's. Verbal expression of negative attitudes (prejudices) may be evident, and

[1] Millie Almy, *Young Children's Thinking* (New York: Teachers College Press, Columbia University, 1966)

some children openly express a dislike for members of certain groups in ways that have been learned at home.

Characteristics of disadvantaged children are receiving special attention. Their language is simpler in syntax, and they use fewer descriptive terms and modifiers than do middle-class children. Few books and magazines are found in their homes, the naming of objects and activities is not emphasized, and they are less able to use language to handle problems. Their perceptions of social situations, authority figures, the school, and other social institutions is conditioned by an environment that provides fewer opportunities for the development of positive attitudes. Even those children whose parents are migrant workers have not developed the time and space concepts that are possible from travel experiences. Compensatory education is needed to develop language power and to nurture the attitudes and values necessary if such disadvantaged children are to function effectively in school and community situations. Special provisions must be made to build the concepts and related vocabulary required in the social studies. A guiding principle is to plan instruction to meet their individual differences rather than to provide a watered-down version of the social studies. Disadvantaged children need the advantages of new social studies instruction (and new math and science), as do all children.

Implications. Beginners need help and guidance in making the transition from home to school. Teachers must show them affection, encouragement, and understanding, and give them specific directions as to what to do, where to work, when to play, when to rest, and how to get and use materials and return them to their places. Overstimulation can be avoided by careful selection and planning of social studies activities interspersed with periods of rest and relaxation. Short work and discussion periods of ten to fifteen minutes should be followed by rhythms, dramatic expression, games, or other physical activities. Blocks, clay work, large illustrative materials, books with large type, simple construction, easel painting, experience charts, story telling, reading by the teacher, rhythms, singing, playing simple instruments, dramatic representation, sharing periods, and observation of activities and seasonal changes in the neighborhood are put to many uses to promote learning in the social studies.

The transition from self-centered activities is facilitated by providing parallel activities in which two children work side by side, partnership activities in which two children build with blocks or make something, small-group activities in which several children use the playhouse or other centers of interest, and whole-class activities in which the entire group shares ideas, sings, makes plans, or discusses problems. Work areas should be small, involving two or three children at first and increasing to five or six as ability to use materials and work with others increase. Concern for others, cooperation, and responsibleness are emphasized through comments made by the teacher, such as: "Now it is Ben's turn," "That is a good way to help," "Paul is finishing his work," "We share materials," and "That's a good way to use our brushes."

As growth in reading ability takes place, the many stories in supplementary readers that deal with social studies topics are utilized in units of instruction, along with experience charts and social studies textbooks. Teachers must give specific attention to developing the social studies vocabulary needed to handle reading materials. Time, space, distance, and beginning map concepts should be introduced in the context of children's experiences and presented in such units as Our Neighborhood and Community.

In Grades II and III, children's growth in reading ability, attention span, language facility, and thinking processes make possible longer work periods and more intensive units of instruction. Broader aspects of community living, contributions of community workers, community services, modes of transportation and communication, and ways of getting food, shelter, and clothing may be studied in greater depth. Relationships between the child's community and other communities, and comparisons of ways of living in communities in other lands may be undertaken to extend concepts and generalizations and to tap interests created by television, other mass media of communication, and contacts with adults. The concepts and generalizations developed in the primary grades become the child's background for studying other peoples and places in later grades.

INTERMEDIATE LEVEL

The transition from Grade III to IV does not represent a sharp break in a child's development. Each child has his own growth patterns, individual differences continue to increase, and there is much overlapping of growth characteristics between grades. Children develop more refined skills, make rapid progress in concept attainment, tend to form more cohesive sets of values, and take a more clear-cut sex role. Physical growth in Grades IV–VI continues to be steady with a lag just before puberty. Some girls enter the puberty cycle, and girls are generally more advanced than boys.

Social development in children is marked by emerging peer values, sex cleavage, formation of groups, and increased interest in cooperative activities. They do not regard adult values as highly as they did in earlier years, and may reject them if they are in conflict with peer values. Children wish to become self-directive, more independent, more self-assertive. Acceptance by their peers becomes more important, and rejection by them may create feelings of insecurity and anxiety. Rejection by adults, or ridicule and sarcasm which lead to feelings of rejection, also creates feelings of insecurity. A major need is to maintain security with adults, and at the same time to gain a place among their peers. Middle-class children are more responsive to long-range goals, more willing to comply with regulations, more respectful, and less fearful of authority and less prone to fighting than are lower-class children.

Piaget's studies of intellectual development indicate that from around the ages of seven to eleven children are in a stage of concrete operations; they can think in terms of concepts and symbols related to objects and actions they have experienced.[2] Children can carry out such internalized operations as classifying objects, putting events in a series, and anticipating consequences without having objects before them, and these operations can be reversed.

Intellectual growth is marked by active curiosity, wider interests, more realistic creative expression of thoughts and feelings, refinement of reading ability, improvement of independent study skills, growth in problem-solving ability, and greater insight into causal relationships. Attention span increases and concentration is given to tasks over a longer period of time. Level of aspiration increases and is reflected in more effective self-evaluation, and in criticism of maps, murals, reports, and other materials prepared by pupils. A rapid growth in knowledge of social studies concepts occurs in Grades IV through VIII. Time, distance, space, and map concepts develop in relationship to the extent to which they are stressed in the social studies program. Chronology and historical time are difficult for children to grasp, and such concepts as latitude and longitude must be intensively taught if they are to be truly learned and put to use. Eye-hand coordination improves, and most children can make accurate and detailed maps, graphs, charts, diagrams, and models.

Social attitudes are sharpening and some children show nega-

[2] J. H. Flavell, *The Developmental Psychology of Jean Piaget* (Princeton, N.J.: D. Van Nostrand Co., Inc., 1963).

The ability to develop cross-cultural understandings may be brought to higher levels in the middle grades. What understandings might be emphasized in a study of Mexico? *(San Diego County)*

Creative expression reaches a high level in the middle grades. What other types of creative activity should be provided in connection with social studies experiences? *(Los Angeles)*

tive attitudes; stereotypes about other groups appear. Children from authoritarian homes tend to be more prejudiced than children from homes with a democratic atmosphere. Children show a growing sense of right and wrong and a willingness to use persuasion and reason in attaining their goals. A more critical sense of justice is expressed in fair-play, teamwork, being a good sport, and helping others. This sense of fair-play contributes much to the success with which teachers can develop wholesome attitudes and appreciations while presenting various units of the social studies.

Implications. A child's transition from primary to intermediate grades must be smooth. Increasing individual differences should be taken into account by including a variety of activities and materials in each unit of instruction, flexible grouping, individualized assignments, variation in time requirements, and variation in what is expected of individual children.

In planning units of instruction, teachers should give direct attention to cross-cultural understandings, geographical relationships, and historical time concepts. Comparing ways of living at home and in other lands, discovering and presenting relationships on maps, blocking out major time periods on charts and time lines, reading to discover relationships and to make comparisons, and classifying ideas under key concepts and generalizations are helpful procedures. The heavy load of terms and concepts in reading materials requires direct instruction in vocabulary development.

Individual study skills and group work skills can be used extensively. Teachers should have clear purposes for individual and group work, and direct instruction should be provided on related skills.

Committees should be organized to gather information on topics related to questions and problems defined by the group. More care is needed to select, discuss, and relate current affairs to basic units of instruction. The use of children's weekly newspapers, clippings, news magazines, newspapers, and radio and television programs should be carefully planned to extend the development of key concepts, generalizations, attitudes, and appreciations.

Thinking processes can be developed through problem solving. Emphasis is given not only to the *what, when, where,* and *who,* but also to the *how* and *why.* Key concepts and generalizations can be used to guide inquiry and organize data.

A variety of creative and esthetic experiences are needed to enrich concepts and develop appreciations. Creative expression should be encouraged through related language activities, art work, construction, musical activities, weaving, making of dioramas, and dramatic representation. The art, music, literature, and folk dances of early America can be used to help children identify more closely with the hopes, feelings, and aspirations of the colonists and pioneers, and similar experiences should be provided as other lands and peoples are studied.

UPPER GRADE LEVEL

The in-between age, the awkward transition from childhood to adulthood, the uneasy shift to more mature forms of behavior —this is adolescence. Many children in Grades VII and VIII are already in its beginning stages and must endure the uncertainties, the vacillation between independence and dependence, the desire for freedom from adult controls yet the need for adult guidance, acting like a grownup one minute and being a child the next, and wanting to do the right thing without revealing that one is not sure just what the right thing is. Yet some seventh and eighth graders, boys more frequently than girls, still exhibit characteristics of intermediate grade children. Their physical growth rates are slower and they have not developed the physical and social characteristics of those who are entering the adolescent period.

Because of differences in rates of maturation, home backgrounds, and the impact of the educational program, individual differences among pupils are great in Grades VII and VIII. Reading ability ranges from primary level to high school level, mental ability shows great variation among children, and a given child may have high linguistic ability yet relatively low quantitative ability. Independent study skills are well developed by some children while others need specific direction as to what to do to handle work in the social studies. Coupled with these differences are variations in energy output, restlessness, posture, awkwardness, social skills, poise, interests, future plans, and personality.

Certain general characteristics emerge in the upper grades. Most children work out a more definite masculine or feminine role. Greater identification with age-mates leads them to differentiate more sharply between their own world and that of adults. Social development is marked by increasing ability to cooperate, a strong desire for group approval, and more critical selection of friends. Concern about self is great and peer values serve as guides to behavior in many situations. Speech is patterned after that of the gang or clique. Self-criticism in terms of peer values, a desire for freedom from adult domination, and eagerness to make one's own decisions are evident. Many are concerned about the future, are searching for values and ideals, and are in need of help in finding a place for themselves as individuals and as members of groups. Students at this age want to be accepted and treated as adults, yet they need guidance and help in handling not only school problems, but personal and social problems as well.

Their interests are broadening. The impact of the mass media in certain ways expands these interests, in other ways channels them. They have greater understanding of contemporary affairs at home and in other countries; at the same time, they are deeply involved in their own styles of language, modes of dress, popular music, and other aspects of the *mass culture* of youth. Hero-worship is typical and the behavior of "ideal types" is copied.

Piaget's studies indicate that children move from the stage of concrete operations to formal operation somewhere between the ages of ten and fourteen.[3] In the stage of formal operations children can carry on hypothetical reasoning, make deductions, and carry out other mental operations without being limited to their own firsthand experiences. They can handle abstractions with increasing facility and can manage a variety of logical operations if appropriate instruction is given.

Intellectual development is characterized by increasing interest in more advanced problems and ideas, rapid concept development, and increasing ability to formulate generalizations. Time and space concepts are more easily grasped, and historical sequences, chronology, and time periods can be presented in greater detail. Individual reading, study, and reporting can be used to advantage in promoting learning and in meeting individual differences. Problems are attacked with increasing skill, group planning and discussion become more advanced, and most students are able to give sustained application to problems.

Implications. The development of increased ability to do abstract thinking, develop generalizations, and use reading-study skills opens new horizons of inquiry. Social, political, historical, economic, and geographic aspects of living in the United States, other lands, and early cultures can be studied in greater depth. Greater use can be made of multiple textbooks, library resources, and individual study projects.

Democratic values and processes should be studied in greater

[3] Jerome S. Bruner, *The Process of Education* (Cambridge: Harvard University Press, 1960).

depth as American history is taught. Practical applications should be made to community living, and to problems of government at the local, state, and national level. The early origins and growth of the democratic idea, the spread of the democratic idea in Europe and the Americas. the extension of democratic principles down through the years, the efforts of new nations to achieve freedom, and the responsibilities of each generation to preserve our democratic heritage are among the key ideas to be emphasized. As the contributions of great men and women are studied, individual responsibilities of citizenship and conceptions of loyalty and patriotism should be clarified and intensified.

Teachers are needed who "understand" and who can meet individual differences without causing embarrassment. Sarcasm, ridicule, and talking down to pupils should be avoided. Pupils at this age want to be treated as adults but they still need much help in handling both problems arising from their school work and the personal and social problems characteristic of this period of development.

Systematic attention should be given to the skills involved in reading, using the library, gathering and organizing information,

The skill children possess at this level can be utilized in map-making activities of various types. (Hays; Courtesy of Monkmeyer)

using maps, and problem solving. Planning for individual differences is imperative so that each child will show maximum growth in utilizing these skills in the social studies.

Teachers should guide students' study of reading materials and other resources in order to help them detect conflicting points of view, clarify issues, and improve their ability to secure reliable sources of information. Substantial progress can be made in the analysis of propaganda and persuasion materials and in contrasting democratic ways of living with those in totalitarian regimes. Criteria for judging materials, points of view, and proposed solutions to problems are useful in improving critical thinking skills; these may be related to pupils' activities and to significant topics in the social studies program through group discussion and planning.

Developing Thinking Processes

Nothing in recent years has stimulated teachers more than the challenge to develop the thinking processes of students. Although the ways of bringing this about have been debated, everyone seems to agree that the cultivation of thinking ability is a basic goal of education. As stated by one group: "The purpose which runs through and strengthens all other purposes—the common thread of education—is the development of the ability to think." [4]

At this point, several questions need to be considered: How is thinking defined? How is it initiated? What types of processes are used in the social studies? What are the outcomes?

A SYMBOLIC PROCESS

Thinking is a process which involves signs, signals, and symbols of events and objects. In the social studies, great use is made of word symbols, and children must be able to distinguish words and to associate meanings with words if they are to use them as symbols in their thinking. Number symbols and symbols on maps, charts, and other graphic materials are also used and must also be distinguished, interpreted, and associated with the various objects and activities they represent.

INITIATION OF THINKING

Thinking processes are initiated by stimulus patterns which

---

[4] Educational Policies Commission, *The Central Purpose of American Education* (Washington, D.C.: National Education Association, 1961).

have meaning for the individual; stimuli may be internal or external in origin. A perplexity, need, want, difficulty, question, or problem may stimulate thinking in the social studies. Children must, however, be able to correctly recognize and associate appropriate meanings with questions, problems, and other stimuli if their thinking is to take desirable directions.

SEQUENCE OF IDEAS

After thinking is stimulated, a pattern or sequence of ideas occurs that may include percepts, images, memories, concepts, and generalizations. An individual's thinking is affected by such personal factors as motives, emotions, attitudes, needs, self-concept, habits, skills, and capacity. In the social studies, thinking is directed by setting purposes, defining problems, and proposing hypotheses, and is enriched by meaningful content introduced through films, study trips, textbooks, and other instructional resources.

TYPES OF THINKING

Six types of thinking are of special importance in the social studies. Perception, association, and concept attainment are the three types prerequisite to higher levels of thinking. The higher levels of thinking are problem solving, critical thinking, and creative thinking.

OUTCOMES OF THINKING

Typical outcomes of thinking in the social studies are solutions to problems, answers to questions, and conclusions. However, there may be many other outcomes such as a clearer definition of terms, new meaning, deeper understanding, enriched or new concepts and generalizations, a grasp of relationships, or a refined classification of objects or events. Outcomes of thinking may also include changes in attitudes, appreciations, and beliefs. Outcomes of critical or reflective thinking may be described as considered opinions, reasoned beliefs, and sound judgments. Another outcome may be the improvement of skill in using cognitive processes. Finally, the new perplexities, needs, wants, difficulties, questions, problems, and hypotheses that result from thinking may lead to the initiation of a new flow of thinking processes.

A summary of the various aspects of thinking is given in the diagram in Chart 1.

A SUMMARY OF SELECTED ASPECTS OF THINKING

Thinking is a symbolic process
Objects and events are represented by
signs, signals, and symbols.

Stimulus patterns initiate thinking
Perplexities   Needs   Wants   Difficulties   Questions   Problems
Their meaning is interpreted by the individual.

A pattern or sequence of ideas is evoked
that may include such materials of thinking as
Percepts   Images   Memories   Concepts   Generalizations
The Pattern or Sequence of Ideas Is Affected By Personal Factors
such as
Motives   Emotions   Attitudes   Needs   Self-Concept   Habits   Skills

One or more types of thinking
may be involved
Perceptual   Associative   Conceptual   Problem Solving   Critical   Creative
Processes that may be involved
include one or more of the following
Discrimination   Interpretation   of   Meaning   Abstraction   Generalization
Induction   Deduction   Hypothesizing
Analysis   Application   Synthesis   Reasoning

Outcomes of thinking
may include
Concepts   Generalizations   Interpretations   Solutions   Conclusions
Definitions   Meaning   Understanding   Classifications   Relationships
Changed. Attitudes   Appreciations   Values
Considered Opinions   Reasoned Beliefs   Judgments
Improved Habits, Techniques, and Skills of Thinking
New Perplexities   Needs   Wants   Difficulties   Questions   Problems

Chart 1

Perception, Association, Concept Attainment

Relationships and differences among perception, association, and concept attainment operate in the social studies as follows: Perception involves the process of discriminating and differentiating the characteristics or properties of objects and events; for example, a child examines a flintlock rifle, or a picture of one, and notices specific details. He may form a percept or mental image which can be recalled later even though the rifle is not present. Association involves the process of relating or linking a percept, meaning, or idea with one or several others; for example, a child may associate the term flintlock rifle with his percept, and he may also associate with his percept a stream of thoughts such as hunting game, defending the fort, and so on. Concept attainment is the process of abstracting or generalizing properties that an object or event has in common with others; for example, the properties that the flintlock rifle has in common with other rifles, guns, or weapons. As children gain experience, concepts and associations become a part of the thinking process as various objects and events are perceived. For example, when an older child first sees a flintlock rifle, he probably wonders what kind of gun it is, how it works, how it is like others, how it is different, and what it was used for.

Several points may be drawn from this illustration. Separate planning and emphasis on each process of thinking is not always necessary and may even interfere with clear thinking, but each type should be recognized and given attention as needed. Specific attention should be given to detailed and precise perception of the characteristics of objects and events that are included in each unit of instruction. If children cannot clearly differentiate objects, words, and map symbols, they will not develop clear and precise meanings. The desired associations that are essential to thinking and learning in the social studies should be stressed by the teacher in setting purposes, directing the children's observation, guiding discussion, and evaluating outcomes. Finally, the class of objects or events to which the item being studied belongs should be clarified, and the item should be placed in the class with others that have similar attributes. Teaching usually begins with questions such as *What is it? How is it used?* and moves to *How is it like others? How is it different?* Related concepts and meanings are drawn in, and the terms that are used to name the object and describe its uses are associated with the object. During this process, the object is being conceptualized or grouped into the class of objects to which it belongs, and the child's concept is said to be growing.

An example involving an intangible concept will further illustrate the relationships among perception, association, and concept attainment. The intangible concept *interdependence* is stressed in the social studies from the early grades on through secondary schools and is given attention in nearly all units of instruction. Perception is involved as children distinguish relationships among members of the family, children in school, farmers and suburbanites, community workers, and people in other settings. Association is involved as words are learned to describe the relationships, and as activities and processes related to interdependence are brought together in meaningful associations. Concept attainment is involved as children discover the many ways in which people depend on one another, and classify them meaningfully. Through reading and study, children develop greater depth and breadth of understanding of people throughout the world.

The teacher-learning process here differs somewhat from that involved in the example on the flintlock rifle. The beginning questions are not *What is it?* and *How is it used?* Rather, attention is directed to subconcepts and related ideas and meanings through such questions as: *How do members of the family depend on each other? What do we get from farms? What do farmers get in the city? What are the contributions of different community workers? How do community workers depend on each other?* Out of the meanings and associations derived from experiences related to such questions comes a beginning concept of how individuals depend on others; this becomes the basis for an ever-growing concept of interdependence that will be limited only by the child's future experiences in analyzing and synthesizing human relationships.

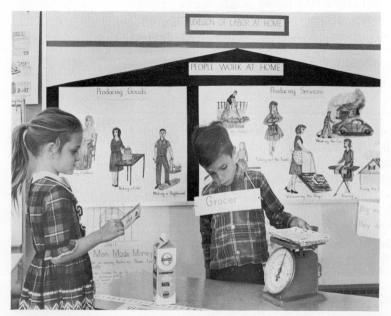

How is associative thinking involved in the learning of terms such as these? What types of experiences are necessary to develop vocabulary and the meanings related to them? *(San Diego City Schools)*

PROVIDING VARIED EXPERIENCES

Activities, such as study trips, construction and processing of materials, and dramatic representation, and resources, such as films, pictures, recordings, and models, provide sensory experiences that may be used to develop children's perceptual, associative, and conceptual abilities. Careful planning and direction is needed to make such activities effective. Teachers should establish readiness—in the sense of *expectancy* on the part of each child— by planning and discussing the items that will be observed and by relating them to past experiences and to possible uses of ideas suggested by the activities. Immediate follow-up activities are needed: the similarities and differences in the observations made by the children may be discussed, and the information obtained may be organized and put to practical uses. Specific guidelines for planning and using sensory activities in the social studies are presented in later chapters.

Although sensory experiences are valuable in building and extending concepts, they alone cannot develop the range of concepts needed for thinking and learning in the social studies. The meanings developed through firsthand sensory experiences must be given depth; this calls for vicarious experiences that take the child far beyond the objects and events that he has experienced directly. As a child builds concepts and is able to think about his experiences without having real things before him, a new world of learning is opened for him. Through books, maps, discussion, individual study, and other vicarious experiences, his thinking and learning can reach ever higher levels.

Teachers can develop various shades of meaning by using literature, rhythms, art, and music. A reading of stirring tales of Daniel Boone extends the meaning of *scout, defending the fort,* and *adventures of early explorers*. Recordings of songs sung by the pioneers as they went west, and carefully selected pictures which depict the joys, sorrows, hopes, aspirations, and tragedies of the pioneers as they established homes and towns, give overtones of feeling to terms such as *husking bees, clearing, attack, homemaking, hardship, courageous,* and *fearless* that can be attained in no other way. Similarly, folk dances help children see how the pioneers enjoyed themselves and provided *recreation*. Such qualitative aspects of concept building must not be overlooked.

Group sharing of experiences through discussion, reporting, and story-telling aids in concept building; pictures, models, and objects should also be used to clarify specific meanings. Children and resource persons who have taken trips to places being studied can tell about them and show pictures and photographs to the class. Materials brought by children that relate to concepts in the unit can be discussed, demonstrated, and used to increase understanding. During a study of Mexico, for example, one child brought *pottery, clothing,* and *jewelry.* In a study of China, two children brought in and demonstrated the use of the *ehru, temple bells,* and a *gong.* Another child brought pictures of Chinese boats and pointed out the differences between *junks, sampans,* and other kinds of Chinese boats.

Without discussion of purposes, clarification of problems, evaluation, and reflection upon relationships to past experience and future action, activities have little value. One child illustrated this point very well during an activity involving construction designed to develop concepts of a Mexican bazaar. When asked what he was making, he said, "I'm just nailing boards to this box." He had not been in on the planning, discussion, and evaluation of the bazaar for use in the study of Mexico. In terms of his experiences he was truly just nailing boards.

Both the number and the difficulty of the concepts must be considered; too many concepts at one time may lead to misconceptions, confusion, boredom, word-calling without meaning, and little or no comprehension. A long, tedious list of ideas to check on a study trip, during a film, or in a dictionary, may result in superficial learning.

In each unit, children need opportunities not only to develop new concepts, but to enrich and extend concepts that they already have. For example, in a well-planned study of colonial and pioneer life, concepts of such terms as these will be learned: *town meeting, dame schools, church services, food, clothing, candlemaking, ways of travel, utensils,* and *weapons.* At the same time, children should extend and enrich their understanding of how the early Americans met their needs for *food, shelter,* and *clothing.*

An effective approach to concept building is to consider the specific experiences in a unit of work and to determine the concepts that are most significant. Their value is shown by the needs for their use which arise in class and by the misconceptions children reveal regarding them. Thus, concepts which are needed in reading materials, films, study trips, construction, dramatic play, discussion, and other experiences may be noted and developed in a manner similar to that used in the following examples.

In a unit on The Farm, a group of lower-grade children developed and used concepts of such words as *silo, corral, feeding, milking, crush, bottle, calf, seeds, garden, barn, chute, hay,* and *fodder* through visiting a dairy farm to see a *silo, corral, barn,* and the *feeding* and *milking* of cows; engaging in and discussing dramatic play related to *chores* on the farm; constructing and using *corrals* and *barns* in dramatic play; collecting *seeds*, planting them, and caring for a *garden*; finding out how *plants* grow with different types of *soil* and varying amounts of sunshine and water; reading and listening to stories related to life on the farm; expressing group and individual experiences through art, rhythms, discussion, group chart making, and songs; and seeing a film on farm life. All of the foregoing were used in connection with significant questions in the unit.

As a result of these experiences, the children expressed several generalizations. Among them were the following:

> There are many different kinds of farms.
> Farmers sell their products and use the money to buy things they need.
> New machines make it possible to farm with fewer workers.
> Farmers change the land and accept the weather.

Problem Solving, Critical Thinking, Creative Thinking

These three modes of thinking are interrelated. For example, problem solving includes critical and creative thinking at various points. And all three processes include various aspects of perceptual, associative, and conceptual processes as they are put to use in the social studies.

PROBLEM SOLVING

Problem solving includes such steps as (1) recognizing and defining problems, (2) recalling past experience and framing tentative solutions or hypotheses, (3) gathering data, (4) appraising, organizing, and interpreting data, and (5) drawing and checking conclusions. Although the foregoing steps may not be followed in the order given above, each usually may be identified in a complete act of thought and in which a problem is solved.

In different units of instruction, problem-solving processes can be applied to a large number of questions and problems, such as: How do we benefit from the work of different community workers? How should we organize and present a program for our parents to show them what we have learned? How has our community changed from early times to the present? How can natural resources be conserved in our state? How are countries working together to help new nations? Such questions and problems may be raised by the children or by the teacher, or they may be found in reading materials, films, and other instructional materials. The important point is that children must understand and be concerned about them if their thinking is to be stimulated by them.

In the study of questions and problems that arise in units, teachers may direct children's thinking through discussion that gets at each of the steps in problem solving. Chart 2 may be used as a model of basic questions to raise with children in the course of solving a problem.

QUESTIONS TO DIRECT OUR THINKING
What is the main question or problem?
Are there related questions or problems?
How is the main problem like others we have studied?
How is it different?
What do we know about it right now?
What additional information do we need?
How shall we obtain the needed information?
What sources of information should be used?
How shall we check the accuracy of information?
How shall we organize the information after it is collected and summarized?
What interpretations can be made of the information?
What conclusions or generalizations can be made on the basis of the information?

Chart 2

CRITICAL THINKING

In critical thinking, emphasis is given to the making of an evaluation in terms of standards or criteria. In addition, critical thinking is more of a logical process than it is a problem-solving process in that the individual examines an object or process in order to determine the extent to which given standards are met. Concepts involved in the standards or criteria must be understood, a clear perception of what is being appraised is essential, judgment must be suspended until the evidence is weighed, and feelings must be controlled if a sound appraisal is to be made.

In many situations in the social studies, critical examinations are made of ideas, proposals, issues, points of view, adherence to work standards, discussion procedures, map making, dramatic play, construction, committee work, statements in reading materials, and ideas presented in audio-visual materials. The initial process may be called deductive in that standards are used to make appraisals or judgments. For example, in evaluating discussion the direction of thinking is set by standards embedded in such questions as: Did we stick to the topic? Did each individual participate? Were different points made? Were important questions raised? While thinking about each question, the child attempts to recall pertinent points and to analyze his behavior and that of others. Specific instances may be remembered; strengths and weaknesses of individual contributions may be recalled; the child's perception of his role and that of others may be considered; feelings aroused during discussion may arise again. All of these may affect the child's judgment as he attempts to make an appraisal of how well he and other children have participated in discussion.

Critical thinking processes also are used extensively in the evaluation of ideas presented in instructional materials. For example, statements in textbooks and current materials, arguments presented on current issues, descriptions of cause-effect relationships, terms and phrases that stimulate emotions, propaganda techniques, and exaggerated and incongruous points may be selected for critical review. Facts may be differentiated from opinions, relevant and irrelevant information may be noted, the evidence for various statements may be examined, and conclusions may be checked against the facts presented to support them. Specific word meanings may be analyzed to get below the surface to the deeper meaning that is intended. Charts 3 and 4 are illustrative.

THINKING CRITICALLY AS YOU READ	THINKING CRITICALLY AS YOU SEE FILMS
Select points that are related to questions and problems.	Look for ideas related to questions and problems we are considering.
Check statements against facts.	Check the facts against other sources.
Separate facts from opinions.	Look for main ideas and supporting facts.
Figure out the writer's point of view on problems.	Watch for terms or scenes that have special meaning.
Find all sides to issues and problems.	Look out for short parts that cover a long period of time or space.
Look out for words that stir feelings.	Look for new and different ways of doing things.
Consider all the evidence before making a judgment.	Make comparisons between the ways you do things and the ways that are shown.

Chart 3   Chart 4

As children gain experience, this type of thinking may be put to use in examining beliefs and values that are meaningful to them. For example, *taking turns, fair-play, equal opportunity,* and *rights of others* may be considered in terms of why we value them, how they improve working relations, and how we can extend them to various situations. Beliefs or values that are just "taken on" because of association with others will not be firmly grounded in understanding. A person who takes on beliefs uncritically is trained, not educated. If the learner reflects, reconstructs, and tests beliefs, he will be more likely to have evidential grounds and not just an emotional basis for holding them. Both the meaning and significance of treasured values and beliefs are thus enhanced.

CREATIVE THINKING

The term *creative* implies something new or original. For a child it may be a new interpretation, a grasp of new relationships, an original synthesis and expression of ideas, a new proposal or hypothesis, or a new way of doing something. Originality rather than conformity, divergent thinking in which multiple responses are made rather than convergent thinking in which unifying responses are made, and production of new ideas rather than reproduction of old ideas are earmarks of creative thinking. Basic to creativity are such traits as sensitivity to problems, fluency of ideas and words, expressional fluency, semantic flexibility and elaboration, originality, perception of objects and activities in new ways, and redefinition of symbols.

The thinking processes involved in creativity may be intuitive at times with bursts of insight and discovery. An individual may arrive at a hunch, idea, or hypothesis without formal analysis, in which thinking proceeds one step at a time. However, analytical processes may be used in checking proposals and hypotheses, and the greater the individual's background of understanding and skill, the greater are the opportunities for him to make new discoveries, proposals, and hypotheses. Imagery, perception of relationships, association of meanings, imagination, restructuring of concepts and generalizations, attitudes, and preferences may be involved as a child searches for a novel solution to a problem or a new way to express an idea.

In the social studies, creative thinking is stimulated as children are encouraged to suggest new ideas or ways of doing things, express thoughts and feelings in original ways, and propose solutions to problems. Examples of experiences in which creative thinking may be developed are the planning and arranging of work centers and displays, framing hypotheses, organizing and summarizing information in new ways on maps and charts, constructing objects, dramatizing, expressing thoughts and feelings through art and music, expressing ideas through oral and written

Sailboats

There goes a sailboat
   out to sea.
Think of the colors
   the sails might be.
In the morning, yellow;
   at evening, brown.
But when it gets dark,
   they all come down.

Grade 4

Along the Trail

Slowly
Autoharp

The trail from dawn to sun-set was dust-y, hard, and long. The

Gaily

pi-o-neer at ev'ning re-laxed with dance and song.

Snowflakes

Down, down, down they
   came,
A few at first, and then
   so many
That when I looked up
   toward the sky,
All I could see was
   whirling, twirling,
Soft white flakes
   of snow.

Louise

Sand Storm

The trees rocked
back and forth.
   The wind howled around
the eaves of the house.
   It blew sand
out of the gutters.
   The screens and doors
slammed and slammed.

Creativity takes many different forms and may be expressed by individuals or groups. What other modes of expression might be used in the social studies? *(San Bernardino County)*

language activities, and planning activities to culminate a unit of instruction.

Creative thinking is not limited to special activities in the social studies; it is an approach to problems or a way of viewing them that can open new horizons to children. For example, as different pictures, films, and other materials are used in units of instruction, questions such as the following will stimulate creative thinking:

What do you see in this picture that is new? In what other ways could it have been shown? How could we express it?

What do you think about that statement? Which words have special meaning? How could it be improved?

How is this film related to an experience you have had? How is it different? How did this part make you feel? How would you tell it or write it to express your feelings?

How is this idea related to that one? How are these ideas alike? How are they different?

What do you think will happen next? How is this related to what happened before? Can you think of several possible outcomes?

How about the conclusion? In what other way could it be stated? Does it lead to other ideas? Is follow-up action suggested?

Questions such as these can be adapted to fit all units of instruction. If used wisely, they will spark creative thinking in children who may, in turn, stimulate others to use a creative approach.

Creative thinking processes also are put to use in creative reading in the social studies. Creative reading takes the reader beyond the literal interpretation to implied meanings, appreciative reactions, and evaluation. The reader visualizes what he reads, identifies himself with characters, recalls his own experiences and compares them with experiences presented in the text, anticipates what is coming, notes biases, searches for new relationships, and tries to bring together ideas from several sources. Charts 5 and 6 illustrate specific points related to creative reading.

A first step in promoting the development of creative thinking is to provide the types of experience which help children develop insights. During this phase, attention is given to the perception of relationships, development of concepts, use of expressive terms and phrases, use of pictures and other materials that stimulate imagery, reading of materials that help to build word pictures, discussion of children's reactions, and consideration of the most significant aspects of the topic under study. A teacher's main purposes during this phase are to sensitize children to creative

CREATIVE READERS

Find special meanings of words and phrases.

Grasp the main ideas and supporting details.

Relate ideas to your own experiences.

Discover hidden or implied meanings.

Think of ways ideas and meanings can be related.

Search for ways to apply ideas.

Put ideas to use in other activities.

Chart 5

GETTING A FEELING FOR OTHERS AS YOU READ

Try to picture how they live.

Look for words and phrases that stir your feelings.

Look for humor, exaggeration, and comparisons.

Try to put yourself in their place.

Try to figure out why they do things their way.

Try to guess how they do things and then check to see if you are right.

Chart 6

possibilities and to provide background experiences that will enable them to approach various activities with freshness and spontaneity.

A closely related phase of creativity is the child's organizing, reorganizing, and consolidating of new learnings. Some preliminary attempts at creative expression may be seen in the discussion, sharing, planning, and evaluation which takes place as children clarify meanings, express reactions, and begin to explore creative possibilities. Fluency of thinking, flexibility in handling ideas, and intuitive processes develop along with increasing depth of understanding and the ability to reorganize ideas into new patterns. In this phase, new thoughts and feelings are structured and restructured in ways that are the child's very own.

Closely related to the process of reorganizing and consolidating the thoughts and feelings gleaned from background experiences is the phase of creative thinking in which new insights and relationships, and possible ways of expressing them, are discovered. Some writers refer to this as the stage of illumination, or discovery, in which the individual says, "I've got it!" For a child it is the discovery of a fresh and original way in which he can express the thoughts and feelings that have been building up within him.

In the next phase, the child proceeds to try out, or verify, the creative idea that he has discovered. His perceptions,

CREATIVE THINKERS

Build up a background of ideas.

Organize ideas in new ways.

Search for original ways to express ideas.

Select the best from the old and new.

Are willing to try new ideas.

Check their ways of working in order to improve.

Chart 7

association of meanings, feelings, imagination, skill in handling various media, aesthetic judgment, background of understanding, and unique way of expressing his thoughts and feelings are a part of his attempts to create a product that is representative of his discovery. In the process of creating something—whether it be a mural, model, dramatic portrayal, picture, a hypothesis— he may change it, redo it, alter a part of it, or start anew as he evaluates and judges the adequacy of his expression of the original idea. Vital elements in this phase are the original conception of the idea, the perception of progress in expressing it, and the integration of various elements into a harmonious whole. The child's self-evaluation as he works is important in determining how he proceeds and what form the final product will take.

Remember that creativity involves more than intellectual capacity, problem solving, critical thinking, and basic skills. Creativeness is a step beyond the conventional to new ideas, new relationships, new expression of thoughts and feelings, new discoveries. It is contributory to individual self-fulfillment and essential to the progress of society.

Strategies for Developing Basic Cognitive Processes

Underlying the types of thinking discussed in the preceding sections are certain cognitive processes that can be developed through systematic instruction. The overall strategy is to plan a sequence that begins with concept building, moves to interpreting and generalizing, moves on to applying concepts and generalizations, includes experiences in analyzing and synthesizing data, and involves processes of evaluating or judging as needed. The basic skills in each cognitive process are developed by asking questions which require the use of skills as well as content. The following examples include major elements in each cognitive process and illustrate questions that may be used to focus attention on each element.

CONCEPT BUILDING

Fundamental to other cognitive processes is the attainment of concepts which are the building blocks of generalizations, inferences, hypotheses, and criteria for use in evaluation. The general sequence of development is as follows:

Identifying and enumerating objects or events to be classified such as foods, resources, products:

What items did you see in the picture? The film? In reading materials?

Discriminating special features and abstracting common elements:

How are they alike? How are they different? What do some items have in common?

Grouping into categories according to common characteristics, qualities, uses, or other criteria:

Which ones belong together? How can we group them? Are there other ways to group them? Which is best for our purpose?

Naming or labelling groups:

What is a good name for each group? How can we find out if we do not know?

The development of concept clusters follows the same general pattern but goes beyond single-concept development to include the linking together of a set of related concepts. For example, the cluster of concepts in *major landforms* might proceed as follows. Examples of *plains* are identified, special features such as flatness are identified and abstracted, grouping of examples of plains takes place, and the term *plain* is applied. Similarly, *hills, plateaus,* and *mountains* are considered with special attention to contrasts and comparisons among them. The next step is to discover what all four have in common, that is, they are landforms of major importance. Now the label of major landforms can be applied and plains, hills, plateaus, and mountains are subsumed under it.

INTERPRETING DATA AND GENERALIZING

These processes require a solid grounding in the content that is to be interpreted and an understanding of the concepts that are to be used in generalizations. After information has been gathered and organized, the following may be used to make interpretations, draw conclusions, and give explanations:

Making comparative interpretations:

What work do different individuals do (members of the family, community workers, and so forth)? How are their jobs alike? How are they different?

What are the main resources in our state? How do they compare with those in other states?

What are the major differences (contrasts) between homes in colonial times and those of the present?

Discovering relationships among phenomena:

How are responsibilities related to duties at home?

How is price affected by supply and demand?

How are climate and vegetation related? Resources and industries?

How are events in this period related to events in the next one?

Drawing conclusions and generalizations from data:

What can we conclude from this report on conservation problems?

How can we state the main idea supported by this evidence?

What is the main thing we have learned about the relationship between industrial growth and the movement of people to cities?

Giving explanations of phenomena:

Who can tell why families must make choices as to what to buy?

How can we explain why Japan has become a leading industrial nation?

How can we explain the differences in the views of this group and that group?

APPLYING CONCEPTS AND PRINCIPLES

The development of this process requires the transfer of learning to new situations. Concepts and principles which the individual understands are applied in the following ways:

Using concepts and concept clusters to compare two or more objects, events, or activities:

How can we use the idea of dividing the work to find out about other families? Other communities? Other nations?

How can we use the concept major landforms to compare our country with Canada?

Using principles or generalizations to make predictions:

What do you think would happen if members of the family did not carry out responsibilities?

What would you expect the jobs of members of the family to be in other places?

What do you think a country with coal, iron ore, and limestone might produce?

If a country is next to an ocean, what effect might this have on climate? What might happen when the winds blow from land to sea? Sea to land?

Explaining and supporting predictions and anticipated consequences:
>Why do you think that would happen? What are your rea-
sons? Can you explain why you think so?
>
>Can you give supporting facts? What is the evidence?
>
>What would cause that to happen? What conditions would
be necessary? Can you think of other conditions that would
be required?

Verifying or checking predictions and anticipated consequences:
>How can we find out if members of the family in other
places really do that?
>
>How can we check or prove which is right? What sources
of evidence are best? Which one that we have used before
may be helpful now?

ANALYZING AND SYNTHESIZING

Analysis is employed to break down events, activities, and
objects into parts, for example, division of labor in the home
or community may be broken down into specific jobs of individuals, the processing of milk or the making of steel may be
considered step-by-step, or a model of a covered wagon may be
analyzed part by part. In addition, analysis is used to check the
meanings of words in different contexts, the assumptions behind
statements, and the extent of error or bias in statements. Synthesis is employed to bring ideas, parts, principles, and events
together into wholes, for example, oral and written reports, plans
for experiments or other activities, a set of related main ideas
about a place under study, or a sequence of historical events
related to growth of the community, state, and nation. In addition, maps, murals, charts, models, programs, and dramatic activities may be a synthesis of key learnings. Basic skills in these
processes and illustrative questions to stimulate their development
are as follows:

Analyzing specific parts or elements:
>What are the main things in this part of the neighborhood?
>
>What are the steps in producing milk? Wool? Lumber?
Steel?
>
>What were the main events in the founding of our commu-
nity?

Analyzing relationships between parts or elements:
>How are homes, schools, and other places linked together?

> How are the steps in milk production related?
>
> How is each event related to the next in the founding of our community?
>
> Selecting elements to synthesize into a whole:
> How can we use these items to make a floor layout of the area around our school?
>
> What events shall we include in a program on the early history of our state?
>
> Showing relationships between parts or elements:
> How can we show the relationships among these events?
>
> What is a good way to organize our reports, program, play, and the like so that the parts are related?
>
> Deciding on a pattern or principles for the synthesis:
> How shall we organize our reports? Around main ideas? Around questions? Most important events? Other ways?
>
> How should we arrange events about colonial life? Around the most important people? Places where events occurred? Within time periods?

EVALUATING OR JUDGING

Evaluating or judging involves the use of criteria to assess plans, objects, activities, and events. Important phases of the process are clarifying what is to be judged, defining criteria, applying the criteria, making the judgments, and checking the judgment with others. Both internal and external standards are used in the social studies as shown in the following examples:

> Evaluating in terms of internal standards:
> Was our discussion to the point? Were different views considered? How can we improve?
>
> Is the report (or map, chart, and so forth) accurate? Is it well organized? How can it be improved?
>
> Evaluating in terms of external standards:
> How does our floor map compare with the table map? Is it as accurate? Complete? Clear? Easy to use?
>
> Were the following standards observed? Fair-play? Respect for views of others? Equal rights?
>
> To what extent were civil liberties respected during this period?

Developing Attitudes

Whether or not we pay attention to their development, attitudes are inevitable outcomes of instruction. Too often in the social studies, little thought is given to them. Many teachers assume that constructive attitudes will develop "naturally" in the course of instruction. This may be true in *some* instances, but too much is at stake to leave the development of constructive attitudes to chance.

A DYNAMIC PROGRAM

Multiple learnings are involved in any learning activity; concepts, appreciations, and attitudes do not emerge one by one. A child searching for necessary information in a study of pioneer life may be learning several things simultaneously: some new facts, how to locate information with greater skill, an appreciation of the hardships of the pioneers, how much easier it is to talk about needed information than it is to find it. Some outcomes may be more potent than those which his teacher had planned to achieve. For example, the teacher's major purpose may be to improve study skills and the child's grasp of certain ideas, but the child *may* be developing poor attitudes toward the activity itself and even a dislike for the social studies.

Because attitudes are rooted in feelings, activities in the social studies should evoke positive emotional overtones for children. Whereas positive attitudes and appreciations flourish in a dynamic learning situation, aversions and negative attitudes may develop in learning situations characterized by a drab recitation of facts. The two examples that follow highlight the importance of a dynamic program of instruction.

First, let us consider a group that is studying the westward movement in a rather dull and stultifying manner. Very little is being done to arouse the children emotionally, challenge their intellectual capabilities, or create motivation from within the content of their study. The purpose of the lesson, in the teacher's plan at least, is to have the class find out how the pioneers obtained their food.

> *Teacher:* Today we are to study ways in which the pioneers secured their food. I have selected a book that contains information on how they got their food. Please read pages 68 to 75 and keep a list of all the ways of getting food that you find in your reading. Raise your hand if you have a question.

In the following situation, the children and teacher are working together and are attacking the same type of problem. Notice the difference, however, in the approach being used.

> *Teacher:* Yesterday as you dramatized life in Boonesboro, sev-

eral of you raised questions regarding the ways in which food was secured. What were your questions?

Child A: Well, I was wondering how they got food outside of the stockade and how they brought it in.

Child B: Didn't they raise it right inside?

Child C: I was wondering how the women helped to provide food.

Child D: I read that they had a hard time getting food in winter.

Child E: I think they ate nuts and berries and deer meat.

Teacher: Those are good suggestions. How do you think we we could find more information on ways and means in which they secured food?

In the discussion that followed, the children themselves proposed many procedures for getting at this problem. The emotional response was especially gratifying. Real interest was evident as the group proceeded to solve problems which were significant to them.

STRATEGIES FOR DEVELOPING CONSTRUCTIVE ATTITUDES

The behavior of those who guide children must reflect positive attitudes. Teachers must be aware of their own attitudes; they must be careful about their remarks, facial grimaces, expressions of likes and dislikes, anecdotes and jokes, and any other evidences of negative attitudes since children are quick to imitate and take on such behavior as their own. When children themselves exhibit negative attitudes toward others, they should be helped to find the reasons behind their behavior and to discover that their behavior is not consistent with such standards as fairplay and respect for others. Acceptance by the teacher of children's negative behavior toward others may be taken as tacit approval, thus leading other children to believe that such behavior is quite proper. A teacher must present a model of positive attitudes toward others and encourage children to do the same.

Knowledge and understanding properly learned and used, not just memorized, can lead to an improvement of attitudes. All of us have heard someone say, "Had I known that, I would have acted differently." Or, "Is that so? Then we must do this." A common error, however, in using knowledge to improve attitudes is the assumption that telling is teaching, or that learning about something inevitably leads to a proper attitude toward it. This error can be avoided in part by centering the gathering of information on key problems as they arise, and by using information to interpret the behavior of others and to solve emotionally charged problems. In addition, children need guidance in interpreting facts in the light of sound values and ideals. If any change in attitudes is to result, then, information must be put to use and interpreted in situations vital to children.

Community activities are part of the attitude-building program. Firsthand participation by children in community activities, cooperation of parents and other adults in developing positive attitudes, use of resource persons in the school program, and use of community resources by the school are illustrative of the many possibilities. Festivals, pageants, holidays, and special events in which individuals of many different backgrounds participate are helpful. The spirit in which these activities are carried on and the skill with which children are made a part of them determine their contribution to changes in attitudes. Properly used, they can promote attitudes of loyalty, respect for others, and ideals of patriotism.

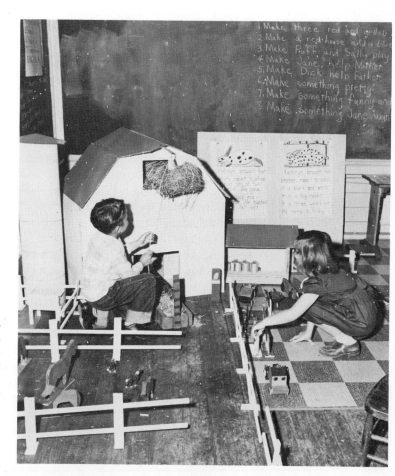

What attitudes might be involved in situations such as this one in which problems of sharing and taking turns arise? How might such situations be used to promote constructive attitudes? (Los Angeles)

Symbolism and ceremony have long been used to develop ideals and attitudes. When developed meaningfully with children, and approached in a way that develops clear insight into their significance, the following have been found to be helpful: flag ceremonies, observance of holidays, pledges and codes, pageants, assemblies, musical programs that emphasize patriotism, exhibits, special television and radio programs, trips to historical shrines, anniversaries, films and film strips, and recordings. These contribute to the development of attitudes and ideals to the extent that children appreciate their significance in their own lives and in the lives of others. Adults must also realize that the way they approach and participate in such activities greatly conditions the way children will react and learn.

As children mature they tend to accept attitudes that *seem* to be the result of their own thinking; they need many opportunities to discover positive examples *on their own*. Discussion, group planning, group decision-making, creative expression, actual participation in ceremonies and community activities, and other skillfully guided activities may be used to help them make discoveries that are their own. Teachers should provide follow-up activities in which their discoveries can be applied, evaluated, and used again.

Not to be overlooked are experiences that kindle the imagination, create upbuilding emotional responses, and arouse positive feelings. Poetry, stories, drama, motion pictures, folk games, art, and music can all be used to create a *feeling tone* that gives warmth, vibrance, and other positive emotional reactions to ideals and attitudes. Unless such feelings are developed, there will be no learning of a permanent nature. This is one of the major reasons why related experiences in art, music, and literature are so important in the social studies.

Individual and group guidance techniques need to be used in some instances to develop wholesome attitudes and to redirect behavior into more positive channels. Individual counseling and small-group discussion can be used as individual needs are discovered. Presentation of problem situations for group analysis, and completion by the class of a story begun by the teacher are effective only if related to problems that have arisen. Group standards and codes of behavior developed before study trips, interviews, and programs help to guide expression of attitudes in a positive way. Simple attitude inventories can be used as a basis for individual counseling and group discussion. Case conferences in which a particular child's difficulties are analyzed by the

teacher and other school workers are helpful in unusual or ex-
tremely difficult cases. In some instances, specialists may be
needed to assist in the development of a long-term program of
therapy. Whenever such techniques are used, they should be tied
in with learning experiences, related to specific problems of children, and personalized.

Dramatic play and role-playing give children opportunities to
improve attitudes, release tension, identify with others, and find
a positive role in group activities.[5] Children may be guided to
try *new* attitudes toward others, and, as roles are played, they
may gradually be helped to take on more positive attitudes, or
reject negative ones. An incident involving a negative attitude
may be "acted out," discussed, and re-enacted in a positive way.
Or, after discussion of an incident, a positive portrayal of a
solution may be tried. Or, through role-playing, a problem situation may be dramatized creatively with a solution emerging as

[5] Fannie R. Shaftel and George Shaftel, *Role-Playing for Social Values*
(Englewood Cliffs, N.J.: Prentice-Hall, Inc., 1967).

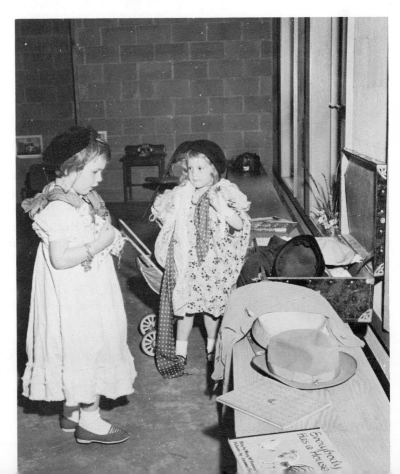

Through dramatic play, children reveal inner thoughts
and feelings as they play
different roles. What at-
titudes toward home and
family life might be re-
vealed through dramatic
play? What should the
teacher's reaction be to differences in attitude? *(Hays;
Courtesy of Monkmeyer)*

children portray what to them seems fair and reasonable. Or, children may act out roles in preparation for a situation they are about to face. Situations may be dramatized depending on the attitudes or problems needing emphasis. Meanwhile, the teacher tries to find clues to the children's feelings, needs, and values. These clues form the basis for discussion, planning, evaluation, and follow-up activities.

Children should not play the same role every time, so that the feelings of others in given situations will become more real to them, and the needs, problems, joys, and sorrows of others will be brought closer. Thus, a child with one background can play the role of another, a leader can be a follower, or a child in one situation can take the part of a child in another. In selecting roles, however, a child should not be given one for which he is unfitted, or which he is unwilling to try. Throughout, teachers should emphasize sincere expression of the roles being acted so that each child gets close to the feelings of the characters he portrays at different times. Once a child grasps how others feel, he may begin to take on more positive attitudes toward them.

Certain procedures are helpful in dealing with examples of prejudice and negative incidents found in reading materials, films, or reports of experiences made by children. After the incident has been summarized and the main details have been noted, possible causes should be discussed and effects on the parties involved should be considered. Children should be encouraged to "get inside the other fellow's shoes." The proposed solution should be evaluated in terms of fairness, respect for the persons involved, and other pertinent values. Specific relationships to situations in the children's own lives should be clarified. Finally, immediate application of generalizations should be made by the group to situations that are vital to them.

Attitudes may be evaluated on several levels according to degree of internalization.[6] The first level is characterized by an awareness of an object, activity, or person. The next level is one of response, and the third involves a deeper feeling that may be expressed as a commitment or conviction. At still higher levels are those attitudes and values that are so deeply internalized that they are an inherent part of a person's way of life. The questions given in the next chapter and the test items given

---

[6] David R. Krathwohl, Benjamin S. Bloom, and Bertram B. Masia, *Taxonomy of Educational Objectives: Affective Domain* (New York: David McKay Co., Inc., 1964).

in the last chapter are illustrative of methods that may be used to assess attitudinal change.

EXAMPLES IN UNITS OF INSTRUCTION

Each unit offers opportunities to develop wholesome attitudes toward others. For example, units on the home and family can be developed so that children can discover many likenesses and common needs, and, at the same time, understand differences among families in size, composition, types of homes, work of fathers and mothers, religious affiliations, and the like. Children can be helped to understand that what is natural to them may be strange to others, and what is strange to them is natural to others. Each family wants to be respected and accepted by others, just as each child wants his own family to be accepted.

In such units as Our Community emphasis can be given to such understandings and appreciations as: Different types of work and services are essential. We share many different things together (parks, playgrounds, stores), and all have a responsibility to make the community a good place in which to live. Many different kinds of people live and work together in a community, and share what they make with different kinds of people in other communities. Rules must be made and followed so that all may have justice and equal opportunity. Communities vary and depend on each other for food, shelter, and clothing. Ideals and contributions of one community are shared with others. There is really no one best kind of community, although we may prefer one kind. The many different kinds of communities (farming, fishing, manufacturing) enable us to share and live more effectively in our own.

Units such as Our State, Region, or Nation provide children with opportunities to discover contributions of others, common needs, examples of sharing, the great range of differences, and the like, on a wider scale. Strength through diversity, power through teamwork, and unity through democratic values should be brought home realistically as reading materials, films, pictures, and other resources are used. A solid beginning can be made in developing appreciation of the contributions of individuals of different ancestry and background, interdependence among regions, respect for the supreme worth of the individual, the need for people with different abilities, and the efforts of those who, from early days down to the present, have tried to extend and preserve the rights of all people.

Units on Mexico, South American countries, Africa, and other areas should be developed in such a way that quaint or bizarre objects and persons are not the main emphasis. The significant ways of living of a people should be considered in the light of present conditions and the traditions and environment of the people. Children should discover and understand why differences and likenesses exist, identify themselves with the people and their problems, and appreciate the attempts that they have made to solve their problems. Needs for education, housing, and hospitals should be understood in the light of conditions, past developments, and current efforts that are being made to provide them. The rosy travel-bureau picture of village life must be tempered by facts that are realistic and descriptive, yet not disparaging. Unfavorable comparisons, ridicule, and jesting should be avoided. What actually exists, and why it exists should be the focus of study.

Guidelines to the Improvement of Learning

From studies of learning and teaching have come guidelines that are helpful in improving children's learning in the social studies. A current trend is for teachers to use a brief statement of selected principles in planning units and in improving classroom instruction at all levels of the social studies course of study. Viewed in this way the principals become guidelines that provide consistent approaches to learning and teaching from level to level, and that enable teachers to focus on fundamental aspects of learning and teaching. Each of the following is elaborated briefly to illustrate specific implications for the social studies.

Clarification of purposes promotes learning. A first step is for teachers to understand the major purposes of the social studies so that their contributions to the overall goals of education are clear. The next step is to clarify the goals of units of instruction and daily plans. As instruction progresses in the classroom, the teacher should set clear purposes for reading various selections, seeing films, making things, taking study trips, and utilizing other resources. Time is wasted and little or no learning results when children do things without knowing *why*, without having specific goals to guide them. Specific purposes can be made clear through group planning, discussion, and evaluation, and by direct comments, questions, and suggestions from the teacher.

A *clearly planned program of instruction improves learning.* Definition of major goals, assignment of topics by grades, gradation of concepts and skills, and provision of related instructional materials are overall aspects of planning the social studies. Each teacher must plan daily lessons and units of instruction in terms of children's capabilities and prior social studies experiences. If planning is done within the overall framework of the social studies during the year and from year to year, children's learning can be continuous, gaps in learning can be avoided, and the purposes of the social studies can be kept in focus.

An active, reflective, inquiry approach improves learning. A student has a greater stake in learning when he has been involved from the initial phases on through to evaluation. Children should be involved directly in clarifying purposes, defining problems, raising questions, proposing tentative solutions, gathering and appraising information, organizing ideas, considering proposals, making generalizations, checking conclusions, and evaluat-

What questions and purposes might be stimulated by an arrangement such as this? How might you arrange a classroom to stimulate basic questions and purposes in a unit? *(San Diego City Schools)*

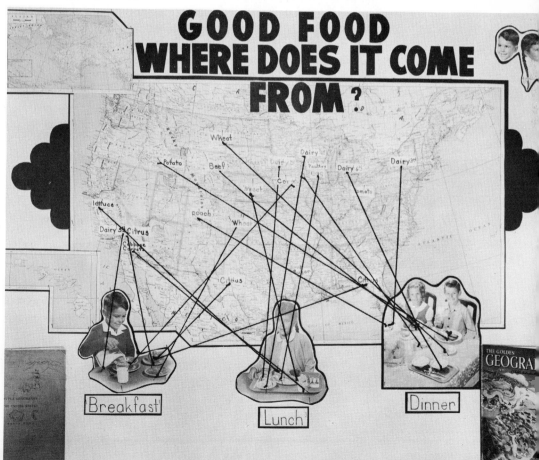

ing progress. Ideas should be set into meaningful patterns: for example, time and distance or cause and effect relationships, or under such topical headings as food, shelter, clothing, transportation, and communication. Each child's thinking capacity must be challenged through individual and group activities that will provide him with opportunities to study and analyze facts and data, synthesize related ideas, utilize concepts, reflect on issues, consider differing points of view, and formulate generalizations.

Critical use of varied activities and materials promotes learning. Key ideas are remembered longer, appreciations are deeper, and interest in the social studies is higher when varied avenues to learning are used. If activities and materials are selected in terms of instructional purposes and individual student capabilities, student interest, effort, and reflective learning are bound to be stimulated. Significant information related to clearly defined problems can be secured from reading materials, audio-visual resources, and community resources. Many different skills can be put to use as ideas are gathered, organized, summarized, or expressed through various language activities, creative activities, and the making of maps, charts, booklets, and other items of a similar nature.

The meeting of individual differences promotes learning. A first principle is to provide varied activities and materials, as was noted above. Other principles that can be applied to gifted, less able, disadvantaged—indeed all—children are as follows: select reading materials each child can handle; vary the amount of time needed to complete activities; use classroom library and other library resources; provide for individual preparation of maps, reports, and other summaries of data; organize small groups with common instructional needs; assign home study related to individual needs; provide different activities for gifted and less able students; vary the amount and kind of supervision, being more specific with less able children; set levels of expectancy or standards appropriate to each child's capabilities; find things to commend and encourage in each child's work.

Suggestions for gifted, less able, and other children should be viewed as a matter of emphasis rather than as exclusive prescriptions. For example, gifted children may be provided more opportunities for independent study, extended reading, library research without denying less able children similar opportunities adjusted to their capabilities. And less-able children may be provided many more concrete experiences and opportunities to get ideas from visual materials without neglecting the need of all children to root concept development in meaningful experiences.

Because of the vital importance of meeting individual differences, several of the following chapters contain specific suggestions directly related to specific materials and activities.

Active teacher guidance promotes learning. The clarification of purposes, use of problem-solving techniques, provision of varied activities and materials, and meeting of individual differences call for more, not less, teacher guidance. Excessive permissiveness leads to confusion and misunderstanding. If a teacher wants to direct children's learning toward specific goals, he must introduce materials as they are needed, raise questions and point out difficulties as they arise, direct discussion, formulate work standards, provide directions for new activities, and guide planning and evaluation.

Systematic evaluation of student progress promotes learning. Teachers should gather data through observation, discussion, appraisal of children's work, testing, and review of previous records. Each child's progress should be studied, with special attention paid to clues for use in planning and directing learning. Student self-evaluation should be encouraged in order to stimulate individual learning and self-understanding.

Helping the child to develop a wholesome self-concept promotes learning. A child's view of himself is especially important in the social studies because it conditions his attitudes towards others, his perception of others, and his participation in group activities. Through successful participation in various activities in the social studies, a child can be helped to develop increasing self-understanding, which in turn contributes to a wholesome self-concept and acceptance of others. Of special importance is that he feel accepted by the teacher, earn recognition from members of the class, become aware of and accept his own strengths and limitations, and develop increased skill in evaluating his own behavior.

A *democratic atmosphere promotes learning.* Mutual respect, concern for others, open-mindedness, responsibleness, self-discipline, respect for constituted authority, recognition of individual differences, critical thinking, adherence to high standards of self-conduct and self-appraisal, individual integrity, teamwork, fairplay—these are the elements that teachers must stress if they are to develop an atmosphere that will be productive of maximum learning on the part of each and every child.

Questions, Activities, Evaluation

1. Discuss the growth characteristics and implications sug-

gested for different grade levels. Visit a class and note other characteristics that might be added to those included in this chapter.

2. Review a unit of instruction and note several concepts and generalizations that are included. What suggestions are given to develop them? What suggestions can you add by drawing ideas from this chapter?

3. Examine one or two children's textbooks and note pictures, passages, maps, questions, problems, and suggested activities that might be used to develop problem solving, critical thinking, and creative thinking abilities. What additional resources would be helpful? Why are a variety of materials needed to develop thinking processes?

4. Indicate ways in which you might develop the cognitive processes noted in this chapter. Prepare questions that might be used in a unit you are planning to teach. Use the examples in this chapter to get started.

5. How might you use the suggestions on attitude development in a unit you are planning?

6. Note practical ways in which you can use the guidelines for the improvement of learning in a unit you are planning. Which are the most difficult to apply?

7. Which of the charts can you use in a unit you are planning? What changes should be made in them to fit your situation? What practical ideas presented in the pictures might you use?

References

Almy, Millie, *Young Children's Thinking*. New York: Teachers College Press, Columbia University, 1966. Review and study of some of Piaget's work.

Black, Millard H., *et al.*, "Critical Thinking and Problem Solving," *Social Studies in Elementary Schools*, 32nd Yearbook, National Council for the Social Studies, pp. 150–75. Washington, D.C.: National Education Association, 1962. Techniques for developing thinking processes in units.

Bruner, Jerome S., *The Process of Education*. Cambridge: Harvard University Press, 1960. Summary of Piaget's studies of stages of intellectual development.

Easton, David, and Robert D. Hess, "The Child's Political World," *Midwest Journal of Political Science*, VI (1962), 229–46. A study of children's political concepts and attitudes.

Educational Policies Commission, *The Central Purpose of American Education*. Washington, D.C.: National Education Association, 1961. Review of basic goals with emphasis on thinking ability as a central purpose.

———, *Education and the Spirit of Science*. Washington, D.C.: National Education Association, 1966. Dominant values that underly scientific inquiry.

Flavell, J. H., *The Developmental Psychology of Jean Piaget*. Princeton, N.J.: D. Van Nostrand Co., Inc., 1963. Detailed review of Piaget's views.

Gagne, Robert, *The Conditions of Learning*. New York: Holt, Rinehart & Winston, Inc., 1965. Discussion of eight types of learning.

———, ed. *Learning and Individual Differences*. Columbus: Charles E. Merrill Books, Inc., 1966. Recent views and studies.

Greenstein, Fred I., *Children and Politics*. New Haven, Conn.: Yale University Press, 1965. Study of political ideas of nine to thirteen year olds.

Hullfish, H. Gordon, and Philip G. Smith, *Reflective Thinking: The Method of Education*. New York: Dodd, Mead & Co., 1961. Principles for basing methods of teaching on reflective thinking processes.

Jarolimek, John, "The Psychology of Skill Development," *Skill Development in the Social Studies*, 33rd Yearbook. Washington, D.C.: National Council for the Social Studies, 1963. Nature and development of skills.

Jenkins, Gladys G., Helen S. Schacter, and William W. Bauer, *These Are Your Children*. Chicago: Scott, Foresman & Company, 1966. Child development through adolescence.

Klausmeier, H. J., and Chester W. Harris, eds., *Analyses of Concept Learning*. New York: Academic Press, 1966. Learning and teaching of concepts.

Krathwohl, David R., Benjamin S. Bloom, and Bertram B. Masia, *Taxonomy of Educational Objectives: Affective Domain*. New York: David McKay Co., Inc., 1964. Objectives and test items related to attitudes and other affective outcomes.

Russell, David. *Children's Thinking*. Boston: Ginn & Company, 1956. A basic reference.

Shaftel, Fannie R., and George Shaftel, *Role-Playing for Social Values*. Englewood Cliffs, N.J.: Prentice-Hall, Inc., 1967. Principles, procedures, and materials for role-playing.

Shulman, Lee S., and Evan R. Keislar, eds., *Learning by Discovery*. Chicago: Rand McNally & Co., 1966. Critical appraisal of discovery learning.

Torrance, E. Paul, *Guiding Creative Talent*. Englewood Cliffs, N.J.: Prentice-Hall, Inc., 1962. Suggestions for developing creativity.

Wallach, Michael A., and Nathan Kogan, *Modes of Thinking in Young Children*. New York: Holt, Rinehart & Winston, Inc., 1965. Examples and implications for education.

The
Disciplinary
Foundations

4

The program of instruction in every area of the curriculum is based on material drawn from fundamental disciplines. The disciplines are sources of content for both the substantive and inquiry aspects of instructional planning. The success with which any program of instruction is implemented depends in large measure on the teacher's understanding of those portions of the disciplines that are included.

Attention is given in this chapter to the disciplines that serve as the basis for planning the social studies. Emphasis is given to the substantive and inquiry components of structure that are used to organize the curriculum. The following chapter deals with the ways in which the components of structure are used to organize instruction. The references at the end of the chapter present additional information that may be used to strengthen one's background of understanding of the social sciences in general and various disciplines in particular.

Core Disciplines

The social studies program of instruction is grounded in the social sciences. Cultural geography, history, economics, political science, anthropology, and sociology are the main sources of content. Some material is also drawn from psychology and philosophy. New attention is being given to aspects of law that should be included, and continuing attention is being given to the use of material drawn from the arts.

A few points about the general nature of the disciplines of primary importance in planning the social studies should be noted. Cultural geography, history, and anthropology are highly integrative disciplines. Geography is rooted in both the physical and social sciences, and in the schools it is used to give a more complete view of areas under study. History includes material from the social sciences and such humanities as art, literature, and philosophy and gives an integrated view of human events in various periods of time. Cultural anthropology is a holistic science that deals with the whole culture of a people, including values, beliefs, social organization, economic activities, authority and other aspects of political life, esthetic and spiritual expression, technology, and artifacts. These three disciplines are used extensively to integrate or relate content: geography in a spatial context, history in a time context, and anthropology in a conceptual context.

Political science and economics are more specialized and focus directly on two of man's most fundamental activities. Material from these two disciplines may be embedded in units based primarily on history, geography, or anthropology, or it may be presented in separate units of instruction. The trend is clearly to include more economics and to give adequate attention to political science at all levels of instruction.

Sociology and social psychology are closely related to anthropology and are sources of concepts that are used extensively throughout the social sciences and in the social studies. Examples are roles, groups, institutions, processes of interaction, individual differences, and social control. These fields contribute much to the study of contemporary societies, social problems, and social change. They also provide, along with anthropology, economics, and political science, many concepts that are used in cultural geography and history.

Philosophy is a humanistic discipline which provides methods of logical analysis and reasoning that are invaluable in the social studies and used throughout the social sciences. The making of inferences, using criteria to make judgments, conflict resolution, hypothetical reasoning, finding fallacies in statements, and studying the grounds for beliefs all call for logical analysis and reasoning. In fact, much of what is done in the social studies in the name of problem solving and critical thinking is relatable to philosophic modes of study.

Several features of the six disciplines from which the bulk of social studies content is drawn are shown in Chart 1. The chart includes concepts that are used as organizing centers for structuring information. Notice that for history a time gap is shown by means of a broken line to highlight the fact that past events are not observable; they must be studied nonempirically by referring to whatever records or other remains are available to the historian. Notice also that historical data may be structured around themes within periods, by areas (such as countries), and around topics (such as the Constitution). The section on geography shows how four central concepts may be used to structure the myriad of detailed information on the location of various phenomena. The other sections include major organizing concepts and illustrate the central focus of four core disciplines. The lines drawn among the concepts are intended to show interrelationships. For example, decisions made in the economic system are central in determining production, income, and other items included to the right and the left of *economic system*. Similarly, patterns of behavior in four major areas of activity are central to the study of culture, as shown in the anthropology section.

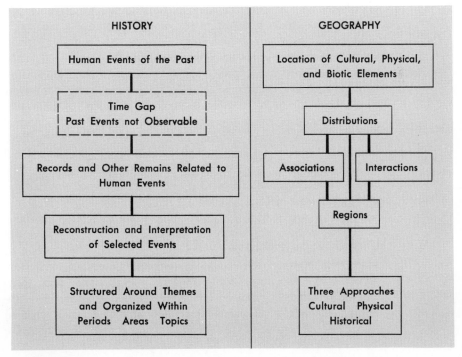

Chart 1

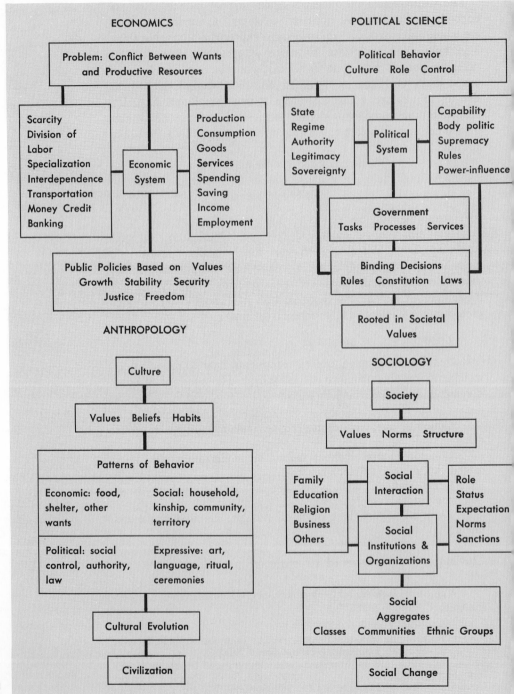

ECONOMICS

Problem: Conflict Between Wants and Productive Resources

Scarcity
Division of
Labor
Specialization
Interdependence
Transportation
Money Credit
Banking

Economic System

Production
Consumption
Goods
Services
Spending
Saving
Income
Employment

Public Policies Based on Values
Growth   Stability   Security
Justice   Freedom

POLITICAL SCIENCE

Political Behavior
Culture   Role   Control

State
Regime
Authority
Legitimacy
Sovereignty

Political System

Capability
Body politic
Supremacy
Rules
Power-influence

Government
Tasks   Processes   Services

Binding Decisions
Rules   Constitution   Laws

Rooted in Societal Values

ANTHROPOLOGY

Culture

Values   Beliefs   Habits

Patterns of Behavior

Economic: food, shelter, other wants

Social: household, kinship, community, territory

Political: social control, authority, law

Expressive: art, language, ritual, ceremonies

Cultural Evolution

Civilization

SOCIOLOGY

Society

Values   Norms   Structure

Family
Education
Religion
Business
Others

Social Interaction

Role
Status
Expectation
Norms
Sanctions

Social Institutions & Organizations

Social Aggregates
Classes   Communities   Ethnic Groups

Social Change

Chart 1
continued

The vastness and the diversity of knowledge in the social sciences have always posed difficult problems for curriculum workers whose job is to select and organize content in teachable form. The knowledge explosions of recent years have increased the need to identify the most significant content and to eliminate trivial ideas. Only the most fundamental and durable ideas from the disciplines are being included in new programs. A widely followed procedure is to identify structural components within disciplines and to select those that are most useful in the social studies.

Identifying Structural Components

A promising development is to provide a concise statement of structural components of core disciplines. Although no uniform agreement exists on a single structure for a discipline, nor is one likely in the near future while scholars hold such diverse views, many helpful statements have been prepared.[1] General agreement does exist that the identification of fundamental ideas is prerequisite to effective instructional planning.

COMPONENTS OF STRUCTURE

Both substantive and inquiry components may be identified in statements on the structure of disciplines. The substantive components may be identified as follows:

Concepts, such as culture, region, values, division of labor, role.

Concept clusters, such as factors of production: land, labor, capital, know-how (entrepreneurship).

Generalizations, such as, culture is a primary determiner of how man uses his environment.

Themes, such as the growth of industry, the westward movement.

The inquiry components of structure are as follows:

Values of inquiry, such as objectivity, open-mindedness, search for truth.

[1] See, for example, John U. Michaelis and A. Montgomery Johnston, eds., *The Social Sciences: Foundations of the Social Studies* (Boston: Allyn & Bacon, Inc., 1965); Irving Morrissett, ed., *Concepts and Structures in the New Social Science Curricula* (Lafayette, Ind.: Social Science Education Consortium, Purdue University, 1966); and Raymond Muessig and Vincent Rogers, *Social Science Seminar Series* (Columbus: Charles E. Merrill Books, Inc., 1965).

Models of inquiry, such as defining the problem, formulating questions or hypotheses, gathering data, testing hypotheses, and making conclusions.

Methods of inquiry, such as experimenting, observing, interviewing.

Most new programs include all of the above in one form or another. Concepts and concept clusters may be identified in all materials that are based on the social sciences. Generalizations and themes are widely used in organizing content and learning experiences in units of instruction. Values, models, and methods of inquiry are used in varying degrees, depending on the extent to which inquiry is emphasized in the program.

Substantive Components of Structure

What is needed by teachers is a concise summary of the components of structure that are included in new materials. Such a summary is helpful as a checklist for instructional planning. Each summary presented below is based on a review of the references cited at the end of this chapter and on materials available to students.

Key concepts have been identified for each discipline. Examples of widely used concept clusters have been included to emphasize the point that many key concepts are multidimensional; they include other concepts that must be given specific attention. The examples of generalizations are illustrative of those that are stressed in new materials; additional examples are presented in the next two chapters in the context of overall program planning and unit construction.

Teachers should add other items to the lists as particular units are planned. One should bear in mind, however, that no single list of ideas from the disciplines can meet all planning needs, although a list is helpful in giving a focus to central ideas. A sound position to take is that of building basic ideas into the program and drawing on others as needed to tackle the problems under study.

Geography

Cultural geography and relevant aspects of physical geography are emphasized in the social studies to develop understandings of how people with different cultures use resources in their environment. Many of the structural components are drawn from anthropology, economics, political science, climatology, and other disciplines. Great care is taken to avoid the outmoded concept of environmental determinism, that is, the notion that the environment determines how people live. Rather, emphasis is given to the importance of culture as a primary factor in determining how people live in families, communities, and regions around the world. Key concepts, examples of concept clusters, and illustrative generalizations are listed below.

CONCEPTS

The earth's surface, earth-sun relationships, location, distribution, association, interaction, region and regionalizing, cultural, physical, and biotic elements, resources culturally defined, dominance of man, the life layer, population, urbanization, culture regions, change, the globe, maps

CONCEPT CLUSTERS

The Earth's Surface: spheres (hydrosphere, lithosphere, atmosphere, biosphere or life layer), human elements (man and his works), physical elements (land, water bodies, climate), biotic elements (plants, animals)

Earth-Sun Relationships: source of energy, rotation, revolution, inclination and parallelism of axis, circulation of atmosphere, seasons, night and day

Location: position (absolute—latitude and longitude; relative —near a known place); site (natural location such as island, continental, or maritime location); situation such as relative location expressed by such terms as strategic, central, or adjacent

Major Landforms: plains, hills, plateaus, mountains

Water Bodies: rivers, lakes, bays, straits, seas, oceans

Natural Resources: water, soil, animal life, plant life, minerals, climate

Factors in Climate: sunlight, temperature, precipitation, humidity, winds, altitude, latitude, major water bodies, mountain systems, ocean currents

Population: size, distribution, centers, density, composition, growth rate, movement, prediction, control, problems, productive potential

Settlement Patterns: isolated, village, town, suburb, city, metropolis, megalopolis

Urbanization: growth of urban centers, location, functions, internal structure (residence, business, industry), interaction with other places, accessibility, changing occupance patterns, migration, invasion, segregation, desegregation, redevelopment, urban planning

Culture Regions: Western, non-Western, European, Soviet, Middle Eastern, North African, Southwest Asian, South Asian, Southeast Asian, East Asian, African, Anglo-American, Latin American, Australian-New Zealand, Pacific

Directions: cardinal, intermediate, north and south along meridians, east and west along parallels

The Globe: land and water areas, the Equator, parallels, meridians, Prime Meridian, International Date Line, Tropic of Cancer, Tropic of Capricorn, high, middle, and low latitudes, hemispheres (northern, southern, eastern, western), land, water, day, night

Maps: data, scale, projection, symbols, legend

Map Symbols: lines, points, colors, signs, words

GENERALIZATIONS

Life on the earth is influenced by earth-sun relationships.

The different climates in a country or region may be explained in terms of temperature, precipitation, and related factors.

The location and productive activities of a community are key factors in its interaction with other places.

People everywhere identify and use resources in ways that are shaped by their culture.

Regions defined in terms of one or more common features may vary as needed in terms of the purposes of inquiry.

Urbanization has necessitated the redevelopment of cities and the advantageous use of space.

Change takes place constantly on the earth's surface.

Four of the spatial concepts listed above merit special comment because they may be used to structure geographic data within regions of varying size. These four concepts are helpful in any unit that deals with the spatial arrangement of surface features, and they can be used at all levels of instruction if they are couched in appropriate language. Because of their great usefulness, definitions and examples are presented below along with questions that illustrate how they may be used to guide the study of topics at various levels.

Spatial Distribution: the pattern or arrangement of phenomena on the earth's surface. Examples are homes around the school, residence and business sections of a community, highways, wheat-growing areas, population, minerals, climates, mountain systems, and drainage systems in selected areas. Illustrative questions are: How are homes arranged around our school? Where is the business section of town? How can we show the distribution of population on our maps? How can we represent the corn belt on a map of the United States?

Areal Association: how distributions are related, how they tend to be found together. Examples are homes and schools, homes

and shopping centers, plains and farming, cattle and corn production, and harbors and shipping. Illustrative questions are:
Why are homes and schools usually found near each other? What
is usually located around a shopping center? How can we show
the relationship between cattle and corn production? How can
we explain the relation between elevation and amount of vegetation in the mountains?

Spatial Interaction: the flow, movement, or circulation of
phenomena. Examples are the movement of children to and from
school, people to and from stores, ideas via newspapers and other
mass media, and goods and people via transportation networks.
Illustrative questions are: How do we get from home to school
and back? Where do people go to buy things they need at home?
What is brought to our community from farms? What are some
ways to map the main shipping routes between our country and
Europe? How are goods, people, and ideas circulated throughout the world?

Region: a defined area that is relatively homogeneous in one
or more characteristics. Examples are neighborhoods in a community, defined areas around the community, regions of a state
or the United States, regions within other countries, and culture
regions of the world. Illustrative questions are: What is in the
area around our school? What are the main neighborhoods in
our community? How may we divide our community into areas
that may be studied in detail? How might our state be divided
into regions for study? How have others defined regions of our
state? How might the fifty states be grouped into regions? What

How should we divide our
state into regions? Will economic, physical, agricul-
tural, or other regions be
best for our purposes?
These are the kinds of
questions that are raised in
new programs. *(Alameda
County Schools)*

regions can we find in reference materials? Can you find the reasons (criteria) that were used to group them? The last question is designed to develop an understanding of regionalizing as the process of using criteria to define regions. Experiences in all grades should contribute to competence in handling the concept of regionalizing as students define regions for various purposes and discover the reasons why others have defined regions in similar and different ways.

History

The social studies program is replete with material from history. Changes in family life from colonial times to the present, growth of the community, state and United States history, and selected historical developments in other countries are usually included. The bulk of the conceptual components of history are drawn from other disciplines and are used to make interpretations of past human events. For example, role, division of labor, resources, and borrowing of ideas may be used to explain changes in family life, communities, and nations in different periods of time. Yet time, process, and organizing concepts are also widely used in historical materials. In addition, special emphasis is given to events and themes as shown in the following list.

CONCEPTS

Time Concepts: time, day, week, month, season, year, decade, generation, century, millenium, B.C., A.D., period, epoch, age, era, prehistoric, ancient, medieval, Middle Ages, modern

Process Concepts: criticism, analysis, and synthesis of primary and secondary sources; reconstruction of events; interpretation; periodization

Organizing Concepts: event, theme, period, place

EVENTS AND THEMES

Events and Themes in Local History: first settlers, homes, school, and church; beginning as a town; growth of population, transportation, communication, business, education, public services, the arts; contributions of individuals and groups; problems of growth

Events and Themes in United States History: discovery and exploration, living in the colonies, gaining independence, establishing a government, living on the frontier, the westward movement, the growth of sectionalism, the Civil War, the period of reconstruction, growth of agriculture and industry, becoming a world power, the growth of cities, problems of minority groups

How can study trips be used to gather data on local history? (Burbank)

How can data gathered from visits to historical monuments be used to reconstruct human events? (San Bernardino County)

INTERPRETATIONS AND GENERALIZATIONS

Changes in communities have been the result of the actions of many individuals and groups.

Interdependence has increased rapidly in recent times.

Social problems and institutions of today have roots in the past.

Ideas about self-government were strengthened on the frontier.

Multiple causes and consequences must be considered in studying events.

Time and space form a framework within which events can be placed.

Economics

Economics education has probably made more advances in recent years than any other segment of the social studies. New materials of instruction include a clearly defined set of concepts and main ideas drawn from economics. Concepts such as division of labor are introduced in the beginning grades as children compare the production of cookies or other items on an "assembly line" where each worker does a special job with complete production of the item by individuals. The differences between producers and consumers and goods and services are discovered as children investigate roles of members of the family, community workers, and people in other places to find out who produces and consumes various goods and services. The opportunity

Concepts of producers, consumers, goods, and services are developed early in new programs. (San Diego City Schools)

cost principle is put to use as children consider such questions as: What does Billy give up if he spends his allowance for candy? What does a family give up when a trip is taken instead of spending the money for other things? What does a country sacrifice when it decides to produce some things and not others? The concept of economic systems begins to develop as students find out about the role of the market in allocating resources to alternative uses, the operation of supply and demand, and how central authorities in some countries make decisions regarding what to produce, how to produce, how much to produce and how to distribute what is produced.

Economists have been quite active in working with school personnel to plan the social studies curriculum. The result has been widespread agreement that the following items should be included in social studies instruction.

CONCEPTS

Conflict between wants and resources, scarcity, division of labor, specialization, interdependence, goods, services, consumers, producers, factors of production, or productive resources, production, consumption, exchange, distribution, market, supply, demand, prices, money, banking, credit, saving, spending, investing, trade, inputs, outputs, economic systems, economic values, opportunity cost principle

CONCEPT CLUSTERS

Basic Economic Problem: conflict between wants and resources, need to make choices, need for an economic system to allocate resources to alternative uses

Specialization: division of labor by occupations, technological applications, and geographic situation; resulting interdependence

Productive Resources: human (workers, managers, know-how), capital (tools, machines, factories), natural (soil, water, climate, minerals, forests)

The Market: means of allocating resources, interaction of supply and demand, use of money, transportation, and communication, modification by policies related to economic values

Economic Systems: market-directed or private enterprise, centrally directed or command, tradition-directed, mixed

Economic Values in Our System: growth, stability, security, justice, freedom

GENERALIZATIONS

Members of families, people in communities, and societies meet the basic economic problem by finding answers to these questions:

What to produce? How to produce? How much to produce? How to distribute what is produced?

Division of labor improves production and leads to interdependence among individuals, communities, states, and nations.

People in a market system have more freedom of choice than do people in a command system.

Firms produce goods and services in a modified market system under policies set by government to protect consumers and producers.

In our system the government provides certain goods and services such as highways, schools, protection, and welfare services.

Political Science

Material from political science has traditionally been included in the social studies under the title of civics. A current trend is to move beyond the narrow civics tradition toward the inclusion of dynamic aspects of the uses of power and authority in the home, school, and other situations as well as in government. The need to provide instruction early in the program has been revealed by studies of political socialization which show that elementary-school children develop many notions about political activity, some of which are erroneous.

Instruction may begin with attention to rule making, rule applying, and the settling of disputes in situations familiar to children. Later these concepts are extended to legislative (rule making), executive (rule applying), and judicial (rule adjudicating) processes of local, state, and national government. Attention is given in community studies to the mayor, city council, teachers, firemen and other public employees, public services such as education, protection, and recreation, city planning and redevelopment, and metropolitan planning to solve transportation and other cross-community problems. State and national studies include such concepts as authority, political party, separation of powers, public services, and processes of government. Historical studies include material on contributions of the Greeks and Romans to government, the Magna Carta and other developments in England, representative government in early America, and great documents such as the Mayflower Compact, The Declaration of Independence, and the Constitution. Studies of other lands include material on leaders in the past and present, roles of authorities and citizens, types and processes of government, and relations with the United States. Information related to the foregoing and to other topics may be structured around the following:

Simulated activities are used to develop concepts and to provide insights into decision making. *(San Diego City Schools)*

Concepts

Power, authority, unit, regime, state, sovereignty, system, demands, decision-making, party, government, constitution, law, rules, political behavior, processes, services

Concept Clusters

Tasks of Government: external security, internal order, justice, public services, freedom (under democracy)

Processes: rule making (legislative), rule applying (executive), rule adjudicating (judicial)

Levels of Government: local, state, national, international

Public Services: police, fire, postal, education, health, welfare, sanitation, conservation, recreation, labor, business

Types of Government: democratic, authoritarian; parliamentary, presidential; unitary, federal

Themes: maintaining civil liberties, the rights of minorities, the general consent of the governed, due process of law, separation of powers

Generalizations

Some wants of people are handled through the political system.

Our political system is rooted in democratic societal values.

The source of authority rests with the people in a democracy.

Governments have the power to enforce laws.

Binding decisions made by authorities apply to all people in our system of government.

Anthropology

An increasing number of concepts and key ideas from anthropology are included in new programs of instruction. This increase is the result of greater recognition of the contributions that anthropology can make to the objectives of the social studies, especially to those attitudes, understandings, methods of inquiry, and skills related to the comparative study of cultures. The inclusive culture concept that brings together values, beliefs, and patterns of learned behavior into a unified view of ways of living is inherent in many units of instruction beginning with comparative studies of families, villages, and communities and moving to studies of selected areas, prehistoric peoples, and early civilizations. Specific units on Eskimos, American Indians, Village Life in Africa, and other peoples include anthropological material on human activities related to food, shelter, clothing, utensils, social organization, arts, crafts, rituals, ceremonies, and other as-

How might artifacts such as these be used in studies of other cultures? (San Diego City Schools)

pects of culture. Units centered on local, state, and national history as well as units centered in the geographic study of selected regions usually include a good deal of material from anthropology. Key structural elements are listed below.

CONCEPTS

Culture, society, values, beliefs, tradition, customs, change, social organization, role, technology, community, civilization

CONCEPT CLUSTERS

Culture: learned patterns of behavior, ways of living, both material and nonmaterial aspects of arts, crafts, technology, religion, economic activities, language, and other aspects of life in a society

Processes of Cultural Change: invention, discovery, diffusion, adaptation

Food-Getting Activities: gathering, hunting, fishing, herding, gardening, agriculture

Societies: folk or preliterate, preindustrial, transitional, industrial

Families: nuclear, extended; functions—biological, affectional, economic, social

Community: territory, common culture, collective action; folk, peasant, urban

Characteristics of Civilization: writing, accumulation of food and other goods for managed use, division of labor, government, arts, sciences, urbanization, trade

GENERALIZATIONS

Culture is socially transmitted in all societies, differs from society to society, and is a prime determiner of behavior.

Families around the world have common needs but vary in the ways that needs are met.

Major differences among people are cultural, not biological.

Food-getting activities of people are closely related to their level of technology.

The culture of modern societies has evolved from the culture of earlier societies.

Sociology

Concepts and key ideas from sociology are included in many units of study. Studies of the family and school, two basic social institutions, are provided early in the program. The positions and roles of members of the family, the teacher, and other school personnel are included. Values and expectations of chil-

What roles do workers have in banks? Are their roles the same in other places? *(International Society for the Study of Education, Tokyo)*

dren, parents, teachers, and community workers are considered in the context of children's relationships to each other and to adults. Norms and sanctions and their relation to social control are discovered in the context of children's own experiences and in units that include material on customs, regulations, rewards, punishments, and laws in communities and other places near at hand and far away. Understandings of processes of social interaction such as cooperation, competition, and conflict are also developed in the context of children's experiences and units of study. Historical and geographic studies centered on the community, state, nation, and other places typically include such concepts as role, groups, institutions, values, and social change.

The structural elements drawn from sociology are closely related to those drawn from anthropology and psychology. However, primary attention is given to society and social structure as shown in the following summary.

CONCEPTS

Society, values, norms, role, status, expectations, social institutions, social processes, groups, social control

CONCEPT CLUSTERS

Values: personal, social, economic, political, religious, esthetic
Social Institutions: family, economic, political, educational, scientific, religious, recreational, welfare, esthetic

Processes of Social Interaction: cooperation, competition, conflict, assimilation, accommodation

Groups: primary, secondary, reference, in-group, out-group

Social Control: dependency, rewards, sanctions, norms, laws

Minorities: foreign, religious, racial, socio-economic

GENERALIZATIONS

The work of society is done through groups formed to achieve common goals.

Societies need a system of social control in order to survive.

Social institutions are shaped by societal values and norms.

The family is a basic social institution in all societies.

Individuals have positions and roles in social institutions.

Psychology

Concepts and key ideas from psychology are embedded in units of study at all levels of instruction. For example, the concept of individual differences is important in studies of families, schools, community workers, and people in other places. How seeing, hearing, touching and other senses help one to observe and to learn may be included early in the program. Understanding of the influence of groups on individual behavior and of the role of individuals in group processes, such as goal setting, planning, carrying out plans, and evaluating group work, may be developed in classroom activities and in studies of other groups. The importance of attitudes, motives, and interests as key factors in human behavior is brought home in both contemporary and historical studies of people near at hand and far away. How to control feelings and what happens when feelings are not controlled are considered in the context of children's own experiences and in studies of others. Direct attention is given to effective ways of learning, how to remember and use what is learned, and how to improve critical thinking and problem solving. All the foregoing are linked to findings and concepts from psychology.

The following are closely related to structural elements in anthropology and sociology, the primary difference being that psychology in general is focused on the individual, and social psychology in particular is focused on the individual in society.

CONCEPTS

Senses, learning, remembering, group processes, attitudes, perceptions of others, personal-social needs, individual differences, intergroup relations, social roles

Using Our Senses to Learn: seeing, hearing, smelling, touching, tasting, balancing

Learning and Remembering: clear purposes, meaning, practice, use, review, application, grouping around main ideas, contrast, comparison, concentration, knowledge of results, ideas in own words

Perception of Others: previous experience, needs, motives, attitudes, expectation, current condition of perceiver, self-concept

Group Processes: goal setting, planning, doing, evaluating, decision-making, valuing

Personal-Social Needs: acceptance, belonging, security, achievement, self-expression, interaction with others, learning, self-actualization

Individual Differences: appearance, personality, role, attitudes, beliefs, family, customs, learning, abilities, habits

Social Roles: leadership, followership, aggression, submission

GENERALIZATIONS

Individual differences exist among members of families, children in schools, and people in communities.

Perceptions of others vary from individual to individual and are conditioned by a variety of factors.

Both individual and group needs may be met through group action.

Learning and remembering can be improved by concentrated effort.

Individuals take different roles in different groups and situations.

Philosophy

Better classified as a humanity than a social science, philosophy is included as a foundation discipline because of the concepts related to values and various aspects of inquiry that are emphasized in the social studies. Wide agreement exists that the conceptual basis of such values as freedom, equality, responsibleness, loyalty, and patriotism should be emphasized along with the positive attitudes and feelings that are needed to give them enduring qualities. Students should also understand the nature of logical fallacies, the meaning of the spirit of science, and the processes involved in making judgments.

The value-related concepts listed below are almost universally found in social studies materials. The concept clusters and generalizations are illustrative of those that well may be emphasized throughout all phases of instruction.

CONCEPTS

Values, moral and ethical principles, right, duty, freedom, equality, justice, rational behavior, human dignity, patriotism, loyalty, free society, free inquiry, common good, individual interest, responsibleness, cooperativeness, creativeness, open-mindedness, concern for others

CONCEPT CLUSTERS

Spirit of Science: longing to know and understand, questioning of all things, search for data and their meaning, demand for verification, respect for logic, consideration of premises, causes, and consequences

Logical Fallacies: appeal to force, argument from ignorance, appeal to pity, emphasis on false cause, snob appeal, neglect of all causes, false premises

Making Judgments: clarifying what is to be judged, defining related criteria, analyzing in terms of criteria, making the judgment, checking the judgment with others

GENERALIZATIONS

The basic value of human dignity underlies our way of life.

Free societies keep open the path of free inquiry for their own well-being.

Criteria should be defined in terms of values and used to decide what is good or ought to be.

Ideas and proposals must be subjected to critical examination if their value is to be determined.

Inquiry Components of Structure

Values, models, and methods of inquiry are dynamic aspects of the foundation disciplines that are used to investigate topics, questions, and problems. Values of inquiry are indicative of the attitudes held by those who truly search for the best new ideas and test old ideas about human relationships. Models of inquiry are helpful guides in the study of problems. Specific methods of inquiry can be put to use in units of instruction at all levels.

VALUES OF INQUIRY

The spirit of inquiry characteristic of social scientists is similar to that of other scientists. Free and open inquiry in the best tradition of the democratic ideals outlined in Chapter 2 clearly underlies the work of any person who wants to find the best possible explanations for cultural and natural phenomena. Individual opinion, tradition, pronouncements of authorities, and other ideas not based on critical study are opened to review and investigation.

Several values of inquiry have been stressed by scholars at work on social studies projects and may be found in new teaching guides and units of instruction.[2] High value is placed on the following which are closely related to the values outlined in a recent report: [3]

Curiosity about the causes and consequences of human behavior and ways of studying human relationships

Definition of terms in precise language so that the meaning is clear to others as well as to the inquirer

Awareness of the effects of one's own background, views, feelings, position, and values on the way problems are viewed, how they are studied, and how findings are interpreted

Objectivity in the study of human problems as well as other problems so that findings will be reliable and can be readily checked by others

Skepticism marked by thoughtful questioning and critical review of methods of study, findings, interpretations, and conclusions

Demand for evidence to test hypotheses, to answer questions, to support conclusions, and to weigh alternatives

Respect for differing views based on evidence gathered through systematic study and through critical analysis of causes and consequences of human events

Regard for logical thinking in defining problems, framing questions and hypotheses, making plans for study, classifying data, interpreting data, and drawing conclusions

Analysis of assumptions, premises, biases, possible errors, and special meanings, ideas behind interpretations, and other subjective aspects of inquiry

Identification of multiple causes of human events, or all of the factors or variables relevant to the study of a problem

Discovery of new and better ideas that can be used to explain and predict human behavior in different situations and under varying conditions

Corroboration or double-checking of findings by repeating studies and making comparisons with the findings of others

---

[2] See, for example, Roy A. Price, Warren Hickman, and Gerald Smith, *Major Concepts for Social Studies* (Syracuse: Social Studies Curriculum Center, 1965); and Edith West, *Project Social Studies* (Minneapolis: School of Education, University of Minnesota, 1968).

[3] Educational Policies Commission, *The Spirit of Science* (New York: National Education Association, 1966).

Values such as these are not attained in the fullest by many individuals, yet they can serve as ideals which guide inquiry into human relationships. A simple beginning can be made early in the social studies program as problems and issues are studied. Curiosity is characteristic of all children and can be kept alive by exploring a variety of problems ranging from differing ways of living in homes and communities to changes taking place in regions throughout the world. Values associated with the clear definition of terms, demand for evidence, and meaningful classification of ideas can be developed as problems and topics are studied in different units of instruction. Objectivity, personal preferences and feelings, thoughtful skepticism, and respect for differing views can be nurtured by considering such questions as: Will we get the same result if we do it again? Are we consistent in the way we do it? Did we control our feelings about it? Is this a good idea because we like it or because it works? Is this a fair statement? What questions do we have about it? Where might mistakes have been made? What is good about that idea? How can we use that idea? Is that a sound argument? The importance of exploring all causes and reasons, searching for assumptions and hidden meanings, and double-checking of findings can be brought out in discussions of events, issues, and problems, and in directing children's study of textbooks, references, films, and other instructional media. In short, values of inquiry should be made a part of each unit of instruction as various models and methods of inquiry are put to use.

Models of Inquiry

A primary reason for considering models of inquiry is to identify elements that may be put to use in the social studies. The educational principle here is that fuller learning will result if the methods of study employed in the social studies are consistent with those used in the social sciences. In other words, children can begin to learn effective ways of investigating topics and problems as well as concepts and generalizations. Models serve as vehicles for putting concepts and generalizations to use in the study of human relationships. Learning is incomplete in the social studies, or in any other area of the curriculum, if models of inquiry are neglected.

Models of inquiry of various types are used in the social sciences to guide the study of topics and problems. Some models are broad general guides while others are designed for particular purposes such as field studies. Some are quite similar to the model of problem solving presented in the preceding chapter. Others are designed for the analysis of issues and problems and involve various aspects of critical thinking. All of them involve creative thinking and the use of the cognitive processes discussed in the preceding chapter.

The function of models is to bring together the concepts, related questions, and procedures of study in a form that can be used to investigate a problem. Concepts such as those presented earlier in this chapter may be used to pose questions. For example, the concept of major landforms may suggest such questions as: What are the major landforms in this region? What part of the area is mountainous? Hilly? Where are plains and plateaus located? What is the relation between landforms and location of people? Once questions (or hypotheses) are clear, a plan is made to gather, evaluate, classify, and interpret related information. This may be followed by the framing of tentative conclusions which can be checked through further study. Additional questions may emerge, and suggestions for additional study may be made.

Special note should be made of the need to use models flexibly and to adapt them to problems under study. The rigid following of predetermined steps of procedure irrespective of new insights that are gained as one studies a topic is the antithesis of sound thinking. Creative thinking is a key ingredient in inquiry and should be employed to the fullest to adapt models to differing situations.

Models of inquiry used in different disciplines have been adapted from the references at the end of this chapter and are presented in Chart 2. Special attention should be given to the following points as they are studied. Notice that the general pattern or sequence begins with identification of problems and ends with the making of conclusions or interpretations and the suggesting of further studies. The importance of helping children grow in the ability to identify problems cannot be overemphasized. Also important is the need to be on the lookout for what to study next. These two elements of inquiry, as well as the others, are directly related to the goal of developing competence in learning how to learn. Notice that the section in the center of the chart contains a listing of common phases of inquiry. Check the points listed in this section with those in the others. Wherever similar items are not listed, one can assume that in general they do apply. At the bottom of the chart are two examples of models that can be used to analyze issues and problems.

GEOGRAPHY	ANTHROPOLOGY
Identify and define the topic or problem to be studied. Consider all factors that may be related. State questions or hypotheses related to each factor. Gather data related to each hypothesis or question. Evaluate and organize data to test hypotheses or answer questions. Interpret findings and draw conclusions. Suggest other needed studies.	Define objectives for the field study. Make a plan for each phase. Gather materials for recording data. Make necessary arrangements. Gather data by direct observation, interview, and participation (if feasible). Organize and interpret data in light of objectives. Summarize findings and draw conclusions. Compare findings and conclusions with those of others.

HISTORY	COMMON PHASES OF INQUIRY	SOCIOLOGY
Define the question or problem to be studied. State hypotheses or questions to guide study. Collect sources of information. Analyze and synthesize data in the sources. Organize findings to answer questions and test hypotheses. Interpret findings in relation to social, economic, and political developments.	Define the problem. Clarify objectives. Relate the study to what is known. Consider related factors. State questions or hypotheses. Make a plan to gather data. Have an adequate sample. Use appropriate data-gathering techniques. Use reliable sources. Evaluate and organize data. Interpret findings. Draw and check conclusions. Suggest further studies.	Define the problem and relate it to existing knowledge. State hypotheses to guide study. Select an adequate sample. Use appropriate techniques to gather data. Organize and analyze the data to test each hypothesis. Interpret findings and draw conclusions. Suggest other studies.

POLITICAL ANALYSIS	ECONOMIC ANALYSIS
Define the problem and clarify related values. Consider different choices or solutions. Evaluate each choice or solution in terms of values, facts, and historical background. Identify possible consequences of each choice or solution. Evaluate the consequences in light of values. Make judgments as to which choice or solution is best.	Define the problem. Where are we in terms of where we want to go? Identify goals and place them in order of priority. Consider the resources available to attain the goals. Consider alternative ways to attain goals with usable resources. Analyze consequences of each alternative. Choose the best alternative in light of objectives.

Chart 2

Careful analysis of the models in Chart 2 indicates that for most purposes in the social studies one can use a generalized model that incorporates the basic features that are common to all of the models. In fact, the general model for guiding group inquiry that is presented in Chapter 8 includes the aspects of inquiry noted in the center of Chart 2.

Sometimes, however, study can be sharpened by relying mainly on two other models. The example given for anthropology is especially useful when field trips are being planned and conducted. Detailed information for the use of field trips is presented in Chapter 11. The models given for political and economic analysis have much in common and are quite useful in analyzing and resolving value conflicts, such as those shown in Chapter 2. Attention is given next to the many methods of inquiry that are drawn from the social sciences and used in the social studies.

Methods of Inquiry

A variety of methods of inquiry may be used in models such as those discussed above, and in units of instruction at all levels. The underlying principle is to use whatever methods of collecting, organizing, and evaluating data are most appropriate in a given situation. In units based primarily on history, extensive use is made of those techniques involved in analyzing and synthesizing data from records and other remnants of human events of the past. In studies of contemporary problems, a variety of methods may be used to gather and process new and up-to-date information. The following methods of inquiry are adapted from reports on various disciplines and may be found in new social studies materials:

Collecting data

Critical study, analysis, and selection of data in such sources as:

Written materials: textbooks, references, letters, diaries, minutes, newspapers, magazines, government reports and documents, business records, biographical materials

Art objects: paintings, murals, tapestries, vases, plaques, medals, jewelry, wall paintings, portraits, ornaments, sculpture

Orally transmitted materials: folklore, legends, sagas, ballads, anecdotes, stories, eyewitness accounts, tales of old timers

Recorded materials: photographs, slides, films, tapes, records, maps, diagrams, graphs, charts

Inscriptions: monuments, plaques, buildings, coins, clay tablets, walls, grave markers, bridges, art objects

Physical remains: buildings, monuments, aqueducts, implements, tools, utensils, weapons, pottery, baskets, clothing, textiles, costumes, furnishings, musical instruments

Content analysis of printed materials, films, and other instructional media to gather data on meanings of terms, changes and trends, uses of resources, use of words to stir the emotions, underlying assumptions, and the frequency of occurrence of other items under study

Field trips to collect data on farming, business activities, conservation, transportation, communication, artifacts in exhibits, and other topics under study

Observation of activities of members of the family, house builders, and other community workers; of the roles of policemen, firemen, and other public officials; of changes in the weather and seasons; of meetings of the city council, school board, and other groups

How can simulated activities such as this one be used to further inquiry? What concepts in addition to producers of services might be developed? *(San Diego City Schools)*

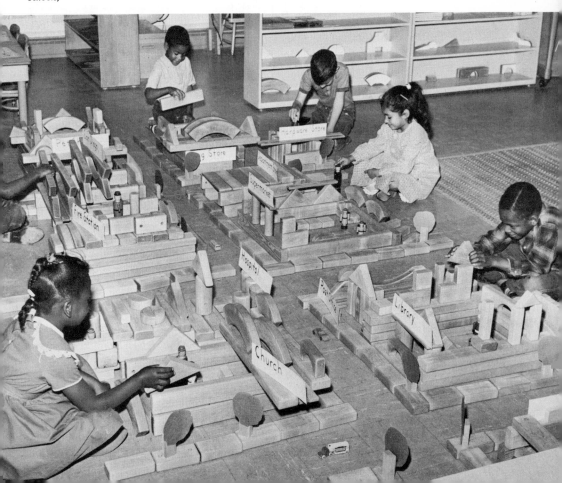

Interviews, polls, and *questionnaires* to gather data from fellow students, parents, community officials, businessmen, health workers, experts on conservation, and other resource persons who are expert on issues and questions under study

Role-playing and *simulation* of activities and decision-making in families, markets, banks, and other situations in which identification with others and involvement in decison-making processes are important

Experiments to determine what happens when different procedures or treatments are used, such as selecting and testing hypotheses about division of labor or presenting objects of varying sizes or colors to find out how one's perception of them changes

RECORDING, ORGANIZING, AND PRESENTING DATA

Making notes or tape recording of data obtained through interviews and on field trips

Construction of maps to show the distribution of homes, businesses, population, resources, and other phenomena, how such distributions as transportation networks and cities are related, and the flow of people, goods, and services between places

Construction of models, diagrams, graphs, tables, and charts of objects and processes under study to demonstrate and explain how they work and how they are used

Preparation of sketches, drawings, displays, and exhibits to illustrate processes, show the uses of objects, and highlight relationships between objects and human activities

Preparation of reports, oral or written, to share findings and conclusions with others

EVALUATING INQUIRY AND MATERIALS

Keeping logs, diaries, or other records for use in evaluating both individual and group activities

Construction and use of rating scales, charts, and checklists to appraise reports, maps, films, other sources of information, and individual and group activities

Participation in discussions to appraise and improve the effectiveness of both individual and group inquiry

Analytical Questions for Inquiry

Analytical questions are used extensively as a part of models and methods of inquiry. Questions are used by the teacher to analyze problems, guide planning, focus attention on items that may be neglected, guide the study of instructional media, and evaluate learning. Questions are used by students to guide their study from the first phases of inquiry on through to the last.

A promising development is to plan questions on different

levels of complexity, beginning with knowledge and moving to evaluation.[4] The purpose of such planning is to rise above the

kind of questioning that remains on the information level. Effective inquiry calls for higher levels of thinking, which can be triggered by well-planned questions.

A useful strategy is to employ the taxonomies of objectives that were presented in Chapter 1.[5] The categories of objectives which represent different levels of cognition and affective response may be used as guides as shown in the following examples:

LEVELS OF COGNITION

Knowledge: What are major landforms?

Comprehension: Can you explain the meaning of major landforms in your own words?

Application: How can we use the concept cluster *major landforms* to compare surface features in eastern and western United States?

Analysis: In what ways are transportation systems adapted to *major landforms*?

Synthesis: How shall we organize and present ideas about *landforms* in the United States?

Evaluation: How can we use the concept *major landforms* more effectively as we compare areas in our next unit on Latin America?

LEVELS OF AFFECTIVE RESPONSE

Receiving (attending): Did you notice any examples of unfairness to individuals in the reading selection?

Responding: What parts were most unfair?

Valuing: What do you feel should have been done?

Questions such as these can be used in units at all levels to sharpen thinking, clarify attitudes and other feelings, and improve inquiry. A basic principle, when new topics are under study, is first to use questions on the basic levels. If this is done, the teacher has a means of finding out if students have the knowledge and comprehension needed to move to higher levels. No student can engage in analysis, synthesis, and evaluation until he comprehends the matters under study.

---

[4] Norris M. Sanders, *Classroom Questions* (New York: Harper & Row, Publishers, 1966).

[5] See Benjamin Bloom, ed., *Taxonomy of Educational Objectives: Cognitive Domain* (New York: David McKay Co., Inc., 1956); and David Krathwohl, *et al.*, *Taxonomy of Educational Objectives: Affective Domain* (New York: David McKay Co., Inc., 1964).

Another principle is to use key concepts, concept clusters, and generalizations as sources of ideas for questions in the cognitive domain. The cluster *major landforms* was used in the examples above. Similar questions could be posed by using cultural change, division of labor, and other concepts noted in the first part of this chapter. In the affective domain, the values cited in Chapter 2 and in this chapter may be used as sources of ideas. For example, concern for others, open-mindedness, and respect for differing points of view may be used to formulate a variety of questions.

Effective questioning is truly an essential element in the development of skills of inquiry. Questions may be used to bring together the substantive and inquiry phases of the structure of the social studies. The higher the quality of the questions, the higher the level of inquiry! Students as well as teachers strive to devise questions that add dimensions of quality thinking, which can be achieved in no other way.

In closing this chapter, we should emphasize that involved in using models and methods of inquiry are a variety of basic skills. Because of their importance in the social studies several chapters are devoted to them in the latter part of this volume.

Questions, Activities, Evaluation

1. Examine two or three children's social studies textbooks and note examples of the following:
   a. Concepts, concept clusters, and generalizations
   b. Models and methods of inquiry suggested in the related teacher's manual
   c. Relative attention to material from core disciplines
2. Examine a course of study and do the same as above.
3. Examine a unit of instruction and do the same as in number 1 above.
4. Which of the models of inquiry presented in this chapter do you prefer? Discuss and defend your choice with others.
5. Which of the methods of inquiry do you think will be most useful in a unit you plan to teach? Note examples of how they might be used.
6. Prepare two or three sample questions on different levels as shown in this chapter.

References

Bailey, Wilfred, and Marion J. Rice, *Development of a Sequential Curriculum in Anthropology for Grades 1–7*. Athens, Ga.: College of Education, 1967. Teacher's guides, materials for students, and tests based on anthropological components of structure.

Berlak, Harold, and Timothy R. Tomlinson, *Development of Elementary School Social Science Curriculum.* St. Louis: Social Studies Center, George Washington University, 1968. Units and pupils' materials based on political science and other disciplines.

Bloom, Benjamin S., ed., *Taxonomy of Educational Objectives: Cognitive Domain.* New York: David McKay, Co., Inc., 1956. Objectives and test items on varying levels of complexity.

Bruner, Jerome, S., *The Process of Education.* Cambridge: Harvard University Press, 1960. A rationale for programs designed to develop insight into structure of disciplines.

English, Raymond, *Greater Cleveland Social Science Program.* Cleveland: Greater Cleveland Educational Research Council, 1967. Guides and pupils' materials based on concepts, themes, and generalizations.

Gabler, Robert E., ed., *A Handbook for Geography Teachers.* Normal, Ill.: National Council for Geographic Education, Illinois State University, 1966. Concepts and other background material for teachers.

Gill, Clark C., and William B. Conroy, *Development of Guidelines and Resource Materials on Latin America.* Austin: College of Education, University of Texas, 1968. Units and guides on Latin America.

Hill, Wilhelmina, ed., *Curriculum Guide for Geographic Education.* Normal, Ill.: NCGE, Illinois State University, 1964. Basic concepts, skills, and other background material for teachers.

Journal of Geography, 66 (January, 1967) 7–40. Entire issue devoted to statistical information on physical and cultural topics; useful as source of data for inquiry.

Krathwohl, David R., Benjamin S. Bloom, and Bertram B. Masia, *Taxonomy of Educational Objectives: Affective Domain.* New York: David McKay Co., Inc., 1964. Objectives and test items on varying levels of internalization.

Lord, Clifford L., *Teaching History with Community Resources.* New York: Bureau of Publications, Teachers College, Columbia University, 1964. Suggestions for the study of local history; related booklets on selected places in the United States.

Michaelis, John U., *Asian Studies Curriculum Project.* Berkeley: School of Education, University of California, 1968. Units on Asian countries based on concepts from the social sciences.

————, and A. Montgomery Johnston, eds., *The Social Sciences: Foundations of the Social Studies.* Boston: Allyn & Bacon, Inc., 1965. Chapters of eight core disciplines; major generalizations from the social sciences in appendix.

Moore, Evelyn, and Edward E. Owen, *Teaching the Subjects in the*

Social Studies. New York: St. Martin's Press, Inc., 1966. Emphasis on geography and history.

Morrissett, Irving, ed., *Concepts and Structure in the New Social Science Curricula.* Lafayette, Ind.: Social Science Education Consortium, Purdue University, 1966. Chapter by Senesh on fundamental ideas in economics, political science, sociology, anthropology, and geography; charts to show relationships.

Muessig, Raymond H., and Vincent R. Rogers, *Social Science Seminar Series.* Columbus: Charles E. Merrill Books, Inc., 1965. Volumes on history, geography, economics, political science, anthropology, and sociology.

New York City Board of Education, *Curriculum and Materials.* New York: The Board, 1965. Generalizations from basic disciplines for a K–XII program.

Price, Roy A., Warren Hickman, and Gerald Smith, *Major Concepts for Social Studies.* Syracuse: Social Studies Curriculum Center, 1965. Thirty-four selected concepts.

Rader, William D., *Elementary School Economics Program.* Chicago: Industrial Relations Center, University of Chicago, 1967. Pupils' materials for Grades IV–VI.

Raths, Louis E., Selma Wasserman, Arthur Jonas, and Arnold M. Rothstein, *Teaching for Thinking.* Columbus: Charles E. Merrill Books, Inc., 1967. Suggestions for applying comparisons, summaries, observations, classifications, and other processes to instruction in the social studies and other areas.

Riddle, Donald H., and Robert S. Cleary, eds., *Political Science in the Social Studies,* 36th Yearbook, National Council for the Social Studies. Washington, D.C.: National Education Association, 1966. Conceptual components and suggestions for program planning.

Sanders, Norris M., *Classroom Questions.* New York: Harper & Row, Publishers, 1966. Sample questions on levels ranging from memory to evaluation.

Senesh, Lawrence, *Our Working World.* Chicago: Science Research Associates, 1966. Materials for children in primary grades based on concepts from economics and other fields.

The Social Studies and Social Sciences. New York: Harcourt, Brace & World, Inc., 1962. Concepts and methods of inquiry in basic disciplines and area studies.

West, Edith, *Project Social Studies.* Minneapolis: School of Education, University of Minnesota, 1968. Units for Grades K–XII based on social science concepts.

Wisconsin State Department of Public Instruction, *A Conceptual Framework, Social Studies.* Madison, Wis.: The Department, 1964. Generalizations from basic disciplines.

Structure
of the
Social Studies
Program

How to structure the social studies curriculum is one of the most difficult problems faced by curriculum planners. The great diversity among the disciplines on which the social studies program is based compounds the difficulty. Many different proposals have been made and many different patterns of organization have been tried. Great effort has been put forth to structure the program in ways that enable teachers at various levels of instruction to contribute to the fullest possible achievement of the objectives of the social studies.

A well-designed plan of organization is helpful to teachers in several ways. Implications derived from the foundations of the social studies can be related to instruction at each of the different levels. Planning for a group can be more effective when definite suggestions are available regarding the units or topics at each level. Needless repetition can be avoided, gaps in learning can be prevented, and a more balanced program can be assured. More appropriate instructional media can be reviewed, selected, and arranged for use. Continuity of learning can be maintained as each teacher builds on what has gone before. Both depth and breadth of learning can be given attention as instruction is planned for topics and units at each level. Key concepts and generalizations can be kept in focus as children progress through the program. Evaluation can be planned and carried out in terms of areas of emphasis at each level.

5

Aspects of curriculum development prominent in the development of new programs are considered in this chapter. Specific attention is given to general trends, specific emphases and trends at each grade level, selected K–XII programs, the structuring of programs to provide for the spiral development of conceptual components, the structure of units, and a summary of guidelines for organizing the program.

Trends in Organization

One of the most significant trends is the use of multiple patterns of organization rather than a single pattern. Patterns of organization may be viewed on a continuum ranging from unified or interdisciplinary approaches, in which disciplines are indistinguishable, to separate-subject approaches, in which history, geography, or other disciplines are singled out for emphasis. Unified approaches are usually found in the early grades in such units as Families Around the World, Our Community, and Communities Around the World; they also may be found in courses in secondary schools that deal with contemporary problems related to urbanization, international relations, or other topics that require the use of material drawn from several disciplines. The separate-subject approach is predominant in high schools in such courses as United States history, world history, economics, and American government.

In between the unified and separate-subject approaches are multidisciplinary approaches that bring the perspectives of different disciplines to bear on topics and problems in such units as Our State, The New England States, Changing Japan, Latin America, and The Middle East. In multidisciplinary approaches the geographic, historical, economic, political, and socio-cultural features of the area under study are considered and relationships among them are highlighted. But each discipline is clearly visible, and the content is not brought together into a mix or amalgam which renders the disciplines indistinguishable.

A variety of patterns of organization may be noted in new programs of instruction. Instead of debating whether unified or multidisciplinary approaches are superior to separate-subject approaches, individuals associated with the development of new programs use whatever approach seems to be best in a given situation. Thus one can find separate-subject approaches used at times in the primary grades as well as in later grades and unified approaches used at various levels, depending on the need to fuse or relate material from several disciplines to the topics under study. Such a strategy seems to be far more useful than one in which *a priori* decisions are made to adopt a single approach and then units and courses are molded to fit the decision. In short, patterns of organization should be designed to support the attainment of objectives. When direct attention is being given to economic, geographic, or other special phenomena, there is good reason to use the conceptual tools and processes of inquiry that are directly relevant. On the other hand, when relationships are being emphasized, there is good reason to use unified or multidisciplinary approaches. The examples of topics and units in new programs that are presented later are illustrative of the trend to use multiple patterns of organization rather than a single one.

Several other developments are related to the structure of the social studies curriculum. In the new programs certain topics and units, ranging from Children in Other Lands in the Kindergarten and Families Around the World in Grade I, to Area Studies of India in Grade IV and the History of Early Man and Greece and Rome in Grades V–VI, are now introduced earlier than under the traditional curriculum. The traditional expanding environment sequence that begins with the child's home, school, neighborhood and community, and moves out to the state, region, nation, and world in later grades is being replaced by comparative studies of families, communities, and regions around the world.

Significant changes may be noted in the content that is included in new programs. Much more economics is taught at all levels of instruction. Material from anthropology is used in comparative studies of families and communities in the early grades and in cross-cultural area studies in later grades. Material from sociology and political science may be found in units centered on family life, community living, urbanization, minority groups, and problems at the state, national, and international levels. Increasing attention is being given to Asian countries, Africa, and minority groups in both elementary and secondary schools.

Concepts and generalizations are widely used as strands or threads to provide for cumulative learning from level to level. Units of instruction are designed to contribute to the development of selected concepts and generalizations in a spiraling sequence that begins with concrete experiences and becomes increasingly more complex and abstract from grade to grade. Main ideas derived from concepts and generalizations are used to structure units of study.

Certain long-term trends are continuing to receive systematic attention in the structuring of the curriculum. Democratic values and processes such as human dignity, equality of opportunity, and concern for others are emphasized in the context of minority groups and problems of newly developing countries. Major societal changes such as population growth, urbanization, and technological developments are included in units dealing with both historical and contemporary aspects of change in ways of living at home and abroad. Thinking processes and related cognitive skills are built into units at each level of instruction. Basic skills involved in map reading, gathering information from other instructional media, and evaluating, organizing, and interpreting data are made an integral part of the sequence of instruction.

Additional information on current trends and developments is presented in the next section in the context of topics and units at each level of instruction.

Overview of Dominant Topics and Units

Of primary concern to teachers are these questions: What main themes or areas of emphasis are included in different grades? What specific topics and units are included? What are the current trends at various levels? Answers to these questions are helpful as background information for reviewing and interpreting local courses of study.

State and local control of educational policies has created many differences among schools throughout the country. In fact, greater diversity may be noted in the social studies than in other areas of the curriculum. Nevertheless, certain similarities in content exist at various levels of instruction. The greatest similarities may be found in the early grades, which include such units as Family Life, The School, Our Community, and Communities Around the World. Great diversity may be noted in Grades IV, VI, and VII. However, even at these levels one can find similar topics and units, but they are placed in different grades. For example, some schools provide for the study of Western Hemisphere Countries in VI and Eastern Hemisphere Countries in VII; in other schools the reverse may be true.

The following section presents a grade-by-grade overview which shows the dominant theme or themes for each grade in italics. This is followed by illustrative topics and units in each grade and a brief statement of recent trends.

Kindergarten. Local Environment Studies: Short-term experiences and units are provided on The Home, The Store, The Service Station, How We Learn, The Airport, Trucks, and other aspects of the immediate environment.

Current trends are to provide deeper studies of The Home, School and Neighborhood, Children and Families in Other Lands, Our Global Earth, and How Man Changes the Neighborhood and Community.

Grade I. Family, School, and Community Life: Illustrative units are The Family, Our School and Other Schools, The Family at Work, Neighbors at Work, Community Workers, The Fire Station, The Supermarket, Families Around the World, Schools Around the World, The Dairy Farm, Farm Life, and How We Learn.

Current trends are to introduce economic, anthropological, and other concepts from the disciplines such as division of labor, extended family, and role, to teach map and globe skills in greater depth, to provide comparative studies of families and schools at home and abroad, and to compare rural and city life.

Grade II. Community Studies: Units and topics include Community Workers, Public Services, How We Get Our Food, The Wholesale Market, Transportation, Communication, Our Community and Other Communities, Living in Different Communities, and Workers Around the World.

Current trends are to provide for comparative studies of communities, to extend map and globe concepts, to study and compare changes in communities, to include some historical material on the community, and to emphasize specialization and division of labor within and among communities.

Grade III. Metropolitan Communities, City Life, Communities Around the World: Illustrative units and topics are Neighboring Communities, Different Kinds of Communities, Transportation, Communication, The Area Around Our Community, Living in Metropolitan Communities, Communities Around the World, Pioneer Communities, Indians, Development of Our Community, and Comparative Studies of Our Community and Other Communities.

Among the trends at this level are increased attention to interdependence among communities, problems of urbanization, historical and current changes in communities, local history, and government of the community.

Grade IV. Our State, Area Studies of Other Lands, Geography of Selected Regions, Great People in American History: Units and topics which illustrate the diversity at this level are Our State in Early Times, Our State Today, The Story of Agriculture and Industry, Living in Different Climatic Regions, Our Global World, Conservation, Area Study of India, Changing Japan, and How Americans Obtain Goods and Services.

Significant trends at this level are to provide cross-cultural comparative studies, to study historical, geographic, and economic aspects of the home state in greater depth, to give more attention to state government, to study the contributions of great men and women to the development of the state and nation, and to include more anthropological content in studies of other lands.

Grade V. Living in Early and Modern America, Regional Studies of the United States, Canada, and Latin America: Illustrative units and topics are Discovery and Exploration of America, Colonial Life, Pioneer Life, Westward Movement, Contributions of Leaders, Regions of the United States, Relationships with Canada, Living in the Americas, and Our Neighbors to the North and South.

Current trends are to teach the history, geography, economics, and political life of the United States in greater depth, to stress relationships among countries in the Americas, to introduce more material on backgrounds of United States history, to study urbanization in different regions, to explore the impact of scientific and technological developments in the past and present, and to give greater attention to the contributions and problems of minority groups.

Grade VI. Global Geography, Western or Eastern Hemisphere: Illustrative units and topics in schools stressing the Western Hemisphere are Early Cultures of South America, The ABC Countries, Argentina, Brazil, Chile, Living in Mexico, Countries of Central America, Historical and Cultural Beginnings in the Western World, and Economic and Social Problems. Illustrative of units and topics in schools focusing on the Eastern Hemisphere are Backgrounds of American History, Western Europe, Central Europe, Mediterranean Lands, Eastern Europe, The USSR, The Middle East, North Africa, Africa South of the Sahara, India, and China. Schools that focus on global geography provide for a selection of units on culture regions and countries around the world.

Trends at this level are to program Grades VI and VII so that students may study both eastern and western culture regions, to highlight interdependence among countries, to explore the problems of newly developing nations, to consider the work of international agencies, to study the impact of culture on ways of living, and to analyze social, economic, and political systems in greater depth.

Grade VII. Eastern or Western Hemisphere Studies, Study of Our State, United States History: The history and geography of Eastern Hemisphere Areas, especially Europe, are predominant with an emphasis on such units and topics as Old World

Backgrounds, Early Man, Early Civilizations, Greece and Rome, The Middle Ages, and Western European Nations. Schools that focus on countries in the Western Hemisphere tend to stress geography and include units and topics similar to those listed above for Grade VI. World Geography is offered in some schools, and Our State is studied in several places in Grade VII instead of Grade IV. Much of the work in Grade VII is planned to provide background for units on United States History in VIII.

Current trends are to include more material on Asian countries, to interrelate state and national history, to give greater attention to minority groups, to explore the problems of new nations, to analyze conflicts between nations, to investigate reasons for the lack of development in nations with traditional cultures, and to study historical, geographic, social, economic, and political aspects of development in greater depth.

Grade VIII. United States History, The Constitution, Federal, State, and Local Government: Specific topics and units include Exploration and Discovery, Colonization, The Thirteen Colonies, The Winning of Independence, The Constitution, Building a Government, Emergence of American Patterns of Living, The Civil War and Reconstruction, Growth of Industry and Agriculture, Enrichment of American Life, Contributions of Leaders, Contributions of Minority Groups, Preserving and Extending Human Rights, Becoming a World Power, Relations with Other Nations, Government at the Local, State, and National Levels, and Geography of the United States. The typical practice is to emphasize the study of early American history up to the Reconstruction Era with about one-third of the time on later American history; the reverse is generally true in Grade XI, in which United States history is studied intensively.

Current trends are to provide fewer units and to study them in depth, to provide primary source materials for analysis and interpretation by students, to give more attention to minorities in the history of the United States, to use concepts from economics and other disciplines in analyzing historical events, to acquaint students with historical methods of inquiry, to emphasize the interrelationships of Federal, state, and local government, to provide case studies on selected aspects of government, to study government as a system, and to contrast democratic and communistic forms of government.

Grades IX–XII. Civics, World Geography, World History, United States History, United States Government, Economics, Current Problems: Civics is required in many schools in Grade IX with special attention to citizenship responsibilities of youth. World geography and world history are electives in most secondary schools in Grades IX and X. United States history is a standard requirement in Grade XI, and many schools require a course in government and current problems in XII. Larger high schools offer electives in such courses as sociology, anthropology, state history, economics, international relations, European history, Afro-Asian studies, Asian studies, and psychology.

Current trends are to provide courses on comparative economic and political systems, to increase the amount of time given to Asian civilizations in world history, to require work in economics, to offer a two-year block in United States history rather than the separate offerings in VIII and XI, to emphasize independent study in which methods of inquiry from the disciplines are put to use, and to view elective courses as capstone offerings which bring together concepts and modes of inquiry included at various points earlier in the program.

This brief overview shows that most programs begin with the child's immediate environment and move outward to increasingly larger and more distant areas. Yet the trend is to introduce the study of other families, communities, and cultures early in the program. Although major attention still is given to history, geography, and political science in current social studies programs, more content is being drawn from anthropology, economics, and sociology.

That a study of the United States is not neglected may be shown by pointing to the study of the local community in primary grades, state history and geography in middle or upper grades, United States history in Grades IV or V, VII, VIII, and XI, and relationships between the United States and other countries at different levels. New countries and new problems are being given attention at various levels.

Recurring topics that are included in the social studies program at different levels are current affairs, holidays, commemorations, controversial issues, and the contributions of great men and women. Specific aspects are selected for study at different levels in terms of the children's background of experience and maturity. More complex aspects are introduced as children progress through school and as efforts are made to develop depth and breadth of understanding of societal changes.

The Organization of New Programs

Several features of new programs can only be revealed by examining selected programs in detail. For example, continuity from level to level, the planning of blocks of instruction over two or more levels, the emphasis given to United States history at different levels, and the scope or breadth of the program all need to be considered in the context of a particular plan or framework. The following examples have been chosen to illustrate current trends and new developments. Each example is preceded by introductory comments that are intended to focus attention on special features.

CALIFORNIA

A sequence recently proposed in California may be characterized as an inquiry-conceptual-topical approach. Inquiry processes such as observation, classification, and comparison are linked with key concepts such as role, division of labor, and urbanization. The inquiry processes and concepts are applied to topics such as the nature of communication, use of the environment, and cultural diversity in California and the New World. The processes, concepts, and topics are arranged by blocks of grades to permit flexibility in grade-level planning at the local level.

The sequence of topics begins with the study of mankind in Grades K–II, moves to cultural and geographic interrelationships in Grades III–IV, and is focused on mankind and men in Grades V–VI: [1]

Kindergarten–II. The Study of Mankind: Physical and Bio-Characteristics, Contrasts to Animals; The Nature of Communication and Symbols; Uses of the Natural Environment; Living in Communities, Contrast between Man and Animals; Man as Producer and Consumer, Roles in the Family, School, Community, Rules and Rule Making, Changes in Roles, Groups, and Social Systems; The Wonderment of Man's Universe, Songs, Tools, Games, Toys, and Personalities, Around the World

Grades III–IV. Man and Land: Cultural and Geographic Interrelationships: Contrast between Human and Animal Adaptations to Land; Human Adaptations to Land in California, Use of Land by Indians and Later Groups; Growth and Development of Selected Towns and Cities; Development of Economic and Political Institutions; Immigrations; Cultural Diversity, Urban and Rural, Comparative Study of Urban Communities, Regional Heterogeneity; Cultural Diversity in the New World to 1830, Comparisons between North and South America, Interaction of Indians,

---

[1] California Statewide Social Sciences Study Committee. *Progress Report, August 1967.* Sacramento: California State Department of Education, 1967.

English, French, Dutch, Spanish, and Negroes, Comparison with Diversity in Local Community and State, Diversity in Urban Centers and in Selected Regions

Grades V–VI. Mankind and Men: Man, A Social Being, Man's Use of Language, Tools, and Technology, Man's Need for Social Organizations, Human Diversity; Cultural Diversity in Modern America since 1830, Immigrations, Regional Heterogeneity; Man as Creature and Creator of Culture, Humanistic Expression as a Lens on the Milieu and the Individual, In a Folk Society, In Periclean Athens, In the Medieval Period or the Renaissance, In a Non-Western Society such as China, In America

Grades VII–IX. American Political System, Economic Systems, Urban Society. Politics and the Formation of the American Political System, Political Behavior, Political Culture and Socialization, Decision Making, The Constitution; Poverty and Abundance, Functions of Economic Systems, The United States from Agrarian to Industrial State, Comparative Systems, Economic Development; The First Cities, Case Studies of Pre-Industrial Cities, Contemporary Urban Life, Improving Urban Life

Grades X–XII. Major Themes in History, American Political System, Capstone Courses: Major Themes in World History; Major Themes in United States History; Study of a Non-Western Country such as China; American Political System; Capstone Electives in Disciplines, Area Studies, and other Courses

NEW YORK STATE

The New York State program includes several features that should be noted. The two-year blocks that include Local Environment Studies in Kindergarten and Grade I, Community Studies in Grades II–III, and Major Culture Regions in Grades V–VI, Our Cultural Heritage and U. S. History in Grades VII–VIII, and World and American History in Grades X–XI provide opportunities for concentration on the development of concepts and generalizations within the defined area. The strong cultural orientation calls for the use of considerable material from anthropology, human geography, and sociology. Notice also that social, economic, and political organizations are emphasized in all of the first seven grades with the exception of the fourth grade.

A recurring emphasis, found in all social studies programs, is the direct attention to patriotism in the first five grades. Included in this phase of the program are The Pledge of Allegiance,

The National Anthem, The Story of the Flag, Democratic Rights and Responsibilities, and Holidays and Festivals.

As in most social studies programs three full years are devoted specifically to the study of United States history. An attempt has been made to avoid overlapping and duplication by emphasizing the contributions of leaders in Grade IV, major periods of U. S. history in VIII, and broad themes in XI. Notice that the program in Grade VIII is preceded by a study of state history, a unit on New York as a part of a megalopolis, and work on local and state government. Grade-level themes and topics are as follows: [2]

Kindergarten. Local Environment Studies: Social, economic, and political organization of family and school, geography, Pledge of Allegiance and other activities to develop patriotism

Grade I. Local Environment Studies: Social, economic, and political organization, families, schools, village and city life, farming, geography

Grade II. Community Studies: Social, economic, and political organization, social, ethnic, and religious groups, community organizations, industries, business, local government, needed services, geography, patriotic activities

Grade III. Community Studies: Geographic introduction, desert communities, northern forest or taiga communities, tropical rainforest communities, mountain communities, prairie farming communities, patriotic activities

Grade IV. American People and Leaders: The people, discoverers and explorers, leaders during colonial, revolutionary, and early government periods, leaders in the fight for human rights, leaders in industry, science and arts, and patriotic activities

Grade V. Major Culture Regions (Western Hemisphere): Geographic and historical introductions, United States, Canada, and Latin America, social, political, and economic organization

Grade VI. Major Culture Regions (Middle East and Europe): Geographic instruction, historical summary, social, political, and economic organization

Grade VII. Our Cultural Heritage: Pre-Columbian period, New World explorations and settlement, colonial period in the Americas, New York in the emerging nation, New York in the age of homespun, New York in the gilded age (to about 1915), New York in a megalopolis society, local and state government and civic responsibility

[2] New York State Department of Education, *Flow Charts for Elementary and Secondary Social Studies Programs* (Albany: The Department, 1965).

Grade VIII. United States History: The new nation (to 1800), the National-Republican period (1800–25), the age of Jackson (1825–40's), division and reunion (1850's–80), economic expansion (1865–1900), United States a world power (1900–40), United States a world leader (1940–present), the federal government and civic responsibility

Grade IX. Asian and African Culture Studies: World cultures today, Africa south of the Sahara—land and people, Africa south of the Sahara—historic trends, South Asia—India and Pakistan, China, Japan, Southeast Asia

Grade X. Modern World History: The cultural heritage of modern Europe, the emergence of modern Europe, the rise of democratic societies, industrialism, nationalism, and Europe's self-confident era, Europe's new age of colonialism, conflicting ideologies, and twentieth century conflict, Europe in the mid-twentieth century world

Grade XI. American History: The American people, government and politics, American economic life, the United States in world affairs, American civilization in historic perspective

Grade XII. Specialized Courses: Economics; government; other suggested courses are African studies, anthropology, ancient history, Asian studies, great issues, Latin American studies, Middle Eastern studies, psychology, sociology

NEW YORK CITY

The proposed New York City program has some interesting deviations from the typical program. The program in kindergarten is focused on the home and school here and in other places. Changes in the community and group living are emphasized in Grade I. Living and working around the world are emphasized in Grade II, and culture studies of people of other times and places are included in Grade III. United States history is included in Grades IV, VII, and XI. A two-year block is provided in Grades V–VI for the study of geographic, economic, historical, and cultural aspects of the Western world. Urbanization is the focus of Grade VIII, and studies of Eastern and Western civilization constitute a two-year block in Grades IX–X. Economics is suggested as a requirement in Grade XII and may be followed by a choice of several elective courses. Specific themes and topics are as follows: [3]

Kindergarten. The Child in Home and School: Family activi-

---

[3] New York City Board of Education, *Curriculum and Materials* (New York: The Board, 1965).

ties, roles and jobs of members, changing structure, rules, work, income, tools, machines, basic needs; orientation to the school, school personnel, mapping the classroom and the school, conserving school resources; families and schools in other cultures; holidays, care of the flag, other patriotic activities

Grade I. Changing Communities. How We Live Together: Family life today and long ago, community workers, community differences, changes, public services, food production; holidays and other patriotic activities

Grade II. How People Live and Work Around the World: Social organization of the community, sources of individual and governmental income, communication, transportation, studies of other communities; patriotic activities

Grade III. How Man Lived at Other Times and in Other Cultures: Desert, plains, mountains, rainforest, marine areas; primitive and advanced peoples; ways in which various peoples are inventive; ways of studying early peoples; people in ancient times; early urban cultures; patriotic activities

Grade IV. American People and Leaders: How the United States Began and Grew: Discoverers and explorers, colonists, people who helped to establish our nation, people who helped to develop our nation before 1900, people leading us into the Great Society since 1900, people who have led America's fight for freedom; patriotic activities

Grade V. The Western World—Geographic and Economic Studies: Geographic principles and tools with a focus on the United States, regional studies of Canada, Latin America, Europe and their relationships to the United States

Grade VI. The Western World—Historical and Cultural Beginnings and Early Development: Work of archeologists and historians in recreating the past, development of modern man, geographic factors, development of government, search for freedom and equality under law, contributions of the past

Grade VII. American History: Colonial times to present, geographic and political settings, coming to the New World, development of democratic government and a democratic society, movements of people, changes in government

Grade VIII. Urban Growth—Challenges of a Changing Society: Metropolitan areas around the world, New York area, megalopolis, urbanization in New York State, problems and challenges; Federal-state relations, the Constitution, state and local government

Grades IX–X. World Studies: Regional studies of Eastern civilization in IX; history and culture of Western civilization in X

Grade XI. American History (American Studies): Government, foreign policy, selected institutions, optional topics (predicated on flexible Regents examination)

Grade XII. Economics in first semester; selection from problems courses, government, behavioral science, Asian studies, Latin American studies, African studies, geography, advanced placement courses

THE GREATER CLEVELAND PROGRAM

The curriculum being developed by the Greater Cleveland Research Council (1967) departs markedly from traditional patterns of organization. For example, globe study and units on children in other lands are included in kindergarten materials. Stories of explorers and discoverers are included in Grade I, and communities of various types are studied in Grade II. Much of the material included in Grade III on Anglo-America is found in Grade IV or V in traditional programs. The attention to metropolitan problems in Grade III is in keeping with the current emphasis on urbanization.

Several departures from traditional practice may be noted in the later grades. Agriculture and industry are singled out for emphasis in Grade IV and the first of several area studies is introduced. The area studies included in subsequent grades provide for a fairly complete coverage of the world. The sequencing of historical studies in Grades V–VIII begins with early civilization and moves down to the present. Direct attention is given to U.S. history in Grade VIII, rather than in Grades V, VIII, and XI, which is the practice in traditional programs.

The following summary includes an outline of major topics for Kindergarten through Grade VIII and the tentative plans for Grades IX–XII.[4]

Kindergarten. The Child Begins to Know His World: School Family, Ourselves, Neighborhood, Services; *Children in Other Lands:* Globe Study, Japan, Mexico, American Samoa, Lapland, Nigeria, Central Congo, England

Grade I. Learning About Our Country: Review of Home, School, Neighborhoods, Map and Globe Skill, Travel in Our Country, A Trip to the Capital, Symbols of Our Nation, Biographies of Washington and Other Americans; *Explorers and Discoverers:* Balboa, Byrd, Columbus, Cook, Cousteau, De Soto, Glenn, Hudson, Magellan, The Norsemen, Peary, Marco Polo

Grade II. Communities at Home and Abroad: Our Own Com-

---

[4] Raymond English, *Greater Cleveland Social Science Program, Publications 1966–67* (Cleveland: Greater Cleveland Research Council, 1966).

munity, Two Different Communities (Aborigines of Australia, Eskimos of Alaska); *Communities in the United States:* Historical (Williamsburg), Agricultural (Webster, Ia.), Recreational-Cultural (Aspen), Apple-Growing (Yakima), Lumber-Paper Producing (Crossett, Ark.), Multiracial (Hawaii)

Grade III. The Making of Anglo-America: Geography, Population, Economic Factors, Exploration, Colonization, The Revolution and Constitution, Westward Movement, Industrialization; *The Metropolitan Community:* Historical Study of Imaginary City, Metropolitan Problems, Metropolitan and Megalopolitan Areas of U.S. and Canada, Principles of Government; *Cleveland, A Metropolitan Community:* Geography, History, Economic, Social, Cultural and Political Institutions (case study to complement preceding unit on imaginary city); *Boston and Brockton— Metropolitan Communities* (for schools in Boston area, useful as a model for metropolitan studies)

Grade IV. The Story of Agriculture: Food Production and Distribution, Relationships to Civilization's Growth, Rice Growing in Java and Texas, American Wheatfields; *The Story of Industry:* Specialization, Research, Investment, Mass Production and Consumption, Semiautomated Food Processing, Automobile Production, Computers, Implications of Industrial-Technological Change; *India—A Society in Transition:* Traditional Agriculture, Modern Industry, Geography, History, Village Life, Growth of Industries, Industrial Cities

Grade V. The Human Adventure I—Ancient Civilization: Geographic Base, Rise of Civilization in the Middle East, Four World Views of the Sixth Century B.C. (China, India, Israel, Greece); *The Human Adventure II—Classical Civilization:* Greece and Rome, Athens under Pericles, Alexander, Republican and Imperial Rome, Early Christianity, Western Civilization as Synthesis of Christianity and Greco-Roman Tradition; *The Human Adventure III—Medieval Civilization:* Islam's Dominance, Latin Christendom in Middle Ages, Mongol Conquests, and Aspects of China's and India's Civilization, Brief Overview of Origins of Science, Age of Discoveries, and Roots of European Prestige; *Area Study of Middle East:* Geography, Role of Islam, Culture, Economics, Sociology, Politics, Egypt, Israel, the Arab Nations, Iran, Turkey

Grade VI. The Human Adventure IV—The Rise of Modern Civilization: Formative Period (emphasis on humanism, capitalism, religious schism, science, monarchies, decline of medieval governments), Opening of New World, Emergence of Russia, Moslem Conquest of India, Japan under Hideyoshi; *The Human Adventure V—Later Modern Civilization:* Changing Mental

Climate in 18th Century, French Revolution, Napoleonic Wars, Revolutions in Industry, Agriculture, Applied Science, Technology, Production and Population Growth, Contrasts to non-Western World, Nationalism and Other Isms of 19th Century, The World of 1918; *Area Study of Latin America:* Geography, Culture, Economics, Politics, Peru and Mexico, Organization of American States, Relations with the United States

Grade VII. The Human Adventure VI—Contemporary Civilization: Totalitarian Revolutions in Russia, Germany, and China, Problems in Western Europe and America to 1939, World War II, the Cold War, Economic Underdevelopment, Population Explosion, Role of the United States; *Principles of Geography:* Planet Earth, Maps and Other Tools of Geography, History of Earth, Cultural Habitats, Distribution of People and Culture Patterns, Economic Geography, Patterns of Circulations, Political Geography; *Area Study of Subsaharan Africa:* Anthropology (tribal society), Economics, Political Developments (emergence of new nations)

Grade VIII. The Human Adventure VII—American Generations, the Young Republic: U.S. History, Narrative Biography Centered on Great Americans, Colonial Times up to Civil War (special attention to Jonathan Edwards, Benjamin Franklin, George Washington, Thomas Jefferson, Andrew Jackson, and John C. Calhoun), Characteristics, Movements, and Accomplishments of Several Generations; *The Human Adventure VIII—American Generations, the Growth of Titan:* Civil War to Early 20th Century (special attention to Robert E. Lee, Abraham Lincoln, Mark Twain, Andrew Carnegie, Theodore Roosevelt, and William Jennings Bryan), Growth into a World Power; *Area Study of North America and the Caribbean:* Geographic, Economic and Political Survey

Grades IX–XII. (Tentative): Comparative Economic and Political Systems, Area Study of Europe and USSR, Research and Problems in IX; International Politics and Economics, Review of History of Civilization, Philosophy and Religion I, and Area Study of Far East in X; Economics and Sociology, History of Civilization, Philosophy and Religion II, and Area Study of the Pacific Ocean and Australia in XI; American Government, Research and Problems in Social Science (revolutions, power politics, race relations, population, and the like) in XII

PROJECT SOCIAL STUDIES, MINNESOTA

The structure of the curriculum in this special project differs from traditional patterns in several ways. The Kindergarten program includes material on map and globe skills, interdependence in the neighborhood, peoples of the world, and ways in which man changes the earth. A two-year block is provided on Families Around the World in Grades I–II, and on Communities Around the World in Grades III–IV. Regional studies of the United States, Canada, and Latin America are presented in Grade V, and Area Studies of Europe, the USSR, China, and India are in Grade XI. United States history is in Grades VI and X, not in V, VII, and XI as in most programs. Grade VII has a heavy sociological and anthropological emphasis with a focus on socialization, the family, the school, and other aspects of "man in culture." Our political and economic systems are presented in Grades VIII–IX. The last year is devoted to such problems as security and freedom, war and peace, and race relations. The specific themes and units in the K–XII sequence are as follows: [5]

Kindergarten. The Earth as the Home of Man: Our Global Earth, A Home of Varied Resources, A World of Many Peoples, Man Changes the Earth

Grade I. Families Around the World: Chippewa, Hopi, Quechua (Peru), Japanese

Grade II. Families Around the World: Boston (18th century), Soviet (Moscow), Hausa (Nigeria), Kibbutz (Israel)

Grade III. Communities Around the World: Rural and Urban (contrasts), Frontier Community (California mining camp), Paris, Manus (New Guinea)

Grade IV. Communities Around the World: Our Own, Soviet, Trobriander Island (exchange system), Village in India (caste system); economic emphasis in each community study

Grade V. Regional Studies: The United States, Canada, Latin America, Small Region of Africa; selected case studies of areas around major cities

Grade VI. The Formation of American Society: Indian America, Colonization, English Settlement, American Revolution, Westward Expansion, Civil War and Reconstruction

Grade VII. Man and Culture: Introduction to Human Behavior and Sociological Reasoning, Biological Bases of Behavior, How We Become Human, The Family, The School, Minority Group Problems

Grade VIII. Our Political System: Need for Government and Law, Political Parties and Elections, Executive, Legislative, and Judicial Processes

[5] Edith West, *Project Social Studies Curriculum Center, Progress Report No. 2* (Minneapolis: University of Minnesota, 1965).

Grade IX. Our Economic System and Socio-Economic Problems: The United States: An Affluent Society? How Our System Works, Farm Problems, Auto Industry, Pockets of Poverty, Selecting an Occupation

Grade X. American History: I. Formation of American Civilization, 1630–1860; II. Modern America, 1870 to Present

Grade XI. Area Studies: Western Europe, USSR, China, India

Grade XII. Value Conflicts and Policy Decisions: Security and Freedom, Underdeveloped Countries, Economic Growth at Home, Race Problems, Africa South of the Sahara, War and Peace, What Is the Good Life?

The Structuring of Programs Around Concepts and Generalizations

Programs such as those outlined above are structured around concepts, themes, and generalizations drawn from basic disciplines. In fact, agreement is widespread that conceptual strands or threads should be used as foci for planning the K–XII program. Continuity of learning from level to level is facilitated by planning for the spiral development of concepts, concept clusters, generalizations, methods of inquiry, and related attitudes and skills. How this is done may be clarified by considering the spiral development of concepts and related generalizations.

An example of the cumulative development of concepts in cultural change and the related generalizations that may be developed at different levels of instruction are shown in Chart 1. Other concepts and various methods of inquiry and skills might be shown in a similar fashion.

Special note should be made of the fact that cultural change is not shown as a single concept because it consists of a cluster of related concepts. If attention is not given to the related concepts, important dimensions of cultural change will be neglected. Instruction at each level is designed to provide for the use of concepts on increasing levels of abstractness and complexity, and for the development of related generalizations that encompass broader domains of content. Yet care is taken to embed instruction at each level in adequate samplings of concrete and familiar material so that cumulative development of each concept is nurtured without gaps or breaks in the child's changing cognitive structures.

PLANNING FOR SPIRAL DEVELOPMENT

The general procedure in planning for the spiral development of concepts and generalizations is to identify applications that

SPIRAL DEVELOPMENT OF A CONCEPT CLUSTER AND RELATED GENERALIZATIONS

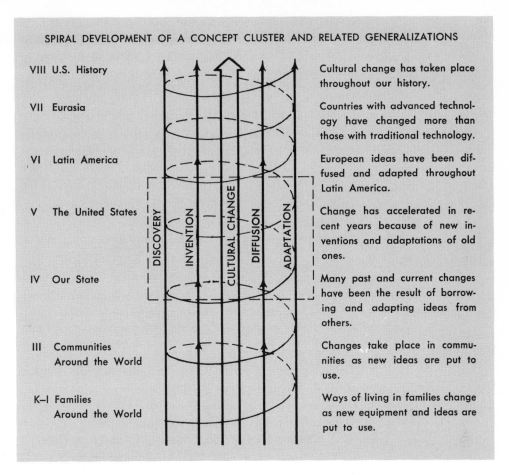

VIII U.S. History	Cultural change has taken place throughout our history.
VII Eurasia	Countries with advanced technology have changed more than those with traditional technology.
VI Latin America	European ideas have been diffused and adapted throughout Latin America.
V The United States	Change has accelerated in recent years because of new inventions and adaptations of old ones.
IV Our State	Many past and current changes have been the result of borrowing and adapting ideas from others.
III Communities Around the World	Changes take place in communities as new ideas are put to use.
K–I Families Around the World	Ways of living in families change as new equipment and ideas are put to use.

DISCOVERY   INVENTION   CULTURAL CHANGE   DIFFUSION   ADAPTATION

Chart 1

can be made to units and topics at each level of instruction. The applications may be noted in different ways, as the examples below show. The first example shows applications of the concept *interdependence* to blocks of grades. The second shows applications of a broad generalization from economics in the form of main ideas at each level. The third shows the types of questions that may be used at different levels to guide learning toward a major generalization rooted in anthropology and sociology.

INTERDEPENDENCE

K and I: Interdependence among members of the family, neighbors, school workers, community workers, producers and consumers, buyers and sellers

II and III: Interdependence among families in communities, among neighborhoods in communities, between communities, between farms and markets, factory workers and transportation workers

IV and V: Interdependence among communities and areas with the state, between industries and government, between states, between regions of the United States, between the United States and other countries

VI and VII: Interdependence among countries in the Americas, in Europe, and throughout the world

GENERALIZATION

Specialization has led to interdependence among individuals, communities, regions, and nations.

Members of the family have special jobs. Each member depends on others for some things.

Community workers have special jobs and depend on each other for many goods and services.

Our community produces some things but depends on other communities for many goods.

States and regions in our country use resources to produce goods that are exchanged with goods produced in other places.

Our country imports and exports a variety of goods. We depend on other countries for some goods, and they in turn depend on us.

Countries around the world have specialized in producing some goods that can be sold to other countries.

GENERALIZATION

Societies require a system of social control in order to survive.

What rules do families have? Why must members of families stick to rules? What happens if they don't? What responsibilities do children have?

What rules do we have in our class? In our school? What might happen if we had no rules? How can the rules be changed? Why must rules be changed at times?

How do safety regulations help to protect us in the community? Food regulations? Others? What responsibilities do firemen have? Policemen? Other public workers? What are our responsibilities?

How do state laws help to protect us? Food inspections? Highway traffic? Business regulations? Others? What responsibilities do officials have? What responsibilities do we and others have?

What responsibilities are taken by the Federal Government for internal control? Law enforcement? Law making? Individual rights? Others? How are local, state, and Federal means of control interrelated? How does our Government participate in controlling international problems?

The Structure of Units

Some of the best examples of the use of structural components from the disciplines may be found in units of instruction. Both concepts and generalizations have been used to organize content and learning experiences in units at different levels of instruction. In state and local programs major use has been made of generalizations.[6] Both concepts and generalizations have been used in social studies projects. The examples below illustrate the kind of analysis that is made. Detailed procedures for the planning of units are presented in chapter 7.

STRUCTURING UNITS AROUND CONCEPTS

Sets of concepts have been used in several different programs to structure units. Chart 2 shows the type of applications that can be made in a unit on Families at Work.[7] Concepts from economics are listed on the left and applications are shown on the right.

[6] See California State Department of Education, *Social Studies Framework for the Public Schools of California*; New York City Board of Education, *Curriculum and Materials*; and Wisconsin State Department of Education, *A Conceptual Framework: Social Studies*.

[7] Lawrence Senesh, *Our Working World: Families at Work* (Chicago: Science Research Associates, 1964).

ECONOMIC CONCEPTS IN A UNIT ON FAMILIES

SCARCITY: Wants are greater than available goods and services.

NEEDS: Needs for food, shelter, and clothing have priority.

CHOICES: Families make choices in light of income, tastes, customs, available alternatives.

GOODS AND SERVICES: Members of the family use both consumer and producer goods and services.

Consumer: Consumer goods include food, clothes, furnishings; services include health care, entertainment via radio and TV, repairs; all members of the family are consumers.

Producer: Producer goods include stoves, sewing machines, tools; services include repairs of tools and equipment; some members of the family are not producers.

Chart 2

DECISIONS:	Families make decisions on what, how much, how to produce, and how to divide what is produced.
What to produce?	Some families produce food, clothing, furnishings, and other items.
How much, and how to produce?	How much and how to produce are related to size of family income, skills, tastes, customs, time, and equipment. How to produce depends on customs and skills.
How to divide?	Consumer goods and services are divided to meet individual and group needs of members of the family.
SPECIALIZATION:	Members of the family specialize; they also benefit from the specialization of others.
Division of labor:	Adults and children have different roles; working members of a family specialize at work and at home.
Technology:	Differences exist among families in the extent to which tools and equipment are used in the home.
Geographic:	Local resources are used by families; specialities from other areas may be purchased.
Occupational:	Members of the family have jobs that require skills and education.
THE MARKET:	Members of the family search for best values in terms of wants, income, tastes, customs.
Prices, Money, Transportation:	Prices vary in terms of supply and demand; money and transportation facilitate the market.

Chart 2 continued

STRUCTURING UNITS AROUND MAIN IDEAS DERIVED FROM GENERALIZATIONS

Main ideas derived from generalizations are used to structure units in many programs. The process is one of preparing statements of subideas that can be applied in a given unit. Chart 3 includes main ideas that have been derived from a set of generalizations drawn from several disciplines. Notice that each main idea is indicative of the kind of content that should be provided in the unit.

MAIN IDEAS IN A UNIT ON FOOD PRODUCTION

GENERALIZATIONS	MAIN IDEAS TO BE DEVELOPED
Basic needs. People work to satisfy needs for food, ⟶ clothing, and so forth.	Every community provides food.

Chart 3

Group action. The work of society is carried on through groups. →	Many groups work to produce and distribute food.
Culture. Individual behavior is influenced by the culture. →	People eat different foods to obtain the nourishment they need.
Interdependence. People depend on others. →	The food store provides a community service.
Technology. Level of technology is related to production. →	Machines, power, and inventions are used to produce and process food.
Standards. People act in accordance with laws and regulations. →	Laws and regulations apply to the production and distribution of food.
Technology. Level of technology is related to production. →	Transportation, refrigeration, and processing plants make possible a wide variety of foods.
Contributions. Others have contributed to our cultural heritage. →	Some foods have been brought from other lands.
Change. Change is characteristic of the social and physical environment. →	Ways of producing food have changed.

Chart 3 continued

EXAMPLES OF MAIN IDEAS IN OTHER UNITS

A variety of derived main ideas may be found in new units of instruction. A helpful practice is to state main ideas in terms that are fairly close to the kind of generalization that children themselves will formulate after a series of learning experiences. Examples of main ideas are given in Charts 4–15. All of them are directly related to generalizations presented in this and the preceding chapter. Other examples are given in the following chapters.

HOME AND FAMILY

Families differ in size and composition.

Everyone at home has work to do.

Changes take place in homes and families.

Money may be earned by one or more members of the family.

Some members of the family produce goods and services.

Chart 4

LIVING ON FARMS

Our country has many different kinds of farms.

Different kinds of work are done as seasons change.

Water, soil, and weather are important to the farmer.

New machines have changed the work of farmers.

People depend upon farmers, and farmers depend on other workers.

Chart 5

LIVING IN OUR COMMUNITY

People work at many different jobs to provide goods and services.

People depend upon one another for food, clothes, and other goods.

Many goods that we need are made in other communities.

Many changes have taken place since our community was founded.

Chart 6

LIFE IN TRIBAL VILLAGES

People make most of the things they need.

Members of the family work to get food, shelter, and clothing.

People depend upon their own skills and their environment more than we do.

Customs and traditions are very important in people's lives.

Chart 7

COMMUNITIES IN OTHER LANDS

Weather, climate, and landforms vary from place to place.

People work for food, shelter, and clothing.

Changes take place as new ideas are put to use.

Some communities are like ours in some ways, but different in others.

Chart 8

GROWTH OF OUR STATE

Industries have been set up to use capital, resources, and labor supply.

Some ways of living brought by early settlers are still evident.

Many people have contributed to the growth of our state.

Changes have taken place faster in recent years.

Chart 9

IN EARLY AMERICA

Many settlers came in search of a better life.

The reasons for coming to America differed among settlers from different countries.

Ways of living in the colonies were related to beliefs, past experiences, and new problems.

The idea of self-government was expressed in many ways.

Chart 10

SOME MAIN IDEAS ABOUT CANADA

The history of Canada is like ours in some ways but different in others.

The heritage left by early English and French settlers is evident in many ways.

Canada and the United States are interdependent in many ways.

Resources, knowledge, trade, and other factors have led to rapid economic progress.

Chart 11

SOME MAIN IDEAS ABOUT JAPAN

The shift from a traditional to a modern society was made rapidly.

New ideas have been combined with old to improve ways of living.

Trade with other countries is essential for many reasons.

Economic activities are related to resources, population, know-how, and geographic conditions.

Chart 12

LIVING IN MEXICO

The distribution of landforms and climates is distinctive.

The diffusion of Spanish traditions has been great.

The population is more dense in the highlands than in the lowlands because the climate is more favorable.

Agriculture is the major industry, but manufacturing is increasing.

Chart 13

IN SOUTH AMERICA

The countries of South America attained freedom from European nations after a long struggle.

Countries in the Americas are interdependent in many ways.

The Alliance for Progress is designed to improve conditions of living.

A single major industry exists in many nations.

Chart 14

GROWTH OF DEMOCRACY

Democratic concepts of government began to emerge early in America.

The Constitution provided the basic framework of government.

Principles of democracy were extended as frontiers were opened.

Many individuals and groups have contributed to the growth of democracy.

Chart 15

A Summary of Guidelines

Summarized in this last section are guidelines that are widely used in planning and organizing social studies programs.

The K–XII program should be based on a clearly formulated point of view. Attention should be given to objectives of the social studies, implications for instruction derived from the social and psychological foundations, ways in which the program is rooted in the disciplinary foundations, characteristics of an effective program, and rationale of the pattern of organization. Of special importance to teachers are guidelines that deal with unit planning, adaptations to local conditions, individual differences, selection of instructional media, teaching strategies, and evaluation of outcomes.

The social studies program should be developed by school personnel with the assistance of resource experts. Scholars from the social sciences are needed to assist in the identification of main ideas, methods of inquiry, and related content. Specialists in child development and learning, current social changes, and democratic ideology may contribute to the grounding of the program in the psychological and social foundations of the social studies. Specialists in social studies instruction may assist in designing the overall program and in planning units of instruction.

The process of planning the social studies program should contribute directly to the professional growth of teachers. Teachers' values, beliefs, and backgrounds of understanding are prime determiners of the kind and quality of instruction that will be provided. Furthermore, teachers have far more reason to accept and implement the point of view underlying the program when they have had a stake in formulating it. Curriculum development in the social studies should be viewed as a basic part of the in-service education program. Professional growth of teachers takes place as they participate in curriculum committees, grade-level meetings, unit planning, selection of materials, experimental try-out of proposals, evaluation of outcomes, and other activities.

The organization of the program should provide for flexibility and should be subject to revision as needed. Flexibility must be provided so that teachers can adapt the program to local conditions and to the educational needs of children. New developments in the social sciences, in societal conditions, and in child development and learning should be reflected in the program. Studies should be made to determine the value of new proposals for the program, and continuing revision is needed to keep the program up to date.

Current curriculum projects and reports in the social studies

*should be studied critically in the light of state and local edu-
cational needs.* Critical appraisals should be made under the
leadership of curriculum workers with the assistance of teachers,
interested scholars, and specialists in the social studies. Special
attention should be given to the following:

Sponsorship of the project, and purposes set up to guide the
development of materials

Extent to which scholars, teachers, and specialists in the social
studies were involved

Care with which materials and proposals were prepared, evaluated, and revised

Evidence of the effectiveness of materials or proposals in improving social studies instruction

Type of students—able, average, less able—for whom the materials are intended, and the extent to which individual differences
can be met

Feasibility of local use in terms of educational needs of children, backgrounds of preparation of teachers, community acceptance,
and time, effort, and expense involved in using the materials and
making adaptations

Effect of use of the materials on maintaining balance and continuity in the curriculum in general, and the social studies in particular

Experimental tryout of materials or proposals should be conducted to answer questions about their instructional value and
to assess teachers' competence in using them. Special attention
should be given to in-service education needs of teachers so that
adopted materials will be used effectively.

*The scope of the program should include fundamental strands
that link the program from level to level.* In essence, the scope
of the program should:

Be comprehensive—provide for instruction as broad as the
range of human relationships that children can grasp.

Be balanced—provide for all areas of study considered most
important in the light of the purposes of the social studies.

Relate to daily living—provide opportunities to deal with edu-
cationally significant problems, events, and activities as they arise.

Promote continuity of learning—provide for recurring emphases
from level to level and the cumulative development of deeper and
broader learnings.

Facilitate the development of relationships—enable the teacher
to provide instruction that draws on content from whatever disciplines are needed to achieve the objectives of the social studies.

The sequence of the program should be planned in the light of both logical and psychological considerations. Guidelines for use in planning the sequence are as follows:

The theme for each grade should indicate the broad area of study to be emphasized and be an extension of preceding experiences. It should not limit learning to the expanding-environment concept.

Units of instruction should be selected critically for each grade in the light of the theme, the capabilities of children, and the objectives of the social studies.

Recurring topics and units should be planned to go beyond earlier emphases and avoid needless repetition and duplication.

At each level, provision should be made for intensive study of new content organized around key concepts and generalizations from the social sciences.

Provision should be made at each level for the strengthening of skills involved in thinking processes, independent study, group work, and use of instruction media.

Opportunities should be provided at each level for the development of positive attitudes and the enrichment of appreciations.

Areas of study at each level must be feasible in terms of teachers' backgrounds and available instructional materials.

The overall sequence must provide for balance, comprehensiveness, and flexibility.

The content of the program should be selected critically. The content of the social studies is drawn primarily from the social sciences, but additional content may also be drawn from current affairs and community activities and, at times, from art, music, science, and other areas of the curriculum. A fundamental principle is to select content which can help achieve stated objectives, content which can deepen and round out basic generalizations, attitudes, and appreciations.

In considering content for the social studies program, we may apply such criteria as the following:

Can it be used to develop generalizations, basic skills, attitudes, appreciations, ideals, and values emphasized in the social studies?

Is it related to the most significant human problems today?

Is it reliable, authoritative, authentic, and up to date?

Is it adaptable to the children's capabilities and backgrounds?

Can it be organized into units of instruction which provide for higher levels of understanding from grade to grade?

Can it be used to develop insights into basic disciplines?

Can it be used to develop increasing understanding of the methods of inquiry used in the social studies?

Is it readily available in textbooks, references, audio-visual materials, maps, and other usable forms?

Care should be taken to meet legal requirements. From our earliest days the popular interest in education has been strong, and this has resulted in many state requirements. Many of these requirements have a direct bearing on the social studies program. For example, most states have specific provisions regarding instruction in United States history, geography, civics, the Constitution, observance of special days, display of the flag, state history and government, loyalty, and patriotism. In addition to state legal requirements, state and local boards of education also impose regulations. Many of these extend and implement state laws.

Every teacher should assume responsibility for carrying out the intent and purpose of existing requirements. Existing provisions may be found by checking the school code, summaries published by the state department of education, the course of study, or the school register of enrollment and attendance. If any provisions appear to be detrimental to the development of an effective program of instruction, they should be called to the attention of the local school authorities who can take steps to bring about appropriate changes.

Statewide curriculum guides should provide a framework for local planning. They should be designed to:

Give direction to the planning, organizing, and developing of the social studies in local school systems.

Indicate basic purposes and characteristics of an effective social studies program.

Set forth basic principles of instruction, newer trends and practices, and legal requirements.

Indicate areas of emphasis and units of work in broad outline which may be adapted and modified to meet local conditions.

Suggest content—knowledge, concepts, and generalizations—of greatest value in the social studies.

Suggest implications for social studies instruction derived from studies of democratic society, changes taking place in society, and child development and learning.

Provide guidelines for the selection of instructional resources, the selection and use of instructional procedures, the evaluation of children's learning, and the appraisal of the social studies program.

The course of study for the local school system should go beyond the state framework to include detailed suggestions for teachers to use in planning, guiding, and evaluating social studies instruction. Among the topics commonly included in courses of study are the following:

1. Point of view or basic beliefs underlying the program
2. The local setting and adaptations to community needs and conditions
3. Objectives of the social studies program
4. Organization of the instructional program
   a. Principles of organization
   b. Definition of scope to show strands running through the program
   c. Sequence of themes and units of instruction for each level
   d. Recurring topics such as current affairs, special days and weeks
5. Basic principles and procedures of instruction
   a. Planning and developing units of instruction
   b. Teaching strategies for developing generalizations, skills, and attitudes
   c. Procedures for meeting individual differences
   d. Techniques for utilizing instructional media
6. Essential instructional media and their place in the program
   a. Textbooks and other reading materials
   b. Maps, globes, films, and other audio-visual materials
   c. Community resources
7. Evaluation of outcomes of instruction
   a. Guiding principles for use at all levels
   b. Techniques for use at different levels

Unit plans—guides for teaching units of instruction—should be provided for teacher reference. Unit plans are an extension of the local course of study; they are the teacher's instructional guide for developing the units assigned to each grade. Specific objectives are included along with the learning experiences, related instructional materials, and procedures of evaluation that may be used to guide and evaluate children's learning.

Daily planning should be carried out to provide instruction directly related to the individual differences and capabilities of children in the class. The program of instruction comes to life in the classroom; it should be based on plans that are designed to provide instruction that will promote maximum learning on the part of each child. Both individual and group work may be included in plans containing specific suggestions related to:

1. Objectives
   a. Teacher's
   b. Pupil's
2. Procedures and Related Materials
   a. Introduction
   b. Development

    c. Conclusion
3. Evaluation of Children's Work

A helpful practice in some unit plans is to include introductory, developmental, and concluding activities for each main idea to be developed. Such a format contributes to the usefulness of unit plans and to daily planning. Examples are given in the next chapter.

Questions, Activities, Evaluation

1. Criticize the general trends and the specific grade-level trends reported in the first sections of this chapter. Which ones do you favor? Oppose? Give reasons for your position.

2. Appraise the selected programs presented in this chapter. How might they be improved to meet conditions in your area? Which parts of each program do you prefer?

3. Plan what you believe to be an ideal social studies program for Grades K–XII. Indicate the theme and topics or units for each grade. Discuss your proposed program with others, getting their views on its strengths and weaknesses.

4. Examine a course of study being used in a nearby school system and review it critically to answer the following questions:

    a. What themes, topics, and units are recommended for each grade? Are any optional units suggested?

    b. Note any suggested topics or units that are not included in the overview presented in this chapter. Do you think they should be included? Give reasons for your position.

    c. What suggestions are made for the spiral development of key ideas and concepts?

    d. What suggestions are made for incorporating key ideas in units?

    e. What legal requirements are noted? What suggestions are made for the observance of holidays and special events?

5. Select three or four concepts, or a concept cluster, from the preceding chapter and show how they might be included in a unit you are planning to teach. Follow the procedures suggested in this chapter. Do the same for a generalization.

References

California State Department of Education, *Social Studies Framework for the Public Schools of California*. Sacramento: The

Department, 1962. An outline of themes and major areas of emphasis for a K–XII program.

Ellsworth, Ruth, "Trends in Organization of the Social Studies," *Social Studies in Elementary Schools*, 32nd Yearbook, National Council for the Social Studies. Washington, D.C.: National Education Association, 1962. A discussion of trends in organizing the social studies.

English, Raymond, *Greater Cleveland Social Science Program: Publications 1966–67*. Cleveland: Greater Cleveland Research Council, 1966. A summary of the K–XII program and available materials.

Fraser, Dorothy M., and Eunice Johns, "Developing a Program for the Effective Learning of Skills," pp. 296–309, *Skill Development in the Social Studies*, 33rd Yearbook. Washington, D.C.: National Council for the Social Studies, 1963. Principles and procedures followed by an Appendix that includes grade placement of basic skills.

Jarolimek, John, *Social Studies in Elementary Education*. New York: The Macmillan Company, 1967. Outline of procedures for planning the social studies program.

Lee, John R., and Jonathon C. McLendon, *Readings on Elementary Social Studies*, pp. 26–57. Boston: Allyn & Bacon, Inc., 1965. A collection of articles on organization of the social studies.

Michaelis, John U., *Teaching Units in the Social Sciences: Early Grades, Grades III–IV, Grades V–VI*. Chicago: Rand McNally & Co., 1966. Three paperback volumes containing units for blocks of grades.

New York City Board of Education, *Curriculum and Materials*. New York: The Board, 1965. Outline of a proposed K–XII program.

New York State Department of Education, *Flow Charts for Elementary and Secondary Social Studies Programs*. Albany: The Department, 1965. Charts showing K–XII program.

Senesh, Lawrence, *Our Working World: Families at Work*. Chicago: Science Research Associates, 1964. A resource unit based on economic concepts.

Taba, Hilda, *Teacher's Handbook for Elementary Social Studies*. Reading, Mass.: Addison-Wesley, 1967. Guidelines and strategies for planning instruction to develop concepts and main ideas.

West, Edith, *Project Social Studies Curriculum Center: Progress Report No. 2*. Minneapolis: University of Minnesota, 1965. Outline of the units included in the K–XII program.

Wisconsin State Department of Education, *A Conceptual Framework, Social Studies*. Madison, Wis.: The Department, 1964. Generalizations from history and the social sciences.

Current Affairs
and
Special Events

In addition to the planned program of units in the social studies, certain recurring topics receive attention from grade to grade. These are *current affairs*—current events, issues, and problems; and *special events*—special days and weeks of local, state, and national importance.

Because of the appreciations, understandings, and skills that children can develop as a result of experiences related to these topics, systematic attention should be given to the planning of instruction in each grade.

Current Affairs Study

In recent years, instruction in current affairs has been given increased emphasis. Among the many factors contributing to this emphasis are the growth and changes in communities, the increased movement and travel of peoples, the population explosion, the emergence of new nations, the tensions in international affairs, the tightening interdependence at home and abroad, the impact of scientific and technological developments on ways of living, the expansion of the mass media, and the effect of social and cultural changes. Coupled with these have been the impact of television on children's thinking and learning and the increased interest of children and adults in local, national, and international affairs. Little doubt exists that if the goals of the social studies are to be achieved, current as well as past human relationships must be studied.

The increased emphasis on current affairs calls for a careful review of their place in the social studies. Care must be taken to maintain balance in the total program. Special consideration must be given to the purposes to be achieved, the principles and newer practices involved in the teaching of current affairs, the ways of relating current affairs to ongoing units of work, the criteria for selecting current affairs and current materials, and the utilization of children's weekly newspapers.

PURPOSES TO GUIDE STUDY

The study of current affairs in the social studies should be viewed in terms of specific contributions that can be made to the achievement of the overall purposes of the social studies. This point of view is based on practical considerations as well as on fundamental principles of curriculum planning. Current affairs should be selected and utilized to promote the development of basic attitudes and appreciations, concepts and understandings, and functional skills and abilities. When fundamental goals are kept in mind, planning is more effective, unity of purpose is maintained, and peripheral matters that sidetrack basic learnings can be avoided. This does not mean that significant events will be overlooked. Rather, it means that each event and issue will be related to an important objective.

The following purposes are frequently cited in courses of study and textbooks for teachers:

To develop wholesome attitudes toward others and an appreciation of democratic processes in daily activities

To help bridge the gap between life in school and life outside of school

To develop and broaden interests in current affairs, to build a desire to keep abreast of new developments, and to reveal the relationships between the present and the past

To update and enrich textbooks, other instructional materials, and units of work

To extend, refine, and apply basic concepts such as interdependence, social change, and fair-play

To improve skills involved in critical thinking, problem solving, reading, and studying

To increase understanding of, and ability to distinguish between, incidents and trends, significant and trivial events, consistent and inconsistent points of view, accurate and inaccurate statements, and straight and slanted news reports

To improve competence in appraising sources of information such as children's weekly newspapers, radio and television programs, newspapers, and magazines

Selecting Current Affairs for Study

With the large number of news items that are always available, the selection of those to be studied is no simple task. Although much help in selection can be obtained by relying on the use of children's weekly newspapers, problems still exist in selecting local news items, adding items not included in the children's periodical, and screening out some that have been included. As with the selection of content for the overall social studies program, teachers should apply such criteria as the following:

Educational Value: Will children learn something significant? Is the event or issue related to fundamental purposes? Will study of it contribute to the development of basic attitudes, concepts, and skills?

Appropriateness: Is it appropriate in terms of the maturity, experience, and competence of pupils? Is it appropriate in terms of community conditions, values, and feelings?

Relatedness: Is it related to past and future learning of the pupils? Can it be related to basic units of study? Can it be tied in with other experiences?

Related Information: If needed, can background information be obtained? Are suitable teaching materials available?

Available Time: Is sufficient time available to obtain adequate depth of understanding?

Reliability: Is accurate information available? Can facts be differentiated from opinions? Can differing points of view be noted?

Timeliness: Is it current? Is up-to-date information available? Is it related to basic trends? Are significant consequences discernible?

Much time can be saved and children's learning can be improved when teachers apply such criteria in selecting current affairs. Every effort should be made to select those most significant for the *particular class in which they are to be used.* Children should be guided so that they will avoid sensational, lurid, and trivial events. In addition, specific attention must be given to the teaching of criteria which children can use, and direction must be provided in the selection of current events to be shared in class. In the following section, several techniques are suggested for this purpose.

GUIDING THE SELECTION OF CURRENT EVENTS

One of the most effective procedures is to direct children's search for current events related to a topic or unit they are studying. Problems and topics in such units as Home and Family, Community Workers, Conservation, Transportation, Communication, Industries, Living in Our State, Regions of the United States, Living in Canada, and Living in Mexico make excellent focal points around which current events selected by children can be organized. When this is done, skills in critical and evaluative reading are enhanced, and selected events are placed in a setting of broader and deeper studies which give meaning to them.

Teachers can apply the same idea to current events bulletin boards, panel discussions, and other activities by setting a major theme or concept to guide the selection of events. Some teachers also make use of basic concepts such as cooperation, interdependence, creative contributions, and man's use of resources. When current events are gathered and discussed in terms of one of these basic concepts, the growth in depth and breadth of understanding that almost invariably takes place is a rewarding sight.

Scrapbooks or notebooks prepared individually, by small groups, or by the class can also be organized around specific topics and themes. At times, an entire scrapbook may be organized around a single topic or problem. At other times a scrapbook may include several related topics or problems with clippings placed in each section. In all cases, pictures, charts, maps, and other illustrative materials should be included to enhance understanding.

The main idea here is to help children relate the selection of current affairs to basic purposes and to the activities that are used in dealing with them. Continuing guidance of children's selection of current affairs is essential and can be improved by utilizing standards that children have helped to formulate. Charts 1 and 2 and those presented in the following section (Charts 3–6) are illustrative.

SHARING THE NEWS	FINDING CURRENT EVENTS
About our pets	Is it important?
About mother's work	Do I understand it?
About father's work	Can I report it well?
About our own work	Will it be interesting to others?
About trips we take	
About community activities	Is it related to other topics?
About changes in seasons	

Chart 1   Chart 2

Approaches to the Study of Current Affairs

Several approaches may be made to the study of current affairs, each one having its strengths and weaknesses. Many teachers use a combination of approaches, depending on the objectives to be achieved, the significance of the events involved, the units under study, and the availability of materials.

RELATING CURRENT AFFAIRS TO BASIC UNITS

As a general policy, a sound procedure is to relate current affairs to basic units of instruction. When this is done, the problem of obtaining background material and giving perspective to current affairs becomes less difficult.

As regional units such as Areas of Our State, Mid-Western United States, and Regions of South America are studied, current events can be selected to highlight recent developments. As historical units are studied, such as Early Times in Our State and Colonial Life, current events can be selected to contrast "then and now." Charts 3–6 show topics in selected units which can be used as guides for finding related current affairs.

WE NEED NEWS ITEMS ON OUR CHANGING COMMUNITY

Activities of people

Housing developments

Highways and traffic

Health and safety problems

Conservation problems

Recreation facilities

Water supply

New schools and libraries

Relations with other communities

Chart 3

WE NEED NEWS ITEMS ON OUR STATE

Population	Government
Industries	People
Agriculture	Cities
Education	Rural areas
Conservation	Health
Recreation	Safety
Transportation	Communication
Relations with other states	Exports to foreign places

Chart 4

FIND ITEMS ON THESE REGIONS FOR FURTHER USE

New England states

Southeastern states

North Central states

South Central states

Rocky Mountain states

Southwestern states

Far Western states

Chart 5

LOOK FOR NEWS ITEMS ON CANADA RELATED TO THESE TOPICS

Cities	Transportation
Provinces	
St. Lawrence Seaway	Communication
Oil pipelines	Government
	Education
Mining	Conservation
Trade and industry	Relations with the United States
Value of the dollar	Relations with other countries

Chart 6

Travel agencies and transportation companies have pictures related to new developments. How might such materials be related to the study of current events? *(Pan American Airway)*

The great problem here is one of timing. As one teacher put it: "So many significant events occur either before or after I teach a unit." Many teachers meet this problem by using current events to launch units, by collecting clippings and having children collect clippings related to units that are to be developed, by timing the introduction of certain units to coincide with holidays, sessions of the state legislature and congress, and other scheduled events, by keeping files of children's weekly newspapers related to future units, by relating events to past units, and by continuing certain strands such as transportation, communication, and conservation from unit to unit.

WEEKLY STUDY OF PERIODICALS

Many teachers provide for the study of children's periodicals during one period each week. It is convenient and relatively easy to assign the reading of articles, carry on discussion, and have children complete activities and tests included in each weekly issue, but dangers exist in this approach. These include routine reading and answering of questions, superficiality of learning caused by an attempt to cover too many topics, and failure to relate current events to basic topics and units. The suggestions

173

presented later in this chapter in the section on weekly periodicals for children are helpful in avoiding these dangers and in getting maximum benefit from the weekly study of current affairs. In addition, a sound procedure is to direct the study of weekly periodicals by stressing points noted in Chart 7.

STUDYING WEEKLY NEWSPAPERS

Skim it first to get a general idea of the contents.

Study pictures, maps, charts, tables, and graphs.

Note articles related to topics we are studying.

Note articles on which background material is given.

Note articles on which background material is needed.

Look up the meaning of any words you do not understand.

Look for facts, opinions, and differing points of view.

Be ready to raise questions and make comments during discussion.

Check your understanding by completing the tests.

Chart 7

MISCELLANEOUS REPORTING

This approach may take the form of daily or weekly sharing of news, or it may be done at irregular intervals. Daily sharing is frequently used by teachers in primary grades and may be found in some middle grades. Some teachers like to have reporting on a weekly basis or at especially assigned times. Items are obtained from newspapers, radio and television newscasts, and children's periodicals. In daily sharing, five to ten minutes may be used, but a full period may be used if a weekly plan is followed. The weaknesses in this approach include the reporting of trivial events, superficiality of learning because of a lack of depth of study, isolation of events from past experiences and basic units of study, and the tendency for discussion to wander. These weaknesses can be overcome in part by directing the selection of current affairs, suggesting better sources of news items, systematically relating current affairs to basic topics and units, holding to discussion standards, and providing for deeper study of more important current affairs.

What at first may appear to be isolated events can sometimes be related to significant topics. For example, a bicycle accident may lead to a discussion of safety rules with emphasis on showing concern for others. Or, a news item on minority groups may lead to a discussion of rights and responsibilities, fair-play, and other democratic values in community living.

Because of television, radio, and discussions with adults at home, children may raise questions which are beyond their level of maturity. Such questions should be dealt with on the level of experience and understanding that is appropriate for the group. After adequate comment or discussion, the teacher should direct the group's attention to other questions, reports, or topics.

At times, particularly in the primary grades, children may report events about family life that are of a personal nature and which are not proper topics for group discussion. When this happens, a tactful and unobtrusive shift should be made to other topics. Sometimes, a wise course is to suggest that a particular topic is one that the child may discuss later with the teacher.

SHORT CURRENT AFFAIRS UNITS

Current affairs of special significance cannot always be dealt with in the daily or weekly period or incorporated in units of work. An important community or state event or problem, a major election, the coming of a nation to the forefront in international affairs, the study of an individual of current national and international importance: any of these may require an intensive short unit in which current materials and related background material are used. Sometimes special units are featured in children's weekly newspapers and, because of their current significance, a more extended period of study is needed. By noting related materials and suggestions contained in the teacher's edition of the weekly newspaper, and by collecting pamphlets, books, films, and other resources, important objectives can be achieved through the study of such special units.

Whichever approach or combination of approaches is used, every effort should be made to obtain the highest possible levels of thinking and understanding on the part of children. Three levels may be identified quickly as one visits classrooms. The first level is the routine reporting of events. Each child has seen,

Use maps and pictures to locate events. How might such a display be changed from week to week? *(Bloom; Courtesy of Monkmeyer)*

read, or heard about an event and shares it with the group with little or no discussion by the class or analysis of relationships to other experiences. The second level involves the reporting of an issue or event followed by discussion of the most interesting points. This level involves more thinking by the class, may prove to be entertaining for the children who participate in discussion, and may stimulate interest on the part of others. Usually it falls short of getting below the surface to basic concepts, trends, and relationships and does not involve critical analysis of related issues and problems. The third level involves the use of problem-solving and critical-thinking skills with attention to the significance of the event or issue, review of supporting facts, consideration of differing points of view, need for additional data, and other pertinent factors. To be sure, this third level cannot and should not be applied to all current affairs. However, when truly significant current affairs are selected for study, usually many ways exist to guide children from level one to three and thus increase the value of the experience.

Activities and Sources of Information

Many activities and sources of information are put to use in the current affairs program. In selecting them, teachers should consider those that can be used by individuals and small groups as well as by the entire class. In fact, good group discussion and analysis of current affairs depend on adequate individual preparation. Children, too, should be concerned about the selection of activities and sources of information appropriate for the event or issue under study. Charts 8–10 suggest activities and sources of information that may be used.

WHICH OF THESE SHOULD BE USED IN OUR CURRENT AFFAIRS PROGRAM?

Individual reports	School intercom	Pictures	News maps
Committee reports	Bulletin board	Charts	Globe
Panel or debate	Quiz games	Murals	Models
Classroom newscasts	News files	Scrapbooks	Exhibits
Tape recorder	Picture file	Cartoons	Dramatizations

Chart 8

FINDING CURRENT EVENTS

Radio and television newscasts

Newspapers and magazines

Interviews of experts

School and neighborhood library

News file

Our weekly newspaper

Bulletin board

Chart 9

PERIODICALS IN THE LIBRARY

Weekly Reader	Newsweek
Newstime	Time
News Explorer	U.S. News & World Report
Young Citizen	The Times
Current Events	Evening Star
Junior Review	Chronicle

Chart 10

Specific guidance must be given to the preparing, checking, and reporting of current affairs. Charts 11–14 illustrate guidelines which can be used.

PREPARING NEWS REPORTS
Note the main ideas.
Select the most important facts.
Have pictures or other items to show.
Be ready to locate it on a map.
Be ready to answer questions.
If possible, relate it to a topic under study.

Chart 11

CHECKING REPORTS
Is it accurate?
Is it up to date?
Who reported it?
Can the facts be checked?
Are their opinions in it?
What do others say?

Chart 12

REPORTING CURRENT EVENTS
Is it important to the group?
Do I know it well?
Can I give illustrations?
Can I give it in my share of the time?
Do I have the main ideas?
Can I relate it to other topics or events?

Chart 13

LISTENING TO NEWS REPORTS
Do I understand it?
Do I have questions to ask?
Is it related to my report?
Is it related to something we are studying?
Is other information needed?
Is it controversial? If so, are all sides given?

Chart 14

CHOOSING CURRENT MATERIALS FOR CHILDREN

In selecting current periodicals for children, one should keep several criteria in mind. One needs to know the children in the class. Particular attention must be given to levels of reading ability so that children will not encounter insuperable difficulties. By selecting periodicals that are written on varying readability levels, one can meet individual needs and at the same time provide a basis for the study and discussion of significant current affairs. The following criteria are illustrative of those generally used in selecting children's weekly newspapers:

Content: ____Significant ____Recent ____Timely ____Related to curriculum

Interpretation: ____Meaningful to children ____Stimulates thinking and discussion

Impartiality: ____Various points of view are presented ____ Free of bias

Background Material: ____Related events presented ____Historical, geographic, economic, or biographic information presented as appropriate

Readability: ____Concepts can be made meaningful to children ____Vocabulary graded ____Sentence structure appropriate ____Vocabulary building aids included

Illustrative Material: ____Pictures add to meaning ____Charts and graphs clear and useful ____Cartoons appropriate ____Maps clear and uncluttered

Pupil Activities: ____Geared to the articles ____Worthwhile ____Designed to develop basic concepts and skills ____Stimulate thinking and discussion ____Useful in evaluating outcomes

Teaching Suggestions: ____Related to significant purposes ____Individual and small-group activities ____Relationships to basic units ____Suggestions on evaluation

Criteria such as these can also be used as teaching guides. For example, if an issue of a periodical does not contain suggestions on relationships to units of work, the teacher and pupils should search for possible applications. Similarly, individual and group activities and other points noted above should be considered in terms of the needs and purposes of the group.

WEEKLY PERIODICALS FOR CHILDREN

Fortunately, well-prepared classroom periodicals are available for use in the elementary school. They are prepared by highly qualified writers, editors, and illustrators, and contain a variety of current affairs that meet the criteria just mentioned. Properly used in the classroom, they constitute an excellent resource to place in the hands of children. The following are used in many schools throughout the country:

American Education Publications, 1250 Fairwood Avenue, Columbus 16, Ohio

> *My Weekly Reader* (Separate editions for each grade from Kindergarten and Grades I–VI)
> *Current Events* (One edition for use in Grades VI–VIII)

Civic Education Service, Inc., 1733 K Street, Washington 6, D.C.

> *Young Citizen* (One edition for Grades V and VI)
> *Junior Review* (One edition for Grades VII and VIII)

Scholastic Magazines, Inc., 33 West 42nd Street, New York 36, N.Y.

> *News Pilot* (Grade I), *News Ranger* (Grade II), *News Trails* (Grade III), *News Explorer* (Grade IV), *Newstime* (Grade V), *Junior Scholastic* (Grades VI–VIII)

All of these are well written and are designed to present the most significant national and international current affairs to children. A special effort is made to select events and issues appropriate for study in the elementary school. Various points of view are presented, related background information is frequently given, trends are highlighted, and related tests and exercises are included. Suggestions for teachers that accompany various issues are to the point and are consistent with sound principles of teaching.

The following guidelines should be observed in the use of children's newspapers in order to get maximum value from them and to avoid misusing them:

1. By selecting editions that are appropriate to the reading levels in a class, individual needs of children can be met. Thus, one may find editions on three or four reading levels being used in the same class.

2. Effective teaching techniques should be used with attention to developing readiness for reading, clarifying purposes, building vocabulary, anticipating difficulties, interpreting maps and graphs, and discussing and summarizing key ideas. As with textbooks, films, and other resources, children's periodicals do not take the place of good teaching.

3. An effort should be made to use each issue of the periodical

at the time when it will be most effective. Although one period each week may be set aside for intensive study, many teachers have found that it is sound procedure to provide for study and discussion at times when the related topics are being studied. Here again, flexibility in the use of instructional resources must be considered as plans are made for their use.

4. The whole-class approach to the study of selected sections of the weekly newspaper may be appropriate at times, but it should certainly be supplemented by individual and small-group study in accord with individual needs and problems.

5. Whenever possible, relationships between current affairs presented in the children's newspaper should be related to basic units of instruction. Isolated items and incidents are soon forgotten, but events and issues related to basic studies become a part of the child's growing background of concepts and knowledge.

6. Both formal and informal evaluation should be made of children's learning resulting from the use of current periodicals. Tests provided in the periodicals, discussion, sharing, reporting, follow-up activities, and observation will yield clues that can be used to appraise basic outcomes.

7. A teacher should not expect a weekly periodical to constitute the entire program of study of current affairs. A need exists for a careful selection of significant local and state news items as well as important national and international items that may not have been included in a particular issue.

8. By maintaining files of back issues, one can provide reference material on topics and units in the basic program.

9. The new and up-to-date maps presented in children's periodicals can be used to improve children's competence in map reading and map making.

CONTROVERSIAL ISSUES

A statement sometimes heard is that "elementary school children have inadequate backgrounds to study controversial issues." Ordinarily, when this statement is made, the speaker has in mind the study of critical issues currently being debated by adults and the achievement of adult levels of understanding. Certainly, adult levels of understanding cannot be achieved and many current issues are beyond children's understanding. But controversial issues, questions, and problems do come up in the social studies, and experienced teachers wisely select some of them for study. This is based on the assumption that issues will be approached as unanswered questions on which there are differing points of view that should be studied in a thoughtful manner. Some may be handled briefly, others may simply be introduced as continuing problems which will be reviewed in the future, and others may be studied in detail because of their importance.

In the primary grades, attention is generally given to issues and problems close to the lives of children, issues and problems that come up in school, in the neighborhood, and in the community. Examples of these would be differences of opinion on ways of carrying out classroom activities, best ways of improving the conservation of resources, utilization of parks and playgrounds, fair-play in the treatment of others, contributions of others, and conflicts between individuals and groups. At times, attention may be given to issues and problems raised by children concerning elections, campaign issues, minority group problems, housing problems, ways of preventing discrimination against others, and other problems growing out of community living. These should not be ignored, nor should they be handled in a way that is beyond the ability of children to understand. A simple answer, an explanation of the problem, a clarification of the issue, or a brief discussion may suffice. The important thing is to keep the way open for such questions, to discuss them on an appropriate level, and to begin to lay a foundation for a deeper and broader study of issues that will come up in later grades.

In the middle and upper grades, more involved issues and problems are encountered as children undertake such units as Our State, Living in the United States, Mexico, Canada, Countries of Latin America, The Middle East, Africa, and Growth of Democracy. In addition, current events periodicals present issues that may or may not be related to basic units of study. Other issues are presented on television and radio programs, discussed at home, and reported in newspapers.

The study of selected current issues and problems is usually governed by policies set by the board of education. The following statement is illustrative of policies now followed in many school systems: [1]

   1. Only significant issues and problems which are understandable to children, and on which children should begin to have an opinion, should be selected for study in the elementary school.
   2. Instructional materials must present differing points of view, discussion should include all points of view, and respect for the views of others should be shown.

[1] National Education Association, *Controversial Issues in the Classroom* (Washington, D.C.: The Association, 1961).

3. Teachers must guide learning so as to promote critical thinking and open-mindedness, and they must refrain from taking sides or propagandizing one point of view.

4. Special attention must be given to a consideration of background factors, possible consequences of various proposals, the need for additional information, and the detection of fallacies of thinking, logic, and argumentation.

5. The importance of keeping an open mind, that is, the willingness to change one's mind in the light of new information, should be stressed.

The criteria listed in the first part of this chapter must be applied rigorously in the selection of current issues and problems for study in the elementary school. Of special importance are those criteria related to educational value, significance, and appropriateness in terms of children's background of experience and community conditions. Generally, issues are not selected if they are offensive to individuals and groups in the community or will place the school in the center of a heated debate.

Checking with fellow teachers and with the principal is a good idea when any doubt exists about the appropriateness of a particular issue. In some instances, committees made up of school personnel and laymen have worked together to define policies that should govern the teaching of controversial problems. This should be done when serious issues and problems appear to be appropriate for study, but are stimulating heated discussion in the community. Ordinarily, such issues arise in the so-called "closed or restricted areas" which include morality and religion, sex, race relations, and certain aspects of economics and politics.[2] Religious freedom, adherence to established codes of behavior in relations with others, racial equality, loyalty and patriotism, and democratic processes are accepted as being basic to our way of life.

Serious problems arise when a teacher becomes a crusader for a cause and goes all out to get students to adopt his point of view. Behavior of this type is a violation of professional ethics and is a misapplication of the concept of freedom in teaching. Teachers at all levels of education are expected to guide the study of controversial issues in an impartial, unemotional, and unprejudiced manner. The teacher's prestige and position in the

---

[2] M. P. Hunt and L. E. Metcalf, *Teaching High School Social Studies* (New York: Harper & Row, Publishers, 1955).

classroom must not be used to promote a partisan point of view. When the teacher is asked to express an opinion, it should be given and noted as his own opinion, and not as the final answer.

The atmosphere in which current problems and issues are studied should be conducive to thoughtful discussion. Free expression is needed in order to examine differing viewpoints. Partisanship and bias should be detected. The quality of evidence should be considered with attention to the inadequacy or unavailability of information, opinions based on limited experience, opinions of experts, purposes of proponents of various points of view, and consequences of various courses of action. At times one must consider why different groups believe that a given point of view is reasonable to them, to see it from their standpoint. At all times one should not be embarrassed to change one's point of view in view of new information. Charts 15–22 illustrate special points to be emphasized in middle and upper grades.

DEFINING ISSUES AND PROBLEMS	CHECKING MATERIALS	DISCUSSING AN ISSUE
How shall we state it?	What is the author's background?	Define it clearly so that all sides are known.
Do we understand each term?	What group sponsors or publishes it?	Consider each position.
What are the subproblems?	What is the group's purpose?	Find facts related to all sides.
What parts are most important?	Are there other points of view?	Verify and organize facts.
Do we have ideas about any part?	What materials present other points of view?	Make and change conclusions on the basis of facts.
Which parts need most study?		

Chart 15   Chart 16   Chart 17

CHECKING POINTS OF VIEW

What facts do I have?

How do I feel about it?

What do others believe?

How do they feel about it?

What would I believe and feel if I were in their place?

Chart 18

WORKING ON PROBLEMS

Recall ideas related to it.

Think of possible ways to solve it.

Find information related to each possible solution.

Check and summarize information.

Try out the best solutions. Select the one that works best.

Chart 19

FORMING CONCLUSIONS

Wait until facts are checked and organized.

Be sure facts are separated from opinions.

Consider outcomes and consequences.

Test tentative conclusions.

Make final conclusions.

Chart 20

WATCH OUT FOR:

Name-calling and not giving the facts.

Making general statements that sound nice but are vague.

Using popular words so that the idea will be accepted.

Saying that so-and-so believes it, therefore we should believe it.

Saying that plain folks believe it, therefore we should.

Giving only those facts that support one side.

Stating that many people are accepting the ideas, so we should too.

Chart 21

FEELINGS AND ISSUES

Control your feelings and help others control theirs.

Try to put yourself in the other person's place.

Try to understand other points of view.

Give facts when stating your own position.

Search for deeper causes of the difficulties.

Try to find reasonable proposals and next steps.

Make tentative conclusions and be ready to change them when feelings calm down.

Chart 22

185

Special Events

Special events—holidays, special weeks, and commemorations—are a vital part of men's cultural heritage. Many have been set aside as a time for celebration and the expression of treasured values, ideals, and beliefs. Through special days and weeks, attention is called to significant events, institutions, documents, great men and women, and customs. By proclamations, statutory requirements, regulations of boards of education, and tradition, various special days and weeks have been made a part of the instructional program in schools throughout the country.

The observance of holidays helps children learn customs and traditions that have been valued through the years. The manner in which special days and weeks are presented to children, the depth and quality of understandings and appreciations that are achieved, the historical perspective that is developed, and the attitudes that result determine in large measure their meaning and significance in the lives of children. Schools have a great role to play in providing instruction on special days and weeks, and the social studies can make a significant contribution because so many special days and weeks are closely related to basic units of instruction, topics, problems, and current affairs included in the program.

CONTRIBUTIONS TO BASIC PURPOSES

The study of special days and weeks contributes in a number of ways to the achievement of the goals of the social studies. Wholesome attitudes and deeper appreciations may be developed as children learn about the contributions of great men and women, discover the deeper meaning of Thanksgiving, learn how to have fun at Halloween and still show concern for others, find out how Christmas and New Year's Day are celebrated in different countries, express friendship and affection for others on Valentine's Day, and discover how they can show appreciation on Mother's Day and Father's Day. Loyalty, patriotism, and responsibilities of citizenship take on deeper meaning as children are directed in their observance of Bill of Rights Day, Constitution Day, General Election Day, Veterans Day, Washington's Birthday, Memorial Day, Flag Day, and Independence Day. Concepts, such as interdependence, cross-cultural sharing, and cultural diversity, are deepened and broadened as children discover similarities and differences in modes of celebrating holidays at home and in other lands. Intergroup understanding may be increased as children observe Brotherhood Week, and join with others in observing

Hanukkah as well as Christmas, a practice becoming increasingly common in recent years. International understanding may be increased as Pan-American Day and United Nations Day are observed. Reading, study, discussion, and other skills are sharpened as children find and share information related to special days and weeks.

Outcomes such as these are achieved gradually and over a long period of time. Beginning in the primary grades, emphasis is given to first-level concepts and understandings, appropriate activities for children, customs of special importance in the community, and modes of behavior that are consistent with the ideals associated with special days and weeks. A careful selection is made of those days and weeks that can be made meaningful to young children. In middle and upper grades, continuing attention is given to holidays introduced earlier, with emphasis on deeper insights and understandings. In addition, special days and weeks involving more advanced learnings are introduced and studied as deeply as the children's backgrounds of experience and maturity will permit. Some of these days are Bill of Rights Day, United Nations Day, and Pan-American Day.

Grade Placement

Two policies are widely followed in the grade placement of special days and weeks. First, certain holidays are considered in all grades beginning in Kindergarten and Grade I. In succeeding grades, opportunities are provided for more advanced learning

What background study is needed to prepare a display such as this? *(Alameda County)*

through background studies, short units, relationships to basic social studies units, and varied activities. Second, certain special days and weeks are assigned to particular grades in terms of the background and experience of children and the basic units in the program.

An examination of grade placement charts usually reveals a pattern similar to the following:

Kindergarten and Grade I: Halloween, Thanksgiving, Christmas, New Year's, Washington's Birthday, Lincoln's Birthday, Valentine's Day, Easter, Mother's Day, Father's Day, Flag Day.

Grades II and III: Continue the above on higher levels and add Columbus Day, Fire Prevention Day, Veteran's Day, Book Week, American Education Week, Arbor and Conservation Day, Memorial Day, Independence Day, and the day our community was founded.

Grades IV–VI: Continue the above on higher levels and add Labor Day, United Nations Day, Constitution Week, Admission Day, Bill of Rights Day, Franklin's Birthday, Susan B. Anthony's Birthday, Hanukkah, Brotherhood Week, Pan-American Day, International Goodwill Day, Armed Forces Day, other special days and weeks of significance in the community or state, and special days of importance in other countries that are studied.

A CALENDAR OF SELECTED DAYS AND WEEKS

In some school systems a calendar or listing of special days and weeks is provided so that teachers may make a selection and do preplanning for their classes. Because practices vary greatly among school systems and among states, the calendar must be developed to fit local and state policies. The calendar in Chart 23 is illustrative; it was prepared by a group of teachers in a social studies workshop.

Differentiating Experiences from Grade to Grade

Because many special days and weeks are given attention in each grade, overall planning is needed to make sure that children develop deeper appreciations and understandings as they progress through the grades. The following example on Arbor and Conservation Day includes activities that may be provided beginning in Kindergarten and on through Grade VI. Notice how many of them can be made a part of such units as The Home, Our Community, Living in Our State, and Conservation.

CALENDAR OF SELECTED DAYS AND WEEKS

September
Labor Day .... first Monday
Citizenship Day 17
Constitution Week .. includes 17

October
Junior Red Cross Enrollment
.... dates announced
Fire Prevention Day 9
Columbus Day 12
United Nations Day 24
Halloween 31

November
Veteran's Day 11
Book Week ... dates announced
American Education Week
.... dates announced
General Election Day ..first
Tuesday after first Monday
Thanksgiving ... fourth Thursday

December
United Nations Human Rights
Day 10
Bill of Rights Day 15
Christmas 25
Hanukkah .... dates announced

January
New Year's Day 1
Franklin's Birthday 17
Inauguration Day 20
Franklin D. Roosevelt's Birth-
day, March of Dimes 30

February
Lincoln's Birthday 12
Valentine's Day 14
Susan B. Anthony's Birthday . 15
Washington's Birthday 22
Brotherhood Week
.... includes Feb. 22

March
Luther Burbank's Birthday ... 7
Conservation Week
.... includes March 7
Arbor Day ...... various dates
Easter Week
.... in March or April
Passover ...... dates announced

April
Pan-American Day 14
Kindness to Animals Week
.... dates announced
National Youth Week
.... dates announced

May
May Day 1
Child Health Day 1
International Goodwill Day . 18
Memorial Day 30
Mother's Day ... second Sunday
Armed Forces Day
.... third Saturday

June
Flag Day 14
Father's Day ..... third Sunday

July
Independence Day 4

August
National Aviation Day 19

Chart 23

ACTIVITIES FOR ARBOR AND CONSERVATION DAY

Kindergarten–Grade II: Taking a nature walk in the neighborhood; making collections of leaves; observing birds and listening to bird calls; observing the growth of certain trees and shrubs; caring for plants and pets; learning about the many uses of wood; reading and hearing stories and poems about trees; writing original poems and stories; making a display of leaves; seeing films on forest animals; drawing pictures of trees, flowers, and animals; taking a study trip to see a house under construction; learning about synthetic fibers, paper, and other things made from wood; making picture books and scrapbooks; participating in a tree-planting ceremony

Grades III–IV: Observing and identifying trees in the community; learning about commercial, recreational, and decorative values of trees; learning about logging and other aspects of the lumber industry; visiting a sawmill; making a collection of different kinds of wood; learning about the importance of trees in the conservation of water, soil, and animal life; learning about our state's watersheds and water supply; learning about new uses of wood in construction, industry, and hobbies; planning a program and sharing it with parents or another class; seeing films on logging, lumbering, reforestation, and water resources; making charts, a mural, or a movie roll box to summarize basic concepts

Grades V–VI: Establishing a nature trail and making signs to mark trees, plants, and other objects; establishing feeding and watering stations for birds; arranging an exhibit of flowers and leaves of common trees and shrubs; inviting conservation experts to discuss questions and problems raised by the class and to report on newer practices; learning about the consequences of poor conservation practices in ancient civilizations in China and the Middle East; learning about present-day problems in the United States; learning how resources are interrelated; discussing the balance in nature and how man must work in harmony with nature; finding out the steps that are being taken to improve conditions; reading and reporting on contributions to the conservation movement of men such as Theodore Roosevelt and Gifford Pinchot; studying and making maps of forest areas and state and national parks; making rules of camping; creating poems, pageants, and programs that highlight conservation needs, problems, and forward-looking practices; seeing documentary films or TV programs; planning and carrying out a tree-planting ceremony to which other classes will be invited; making scrapbooks containing pictures, clippings, and notes on conservation

PRACTICES IN PRIMARY GRADES

In the primary grades, major emphasis is given to the introduction of customs, traditions, ceremonies, rituals, special meaning of terms, and the significance of selected special days and weeks. Activities and materials are selected in terms of the maturity and background of experience of the children in a given class. Beginning with story-telling, simple art activities, and participation in classroom and school activities, the program moves to the reading of stories, reporting and sharing of ideas found by children, and more advanced activities as children develop basic skills.

Units of instruction in the social studies provide many opportunities for deeper study of special days and weeks. The Home and Family unit gives background to Mother's Day and Father's Day. The contributions of many different workers, a key learning related to Labor Day, takes on greater meaning as School and Community Workers are studied. Thanksgiving activities may be made a part of units on Indians or Pilgrims. Valentine's Day is made a part of the study of the Post Office in many classrooms. As Communities in Other Lands are studied, attention may be given to ways in which New Year's, Christmas, and other holidays are celebrated. Arbor Day activities may be related to the study of conservation, which is a basic strand in many units from grade to grade.

Classroom parties may be held as a part of activities related to such special days as Halloween, Thanksgiving, Christmas, Valentine's Day, and Easter. Children plan and make room decorations, greeting cards, party favors, hats, masks, and other items. Appropriate songs, games, rhythms, poems, and stories are enjoyed. Bulletin board displays, flower arrangements, centers of interest, and exhibits may be arranged. Murals, movie box rolls, and programs may be planned and shared with others.

Gifts and greeting cards may be made in connection with such special days and weeks as Junior Red Cross Week, Veteran's Day, Christmas, Valentine's Day, Easter, Mother's Day, and Father's Day.

Firsthand participation in ceremonies, assemblies, parades, and pageants is possible in connection with many special days. Films, television and other audio-visual resources, reading materials, interviewing individuals in the community, creative activities, and study trips to places in the community also are utilized. Other examples of activities and materials are presented in the checklist at the end of this chapter.

MORE ADVANCED LEARNING IN LATER GRADES

Instruction in middle and upper grades should be planned to increase children's depth and breadth of understanding. Both the teacher and the class should search for new stories, poems, pictures, articles, and activities related to special days and weeks. After discussing what children have learned in earlier grades about

Have children locate the place of origin of special days. How else might maps be used in the study of special days and weeks? (Fresno)

Major events of the past are highlighted in instructional materials and may be summarized in a variety of ways. Can you think of displays that might be arranged to highlight events in other ways? (Monkmeyer)

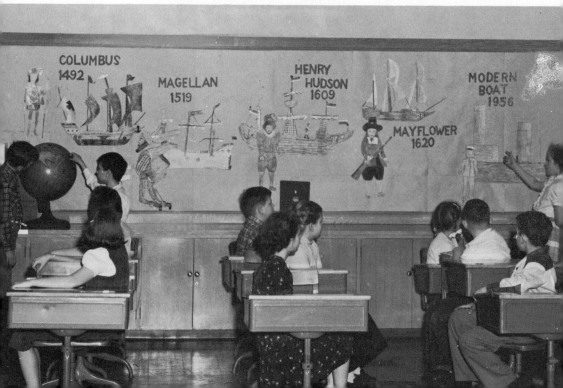

a given day or week, some teachers set leading questions to guide the search for new ideas and materials. For example:

How did this special day originate?
How was it celebrated in early times?
What early customs have we kept for our own?
How is it celebrated in other lands?
What individuals worked to make it a holiday in our country?
What are some famous stories and poems about this holiday?

Questions such as these can be applied to a large number of special days and weeks. In addition, other specific questions relate to particular holidays. These have to do with special meanings of terms, specific reference to individuals, and whether the holiday has civic, religious, or personal-social significance. The examples that follow illustrate questions that can be used to guide children's study of background material related to different types of special days.

Veteran's Day: When was Armistice Day first proclaimed? Why was Armistice Day changed to Veteran's Day? Why is the unknown soldier honored each year at the National Cemetery in Arlington? What is meant by "preservation of fundamental principles of freedom"? What obligations should each individual assume for the peace, welfare, and security of our country?

Thanksgiving: What were harvest festivals like in ancient times? Why did people have them? What was the first Thanksgiving like in our country? How was it different from earlier harvest festivals? Who was Sarah Joseph Hale, and what did she do to make Thanksgiving a national holiday? Which President issued the proclamation that made Thanksgiving a national holiday? What are your favorite stories and poems about Thanksgiving? Can you find some new ones?

Christmas: What is the origin of the word Christmas? Where did we get the customs of having holly, mistletoe, and the yule log? Where did the composers of our favorite Christmas carols live? How is Christmas celebrated in Mexico? In other lands?

Washington's Birthday: Where did Washington live as a boy? What was his home like? How was he educated? What are the main periods of his service to our country? What traits of leadership caused his countrymen to call on him to be the first President? Why is he honored as "the father of our country"? What is meant by "first in war and first in peace"?

Mother's Day: What country first had a special day for mothers? Who was Anna Jarvis, and how did she contribute to the establishment of Mother's Day in our country? Which state was the first to have Mother's Day as a state holiday? Which President signed the resolution of Congress establishing Mother's Day? How did the custom of wearing carnations originate?

Certain special days and weeks are given detailed study at a time when they may be made a part of units of work; this may be in addition to a short observance that is held as a part of classroom or school activities. For example, Constitution Day, Bill of Rights Day, United Nations Day, and the contributions of Franklin, Lincoln, Washington, and other historic leaders are included in units on the United States and the Growth of Democracy. Pan-American Day and International Goodwill Day take on deeper significance when tied in with such units as South America and Other Lands. Great men and women and special days of importance in the child's state should be included in the unit, Our State.

Sometimes it is a good idea to provide for short-term units to give background to a special day or week. Examples are Fire Prevention, Red Cross Activities, Community Chest Activities, and The Parent-Teachers Association. Short units on topics such as these give children the background they need to understand the purposes and activities of organizations and agencies that render services that benefit both children and adults. Other short-term units may be developed on great men and women, special weeks, or days of special importance in the community or state.

More and more, individual study and preparation of reports on related background information are being used to develop greater depth of understanding. The following are examples of reports written by children in Grade V.

Harvest Festivals Before the Pilgrims Had Their First Thanksgiving

Long ago, before the Pilgrims landed, people had celebrations at harvest time. They were happy to have a good harvest. Some would make offerings to the spirits and gods that they thought made seeds fertile and made the crops grow.

The oldest known harvest festival, Succoth, was in Israel. Thanks were given for finding a place to live and for the harvest.

In ancient Greece there was a celebration that lasted nine days. It was in honor of the goddess of the harvest called Demeter. Demeter was also the goddess of corn.

The festival of the harvest moon was held in old China long ago. The Chinese would bake moon cakes. They also thought that a rabbit lived in the moon.

Some of our early settlers had learned about harvest festivals in England. The English would have feasts and share what had been raised. People in the villages would get together and each family would buy something.

The peasants in Old Russia had feasts and dancing. One custom was to place a wreath of grain by the house. A new one was put there each year. They thought it would help make a good harvest.

The Iroquois Indians had feasts at different times. One was in the spring at maple syrup time. Another was at planting time. Still another was at harvest time. They also had a bean and a corn festival. All together they had about seven festivals a year.

What Susan B. Anthony Did

Susan B. Anthony worked hard to get the right for women to vote. She also wanted equal rights for women in other things. She was a teacher once and only got paid $10 a month while men teachers were getting $40 a month. She said that this was not fair. She also said that women should choose their own jobs and take care of their own property. She also said that they should be able to go to college just the same as men.

I didn't know that women never used to have all these rights. It is a good thing that Susan B. Anthony came along. My mother says that some women take these rights for granted. They should remember what Susan B. Anthony did. I am going to remember her birthday on February 15.

Some teachers take time before the school year ends to consider special days that occur during summer vacation. For example, Independence Day and the events leading up to it can be studied as a part of units on the United States. Children can be asked to watch for special reports and activities as celebrations take place during the summer. National Aviation Day, August 19, should not be overlooked as an opportunity for children to collect clippings and other materials for use in Transportation and Aviation units when school starts in the fall. Similarly, Labor Day celebrations and activities in early September are sources of experience and information that can be put to use at the beginning of the school year.

The checklist that follows is a summary of activities and materials for special days and weeks.

Activities and Materials Checklist

Listening: individual and group reports, material read by others, tapes, records, guest speakers, panel discussions, radio programs

Viewing: films, filmstrips, slides, stereographs, photographs, painting, television programs, picture files, exhibits, demonstrations

Reading: stories, articles, poems, essays, biographies, autobiographies, diaries, local documents and pamphlets, reference materials, clipping files, items on bulletin boards

Writing: songs, poems, plays, skits, quiz games, reports, stories

Designing and Making: room decorations, greeting cards, greeting card boxes, costumes, hats, masks, costume dolls, maps, puppets, gifts, gift wrappers, party favors, booklets, scrapbooks, shadow boxes, peep boxes, movie box rolls, dioramas, sandbox displays, time lines, murals, picture files, clipping files, charts, labels

Arranging: bulletin boards, flowers for special occasions, room decorations, the classroom for parties and programs, special centers of interest, exhibits of book jackets, products, and other items related to special days

Visiting: museums, special exhibits, historic places, homes of famous people, special agencies, and organizations

Interviewing: old timers, writers, scholars, experts on conservation, resource persons from special agencies, and organizations

Participating in or Witnessing: school assemblies, ceremonies, parades, pageants, plays

Investigating: the origin of holidays, contributions of great men and women, holidays in other lands, customs brought from other lands around the world

Sources of Information

Children's weekly newspapers and monthly magazines include stories and articles on great men and women, holidays, and special weeks. At times they feature new stories and activities that may be used to provide fresh learning experiences. The teacher's guides that accompany weekly periodicals occasionally list related films, filmstrips, television programs, books, pamphlets, and other materials.

Children's encyclopedias are excellent sources of information. The background material, stories, pictures, time lines, reading lists, dates of holidays, and other information which they contain can be used for individual study and reference.

The World Almanac lists the dates set for holidays each year and includes information on holidays observed in different states and public days in Canada.

The *Grade Teacher* and *Instructor*, magazines for teachers, include stories, articles, units, bulletin-board suggestions, construction activities, reading lists, bibliographies, and other material. Excellent sources for teachers, they are also useful to more able children who are pursuing individual studies or who wish to find directions for making things related to a particular holiday.

Television and radio programs should be checked in newspapers, weekly program guides, and program bulletins issued by broadcasting companies and school systems.

Newspapers and magazines for adults feature special reports and articles that can be read and shared by many children.

Finally, specific suggestions on special days and weeks are included in courses of study, units of instruction, and bulletins on special days made available by state departments of education and many local school systems.

Questions, Activities, Evaluation

1. Which of the purposes for studying current affairs do you believe most difficult to achieve? Which the easiest? Which are most significant in early grades? Later grades?

2. Apply the criteria for selecting current affairs to two or three items from the local newspaper. Which criteria are most difficult to apply? Which criteria do many articles *not* meet?

3. Next, check the articles in one or two of the children's periodicals listed in this chapter. Do all articles meet the criteria?

4. Which approach to the teaching of current affairs do you believe to be the best for general use? Might times occur when other approaches should be used? Give examples.

5. Which of the activities suggested for use in current affairs might you use in a unit of instruction you are planning?

6. Review several periodicals for children and identify articles, maps, charts, test items, and other material that you might use in a unit of instruction.

7. Examine a bulletin on special days and weeks issued by a local school system of the state department of education. Which days and weeks are included? What learning activities are suggested? Which activities might you use in a unit you are planning?

8. Make a calendar of special days and weeks that is appropriate in your community. Indicate the grades in which certain days and weeks might be emphasized.

9. Which of the charts presented in this chapter might you put to use in your teaching? What adaptations might be made in them to meet the needs of children in different grades?

References

Adams, Florence, and Elizabeth McCarrick, *Highways and Holidays.* New York: E. P. Dutton & Co., Inc., 1960. A compilation of poems related to holidays throughout the year.

Anderson, Howard R., ed., *Approaches to An Understanding of World Affairs*, 25th Yearbook, National Council for the Social Studies. Washington, D.C.: National Education Association, 1954. Principles and procedures for the teaching of world affairs.

Burns, P. C., "Check List for Teaching about Holidays," *Instructor*, LXXI (February 1960), 89, 99. Guidelines for planning holiday observances and a list of references on special days and weeks.

Dupuy, Trevor N., ed., *Holidays: Days of Significance for all Americans*. New York: Franklin Watts, 1965. Background information.

Fraser, Dorothy M., "Current Affairs, Special Events, and Civic Participation," *Social Studies in Elementary Schools*, 32nd Yearbook, National Council for the Social Studies, pp. 131–49. Washington, D.C.: National Education Association, 1962. Principles and procedures for teaching current affairs, holidays, and civic participation.

Hunt, M. P., and L. E. Metcalf, *Teaching High School Social Studies*, pp. 6–8 and Ch. 11–16. New York: Harper & Row, Publishers, 1955. Useful in upper grades.

Jarolimek, John, "Teaching of Current Affairs," *Social Studies in Elementary Education*, Ch. 14. New York: The Macmillan Company, 1967. General principles and specific methods.

Kravitz, Bernard, "Factors Related to Knowledge of Current Affairs in Grades 7 and 8," *Social Education*, XXVI (March 1962), 143–45. A report on the relationships between achievement in current affairs and reading achievement, social studies achievement, and mental ability.

McSpadden, Joseph W., *The Book of Holidays*. New York: Thomas Y. Crowell Company, 1959. Suggestions for observing special days and weeks at home and in other lands.

National Education Association, *Controversial Issues in the Classroom*. Washington, D.C.: The Association, 1961. Guidelines for selection and use.

Pannell, Lucile, and Frances Cavanagh, *Holidays Round Up*. Philadelphia: Macrae Smith Co., 1950. Suggestions for observing holidays throughout the year.

Teaching Current Affairs. Washington, D.C.: Civic Education Service, 1966. Practical suggestions.

Wesley, Edgar B., and Mary A. Adams, "Utilizing Current Affairs," *Teaching Social Studies in Elementary Schools*, Ch. 20. Boston: D. C. Heath & Company, 1952.

For specific suggestions on holiday observances see current issues of the following: *Instructor, Grade Teacher, School Activities,* and *School Arts.*

Planning Units
of
Instruction

A unit of instruction is a plan to achieve specific objectives through the use of content and learning activities related to a designated topic. Objectives for the unit are clearly stated and are consistent with the purposes of the social studies. Content and learning experiences are selected to develop concepts, concept clusters, generalizations, attitudes and appreciations, thinking processes, and basic skills. Techniques of appraisal are included or suggested so that systematic evaluation can be made of outcomes. A list of books and other instructional media for children and background materials for teacher reference are also included.

7

Recent Trends

Several trends are evident in unit planning. Key ideas and methods of inquiry drawn from the disciplines are included in new units. Increasing attention is being given to thinking processes and underlying cognitive processes. Some new units, or major sections within them, deal primarily with a single discipline such as economics, geography, or history, for example, Working Families, Geography of Our State, and Growth of Our Community. Other new units draw from many disciplines, having such titles as Families Around the World, Area Study of India, and Changing Japan.

The trend is clearly away from the planning of units on the basis of immediate interests and desires of children and toward planning in terms of study areas considered most significant at various stages of development. This trend is in keeping with the current emphasis on the social studies as a developmental area of the curriculum which has definite form and substance at each grade level. Questions and problems of children are considered within the framework of the units suggested for emphasis in each grade. Thus attention is given to background experiences of children without neglecting the developmental strands—concepts, generalizations, attitudes, skills—that run through the social studies program.

Another trend is to prepare unit plans that are more specific and directive concerning initiation, developmental activities, and instructional materials and procedures. In many recently developed units, specific attention has been given to the preparation of teaching guides which may be used in different classes with fewer adaptations and changes than are necessary when broad, general resource units are provided. Materials and learning experiences for more-able, average, and less-able children are included to meet individual differences.

Another trend is to provide units of instruction which have been prepared by a group of teachers with the assistance of specialists. If areas of study included in the social studies are to be taught effectively, teachers must have unit plans which include materials and learning activities of greatest value. Individual teachers need not prepare detailed teaching guides for each and every unit to be taught, but they should understand unit organization, develop the backgrounds necessary to teach different units, and make necessary adaptations to the capabilities of children in the class.

Another trend is to differentiate more clearly between units of instruction in the social studies and guidance and help given to children on personal-social problems. Units are designed to provide opportunities for children to develop basic learnings as outlined in the curriculum. Guidance and assistance given to children on personal-social problems may take place any time during the school day as needed but cannot take the place of units in the social studies.

The trend in the middle and upper grades, and to a degree in the primary grades, is clearly away from the combining of content from several areas of the curriculum except when necessary because of the problems under study. For example, broad units in which content is drawn together from science, health, literature, social studies, and other areas are not being emphasized at

FOODS COME FROM SEEDS

Seeds

Many plants have seeds now. Most plants make seeds in the fall. We plant some seeds.

Every seed has a tiny plant in it. Every seed has in it some food for the little plant to live on as it is starting to grow. Every seed has a seed coat to help protect the little plant inside it.

We make many different foods from seeds. Animals store nuts and seeds. We store nuts and seeds, too.

Nuts   Grains   Vegetables

Do not overlook related science experiences that are essential to effective problem solving in a unit. What science experiences are appropriate in a unit you are planning? (San Diego City Schools)

the present time. Educators recognize that units of instruction must be planned for each basic curriculum area if the stated purposes of each area are to be achieved. However, in certain instances content from other areas of the curriculum may be drawn in to help solve problems, answer questions, or round out learnings in a unit. But the purpose is to improve learning and problem solving, not merely to combine areas of the curriculum. For example, in area studies of Mexico, Africa, Japan, Indians of the Southwest, and the like, one must study arts, crafts, and music as well as history, geography, economics, and government, if depth and breadth of understanding are to be achieved.

A continuing trend is to apply criteria in selecting, planning, and developing units of instruction. Criteria are derived from the point of view underlying the social studies program and are applied to units by individuals and groups at work in producing them, and by individual teachers as they select and use them in their classrooms. Criteria may be stated as characteristics of effective social studies units and thus serve not only as a checklist for appraising prepared units, but also as general guidelines for unit planning.

Criteria

The criteria discussed below are typical of those employed in selecting, planning, and developing units of instruction in the social studies.

Each unit should contribute to the achievement of the purposes of the social studies. Although the emphasis may vary from unit to unit, attention typically is given to the concepts and generalizations, attitudes and appreciations, and basic skills that may be developed or extended.

Each unit should deal with a significant area of study that is both meaningful to children and based on vital content which can be used to develop generalizations. It should challenge the capabilities of children, meet individual differences, and contribute to depth and breadth of understanding of basic concepts and generalizations.

Each unit should provide opportunities to develop problem solving, critical thinking, creative thinking, and reading-study skills to increasingly higher levels. By employing problem-solving processes one can utilize reading, writing, note-taking, outlining, reporting, interviewing, measuring, computing, and other skills, in ways that promote thinking abilities and highlight basic skills.

Each unit should provide opportunities to develop positive attitudes, appreciations, democratic values, and democratic behavior. Such outcomes may be achieved through a combination of individual and group work in which there is planning, discussion, action, sharing, and evaluation, coupled with opportunities to make decisions, choices, and judgments in the light of democratic standards and values.

One should be able to relate each unit to children's past experiences, to build on these experiences, and to lead on to broader and deeper experiences. Continuity of learning should be maintained within each unit and from unit to unit.

Each unit should include learning experiences and suggested instructional resources that are sufficiently varied to meet the full range of individual differences to be found in any class. Opportunities should be provided for each child to attain significant outcomes through independent and group study.

Each unit should provide opportunities for creative expression. Children's creativeness may be given outlets through individual and group work, planning, organization and expression of ideas, discovery of relationships, interpretation and application of ideas to new situations, evaluation, and other activities calling for original responses. Varied modes of expression should be employed such as art, music, rhythms, dramatic representation, construction, and oral and written language.

Each unit should be practicable from the standpoint of available time and instructional resources. Adequate time is essential to the development of depth and breadth of understanding, and needed reading materials and audio-visual and other resources should be available.

Each unit should include suggested principles and procedures for evaluating outcomes. Suggestions for teacher evaluation and pupil self-evaluation should be included and related to the appraisal of information, concepts, generalizations, skills, attitudes, and appreciations.

In order to select, plan, and develop units that possess these characteristics, teachers must know what is contained in various sections of a unit plan and the procedures involved in unit planning. These factors are considered in detail in the following sections.

The Unit Plan

The unit plan is an outline of purposes, content, main ideas, learning experiences, and instructional materials. It is a teaching guide from which are drawn the particular experiences that will be most profitable for a class. The unit plan does not take the place of daily planning, but it does serve as a storehouse of ideas, activities, and materials which may be used to facilitate planning for a particular group of children. A distinction is customarily made between teaching units and resource units. A *teaching unit* is used to provide instruction for a particular class; it contains the activities and materials to be used with the group. A *resource unit* is a rich source of content, activities, and materials from which a teacher can select those to be used.

Although unit plans vary considerably in different school systems, the following major sections are typical of most of them.

The Title. The title of the unit is descriptive of the major area of study to be included. Titles may be expressed as themes, problems, or topics such as Living At Home, Living in the Community, The Farm, How We Obtain Food and Clothing, History of Our State, Colonial Life, Living in Brazil, Area Study of India.

Background Information. This section is sometimes included as a reference aid for the teacher. It may be an outline of content, a summary of information related to main ideas or generalizations, or a listing of key ideas related to such basic activities as transportation, communication, and production of goods. It should be accurate, up to date, and directly related to the topics selected for detailed study.

Objectives. The objectives of a unit are usually stated succinctly under such headings as concepts and generalizations, attitudes and appreciations, and basic skills. The objectives should be related to the purposes of the social studies but should not be a repetition of them. Rather, they should be stated to indicate the specific contributions the unit can make to the achievement of overall purposes.

Initiation or Approach. This section states specific ways in which the unit may be introduced. The initiation is planned to start the unit on a series of meaningful learning experiences. Questions, problems, and learning possibilities are opened up, and an effort is made to stimulate and challenge each child. Subsequent activities flow out of the initiation in a sequence that contributes to maximum learning on the part of each child.

Problems to Be Investigated, or Main Ideas to Be Developed, and Related Learning Activities. This is the main section of a unit. It includes: (1) problems, questions, or main ideas to guide study; and (2) related learning activities and materials to be used by children. Many different patterns of organization are used in this section, for example, a single column with a listing of problems and experiences, a double-column arrangement with problems in one and experiences in the other, a triple-column arrangement with problems, activities, and instructional materials listed side by side.

In some unit plans, problems or main ideas are listed separately from related learning activities and materials. For example:

PROBLEMS TO BE INVESTIGATED

To find out how the pioneers obtained their food
To find out how the pioneers obtained their clothing
To find out how the pioneers traveled
And so forth

LEARNING EXPERIENCES

Collecting pictures for use in discussion and in making notebooks
Providing for the reading of textbooks, supplementary materials, and library books
Setting up committees to work on each problem
Showing filmstrips and motion pictures, for example, *Travel in Pioneer Days, Westward to the Mississippi, Long Journey West, Pioneer Home Life*
And so forth

In other unit plans, each problem, question, or main idea is listed separately and followed by suggested activities and instructional materials to be used. For example:

PROBLEM

To find out how the pioneers traveled

LEARNING EXPERIENCES

Arrange a display of pictures showing flatboats, stagecoaches, and wagons. Provide for discussion of the pictures around such questions as: Where were flatboats used? What kinds of roads were available? What difficulties were encountered?

Provide for reading such references as *Makers of the Americas*, pp. 122–124, and *Our Country's Story*, pp. 90–91.

Examine a wall map and have the group search for best trails or water routes to use in moving from established colonies.

Read *Exploring Our Country*, pp. 217–218, and discuss these questions: Who went with Boone to North Carolina? Why did they go?

Show one of these motion pictures: *Long Journey West, Pioneers Journey Across the Appalachians, Flatboatmen of the Frontier*
And so forth

Most teachers seem to prefer some form of the second type of arrangement because learning activities and instructional materials are directly related to each problem or main idea. Textbooks, references, audio-visual materials, and other resources are made a part of the sequence of activities to be used to solve each problem or to develop each main idea. Because such an arrangement is more functional and practical than that in which problems are listed in one section and learning experiences in another, additional examples and planning suggestions are given later in this chapter.

Concluding and Culminating Activities. Although some writers use the terms *concluding activities* and *culminating activities* synonymously, in this chapter a differentiation is made between them as noted in this paragraph. (Specific examples of each type of activity are given in later sections.) Two distinct practices are evident in recently published units. First, in some units concluding activities are made a part of the learning experiences related to each problem or main idea. This is done to summarize learnings and to formulate generalizations. Second, in some units culminating activities are suggested for summarizing and evaluating the overall unit of instruction, for example, a play, pageant, program, exhibit, or quiz program. In other units, culminating activities may not be suggested, but possible leads to other units may be given.

Evaluation. This section of a unit plan includes procedures and devices that may be used to evaluate children's learning. Examples of charts, checklists, test items, and other means of appraisal are given. In some units, evaluative devices are distributed throughout the unit and made a part of learning experiences under each problem or main idea. In general, this is a sound procedure since evaluation should be a continuing phase of instruction from the very beginning of each unit. When this is done, only those procedures and devices that are applicable at many different points throughout the unit should be included in a separate section.

Bibliography. This section includes a list of available instructional materials for children, background references for teachers, community resources, current materials, audio-visual resources, and other instructional materials. Complete bibliographical information should be given so that teachers will have no difficulty in locating and obtaining listed materials.

Although different terms are sometimes used, the foregoing are the major sections of a unit of instruction. The following excerpts from a unit on Japan are illustrative of each section.[1]

EXCERPTS FROM A UNIT ON CHANGING JAPAN

Objectives

Generalizations or Main Ideas to Develop:

Japan is a mountainous island nation with diversity in the natural environment.

The Japanese have a distinctive culture that is related in diverse ways to modes of living of other people.

Basic Skills and Methods of Inquiry:

To develop competence in using such methods of inquiry as content analysis, making and interpreting maps, interpreting pictures, and making comparisons.

To improve skill in locating, organizing, summarizing, and interpreting information, hypothesizing, making inferences, forming generalizations, and thinking critically.

Attitudes and Appreciations:

To develop understandings and appreciations of the richness of Japanese culture and how it has changed over the years.

Initiation

Arrange a display that includes news articles, pictures, and objects placed around a large map of Japan.

---

[1] John U. Michaelis, *Changing Japan* (Berkeley: Asian Studies Project, School of Education, University of California, 1967). For other examples, see John U. Michaelis, *Teaching Units Based on the Social Sciences* (Chicago: Rand McNally & Co., 1966).

Provide time for group discussion of the materials on display. Use questions during discussion that will bring out children's background of understanding: What have you heard or read about Japan recently? What have you seen on television?

Developmental Activities

Each main idea will be developed by providing learning experiences as shown in the following example:

MAIN IDEA: THE JAPANESE HAVE DEVELOPED CRAFTS AND ART FORMS TO A HIGH LEVEL OF CREATIVITY.

Notes and Concepts	*Learning Experiences*

Note: Use the following concept cluster, which includes both hand and factory-made crafts, to find out about crafts in Japan and your own area: handcrafts, ceramics, cloisonné, lacquer, porcelain, woodcarving, doll making, bamboo work.

Opener:
1. Arrange a display of pictures and objects of crafts from Japan and at least two other cultures. Guide children to identify the major crafts shown. Define crafts. Which ones do you think are Japanese? Why? Why are crafts an important part of a culture?

A. Japanese craftsmen make useful and beautiful things by hand.

1. Craftsmen still make many art objects: ceramics, lacquer ware, porcelain, cloisonné, dolls.
2. Factory production is more prevalent.
3. Ceramics is one of Japan's oldest crafts:

    a. Clay prepared by kneading.
    b. Clay shaped; freehand; coil or potter's wheel.
    c. Object dried and fired.
    d. Design applied.
    e. Fired in kiln.
    f. Porcelain finest chinaware, nonporous clay used, fired at high temperature, translucent.

Development:
1. Show MP handicrafts, beauty of Japan. Discuss the different kinds of crafts and have the children classify them. Are all crafts handcrafts? Have children compare crafts produced in Japan and in their own area.
2. Find out more about pottery-making in Japan. Read Minugh and Cory, pp. 149–50, and Pitts, pp. 134–35.
3. Take a study trip to a local pottery to gather information on processes that are used.
4. Discuss pictures in Johnes, *Japanese Art*, pp. 23–40.
5. Make a pottery bowl, using Japanese designs.
6. Show MP Ceramic Art of Japan and have children identify the processes used to produce ceramics.

4. Cloisonné ware is made of metal; includes bowls, vases, small boxes:

   a. Designs formed on objects with silver, gold, or brass wires.
   b. Wires heated.
   c. Shiny paint applied between wires.
   d. Objects baked and polished.

5. Lacquer ware made of cypress wood, used for trays, bowls, dishes, furniture:

   a. Lacquer tapped from trees:
     (1) Sap mixed with iron powder, other minerals.
     (2) Colors: black, red, or green.
   b. Cloth stretched over object.

7. How is cloisonné ware made? S Minugh and Cory, p. 148. What o jects may be decorated with enamel?
8. How is lacquer ware made? See Minu and Cory, p. 144, and Pitts, pp. 12 31. What kinds of things are made lacquer? Do we make lacquer ware a cloisonné? Why or why not? Why these wares expensive? Discuss time, tience, and skill involved.

   .   .   .

Conclusion:

1. Discuss features of Japanese arts a crafts that are popular in our country
2. Have children add pictures and short ports on arts and crafts to the cl notebook.

Culminating Activities

   A program in which children share and discuss pictures, drawings, maps, and other materials related to each main idea in the unit.

   A book fair in which children's favorite books are arranged in a display, and each book is opened to show illustrations that highlight the main ideas. Students should be prepared to tell about each book.

Evaluation

   Evaluation is carried on throughout the unit and includes such techniques as observing children at work, giving and discussing, tests, and using charts in self-evaluation.

Children's Books

   Minugh, Lena S., and Nancy C. Cory, *Japan*. Pasadena: Franklin, 1963.
   Pitts, Forrest R., *Japan*. Grand Rapids: Fideler, 1965.

References for Teachers

   Norbeck, Edward, *Changing Japan*. New York: Holt, Rinehart & Winston, Inc., 1965.
   Reischauer, Edwin O., *Japan, Past and Present*. New York: Alfred A. Knopf, Inc., 1964.

Films and Other Materials

Japanese Consular Offices (in New York, San Francisco, and other major cities).

Ceramic Art of Japan, Living Arts of Japan.

(Listing of other films and charts, slides, recordings, booklets, and other free or inexpensive materials).

The foregoing excerpts have been presented to illustrate the type of content included in various sections of a unit of instruction. However, unit plans vary considerably among school systems even though common elements may be found in them. A helpful procedure is to review units that are available in local school systems and to note the pattern of organization that is used. Such a review is quite helpful in the planning of a unit.

A current trend is to provide kits that contain instructional media for basic units. Check to see if kits are available in your area. (MATCH Box Project, Children's Museum, Boston)

Collections of units for teacher reference are available as noted at the end of this chapter.

Guidelines for Planning

SELECTING A UNIT

The most widely used selection procedure is to refer to the course of study, note the units proposed for each grade, and select a unit in the light of the backgrounds and capabilities of children in a given class. This procedure avoids repetition, promotes the use of appropriate instructional materials for each unit, and prevents the selection of insignificant units. Basic or required units are usually listed in the course of study, and one or more optional units may be suggested. The criteria discussed in the first part of this chapter should be applied in selecting optional units. Special attention should be given to the educational backgrounds and growth characteristics of the children for whom the unit is intended. Among the most helpful specific items of information about children in the class are the following:

Units studied in previous grades

Levels of intelligence

Levels of reading ability

Oral and written language skills

Independent study and group work skills

Special talents and interests

Intellectual curiosity

Home study and library skills

Cultural background—travel, socio-economic level, home background, and the like

Such information may be obtained by reviewing cumulative records, observing children in class, and conferring with former teachers and the principal. If a teacher is planning a resource unit and is unacquainted with the class (preplanning before the opening of school), he should review the growth characteristics of children at the level for which the unit is being planned. (See Chapter 3.)

THE TEACHER'S BACKGROUND

An essential step in the planning of units after the topic is selected is the building of a rich background of experience by the teacher himself. Units developed by others should be studied for suggestions. Texts, pamphlets, and references available for children, and background materials for the teacher, should be read and annotated. Audio-visual materials should be previewed, and notes should be made regarding their contributions to the unit. If time permits, community resources should be checked, trips should be taken to those places in the community that may be used for study trips, and interviews should be held with potential resource visitors. Pictures, photographs, maps, sketches, charts, and diagrams should be collected and filed with notations regarding their use in the unit. Some teachers take pictures to use in the unit. Related art processes, experiments, and demonstrations should be tried out. Collections should be made of songs, records, poems, stories, paintings, and realia. Weapons, utensils, clothing, and other realia should be secured. If they are unavailable, the teacher should endeavor to get pictures of them and to see them in a museum. An annotated bibliography containing children's references, teacher's references, and audio-visual materials should be compiled. An outline of basic content and activities should be prepared. Now the teacher is ready to do specific planning for a given class or for children at a given level. To try to plan or teach a unit without a rich background of information is wasteful of time and energy on the part of both the teacher and children.

STATING OBJECTIVES

After a teacher has built up a rich background of knowledge and experience, he should set specific purposes in accordance with the maturity of the children for whom the unit is intended. Types of questions to be answered are: What can the group accomplish in this unit? How can this unit contribute to the purposes of the social studies? What concepts and generalizations can be developed? What attitudes and appreciations can be emphasized? What skills can be further developed? In answering these questions, the teacher should state objectives that are practical, to the point, attainable by children, and that can be used to evaluate children's learning. General purposes such as *the improvement of character* and *appreciation of the growth of our country* have little value as unit objectives. Rather, the specific contributions that the unit can make to basic goals should be stressed as shown in the following examples.

OBJECTIVES OF A UNIT ON THE FAMILY

Terms, Concepts, Generalizations

To develop an understanding of terms and concepts related to the home and items in it, for example, different rooms, appliances, food, clothing

To develop the following main ideas:
Homes and families differ in some ways and are alike in others.
Each member of a family has responsibilities.
Families are supported in different ways.
Recreational activities vary among families.
Regard for the health and safety of others and care of property improve family welfare.

Skills and Abilities

To promote skill in sharing, planning, discussing, carrying out, and evaluating learning experiences related to family living
To improve each child's ability to listen, report to the group, and take turns
To establish habits of safety, cleanliness, and courtesy

Attitudes and Appreciations

To develop respect for the work of mothers, fathers, and other members of families
To instill in children a desire to discharge their own responsibilities
To develop an appreciation of likenesses and differences among families
To develop an appreciation of the importance of the home in daily living

OBJECTIVES OF A STUDY OF LIFE IN EARLY AMERICA

Terms, Concepts, Generalizations

To develop terms and concepts related to ways of living of early settlers, for example, trencher, Betty lamp, sampler, town meeting
To learn how the ideals of early settlers were made a part of early documents, government, education, and other activities
To develop the following main ideas:
Differing purposes and values of colonists were reflected in differences in ways of living.
Distinctive patterns of living emerged in different regions.
Democratic concepts of government began to emerge early in America.
Many different individuals and groups contributed to early American culture.
The sacrifices made by early settlers contributed to our heritage in many ways.

Skills and Methods of Inquiry

To develop skill in defining problems and locating, gathering, summarizing, and interpreting historical information drawn from a period far removed from the present

To improve children's ability to interpret maps and photos of travel routes, settlements, and other phases of life in early America

To improve skill in identifying oneself with others through reading, use of films and other audio-visual resources. independent study, and group work

Attitudes and Appreciations

To develop enlightened loyalty and patriotism based on an understanding of early contributions to our American heritage

To inculcate a feeling for the ideals of freedom held by early Americans

To develop high regard for the place of the home, church, and government in early America

THE INITIATION OR APPROACH

The initiation of a unit should be planned to stimulate thinking, learning, and planning; it should open up truly meaningful ways to begin the study of a unit. Problems and questions that grow out of the initiation should be discussed and defined so that thinking-learning processes will be directed along profitable lines. Active participation of each child should be obtained from the very beginning so that maximum individual learning and growth will take place. In order to serve such purposes, a good initiation:

1. Stimulates keen interest and arouses questions and problems in the mind of each child

2. Provides opportunities for pupils to become directly involved in planning and discussing learning opportunities

3. Starts the unit in worthwhile directions on significant questions, problems, or the development of a main idea

4. Does not create confusion by stimulating interest in too many problems at one time, or in problems and questions beyond the capabilities of children in the group

5. Focuses attention on the central topic to be studied and serves to set the scope of the study

Many different approaches, or combinations of approaches, are used in units of instruction. The following examples are presented to clarify the use of different techniques and materials in the initiation of a unit.

On-going Study. One of the most effective approaches is that in which a unit grows out of the preceding unit as an on-going study. For example, a study of The Wholesale Market may be an outgrowth of the study of The Farm and lead on to a study of The Supermarket. Other examples are a study of The Community growing out of a study of the Neighboring Communities, a study of Transportation leading on to a study of Communication, and a study of Colonial Life leading on to a study of Pioneer Life and Westward Movement. The essence of this approach is the clarification of relationships between final activities in one unit and beginning activities in the next so that a smooth, uninterrupted transition is made. These relationships may be made by raising questions and problems that stimulate children to think of next steps and learning experiences growing out of activities in the unit just completed.

Teacher Suggestion. In some instances, direct teacher suggestion is used to initiate a unit, for example, basic units that are required, optional units that are appropriate for the class, or units on current affairs that are truly significant. To be effective, this approach should be planned to get involvement and participation on the part of children. Challenging questions may be raised, problems may be posed, related past experiences may be shared, an attractive display may be arranged and discussed, a film may be shown to open up questions, reasons for undertaking the unit may be discussed, or other activities may be employed to involve children.

Incidents. A unit may be initiated as a result of a significant incident that has occurred in the community, state, nation, or other lands. For example, an election, a new invention, a new transportation speed record, or the emergence of a new nation may be used as a springboard to a more intensive study. The great problem is one of timing, which can be met only in part by planning certain units to coincide with elections or other planned events. Because of this difficulty, most teachers make other plans to initiate units but do make use of incidents when the problem of timing can be met.

Pretest. A pretest may be used to initiate a unit if it is designed to open up questions and problems and is followed by discussion that is well directed by the teacher. Children's backgrounds of understanding can be assessed quickly, and areas in need of further study can be identified. However, many children will profit from further stimulation such as discussing pictures that highlight topics to be studied or seeing a film or filmstrip that opens up questions and problems. If a pretest is to be used, generally it should be used with other procedures to initiate a unit.

How might such a display be used to initiate a unit? (Education Workshop, University of California, Berkeley)

Books. Books that are new to the group are sometimes used to initiate a unit. Displays of textbooks and library books may be discussed, selected pictures may be shown, and passages may be read to the group. Special comments may be made on supplementary materials in relation to interesting information and ideas presented in them. Books of interest to individuals in the group also may be discussed. A difficulty in this approach is that of developing a common background for planning and discussion. This difficulty can be met in part by having a variety of books and by discussing a wide sampling of material and pictures contained in them. Generally, this approach works best if supplemented by other materials along with the books.

Audio-visual Materials. A motion picture, filmstrip, set of slides, radio program, television program, recording, map, or display of

215

pictures may be used to initiate a unit. For example, one teacher used a motion picture that gave an overview of village life in India to stimulate a discussion of related problems; another used a carefully selected set of slides to open up problems of Living in Africa; still another guided discussion of a set of pictures on The Farm. To be avoided in these approaches are such pitfalls as failure to secure the motion picture at the right time, presenting so many ideas that the group does not sense immediate problems to attack, failure to stimulate thinking on the part of all the children, and passive reception by the group instead of active participation. These difficulties can be avoided by careful preplanning and by formulating questions and comments to guide children's use of the resource and to direct follow-up discussion.

Community Resources. A study trip or a resource visitor may be used to initiate a unit. If careful plans are made, a common experience that focuses on selected problems and stimulates thinking on the part of each child can be provided. Generally speaking, community resources are more effectively used when the class plans for their use in relation to specific questions and problems that are under study. However, they are most effective as an approach to a new unit when used as an on-going activity growing out of the preceding unit. For example, one group in concluding a study of Life on the Farm made plans to visit a wholesale market in order to find out how farm produce was processed and distributed. The visit to the market initiated the unit on the Wholesale Market in a smooth, on-going manner, and with no interruption in the overall emphasis for the year on How We Secure Food, Shelter, and Clothing.

Arranged Environment. The arrangement of materials to initiate a unit is one of the most widely used approaches. The classroom is attractively arranged with pictures, realia, maps, books, pamphlets, and other materials related to the first problems to be considered. Children are given an opportunity to examine the materials and to raise questions about them, and so are able to participate actively in the initiation. A film, story, or recording also may be used. During discussion, questions and problems are clarified and may be listed on the chalkboard or on a chart. The teacher may raise further questions to make sure that important points are not overlooked and to guide thinking in directions that are most profitable for the group. Even when an on-going study is the main approach, arranging materials that focus attention on the next unit is helpful.

A brief description of an arranged environment, and responses of children to it, may serve to clarify its use in the initiation of a unit. The following example is taken from a unit on The West-ward Movement. The classroom was arranged as follows:

1. Pictures of scenes in an early pioneer town on the Missouri River were posted on the bulletin board. They included a general store, a wagon being loaded, a blacksmith shop, a general street scene, a covered wagon being built, and a wagon leaving the city for the West.

2. Another section of the bulletin board had pictures related to the Oregon Trail, including a caravan fording a river, life in a camp, a herd of buffalo, three Indian scouts watching a wagon train, wagons crossing the plains, and pioneers building cabins.

3. Another section of the bulletin board showed several pictures of Plains Indians, including the hunting of buffalo, an attack on a wagon train, and Indian scouts.

4. On a table in a corner of the room there were several articles that children could handle. These included a model of a covered wagon, pioneer dolls (a man, a woman, child), a powder horn, a flintlock rifle, candle molds, a water pouch, shot pouches, buffalo horns, a bull whip, arrows, bows, a corn grinder, and flint used in making arrows.

5. In another section of the room was a large map of the United States, showing various mountain barriers, rivers, and trails.

6. In the library corner, attractively displayed, were several books about Indians, pioneers, covered wagons, cities in the early West, and traveling in pioneer days.

As the children eagerly examined the different items in the arranged environment, the teacher noted their comments, questions, needs, interests, desires, and problems. Typical comments and questions included the following:

What kind of gun is this? How did they work it?
Look at these wagons. Would they hold very much?
I'll bet it was hard to ride in these wagons. They're different from cars, aren't they?
I wonder if it's hard to make a covered wagon.
How did they carry their food and water in these wagons?
Look at the clothes they wore!
Oh! I see how they got across rivers with the covered wagon.
See how this town is different from ours?
Look at the store and the man making covered wagons.

The teacher noted these and other questions and problems raised by the children. These were clues for the development of significant experiences in the unit. After the children had examined the materials, the teacher and the group engaged in a lively discussion of the many interesting materials and activities related to the westward movement. Through group planning, subsequent interests and problems were identified, and specific plans were made for working on them. Thus, the unit was begun in an exciting and challenging manner.

Which type of initiation is the best? One cannot say that one approach is best for all situations. Sometimes a film may be available, an incident may occur, or a field trip is possible, while other resources may not be available at the moment. In other situations, a discussion of common experiences during the summer may lead to a rich study of some aspect of community living, transportation, or conservation. A teacher must be alert to these possibilities and use them creatively. In general, however, the arranged environment and the initiation growing out of another unit as an on-going activity are the two most effective approaches. In each unit that is planned, a sound procedure is to consider previous experiences of the group so that each unit

A well-arranged classroom environment can be used to initiate a unit because it opens up problems for study. What questions might arise after examination of these materials? (Alameda County Schools)

can be an on-going activity, and to plan an arranged environment that can be used to get off to a successful beginning. Then the teacher is prepared to launch the unit and does not have to wait for other possible approaches. After he has decided on an approach, he should plan and guide the initiation so that it creates keen interest in the unit, provokes significant questions, provides for pupil participation, employs a variety of materials, leads to group planning, and starts the unit in profitable directions.

Planning Learning Experiences

As noted earlier, learning experiences should be organized around major problems to be investigated, or around main ideas to be developed. Because of the increased interest in developing main ideas or generalizations, several examples are presented in the following section. We should point out, however, that the procedures are similar for organizing learning experiences around major problems or questions. The basic difference lies in the method of statement. For example, consider the following organizing idea stated as a *problem, question,* and *main idea:*

> *Problem:* To find out how food is provided in the community
> *Question:* How is food provided in the community?
> *Main Idea:* Every community provides food.

Any one of the above may be used as a basis for organizing learning experiences. Some prefer the first two forms because they are closely related to statements that are developed through discussion and planning during initial phases of problem solving. Others prefer the last form because it serves as a guide for the teacher to use in developing generalizations, and questions or problems related to it can be developed through opening activities, as will be seen in the following section. Whichever form is used, children must grasp both the meaning and significance of the topics to be investigated and the sense in the learning experiences that are employed. They must also develop generalizations as a result of the experiences that are provided.

PLANNING UNITS AROUND MAIN IDEAS

The first phase in planning units around main ideas or generalizations is to identify the main ideas to be emphasized. This is usually done by referring to a master list of generalizations and noting selected main ideas as shown in Chapter 4, and noting generalizations related to the content in textbooks and instructional materials that are to be used in the unit. Both methods of identifying main ideas should be used. Reference to a master list of generalizations gives focus and a point of departure for spotting main ideas that can be brought to higher levels in each grade. Instructional materials must be reviewed to identify main ideas and the related content that can be used to develop them.

The second phase in planning units around main ideas is to organize related content, learning activities, and instructional materials, around each main idea. A pattern or organization that has been found quite useful is shown in the following examples. As you read them notice that the sequence of learning experiences begins with openers or initiating activities, moves to developmental activities, and ends with concluding activities.

A point that should be reiterated is that although the main idea is stated first in the unit plan, teachers are not expected to pass it on directly to the children. Rather, the main idea is noted for teacher reference in guiding learning experiences. The development of the main idea is a *goal* toward which the teacher works.

A helpful strategy is to prepare a focal question that can be used to guide inquiry toward the development of the main idea as shown in the following example:

Main Idea: Japan has made progress in providing health services, education, and democratic government.
Focal Question: What has Japan done to meet health needs, provide schools, and improve government?

Notice that the focal question directs attention to the three key concepts in the main idea. The use of such questions promotes inquiry and discovery on the part of children and enables teachers to avoid the pitfall of fact gathering to prove a foregone conclusion. Such questions are also helpful in guiding inquiry in different parts of the unit. For example, one part may deal with health needs, another with schools, and another with government.

The following example illustrates these and other points related to unit planning.[2] The main ideas to be developed in a

---

[2] John U. Michaelis, *Changing Japan* (Berkeley: Asian Studies Project, School of Education, University of California, 1967).

unit on *Changing Japan* are presented first to show the scope of the unit. This is followed by one main idea which is presented in detail. The specific readings and other instructional materials related to the main idea are presented first along with suggestions to teachers, a procedure that teachers find far more helpful than the practice of including references only at the end of the unit. Placement of the readings and instructional materials at the beginning of each main idea enables the teacher to select or request needed instructional media. Notice how the related content is lined up opposite learning experiences for easy reference. Notice also that key questions related to the main idea and the focal question are placed at different points to guide inquiry.

CHANGING JAPAN

Identification of Main Ideas. The following were selected after reviewing concepts, concept clusters, and generalizations (such as those presented in Chapter 4), and the instructional materials to be used in the unit:

1. Japan is a mountainous island nation with diversity in its natural environment. (Focal Question: What are the main features of Japan's natural environment?)

2. The history of Japan is distinctive in many ways, yet it has been greatly influenced by other peoples. (Focal Question: How did contacts with other people influence Japan in the past?)

3. Japan has made rapid progress in providing health services, education, and democratic government. (Focal Question: What has Japan done to meet health needs, provide schools, and improve government?)

4. Japan is an industrial nation with a variety of economic activities. (Focal Question: How can Japan be an industrial nation with such limited natural resources?)

5. The Japanese have a distinctive culture that is related in many ways to modes of living of other people. (Focal Question: How is Japan's culture related to other cultures?)

6. The Japanese have developed crafts and art forms to a high level of creativity. (Focal Question: What are the distinctive features of arts and crafts in Japan?)

7. The Japanese engage in a variety of native and adopted recreational activities. (Focal Question: What recreational activities are popular in Japan?)

Each of the above main ideas was used as a basis for organizing related content, learning experiences, and instructional materials. The following example for the third main idea shows the pattern of organization.

MAIN IDEA: JAPAN HAS MADE RAPID PROGRESS IN PROVIDING HEALTH SERVICES, EDUCATION, AND DEMOCRATIC GOVERNMENT.

(Focal Question: What Has Japan Done to Meet Health Needs, Provide Schools, and Improve Government?)

Readings, References, Audio-Visual Materials, and Tips to Teachers

---

Suggested Reading: *
Dearmin and Peck, *Japan, Home of the Sun*, pp. 208–234.
Minugh and Cory, *Japan*, pp. 105–130.
Pitts, *Japan*, pp. 114–20, 147–57.

Supplementary Reading:
Caldwell and Caldwell, *Let's Visit Japan*, pp. 55–63.
Cavanna, *Noko of Japan*, pp. 32–57.
Hayes, *The Boy in the 49th Seat.*
Mears, *The First Book of Japan*, pp. 46–47.
Schloat, *Junichi, A Boy of Japan*, Part I.

Teacher Reference:
Burks, *The Government of Japan.*
Consulate General of Japan, *The Japan of Today* and *Facts About Japan* (latest issues on government, health, and education).
Reischauer, *Japan, Past and Present*, pp. 201–296.
Seidensticker, *Japan*, pp. 43–59, 77–87, 133–43.
The Statesman's Yearbook, annual, recent data on government and education.

Audio-Visual Materials: *
MP Education in Japan (Ideal Pictures or Japanese Consulate)
MP Japan: The Yukawa Story (United World Films, Inc.)
MP Little Masaki of Japan (Stillfilm Inc.)
MP School Life in Japan (Ideal Pictures or Japanese Consulate)

Audio-Visual Materials: *—Continued
MP Schools in Japan (Ideal Pictures or Japanese Consulate)
FS At School in Japan (Bailey Films)
Elementary Schools of Japan (chart from Japanese Consulate)

Tips to Teachers:
Give attention to education as a primary culture bearer and as a force in social change and technological advance.

Make frequent comparisons between school activities in Japan and in local schools.

Bring out the fundamental importance of health services, education, and government in improving both individual and group welfare.

Weave into instruction the key idea that the functions of government are "to serve and regulate in the public interest," rather than the idea that "the government rules."

Give special attention to concepts introduced in this section: compulsory health insurance, literacy rate, calligraphy, general welfare, branches of government, the Diet, prime minister, prefecture.

Enrich instruction by considering current events that deal with health, education, and government in Japan.

Some teachers prefer to do the section on government first.

---

* The original unit contains complete bibliographic citations; it may be obtained as noted in the end-of-chapter references.

MAIN IDEA: JAPAN HAS MADE RAPID PROGRESS IN PROVIDING HEALTH SERVICES,
EDUCATION, AND DEMOCRATIC GOVERNMENT.

(Focal Question: What Has Japan Done to Meet Health Needs,
Provide Schools, and Improve Government?)

Notes, Concepts, Related Content	*Key Questions and Learning Experiences*

Note: Have the class make a list of important services. Include health, education, safety, security, water supply, courts, government. The list may be used to guide study of the question: Are similar services provided in Japan?

A. Japan has met serious health problems.
  1. Reduction of major diseases
  2. Problems owing to crowdedness
  3. Need for doctors, nurses, hospitals
  4. Keeping large cities clean
  5. Providing pure water
  6. Compulsory national health insurance for medical and hospital care
B. Education is one of the most important services for both individual development and group welfare.
  1. High regard for education
  2. Improvement of education during Meiji era
  3. America's contributions, including independent thought, education for women, new schools, changes in high school and college studies
  4. Class size of forty-eight as government standard
  5. Construction of new schools
  6. Compulsory for nine years
  7. Literacy rate among highest in world, over 98 per cent
C. The school program is well planned and varied.
  1. Traditional respect for teachers
  2. School uniforms worn by many children
  3. Lunch programs in many schools

Opener:
1. What services of government are important to all of us? How about health? Education? Other services?
2. Do you think that similar services are provided in Japan?

Development:
A. How are health needs being met?
  1. What health problems are of concern in Japan? Have students suggest problems that can be used as hypotheses to guide study.
  2. Read Dearmin and Peck, pp. 209–214.
  3. Discuss major health problems, noting similarities and differences in our country. Point out that Japan has recently set up a national compulsory health insurance program to provide hospital and medical care. Summarize steps that have been taken to meet health problems.
B. How are schools in Japan alike and different from ours?
  4. Why must a country provide a good program of education if it is to make progress? Have students consider individual as well as group values of education.
  5. Let's find out how the program of education has been changed in Japan. Do you think that Americans were involved in any way?
  6. Read Dearmin and Peck, pp. 217–21. Discuss early contributions during the Meiji period, later contri-

4. Provision of free textbooks, Grades I–IX
5. Typical school week of five-and-a-half days
6. Basic subjects
   a. Arithmetic
   b. Arts and crafts
   c. Music
   d. Health and physical education
   e. Science
   f. Social studies
   g. Japanese language
   h. Home economics
7. Different forms of Japanese writing
   a. Romaji, using English alphabet
   b. Hiragana, using Kana characters for native words
   c. Katakana, using Kana characters for foreign words
   d. Kanji, using Chinese characters
D. Government provides for voting, defense, internal order and justice, general welfare, and relations with other nations.
E. Three main branches of government are the legislative, executive, and judicial.

Note: Bring out the idea that democratic government has many forms. Japan, United States, Britain, and other countries are democratic, but have differences in form. The Japanese parliamentary system is like the British. In our system we have a clearer distinction between the executive and legislative branches. However, certain freedoms and values are important in all democracies.

F. The Japanese have a democratic form of government.
   1. New constitution includes the basic structure of government, renounces war, and guarantees human freedoms
   2. Symbolic role of Emperor and royal family
   3. Diet, sole law-making body
      a. House of Councilors, 250 members

butions of Americans, and recent improvements.
7. Ask students if they think a school day in Japan is similar to our school day. Show FS At School in Japan. Read Minugh and Cory, pp. 105–130, and Schloat, Part I, Pitts, pp. 114–20, and Hayes. Guide interpretation of the photographs in each book, comparing dress and school activities with their own.
8. Discuss the large picture chart *Elementary Schools of Japan*, guiding students to make comparisons with their own school.
9. Show MP School Children of Japan (from Consulate General of Japan, address in Appendix).
10. Have individuals read Cavanna, pp. 32–57, and report on highlights of the extended study trip to Kyoto and Nara. Discuss why study trips are helpful in learning about one's country.
11. Invite someone who has visited schools in Japan to show slides and report to the group.
12. Read Mears, pp. 46–47. Discuss the difference among Romaji, Kana, and Kanji characters. Have able students investigate and report on Hiragana and Katakana writing.
13. Make a summary chart to compare education in Japan and here.
C. What kind of government does Japan have?
14. What do we expect our government to do for us? Do you think the Japanese expect their government to do similar things?
15. Ask students if they know the three main branches of government. Discuss the role of the President, Congress, and the Supreme Court. Ask students if they think Japan has a similar setup.
16. Discuss the meaning of freedom to

b. House of Representatives, 467 members
4. Prime Minister chosen by Diet
5. Cabinet of sixteen ministers
6. Supreme Court of fifteen judges
7. Local self-government in prefectures, cities, towns, and villages
8. Voting by men and women at age twenty

G. Japan and the United States are "good" neighbors because they work together, exchange ideas and products, and respect each other
1. Separated by the Pacific, but only thirteen hours away by jet
2. Democratic and industrialized nations
3. Japan with a long history in a small area
4. United States with a short history in a large area
5. Japanese contributions in art, architecture, science, agriculture, education, products
6. Cooperation since W.W. II in trade, education, international relations, defense, exchange of ideas, efforts for world peace
7. Some disagreements over Okinawa, Vietnam, and Red China

vote, express ideas, and worship. Why are these important in Japan, the United States, and other democracies?
17. Read Dearmin and Peck, pp. 225–27, and Pitts, pp. 147–57.
18. Have students make a chart to show the main features of government in Japan and in the United States:

JAPAN	UNITED STATES
Constitution	Constitution
Diet	Legislature
Councilors	Senators
Representatives	Representatives
Prime Minister	President
Supreme Court	Supreme Court
Cabinet	Cabinet
Political Parties	Political Parties

D. In what ways are Japan and the United States good neighbors?
19. What does it mean to say that two countries are good neighbors?
20. Why can we call Japan a neighbor when she is so far away?
21. In what ways are Japan and the United States alike? Different? Read Dearmin and Peck, pp. 231–32.
22. What are some contributions of Japanese who have settled in the United States?
23. How have Japan and the United States cooperated since World War II?

Conclusion:
1. Summarize ways in which the Japanese are improving health services, providing education, and extending freedom through government.
2. Have students make a large chart, mural, or movie roll showing major changes in health, education, and government.
3. Have students add sections to the scrapbook on health, education, and government.

RELATIONSHIPS TO PROBLEM SOLVING

The basic sequence of activities in the foregoing example should be noted. In general, the phases of problem solving discussed in Chapter 4 and the sequence of basic activities—openers, developmental activities, and concluding activities—are closely related. The following outline shows the relationships.

LEARNING EXPERIENCES	PROBLEM SOLVING
Initiating and opening activities	Recognizing, clarifying, and defining problems
	Recalling related information and proposing solutions or hypotheses
Developmental activities	Planning ways to solve problems
	Locating, appraising, and selecting information
	Organizing, summarizing, and interpreting information
Concluding activities	Forming generalizations and conclusions
	Evaluating the effectiveness of individual and group work

As learning experiences are provided in each unit of instruction, the various phases of problem solving are used as needed. In some instances, certain phases may be given greater emphasis than others. For example, as opening activities are provided, primary attention may sometimes be given to the recall of related information in order to assess children's backgrounds of understanding. This may be followed by locating, selecting, and organizing information needed to answer questions or to solve problems. In other instances, attention might be given first to the setting of hypotheses, and then to planning of ways to test them, collecting data, and forming tentative conclusions. Evaluation of individual and group work may be a part of opening and developmental activities as well as a part of concluding activities. Questions and problems may be further clarified during developmental activities even though attention was given to them during initiating or opening activities. The point to remember in unit planning is to be sure to include learning experiences that will enable children to put the full range of problem-solving skills to use as needed. Then, as each unit of instruction is developed in the classroom, adaptations can be made to assure the development of problem-solving skills. The list of activities that follows will help to clarify relationships to problem solving and may be used as a checklist in unit planning.

ACTIVITIES

Opening Activities. Openers, or initiating activities, are provided to open up questions or problems, to find out what children know about the topic, to recall relevant information, to relate present learning to past learning, and to set the stage for activities that are to follow. Among the activities used in this introductory phase are the following:

Have children draw pictures, tell about earlier experiences, report on places they have visited, examine and discuss pictures, or recall ideas related to questions raised by the teacher in order to reveal their background of understanding.

Show a film, filmstrip, pictures, maps, or objects followed by a discussion.

Have children say what they would do if they were in a particular situation.

Start a chart, scrapbook, time line, map, or bulletin board display which children are to complete.

Pose a problem, question, or issue for the group to discuss.

List questions, problems, or things to do on a chart or on the chalk-board.

Ask children to report what they have done, or others have done, in a given situation.

Have children interview someone, take a study trip, or dramatize an event.

Arrange pictures, books, and objects to stimulate discussion and to elicit comments and questions from the group.

Have the group read an introductory section of their textbooks, review scrapbooks and materials prepared by others, or examine maps to identify questions and problems for study.

Have children attempt to complete an unfinished story, write a statement or paragraph related to a topic, or complete an unfinished sentence.

The main point to remember in planning openers is to select activities that will reveal children's backgrounds of understanding and lead to developmental activities which give depth and breadth of meaning to the main idea. A teacher should watch during opening activities for both misconceptions and well-founded ideas.

Developmental Activities. Developmental activities are selected and used to plan ways of working, to locate, appraise, and organize information, to summarize and interpret information, and to evaluate progress. The full range of problem-solving techniques is used to solve problems and develop main ideas. Each learning experience should grow out of the preceding one and lead on to the next in order to provide a smooth sequence. The following developmental activities drawn from different units of instruction are illustrative:

PLANNING WAYS TO SOLVE PROBLEMS

Displaying books, and other materials to stimulate thinking and planning

Asking questions to focus children's thinking on the main ideas to be developed, problems to be solved, or questions to be answered

Reviewing ideas and materials which are related to problems under study

Listing questions and problems to guide study as they are proposed in group discussion

Considering possible sources of information such as reading materials, films and other audio-visual materials, and community resources

Giving a test to assess children's backgrounds and to open up topics for further study

Collecting available books, pictures, maps, and other materials

Finding out about related radio and television programs

Planning an imaginary trip to a place that is to be studied

Locating on a map places to be studied, and sharing known information

Explaining terms, phrases, concepts, work standards, and procedures to be followed

Deciding on ways of working as individuals, and as members of small groups

Considering individual, small-group, and whole-class activities

Formulating rules and standards to guide both individual and group work

Listing needs for materials, steps to take to solve problems, and individual responsibilities

LOCATING, GATHERING, AND APPRAISING INFORMATION

Sharing information on references that have been located by the children or by the teacher

Using tables of contents, indexes, study guides, and reading lists

Building a card file on topics that may be found in textbooks, library materials, periodicals, pamphlets, yearbooks, almanacs

Setting up individual and small-group projects to gather needed information

Deciding on the form for organizing information as it is gathered

Reading textbooks, references, periodicals, pamphlets, charts, graphs, diagrams, encyclopedias, yearbooks, almanacs, other pertinent materials

Listening to reports, stories read by the teacher or other pupils, radio programs, recordings, resource visitors

Writing letters to request information or materials related to topics under study

Seeing films, filmstrips, slides, stereographs, pictures, exhibits, displays, television programs, dioramas, panoramas, demonstrations

Studying maps, the globe, and atlases

Photo interpretation skills are put to use in many units. How might you use them in a unit? *(San Diego City Schools)*

Utilizing community resources through study trips, interviewing experts, doing field studies, participating in service projects, finding documentary materials

Observing demonstrations, experiments, individuals at work, seasonal changes, community activities

Collecting news articles, pictures, maps, graphs, objects

Examining collections, models, specimens, textiles, instruments, costumes, utensils

Learning songs, games, rhythmic expression, folk dances, musical accompaniments, and how to play instruments related to the area of study

Tabulating information obtained from interviews, reading, field studies, experiments

Taking notes, outlining material, adding to scrapbooks, notebooks, and classroom charts

Recording information on tapes, charts, graphs, maps, diagrams

Keeping a log or diary of experiments, activities, events, seasonal changes

Appraising information by checking one source against another, finding proof for statements, asking experts, reviewing materials

Contrasting and comparing ideas, events, activities, processes, ways of living

Discussing information and selecting ideas related to topics and problems under study

ORGANIZING, SUMMARIZING, AND INTERPRETING INFORMATION

Discussing and pooling ideas obtained from different sources

Discussing reasons underlying likenesses and differences in ways of living, customs, traditions, beliefs

Conducting class panel discussions, debates, forums, and round-table discussions

Listing items of information related to questions and problems

Classifying information under appropriate headings

Preparing and sharing outlines, summaries, reports, reviews, notebooks, scrapbooks

Writing descriptive statements, classroom newspaper articles, stories, and playlets

Making charts, maps, time lines, diagrams, tables

Arranging displays, bulletin boards, pictures in sequence, exhibits, files of related material

Drawing or painting pictures, murals, cartoons, posters

Modeling objects out of clay, papier-maché, or other material

Engaging in industrial and fine arts experiences such as processing raw materials, bookmaking, weaving, stenciling, sketching, illustrating, lettering, labeling

Making costumes and scenery for use in a skit or play

Dramatizing or pantomiming events, activities, processes

Constructing objects, models, looms, movie box roll, puppets, marionettes, other items

Creating original rhymes, stories, poems, songs, musical accompaniments, rhythms, dances, plays, skits

Interpreting moods and feelings through dramatic play, rhythmic expression, singing, playing instruments, folk dancing, playing folk games

Concluding Activities. Closely related to activities involved in interpreting information, and frequently flowing out of them, concluding activities are designed to focus on the main idea, problem, or questions under study, and should help children pull together related information in order to formulate generalizations. In addition, concluding activities provide opportunities for evaluating children's depth and breadth of understanding, attitudes and appreciations, and basic skills. At times, teachers may use direct procedures such as having children draw conclusions or formulate generalizations; at other times indirect procedures may be used as noted in the examples below. In either instance, primary attention should be given to the development, clarification, and extension of the main idea.

Group discussion and evaluation of individual and committee reports prepared by the children

Writing and sharing summaries, digests, reviews, interpretations, and reports centered on main ideas, questions, or problems

Completing unfinished statements or stories

Engaging in debates, round-table discussions, and panel discussions

Taking and discussing tests containing items related to the main idea developed in the unit

How can authentic costumes and other realia be used to increase depth of understanding and appreciation? How might those shown in this picture be used in concluding activities? (Los Angeles)

Selecting and discussing pictures, maps, charts, and other items that highlight the main idea

Planning and putting on a skit, quiz program, puppet show, choral reading program

Planning demonstrations and presentations that focus on the main idea, problem, or question

Using a motion picture or a study trip as a basis for discussing relationships between activities, content, and the main idea or problem in the unit

Completing charts, maps, notebooks, scrapbooks, murals, or other items that are used to organize information around the main idea

Formulating generalizations based on information that has been summarized

Discussing likenesses and differences between the main idea under consideration and main ideas formulated during preceding activities or units

Evaluating depth and breadth of understanding through tests, checklists, discussion, self-evaluation, and other procedures

Culmination of a Unit. Culminating activities are used to summarize and organize the high points, main ideas, or major outcomes of a unit of instruction. To be stressed are relationships among main ideas or problems, appraisal of larger outcomes, review of major topics, synthesis of information around basic concepts, and sharing of key learnings. In some units that include a series of concluding activities related to each main idea or problem, little or no time may be given to the culmination of the unit. In other units, the culmination consists of a directed discussion of relationships to the next unit, and thus serves as an on-going activity from unit to unit. In still other units various possibilities are suggested for culminating the unit. In all instances, a teacher should ask himself such questions as the following to determine whether to have a culminating activity:

Will a culminating activity help to clarify relationships among main ideas or problems?

Will it contribute to children's ability to organize and share information around basic concepts and generalizations?

Will it provide for a review of fundamental learnings and contribute to evaluation of objectives set for the unit?

Will it provide additional learning opportunities for each child?

If a careful study of these questions indicates that a culminating activity *will* have real educational value for the group, then one should be used. However, if a culmination is to be used merely to "put on a show," then it will have little instructional value in terms of the objectives of the unit.

Listed below are examples of culminating activities that have been successfully used in different units. Notice that many of them are similar to concluding activities presented in the preceding section. The main differentiating feature is to be found in their breadth or scope. Culminating activities are more inclusive and draw together key learnings from the entire unit rather than from one major part of it.

Displaying pictures, maps, charts, objects, and other materials in arrangements that highlight main ideas or problems that have been investigated

Having children report main points related to each main idea or problem with emphasis on interrelationships

Presenting summary reports related to pictures arranged in sequence, or related to scenes depicted in a mural

Presenting a program or pageant in which songs, rhythms, folk dances, commentary, pictures, and other materials are used to highlight main ideas

Dramatizing major events, episodes, or activities studied during the unit

Having a round-table or panel discussion in which key points related to each main idea or problem are discussed

Having a quiz program in which the questions used relate to different main ideas or problems

Planning and taking a study trip to see a group at work; for example, city council meeting, state legislature

Putting on a mock meeting; for example, a New England town meeting, a city council meeting, a meeting of the UN

Deciding on the logical topic to study next and moving on to the next unit

Giving and discussing tests that include items on each main idea or problem included in the unit

Preparing summary sections of notebooks or scrapbooks

EVALUATION

Evaluating Outcomes. Evaluation is an essential process in all phases of the unit from the initiation through the culmination. Preplanning is as necessary for evaluation as it is for other instructional activities. The objectives of the unit should be kept in mind as children's learning is appraised in a variety of situations. Information obtained through evaluation should be used to improve daily planning, individual and group work, the selection of appropriate materials, the extension of concepts, the correction of errors, and the meeting of needs of individual children. At times, summaries may be made and filed or recorded in cumulative records. The entire process of evaluation should be seen as an inseparable part of learning experiences provided in the unit.

A variety of evaluative devices should be used to appraise different outcomes. Some devices are prepared as the unit progresses, for example, charts on work standards, informal rating devices for use in observation by the teacher, and checklists for the children to use in self-evaluation. Many devices may be prepared ahead of time even though some changes may have to be made in the light of changes that have been made in the unit. The following list is illustrative of devices or procedures that may be used (examples of test items are presented in the last chapter):

Objective tests	Reviewing files of each pupil's work
Essay tests	Teacher analysis of tape recordings
Teacher observation	Pupil analysis of tape recordings
Group discussion	Keeping logs or diaries, individual and group
Individual self-checking	Attitude and interest inventories
Checking by a partner	Anecdotal records on selected individuals
Checking of written work	Rating scales and checklists

Keeping a Log to Evaluate the Unit. An item that needs special comment is the keeping of a log by the teacher as the unit is developed. Teachers who have kept a log report that it is a great help in evaluating the unit, and for gathering ideas to use in revising the unit. A satisfactory log is a simple, brief, running account of the unit, that includes notes on strengths and weaknesses of instructional materials, changes to be made in learning experiences, and other ways in which the unit should be modified. Items may be jotted down during, or at the end of the day, and kept in a folder the same way anecdotal records are. After a main idea or major problem has been studied, related notes may be summarized and organized for future use. Periodic summaries of this type are helpful in noting needed changes and improvements while ideas are fresh in mind. A log may also suggest improvements to make in the series of learning experiences related to the next main idea or problem. After the culmination of the unit, notes related to all main ideas or problems should be brought together and used as a basis for revising the unit.

PREPARING AND COLLECTING MATERIALS

The teacher should prepare and collect as many materials as possible before the unit is initiated. Pictures, maps, pamphlets, models, art materials, construction materials, and certain audio-visual resources can be secured in advance. Materials that can be prepared include such items as charts, study guides, adult material rewritten on children's reading level, scrapbooks, check-lists, directions for processes, plans for construction, items for demonstrations, and evaluative devices. After materials are col-lected, they should be organized in a box or a file so that they are readily accessible for reference and use. The arrangement of the materials in the file may well be in the order in which they are expected to be used in the unit.

SUMMARY OF UNIT PLANNING

Although their order may vary, the following steps are essen-tial in the planning of units of instruction:

1. The unit is selected after a review of the course of study and a study of the capabilities and growth characteristics of the chil-dren for whom it is intended.

2. A rich background of experience is developed by the teacher through reading and annotating references, interviewing, visiting, trying out processes and experiments, making collections, previewing audio-visual materials, and reviewing units prepared by others.

3. An outline is made of objectives, main ideas or problems, related content, and related learning activities and materials.

4. The initiation or approach is planned.

5. Each main idea or problem is placed in sequence.

6. Related learning experiences are listed under each main idea or problem.

7. Ways of evaluating outcomes are noted.

8. A list of materials is prepared for both the children and the teacher.

9. Needed materials are prepared or obtained and organized in a box or file.

10. A simple plan is made for keeping a log of the unit.

The following checklist contains a summary of specific points in planning and reviewing units. The items included in it may be readily adapted to fit different patterns of unit organization.

CHECKLIST FOR UNITS OF INSTRUCTION

Title: _____Descriptive of a major area of study. _____Focused on a topic, problem, or theme.

Background Information: _____Indicative of content to be em-

phasized. _____Related to main ideas, problems, or questions. _____
Accurate and up to date.

Objectives: _____Related to purposes of the social studies.
_____Directly related to the unit topic. _____Terms, concepts, generalizations. _____Basic skills. _____Attitudes and appreciations.

Initiation: _____Focused on main idea or problem to be studied first. _____Outgrowth of the preceding unit. _____An arranged environment. _____Teacher suggestion. _____Current happening.
_____Community or audio-visual resources. _____Other._____

Main Ideas, Problems, or Questions: _____Main ideas identified as organizing centers for content and learning experiences.
_____Or, problems identified. _____Or, questions identified. _____
Arranged in a sequence.

Learning Experiences: _____Critically selected. _____Related to main ideas, problems, or questions. _____Related instructional materials noted. _____Arranged in a sequence as follows:

> *Openers:* _____To introduce each main idea, problem, or question. _____Different types suggested such as _____Recalling related earlier experiences. _____Examining and discussing related pictures and objects. _____Other._____
>
> *Developmental Activities:* _____Related to each main idea, problem, or question. _____Outgrowth of opening activities. _____Arranged in a problem-solving sequence. _____Varied activities suggested such as _____Reading. _____Independent study. _____Group work. _____Creative writing. _____Reporting. _____Dramatization. _____Rhythmic expression. _____Art. _____Music. _____Construction. _____Other.__
>
> _____
>
> *Concluding Activities:* _____Related to each main idea, problem, or question. _____Designed to lead to the development of generalizations. _____Different types suggested such as _____Completing charts. _____Sharing reports. _____Dramatization. _____Quiz program. _____Class newspaper. _____ Completing notebooks. _____Other._____
>
> *Culmination:* _____Needed to round out and summarize key learnings stressed throughout the entire unit. _____Provision for participation of each child. _____Contributory to evaluation of objectives set for the unit. _____Different possibilities suggested such as _____Leads to the next unit. _____Program. _____Pageant. _____Other._____

Instructional Materials: _____Critically selected. _____Related to each main idea, problem, or question. _____Different types suggested such as _____Books. _____Periodicals. _____Maps and globes. _____Community resources. _____Audio-visual materials. _____Art. _____Music. _____Construction. _____Demonstration. _____Other.

_____

Evaluation: _____Related to objectives. _____Made a part of experiences related to each main idea, problem, or question. _____

Different techniques suggested such as ____Tests. ____Charts. ____Checklists. ____Discussion. ____Observation. ____Other.

____

Bibliography: ____Materials for children listed. ____Background materials for teachers listed. ____Complete information given.

Where to Obtain Units of Instruction

A large number of preplanned units of instruction are available and they may be obtained from sources such as the following:

1. Units contained in local, county, and state courses of study
2. Units in libraries and curriculum laboratories in local, county, and state school libraries, and in libraries of colleges and universities
3. Short units in magazines, for example, *Grade Teacher, Instructor,* and *Junior Scholastic* (For a detailed list, check *Education Index* under the subheading "Units.")
4. Units published by commercial organizations:
   Compton's Pictured Encyclopedia, 1000 North Dearborn St., Chicago, Ill.
   Pan-American Airways, P.O. Box 1908, New York 17, N.Y.
   World Book Encyclopedia, Merchandise Mart, Chicago, Ill.
(For other examples, check the sources of information on free or inexpensive materials listed in Chapter 9.)
5. Hill, Wilhelmina, *Selected Resource Units,* Curriculum Series Number Eleven. Washington, D.C.: National Council for the Social Studies, National Education Association, 1961. (A collection of twenty-one units for Grades K–VI.)
6. Michaelis, John U., *Teaching Units Based on the Social Sciences.* Chicago: Rand McNally & Co., 1966. Three paperback volumes, one for Grades K–II, II–IV, & V–VI
7. Unit outlines presented in teacher's manuals accompanying social studies textbooks
8. Units contained in professional textbooks for teachers (see the references listed at the end of this chapter).

Questions, Activities, Evaluation

1. Obtain a unit of instruction from one of the sources noted above and do the following:
   a. Note the contents of each major section. Does the unit include the same general sections as noted in this chapter?
   b. Evaluate the unit in terms of the criteria presented in the first part of this chapter.

    c. Summarize the opening, developmental, and conclud-
ing activities that you believe to be most helpful.

    d. Note techniques of evaluation that are suggested.

    e. Note references that may be useful in your own fu-
ture planning.

2. Begin to make a plan for a unit of your choice. Include
ideas for each section of the unit. Review as many related instructional resources as time permits. Add to the unit as ideas
are obtained from subsequent chapters.

3. Prepare a kit, or box, of materials that can be used with
the unit you are planning. Include pictures, maps, free or inexpensive materials, songs, directions for arts and crafts, and other
resources.

4. Arrange to visit a classroom in which a unit of instruction of interest to you is in progress. Try to visit several times
in order to observe the initiation, subsequent activities, and the
culmination. Discuss questions that you would ask the teacher
in charge.

5. Check the section of this chapter that is titled "Relationships to Problem Solving" against the phases of problem solving
discussed in Chapter 4. Do other relationships exist between
activities in units and phases of problem solving that should be
stressed? What other activities might be included under each
phase of problem solving?

References

Burton, William H., *The Guidance of Learning Activities*, 3rd ed.,
Ch. 13, "The Unit," Ch. 14, "Planning and Developing Units,"
Ch. 15, "The Analysis of an Illustrative Unit." New York:
Appleton-Century-Crofts, Inc., 1962.

Fraser, Dorothy M., and Edith West, *Social Studies in Secondary
Schools*, Ch. 6, "Planning and Teaching a Unit," Appendix B,
Master Checklist of Activities. New York: The Ronald Press
Company, 1961.

Hanna, Lavone A., Gladys L. Potter, and Neva Hagaman, *Unit
Teaching in the Elementary School*, Ch. 5, "The Unit of Work,"
Ch. 6, "Developing a Unit of Work." New York: Holt, Rine-
hart & Winston, Inc., 1963.

Hansen, Henry R., and Lelia T. Ormsby, "Incorporating New Content in Units of Study," *Social Studies in Elementary Schools*,
32nd Yearbook, National Council for the Social Studies, pp.
270–84. Washington, D.C.: National Education Association,
1962. Principles and procedures for keeping the content of the
social studies program up to date.

Group Inquiry
and
Related Skills

The success of the social studies program depends on the teacher's skill in guiding group inquiry and in using various group techniques. The bulk of instruction in the social studies is provided in groups, and much of the child's independent study grows out of group activities. Various strategies are employed to bring together thinking processes, democratic values and behavior, and other facets of the instructional program. Concepts and methods of inquiry are woven together into workable patterns of group inquiry. Value conflicts are considered, and specific techniques of group work are put to extensive use.

Four critical aspects of group work are considered in this chapter. First, attention is given to values and limitations of group work. This is followed by a consideration of a model for guiding group inquiry. Next strategies and a model for dealing with values and value conflicts are presented. The last section includes suggestions for applying the group techniques most widely used in the social studies.

Values and Limitations of Group Work

VALUES OF GROUP WORK

Well-directed group work may be used to improve individual and group study. More effective learning may be secured by having a group of children discuss, evaluate, challenge, revise, and share ideas, suggestions, activities, and problems. Concepts can be clarified, hypotheses can be stated, generalizations can be formulated, and higher levels of thinking can be reached. Motivation can be secured and directed toward the attainment of worthwhile objectives. Feelings of belongingness, security, acceptance, respect, and mutual trust can be developed. Study can be more productive as the best thinking of individuals in the class is tapped. A constructive and experimental approach to learning can be nurtured, and the excitement of discovering and sharing ideas with the group can increase the depth and breadth of children's learning. Democratic attitudes and behavior patterns such as open-mindedness, responsibleness, creativeness, concern for others, and cooperativeness can also be developed.

LIMITATIONS

Teachers should know the limitations as well as the values of group work. First, the use of group work should be limited to activities which have some purpose that can be shared by members of the group. Without commonly shared purposes, individuals in the group will waste time and derive little or no benefit from the activity. Second, group work should be limited to activities in which children possess or can be taught the skills needed to carry out the group activity. If children are to benefit from such activities as panel discussion and committee work, for example, they must possess certain skills, which are noted later. Third, group work should be limited to activities in which cooperative action is needed to achieve stated purposes. If an activity can be completed by an individual, or by several individuals working independently, there is no need to organize a working group. Fourth, group work should be limited to activities in which effective working relationships can be maintained. If interpersonal conflicts and differences in points of view cannot be reconciled, progress cannot be made by forcing individuals to work in a group. Fifth, group work should be limited to situations in which the diverse talents of children can be put to use. If each child is required to do the same thing in an activity, individual differences will be neglected and unique contributions will not be obtained from each child. Principles and procedures that teachers may use in dealing with these limitations and in achieving the values of group work are presented in the following sections of this chapter.

A Problem-Solving Model for Group Inquiry

A problem-solving model is used in nearly all well-designed social studies programs. Most models are based on phases of inquiry, discussed in Chapter 4, and processes of thinking, discussed in Chapter 3. They are used flexibly and adapted to meet a variety of situations that arise in the social studies, ranging from problems of immediate concern to the group to the systematic study of an area such as Latin America.

Of all the models of problem solving reviewed by the author, the following, which contains the key phases of effective inquiry, has been found to be the most useful:

1. Clarifying and defining questions and problems
2. Recalling relevant information and proposing solutions
3. Group planning of ways to solve problems, obtain answers to questions, or test hypotheses
4. Locating, appraising, and selecting information
5. Organizing and summarizing information
6. Interpreting information and forming generalizations
7. Evaluating processes and outcomes

Let us now consider each of the major phases of this model to illustrate how it is used in group inquiry in the social studies.

CLARIFYING AND DEFINING QUESTIONS AND PROBLEMS

This is the first step as new units are introduced and as different problems arise in a unit that is under way. The purpose here is to get pupils to recognize and understand the problems or questions to be studied. During the initiation of a unit, selected materials may be used to stimulate children's thinking. Pictures, maps, objects, and other resources may be arranged to highlight significant questions or problems. After the children have examined the materials, there should be a discussion to decide which questions or problems are to be attacked first. And, to direct children's thinking toward the most significant aspects of the unit, teachers should supplement class comments and suggestions with questions and comments of their own.[1]

After first problems are defined and clarified, they may be listed on the chalkboard or on charts as illustrated in Charts 1–3.

---

[1] Other procedures for use in introducing units are presented in Chapter 7.

WORK AT HOME	EARLY TIMES IN OUR COMMUNITY
What does mother do? What does father do? What can children do? What do others do?	Who were the first settlers? What were the first buildings like? Where was the first school? Where were the first streets? When was the railroad begun? What changes have taken place?

Chart 1

BOONESBORO
Why was it built? Who built it? Where was it? When was it built? How was it built? How did people travel to it?

Chart 2   Chart 3

Recognition and clarification of problems are not emphasized only at the beginning of units of instruction. As the unit progresses, new problems and questions need to be identified and clarified. Each unit should become a series of problem-solving experiences with a smooth transition from one problem to the next. For example, moving from the work of members of the family on to how the family obtains food calls for a definition of new questions and problems. Similarly, in units on Our Community, Our State, Westward Movement, and Other Lands, a series of specific questions and problems should be defined with one growing out of another. To expect children to outline all of them at the very beginning of a unit is asking too much. As noted in Chapter 7, a series of questions and problems or main ideas should be included in each unit along with related activities and materials. This practice is consistent with what is known about thinking-learning processes and enables the teacher to plan ahead so that problems, materials, and learning experiences will be related.

RECALLING RELEVANT INFORMATION AND PROPOSING SOLUTIONS

This phase of the problem-solving approach should be creative and spark children's thinking. Previous learning plus information

How might such a display be used to stimulate inquiry? What questions and problems might be summarized and used to guide later study? *(Alameda County)*

introduced during the initiation of the unit, or as a part of it in the case of subsequent problems, is brought to bear on questions or problems that have been listed for study. A teacher could ask such questions as these: What do you think? What ideas do you have on this? What do you think we will find? What have you learned in other units that may apply here? The purpose of such questions is to draw on the children's backgrounds of understanding, to elicit proposals that may be investigated, to detect misconceptions and erroneous ideas, and to clarify needs for additional information.

In some instances, a class may not have an informational basis for suggesting tentative solutions or proposals and, therefore, should list specific questions to guide their search for information. In most instances, however, children come forth with proposals and hypotheses that can be checked through further study and investigation. In either case, whether proposals or specific questions are listed, the excitement of discovery is added, and children have questions or proposals to direct their thinking. As Bruner has indicated,[2] the discovery method can be used in the social studies as well as in science and mathematics education. After citing an example in which children proposed hypotheses

[2] Jerome S. Bruner, *The Process of Education* (Cambridge: Harvard University Press, 1960), pp. 21–22.

related to the location of a city, Bruner noted that they showed greater interest and a higher level of conceptual sophistication than did children in other classes in which no hypotheses were formulated.

Teachers sometimes ask whether tentative answers or hypotheses should be proposed for every problem that arises in the social studies. No! In some instances the best procedure is to attack a question or problem, solve it, and move on to others. But, if a review of related information and the stating of proposals to sharpen thinking are clearly needed, then this should be done. Each unit of instruction offers many opportunities for this. Opportunities arise in connection with narrative and descriptive content that is to be interpreted, as well as with procedural problems related to map making, dramatic activities, expressing ideas creatively through various media, and other activities. Because this is a neglected phase of the problem-solving approach, the following examples are included to illustrate the nature of children's proposals or hypotheses in different units of work.

In a unit on The Home, a procedural problem arose: How can we get furniture for our playhouse? The children's suggestions were: "Maybe the custodian has some. We can bring some from home. We can make some. We will need help to make some."

In a unit on the Post Office, the question was: What happens to the letters that are put in mail boxes? The children's comments were: "They are picked up by a mailman and delivered to the right place. They are picked up by a mail truck and taken downtown. The letters are sorted by workers in the main post office. Each mailman takes the letters that go to places on his route."

In a unit on Living in Early America, the problem of securing clothing was being considered, and the class had discovered that flax sometimes was used to make clothing. The specific question was: How did the early settlers make clothing out of flax? The children suggested the following: "The flax was pounded and cut into strips. The flax was dried and then shredded. The flax was soaked and then pressed flat. After it dried, it was ripped into thin strips. The outer layer was scraped off and the stringy fibers were pulled apart."

In a unit on Westward Movement, this problem on travel routes was posed for the children to consider: Check the relief map of the United States and plan a route to California from St. Joseph, Missouri. Then check to see if your proposed route is the same as one of those used by early settlers. The children made the following proposals and comments: "(1) Go straight across the plains and mountains to San Francisco. If you go this way, you would have to find mountain passes through the Rockies and Sierras. (2) Go along the Missouri to the Platte River and on to the coast across Utah and Nevada. If you would keep close to rivers, you could get water and there would not be many steep grades. I heard that some railroads and highways are built along water level routes. (3) Go along south to Santa Fe and on to Los Angeles across New Mexico and Nevada. This would be a good route in the winter. (4) Why couldn't we start our trip in St. Louis? Then we could use boats all the way to San Francisco."

In all of these examples, the teacher was guiding the children to draw on previous learning in order to propose tentative solutions or hypotheses. Creative thinking was involved as the children tried to relate past experiences to new problems. Divergent thinking was involved as they made multiple suggestions and considered different proposals. Critical thinking was involved as they evaluated the proposals and ideas suggested in support of them. Suspended judgment was emphasized and needs for additional information were established. The question or problem was further elaborated and clarified, and the stage was set for group planning of ways to solve the problem.

GROUP PLANNING

Closely tied to the preceding phase, the group-planning phase often provides clues both to tentative solutions and hypotheses, and to the best ways to proceed. Ways to gather information, possible sources of information, and assignment of responsibili-

SOURCES OF INFORMATION		PROCEDURES TO USE	
Textbooks	Pictures	Reading	Drawing
Clippings	Films	Note taking	Mapping
Magazines	Filmstrips	Observing	Processing
Newspapers	Slides	Collecting	Constructing
Maps and	Study trips	Demonstrat-	Writing for
globes	Visitors	ing	information
Encyclo-	The library	Experiment-	Outlining
pedias	Find others	ing	Find others
		Interviewing	

Chart 4   Chart 5

ties are considered. Questions such as the following are raised: How shall we proceed? What are the next steps? How can we obtain needed information? What sources of information should be used? Should any jobs be assigned to individuals or small groups? Does everyone know just what he has to do? Attention may be given to a wide range of sources and procedures, as is noted in Charts 4 and 5. A careful selection is made of the best possibilities, and children are urged to be on the lookout for others.

LOCATING, APPRAISING, AND SELECTING INFORMATION

With the plans in mind, each pupil proceeds to gather information related to the specific questions, problems, or hypotheses that have been listed. Study skills are put to use to collect data, and critical reading skills are employed to appraise and select information related to each question. Different sources of in-

SELECTING
INFORMATION

Is it related to the problem?
Can it be used to support or reject proposed solutions?
Is it information that we do not have?
Does it explain new terms?
Does it help to clear up ideas?

Chart 6

CHECKING
INFORMATION

Check one source against another.
Check facts and figures by comparing notes with the original reference.
Compare ideas presented in films and in books.
Read it a second time if doubt exists about what was said.

Chart 7

formation are checked. Double-checking may be necessary if differences are noted in statements, or if doubt exists as to the accuracy of information. At times it may be necessary to reshow a film, reread a section of a reference, check one reference against another, or interview an expert in order to resolve a difference in fact or opinion. Charts 6 and 7 show the points that are emphasized during this phase of inquiry.

ORGANIZING AND SUMMARIZING INFORMATION

This phase begins during group planning, continues as children collect data, and is completed after needed information has been gathered. Organization and summarization help the class to interpret, present, share, and use information as a basis for generalization. Such questions as these may be used in group discussion: How should we organize our findings? What ways of presenting information will be most effective? Should we use a chart? Should we make a scrapbook? How about a mural or a display? What about bulletin-board arrangement? Which are best for our purposes? Are there any other suggestions?

Critical thinking skills can be effectively used as children consider different possibilities. If directions or steps for carrying out a process or making something are needed, they may be listed on a chart, the chalkboard, or work sheets. If relationships between physical and man-made surface features are to be shown, then a floor layout or arrangement of objects on a map on a table may be used. If major activities during historical periods are to be shown, then a mural, time line, or sequence chart may

Here is one way to organize and summarize ideas. What others might be used? *(Lew Merrim; Courtesy of Monkmeyer)*

HOW SHOULD WE ORGANIZE AND SHARE INFORMATION?		
Discussion	Floor layouts	Dramatization
Oral reports	Table arrangements	Movie box roll
Written reports	Exhibits	Demonstrations
Scrapbooks	Pictures	Quiz games
Charts	Murals	Radio or TV programs
Maps	Diagrams	Rhythmic expression
Displays	Graphs	Musical expression
Models	Construction	Art media

Chart 8

be made. An outline, a summary of notes, or simply sharing ideas through discussion may be adequate for other purposes. At times, different suggestions may be tried out and evaluated. The important point is to guide children so that they develop increasing understanding and skill in organizing information in ways that will facilitate meaningful interpretation.

INTERPRETING INFORMATION AND FORMING GENERALIZATIONS

In this phase of group inquiry, original questions, proposals, and collected information are considered in order to make interpretations, note limitations, and form generalizations. Interpretation involves a consideration of the meaning and significance of data. Is the meaning of the data clear? Can certain ideas be related to others? What cause-effect relationships can be discovered? How can various ideas be put to use? The class may consider limitations such as needs for additional information, controversial points still not resolved, information that is based primarily on opinion, and points of disagreement in sources of information. At times the class may change or discard original proposals and hunches and search for additional information. If available data appear to be adequate, the children may make and check tentative conclusions. The forming and checking of conclusions involve such processes as relating information to each question or proposal, stating a conclusion that is consistent with available information, and checking conclusions with others. If tentative conclusions do not check out, the teacher must emphasize suspended judgment and help the class to find ways to gather additional data.

In order to illustrate this phase of inquiry the following examples are presented. In a unit on The Growth of Our Community, one group of children made the following interpretations and generalizations.

1. The growth of population was slow at first. It speeded up after 1946. Many houses have been built since then. New businesses also have come to town. As more people move here, more homes and businesses will be needed.

2. In early days there was only one road through town with a few side streets. Now we have many streets and a new superhighway between our community and others. New streets are being laid out in sections where new houses are being built. More streets and roads will be needed as more people move here.

3. The first school had only one room for all grades. As more people moved here, more schools were built. Now we have schools for 15,000 pupils. In eighty years the number of pupils increased from twenty to 15,000. Eighty years is about ten times longer than our average age. More schools are to be built in the area where new houses are being built.

4. Generalizations were made as follows:
   a. Schools, stores, roads, and many other things have changed in our community.
   b. Changes have been faster in recent years.
   c. More changes will occur in the future.
   d. Some changes were made because many people moved here.
   e. Some changes were made because of inventions and better ways of building houses, roads, and doing other things.

The next examples illustrate the interpretation of information and the forming of generalizations that involved a series of relationships, a type of analysis that is often used in the social studies. The examples are drawn from a unit on conservation in which the class had concentrated on problems of flood control. In interpreting information, attention was given to the following:

1. Clarification of the importance of watersheds in preventing floods

2. Ways to prevent flooding, for example, dams, levees, terracing and contour plowing

3. Relationships between floods and surface features, land use, river systems, and weather conditions

4. The effects of floods on land, property, and human activities

5. The significance of planting trees and grasses in certain areas to hold the topsoil

6. The relationship between building dams and hydroelectric power

7. Among the generalizations made by the group were the following:

    a. How man uses the land is an important factor in flood control.

    b. Conservation of resources and flood control are related in many ways.

    c. Some of the things that are done to prevent floods also help to improve agriculture and industry.

EVALUATING PROCESSES AND OUTCOMES

Evaluation is a continuing phase of group inquiry that begins with the definition of the problem and moves right on through to the forming of generalizations and final appraisal of the effectiveness of individual and group work. During each phase of the problem-solving approach attention is given to evaluation. During the definition of problems, for example, the teacher may ask: Is the problem clear? Have main parts of the problem been considered? Or, during the planning phase: Have good sources of information been noted? Does each individual know what he is to do? Similarly, during the organization of information: Are facts related to main ideas? Are relationships shown? Have we selected the best means of summarizing information? By getting clues through the observation of children at work, the teacher raises questions and makes comments that help children to appraise and to improve the skills and processes used in the problem-solving approach.

In addition to the on-going evaluation that is part of daily activities, attention may be given to periodic and systematic appraisal of various aspects of children's thinking and learning. Teachers may use tests to check children's grasp of vocabulary, concepts, basic information, reading skills, and study skills. Charts, checklists, and other devices may be used to appraise work habits, use of materials, discussion techniques, committee work, outlines, reports, maps, and other activities and products. Charts 9, 10, and 11 are illustrative. Both self-evaluation and teacher appraisal are used to improve the attitudes, skills, and understandings that are essential to effective thinking. A detailed discussion of principles and procedures of evaluation is presented in Chapter 18.

Teachers should be able to recognize certain common errors

APPRAISING SOURCES OF IDEAS	JUDGING FACTS AND OPINIONS	APPRAISING TALKS AND REPORTS
Is it related to the topic? Is it recent enough for our purpose? Is it reliable? Valid? Is it published by a special interest group? Does it contain enough information? Can it be checked against reliable sources?	Is it related to our questions? Is the source reliable? Is it consistent with related ideas? Is it supported by evidence? Is it too general to be useful? Is it advanced for a worthy cause?	Is the title descriptive of the topic? Does the introduction set the stage? Are the ideas in good order? Are main ideas supported by facts? Are opinions distinguished from facts? Do conclusions tie ideas together?

Chart 9   Chart 10   Chart 11

and difficulties in thinking as they evaluate children's work, and a knowledge of them is useful in planning as well as in evaluation. A basic teaching principle would be to give attention to them as they arise in children's thinking since it seems valueless to consider them out of the context of children's experiences. Among the more common errors in thinking are confusing the real and the fanciful, mixing facts and opinions, generalizing in terms of purely personal experience or from just a single instance, taking an "either-or" position when clear-cut alternatives do not exist, failing to check information, making errors in observation, organizing ideas to favor a point of view, and failing to consider consequences.

Young children tend to be egocentric and to state problems, select ideas, and make conclusions in terms of their personal interests and wishes. They may jump to conclusions, think that one thing causes another because they happened together, and, failing to see degrees and shades of difference, judge in terms of absolutes. They may make interpretations and conclusions on the basis of what "I saw," "I heard," "I like," or "I want." They have difficulty in handling abstract ideas and relationships (particularly cause-effect relationships), making generalizations, reasoning from the general to the particular, and thinking in terms of different points of view. Development of thinking abilities appears to proceed from the concrete to the abstract, from the simple to the more complex, and from the specific to the more general.

As children gain in experience and begin to develop a "we" feeling, they give increasing attention to the views of others. They also discriminate parts from the whole more effectively, abstract and generalize more easily, and grasp more involved cause-effect relationships. After they have identified errors and difficulties in their own thinking and problem-solving activities, they need experience in applying what they have learned to new situations. Charts 12 and 13 illustrate points that may be given direct attention in discussion and used both in self-evaluation and in teacher appraisal.

LOOK OUT FOR THESE ERRORS IN THINKING	DID YOU REMEMBER TO DO EACH OF THESE?
Mixing up the real and fanciful. Believing that there is only one way to do it. Thinking that one example "proves the rule." Confusing facts and opinions. Believing that one thing caused another because they happened together. Letting our feelings hide some of the facts. Can you find others?	Get facts on all sides of the question. Check facts from different sources. Summarize information so that it is clear and easy to use. Check the meaning of terms and phrases that are not clear. Compare your findings with others. Make tentative conclusions that can be checked.
Chart 12	Chart 13

Group-Work Techniques

Certain techniques are widely used to promote group inquiry in each unit of instruction. Most important from the teacher's point of view are grouping techniques, and strategies for guiding committee work, group planning, discussion, group activities, and group evaluation. All group techniques should be viewed as integral parts of group inquiry so that inquiry will have an on-going quality that blends the various elements into a smooth flow of related experiences.

FUNCTIONAL GROUPING

Various kinds and sizes of groups are used in the social studies depending on the problems to be solved, available space, equipment and materials, and needs discovered in planning. The entire group should work together during such experiences as planning, taking study trips, using audio-visual materials, sharing reports, and evaluation. Small groups may be used during such experiences as making a mural, writing script for a play, writing letters, making a wall map, or doing research on a topic. Small groups of this type provide many opportunities for developing leadership and followership qualities. At other times, small groups may be organized to provide help on special needs, such as reading, outlining, use of tools, or interviewing. Finally, individual responsibilities may be delegated, such as research on a special topic, preparation of a report, interviewing an expert, making a loom, or designing a costume.

Grouping can be facilitated by working out room arrangements to accommodate groups of different size. If movable classroom furniture is provided, arrangements can be changed as special needs arise. The suggested arrangements on pages 254–255 are illustrative of those that provide a high degree of flexibility.

COMMITTEES

In forming small groups or committees, attention should be given to several factors. The chairman may be selected by the group or the teacher after due consideration of needed qualifications. Clear plans should be formulated and checked before the beginning of committee work. The committee should be composed of a congenial working group that is interested in the job to be done and balanced in terms of needed abilities and talents. Provision should be made for needed materials, adequate working space, and sufficient time to make an effective beginning or to complete the job. Work standards should be developed beforehand and used by the committee as responsibilities are carried out.

Each committee member should know what to do so that confusion and excessive noise can be avoided. Many teachers give a demonstration of good committee work after real needs have arisen for guidance. This can be done by selecting a group to demonstrate for the class, or by using the class as a committee with the teacher as chairman. Standards should be developed and placed on the chalkboard or on charts as real needs for standards are sensed by members of the class. Charts 14, 15, and 16 are illustrative.

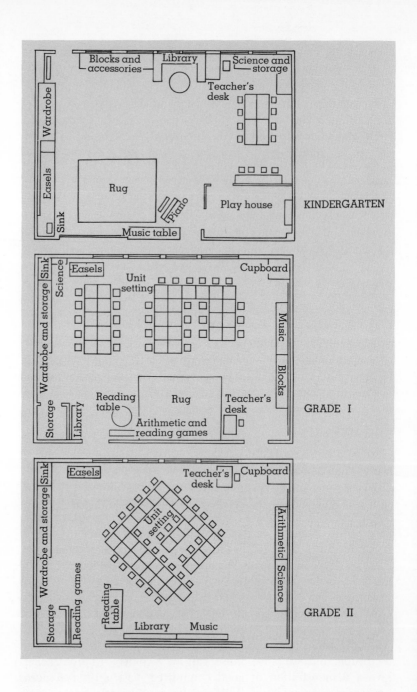

Suggested room arrangements. *(Source: Curriculum Guide for the Elementary Schools, p. 7. Pasadena: City Schools)*

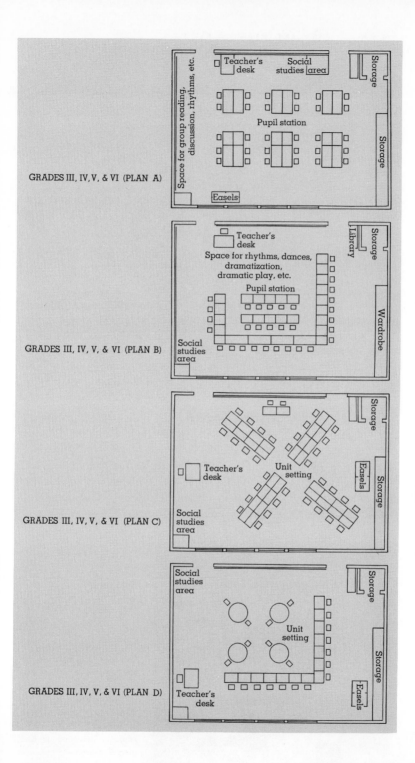

GRADES III, IV, V, & VI (PLAN A)

Teacher's desk

Social studies area

Storage

Storage

Space for group reading, discussion, rhythms, etc.

Pupil station

Easels

GRADES III, IV, V, & VI (PLAN B)

Teacher's desk

Storage

Library

Space for rhythms, dances, dramatization, dramatic play, etc.

Pupil station

Wardrobe

Social studies area

GRADES III, IV, V, & VI (PLAN C)

Storage

Teacher's desk

Unit setting

Easels

Social studies area

Storage

GRADES III, IV, V, & VI (PLAN D)

Social studies area

Storage

Unit setting

Storage

Teacher's desk

Easels

255

COMMITTEE MEMBERS

1. Know what to do.
2. Divide the work.
3. Do each job well.
4. Discuss problems quietly.
5. Plan the report carefully.

Chart 14

COMMITTEE CHAIRMEN

1. Keep the main job in mind.
2. Get ideas from all members.
3. See that each member has a job.
4. Be fair and do not talk all the time.
5. Urge everyone to do his best.
6. Say *our* committee, not *my* committee.

Chart 16

COMMITTEE REPORTS

1. Stick to the questions.
2. Use pictures, objects, and maps.
3. Be ready to answer questions.

Chart 15

As established committees proceed with their work, the teacher should move from committee to committee. Guidance should be given as needed; points should be noted for use in evaluation; suggestions for improving reports by using pictures, charts, maps, and the like should be offered; and the interest and seriousness of each child in being a good committee worker should be noticed and commended. Through careful observation and direct

Committee reports can be made more effective and more interesting through the use of charts and other media. In what ways may other resources be used to improve reporting in the group? (Burbank)

guidance as committees work, the teacher can bring about rapid growth in group work skills. And this is really what is needed: competence in significant group activities set up to achieve vital purposes!

DISCUSSION

Discussion is one of the most valuable techniques used in group work. Its use is essential to effective clarification of goals, planning, and evaluation. Discussion provides a practical opportunity to set purposes, state hypotheses, raise questions, and appraise various experiences in the social studies. Social amenities are put to practical use, critical thinking is sharpened, and attention is focused on common problems. Ideas are shared, points of view are expressed, leaders are selected, responsibilities are delegated, and respect is shown for the right of others to express themselves. Discussion is truly an essential technique of democratic education.

Group discussion provides opportunities for the teacher to note children's behavior, attitudes, and abilities to express ideas. Creativeness of contributions, sharing of ideas, respect for the opinions of others, consideration of differing points of view, shyness, boldness, and the like can be observed and given attention as individual needs arise. Many teachers find discussion situations to be a most valuable source of information regarding children's needs, potentialities, and backgrounds.

The teacher's role in group discussion is of crucial importance. A supportive atmosphere is essential so that each child will feel that his contributions are valued by the teacher and the group. Shy children should be given encouragement, and children who tend to monopolize the discussion should be guided in learning to share discussion time with others. The major problem to be discussed should be clarified and kept in mind throughout. Questions, illustrations, and comments should be called for as particular items need clarification. Adequate time must be given for thinking about points that are made and questions that are raised. To be avoided are such pitfalls as not sticking to the point, failure to clarify the problem, waste of time on side issues, repetitious comments, embarrassment of participants because of rejection of contributions, omission of key ideas, and domination of the discussion by a few individuals. If a summary of the discussion is essential, it may be recorded on the chalkboard or on a chart for use by the group. The spirit of group discussions should always be one of mutual interest and helpfulness. Emphasis should be given to the development of a feeling typified

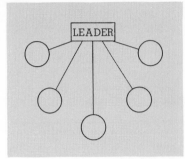

Chart 17

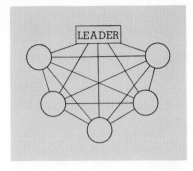

Chart 18

by such expressions as "Let's talk it over," "What's the best thing to do?" and "How shall we proceed?" At no time should the mechanics, techniques, or evaluation of discussion interfere with the development and maintenance of fine group feelings and constructive approaches to learning.

A point needing emphasis is the role of the teacher (or discussion leader) in securing maximum participation of members of the group. Too often, discussion is merely a conversation between the teacher and individuals in the group. For example, the teacher raises a question and gets a response; the teacher responds and another child contributes; this is followed by a rhythm of teacher to child to teacher to child, and so on, with the teacher

DISCUSSION LEADERS	GROUP SHARING	SMALL DISCUSSION GROUPS
1. Call the group to order. 2. Clear up the problem. 3. Get ideas from the group. 4. Have the secretary keep notes. 5. Call on different children. 6. Stick to the point. 7. Get answers to questions from the group. 8. Summarize the discussion.	We share pictures, stories, and other items related to our unit. We hold objects so that all can see them. We speak clearly so all can hear. We watch and listen courteously. We take turns and use only our share of the time.	Each group has a topic or question to discuss. Each group includes four to six pupils. Seats are arranged so that each member of the group can see the others. The chairman opens the discussion. The recorder keeps notes and reports back to the class.

Chart 19

Chart 20

Chart 21

PANEL DISCUSSION

The members of the panel sit in a half circle facing the class.

The chairman presents the topic for discussion.

Each panel member presents his part of the discussion.

Members of the class take notes on questions to raise.

The chairman asks for questions after the panel members report.

The chairman has panel members answer the questions.

The chairman makes a summary of the discussion.

Chart 22

GROUP REPORTS

The topic is broken into subtopics.

Each member of the group prepares a report on a subtopic.

Each report is reviewed to avoid repetition.

The length of time for each report is decided.

Questions that may be raised are considered.

Maps, pictures, and other materials are selected to illustrate reports.

The reports are given according to the plan, and questions are discussed.

Chart 23

making 90 to 95 per cent of the contributions. In sharp contrast is the situation in which the teacher makes a contribution and several children make comments before the teacher or the leader intervenes. Charts 17 and 18 illustrate this point. The rectangle represents the teacher (or leader) and the circles represent the participants. The lines indicate the flow of discussion from one individual to another. Chart 17 illustrates teacher (or leader) domination; Chart 18 illustrates group interaction.

Sometimes children should lead the discussion, particularly in intermediate and upper grades. When this is done, attention must be given beforehand to the development of guidelines for leading the discussion. Chart 19 shows guidelines which were developed by a group in Grade V in order to meet problems that had arisen.

Discussion takes a variety of forms and may be improved through the use of special reports and small-group techniques. Group sharing of experiences and objects, group reports on special topics, and panel presentations are used in many units in the social studies. Small discussion groups, sometimes called "buzz sessions," also may be used at times to summarize ideas on specific questions or topics. Charts 20–23 illustrate standards and guidelines that have been used successfully with children.

DISCUSSION

1. Take turns.
2. Help make plans.
3. Listen to others.

Primary

Chart 24

DISCUSSION

1. Help state your problem.
2. Give your ideas.
3. Consider other ideas.
4. Listen carefully.
5. Help to make a plan.

Intermediate

Chart 25

DISCUSSION

1. State problems clearly.

2. Stick to the point.

3. Respect ideas of others.

4. Make a contribution.

5. Weigh the evidence.

6. Raise questions on issues.

7. Help in making decisions.

8. Help in summarizing.

Upper

Chart 26

Evaluation of discussion should be carried on by both the teacher and the group with specific attention given to points and problems that have arisen. The teacher should keep in mind both the essential elements of effective discussion and the maturity of the children. The discussion itself can be appraised in terms of the items listed on Charts 24–26 and in Checklist 1, page 261.

The maturity of the group is an essential consideration in guiding and evaluating group discussion. Charts, checklists, and group evaluation should take levels of growth into account. Charts 12–14 show how adaptations can be made to groups at various stages of development.

In addition to evaluation carried on by the group, the teacher must consider each child's role in discussion so that effective planning and guidance can be carried out. The checklist in Fig. 8-2 suggests several points to keep in mind as each child's growth in discussion ability is considered. Others may be added or some may be deleted, depending on the maturity of the group and the specific needs requiring attention.

GROWTH IN DISCUSSION

Note: Check each child two or three times during the term
to see if growth is taking place.

Behaviors to Be Checked	Names of Children				
Understands the problem					
Listens while others speak					
Is an interested and willing listener					
Interjects ideas at appropriate points					
Considers ideas contrary to his own					
Sticks to the topic					
Does not repeat ideas given by others					
Gets to the point without delay					
Speaks clearly and distinctly					
Uses appropriate language					
Uses concepts accurately					
Is interested in comments of others					

Checklist 1

GROUP PLANNING

Group planning of ways to achieve goals is essential in democratic group action. How to solve a problem, what to do next, and delegation of responsibilities are key aspects of planning. Many ideas and procedures are suggested as children formulate goals and purposes. Others emerge as the children define the problem, decide what materials are needed, raise questions, discover difficulties, try out various proposals, and evaluate progress. Out of planning discussions are developed the specific procedures and responsibilities essential to the achievement of group-made goals.

In guiding group planning, cooperative procedures should be used. All members of the group should participate, and the unique contributions of each individual should be sought. Needs and purposes that have grown out of group activity should be given attention. Suggestions regarding needed information and material should be considered and evaluated by the group. Work standards, individual responsibilities, and small-group responsibilities should be discussed and agreed upon. Differences of opinion need consideration, and efforts should be made to secure a consensus. Experimentation may require consideration if two or more procedures of equivalent worth are proposed. Records, such as charts, notes, directions, and minutes, should be kept as needed to guide activities.

Planning and replanning as new problems arise are features of effective group work. Initial planning is carried out in group discussion, with special attention to questions, problems, and responsibilities. Replanning is necessary as new needs arise and as special problems are presented for consideration. Both initial planning and replanning should involve more than a search for sources of information. For example, attention may well be given to such items as formulating problems, devising ways to secure data, setting up work standards, deciding on things to construct, considering ways to secure and use materials, overcoming obstacles, helping others, extending interests, investigating proposals, submitting suggestions, asking for help, and finding out about opinions and ideas of others. Planning is also essential in getting ready for research activities, construction, dramatic play, processing of materials, field trips, and creative expression through art, music, literature, and rhythms.

In guiding group planning, teachers should keep the following principles in mind:

1. All should share in planning so that the best ideas of each member of the group are brought to bear upon the problem.
2. Problems and questions expressed by the children should receive major attention. Problems neglected by the children can be pointed out by the teacher.
3. The teacher should create a feeling of freedom and responsiveness by showing utmost respect for each child and his contributions.
4. Constructive suggestions should be secured from the group; negative comments should be redirected into positive suggestions.
5. Techniques of clear thinking are essential; examples of these techniques are: getting the problem clearly in mind, hearing

all suggestions, accepting best suggestions, forming tentative conclusions, determining needs for additional information and sources of information, and basing plans of action on sound conclusions.

6. The teacher, or leader, should participate actively to guide planning and should give help when encouragement is needed, impasses are reached, or too difficult problems arise.

7. Standards for planning should be developed and used as needs arise.

8. Records should be made and kept as needed to further group action; examples are charts, directions, reading guides, work sheets, notes, and minutes.

9. Group decisions growing out of planning should lead to specific plans of action.

10. Group planning is effective when each child understands what he is to do, knows where he is to do it, knows what tools and materials he is to use, knows how to proceed with his work, understands group-made standards, knows where to get help if problems arise, and knows with whom he is to work.

GROUP ACTIVITIES

Group activities growing out of planning are most effective when each individual carries out his responsibilities in line with group purposes. After planning is completed, individual and small-group responsibilities should be accepted and carried out with dispatch. A willingness to help others and to secure help when needed is essential. Each individual should work as a member of the group, hold to plans, try to understand the role of others, and control his behavior with reference to established goals. Available time and materials should be used wisely and in accordance with group plans.

As children engage in group activities, the teacher should observe carefully in order to get information for use in group evaluation. Attention should be given to acceptance of responsibilities, cooperation, courtesy, and self-control. Attention should also be given to the various materials that are being used, techniques that need to be improved, and misconceptions, erroneous ideas, and errors that arise.

As children engage in group work the teacher has many opportunities to move about and to give help as needed. A child may be having difficulty in locating material in a given reference, or some children may be having difficulty using tools and materials. By giving judicious assistance, the teacher can make sure that effective learning takes place. For example, in a unit on Pioneer Life, one teacher noticed during a research period that several youngsters were having difficulty in using the table of contents. Others were not sure of the topics to locate in the index. Notes were made of these items, and they became important problems in a later discussion that centered on skills involved in the location of materials. Another example can be taken from a construction period in which model covered wagons were being made. The teacher noticed that several children were not holding the saws correctly, some were not using the C-clamps to hold boards properly, and others were having difficulty in selecting appropriate materials. The teacher moved about the room and gave suggestions as such needs were detected. By giving help at a point of real need, richer learning was possible for each child.

Notice the concepts from economics being used in this group discussion. How might you extend the development of key concepts through group activities? *(San Diego City Schools)*

The way children use the work standards which they have helped to set should also be noted by the teacher. Commendation should be given to those children who are carrying out group-made standards and who help others to do so. In some cases, the teacher may have to ask a child to stop an activity for a few minutes until he has thought through the significance of group standards with reference to his own behavior. In a few instances, some children must be excluded from the group until they realize that they must accept all of the responsibilities involved in the activity. Following the work period, time should be given to a careful reconsideration of the group standards and ways in which they can be used by each member of the group.

Particular attention must be given to those few youngsters who appear to be at a loss as to just what they should do in an activity. If the planning period has been carefully organized, very few children will not have clear purposes in mind. During the work period, be it research, dramatic play, or construction, the teacher may need to give further guidance to children who do not have clear purposes in mind. Frequently, children in the room volunteer to help others who are not sure what they should do to complete an activity. This is a good indication of cooperative behavior and should be encouraged by the teacher. However, careful planning at the beginning of the work period is the most effective technique to use in order to assure active participation on the part of all members of the group.

The ways members of the group use materials should also be noted. Courtesy and sharing, taking turns, proper use of tools, proper selection of material, and the ways children help others use materials are of particular importance. Toward the end of the work period, materials and equipment should be put in their proper places. Careful attention should also be given to the clean-up period and placement of materials in cupboards. The learnings that grow out of the proper care of materials should not be neglected in group work.

GROUP EVALUATION

Group evaluation is an essential element in all phases of democratic group action—from initial definition of problems to appraisal of the effectiveness of group work. During evaluation, the group answers such questions as: Is each individual doing his part? Are the plans effective? Are leadership responsibilities being carried out? Are our goals being achieved? Are additional resources needed? What next steps should be taken? In making appraisals, the group may use discussions and charts or checklists, refer to a log or diary of activities, get assistance from the teacher, examine work materials, or use other evaluative devices.

During group evaluation, the teacher guides the children to a critical consideration of the key problems that have arisen in a work period. The children themselves should make suggestions for the improvement of their work, for better use of materials, and for a better application of group standards that have been set. New purposes and goals should be established, needs for other materials and tools should be considered, and next steps should be charted. Much self-evaluation by the pupils themselves is essential.

Questions, Activities, Evaluation

1. Evaluate the model of group inquiry in terms of the following questions: How can it be adapted for use in different units of instruction? How can key concepts and methods of inquiry discussed in Chapter 4 be included at various points? How can the learning experiences presented in the preceding chapter be used in connection with different steps of inquiry? How might the model be improved?

2. Consider group work skills in terms of their use in a unit of instruction you are planning. In what ways might you use the techniques suggested in this chapter?

3. Which of the limitations of group-work skills in the social studies do you believe to be most significant? Why? What do you think are some dangers in overemphasizing them at the expense of individual study skills? How can you use the unit-planning suggestions presented in Chapter 7 to plan for a balance between individual and group work skills so that both will be strengthened?

4. Which of the suggestions made regarding committees are apropos of a group of children you are teaching or observing? Are other points more pertinent because of specific problems that have arisen in their committee work? Always try to make specific adaptations to the particular children with whom you are working.

5. Consider the section on discussion techniques in the same light as suggested immediately above. What changes or adaptations should be made?

6. Reread the sections on group planning, group inquiry, and group evaluation. Is the teacher's role clear? Visit a classroom and observe a teacher guiding a group of children in planning and evaluation. Which techniques were used? Was guidance

given to individual children? How were individual questions handled? Was commendation used to accentuate desirable behavior? Were specific points brought out in evaluation in a constructive manner? What points did you gain through the observation?

7. Which of the charts presented in this chapter might you use in a unit you are planning? What adaptations or changes should be made in them to meet the needs of children in different grades?

References

Bigge, Morris L., and Maurice P. Hunt, *Psychological Foundations of Education*, Ch. XIX, "Why Is Climate Making a Part of Method?" New York: Harper & Row, Publishers, 1962. Principles for building an effective classroom atmosphere.

Cartwright, Dorwin, and Alvin Zander, *Group Dynamics: Research and Theory*, 2nd ed. Evanston: Row, Peterson, 1960. A summary of studies of group dynamics.

Dunfee, Maxine, and Helen Sagl, *Social Studies through Problem Solving*. New York: Holt, Rinehart, & Winston, Inc., 1966. Principles and techniques of group problem solving.

Jarolimek, John, *Social Studies in Elementary Education*, chap. vii, "Developing Skills Needed in Group Situations." New York: The Macmillan Company, 1967. Group work techniques.

Jensen, Gale E., *The Dynamics of Instructional Groups*, Fifty-Ninth Yearbook, National Society for the Study of Education, Part II. Chicago: University of Chicago Press, 1960. A summary of theory and practice related to group processes.

Lifton, Walter M., *Working With Groups: Group Process and Individual Growth*. New York: John Wiley & Sons, 1961. Principles and procedures for guiding group work.

Merritt, Edith P., *Working With Children in Social Studies*, Ch. V, "Group Guidance in Social Studies." Belmont, Calif.: Wadsworth, 1961. Group work techniques.

Muessig, Raymond H., and Vincent R. Rogers, "Developing Competence in Group Participation and Human Relations," *Skill Development in the Social Studies*, 33rd Yearbook, National Council for the Social Studies, pp. 230–51. Washington, D.C.: National Education Association, 1963. Principles, techniques, and illustrative activities.

Olson, Willard C., *Child Development*, Ch. VIII, "The Human Relations of the Classroom." Boston: D. C. Heath & Company, 1959.

Quillen, I. James, and Lavone A. Hanna, *Education for Social Competence*, Ch. XIII, "Small Groups in the Social Studies Classroom." Chicago: Scott, Foresman & Company, 1961. Useful in upper grades.

Rehage, Kenneth, "Group Work Skills," *Social Studies in Elementary Schools*, 32nd Yearbook, National Council for the Social Studies, pp. 187–96. Washington, D.C.: National Education Association, 1962. Principles and procedures for developing group-work skills.

Independent Inquiry and Related Skills

A current trend is to give increased attention to the skills involved in independent inquiry and study. This trend is the result of the emphasis on new content and methods of inquiry from the social sciences, the cultivation of thinking processes, the individualization of instruction, the stress on learning how to learn, and the balancing of individual and group inquiry. In addition, home study calls for the development of independent study skills if it is to contribute significantly to children's learning.

The skills involved in independent inquiry are closely related to reading skills, other language skills, and thinking abilities. The development of skills in the language arts program determines in large degree the extent to which they can be put to use in the social studies. Children need special help and planned instruction that is designed to transfer and apply language and other skills to problems in the social studies. A useful strategy is to use topics and content from the social studies as a basis for experience in using study skills, thus promoting the development of fundamental ideas as well as the improvement of basic skills.

A trend in the development of independent study skills has been to give these skills earlier emphasis in the instructional program. In addition to providing earlier grade placement of study skills, such a program offers more-able children in every

9

grade the opportunity to move far beyond usual grade expectancies. For example, there are children in Grade III or IV using references, making outlines, and preparing reports that in former years would have been found only in upper grades.

Two other related trends of significance in the social studies are the use of multiple sources of information in order to obtain varying points of view, more complete information on selected topics, and deeper understandings and appreciations; and an increased use of the skills involved in gathering and organizing information. The use of multiple sources of information has accentuated the need for developing skills in using the aids in textbooks and references. Emphasis on gathering and organizing information has accentuated the need for such skills as finding and arranging material in alphabetical order, note taking, outlining, pooling information from various sources, and preparing reports. Specific attention is given to these skills in this chapter.

Developing Needed Skills

Effective use of the many different aids in textbooks and references calls for the development of a number of specific skills and understandings. Too often, little or no attention is given to the aids in textbooks and references, or an incidental approach is used and children are left on their own to develop the needed skills. By giving attention to the various parts of books, and by planning instruction that leads to effective use of each part, essential skills can be brought to a high level of development. At the same time, textbooks and references will be used more effectively in improving critical thinking and problem-solving abilities.

Learning the Parts of a Book

Learning the parts of a book is begun in the primary grades. For example, when a textbook is introduced to the group, the title page may be discussed, the year of publication may be noted, and the list of stories in the table of contents may be checked. A teacher might ask such questions as these: What is the title of this book? What does the title tell us about the book? Can you find the name of the author? When was this book printed? How old is it? Turn to the table of contents. What is the name of the first story? The second? What does the table of contents help us to find?

GETTING ACQUAINTED WITH THE PARTS OF A BOOK	CAN YOU FIND THESE IN TEXTBOOKS AND REFERENCES?
Front Matter 1. Find the authors on the title page. 2. Find the copyright date and the publisher. 3. Look for special points made in the preface. 4. Get an overview from the table of contents. 5. Check the list of maps. *The Body* 1. Chapters are in the body. 2. Notice how chapters are arranged. *Appendix* Check the tables and charts. *Index* Use it to find topics in the book.	1. Title page 2. Author 3. Copyright 4. Preface 5. Acknowledgements 6. Contents 7. List of maps 8. Additional references 9. Activities and exercises 10. Reference tables 11. The appendix 12. Glossary of terms 13. The index
Chart 1	Chart 2

In the middle and upper grades, instruction is more detailed and is paced with the increasing complexity of the books and references that are used. The main purpose is to develop the habit of checking and using the many different special aids in the books available to the group. Special attention is called to the title page, author, copyright date, preface, acknowledgments, and other "front matter." Children also learn that *the body* of the book is made up of the chapters and that valuable reference tables may be included in the *appendix*. Charts 1 and 2 are illustrative of specific points to be taught.

THE TABLE OF CONTENTS

The table of contents of a textbook is a valuable aid that children should use in all grades. For example, in a unit on The Home, children can find stories about Work of Mother, Work of Father, How Children Can Help, and How the Family Has

Fun Together. As The Community is studied, children can locate such chapters as How We Get Our Food, Our Water Supply, and How Goods Are Transported. As Living in Early America is studied, children can locate chapters dealing with such topics as The First People in America, The Early Explorers, How Columbus Discovered America, and The First Colonies.

Although the skills involved in using the table of contents are not difficult to acquire, specific instruction is needed on the following items: (1) its location in the front of the book, (2) its usefulness in finding major sections and chapters, not specific topics, (3) its usefulness in getting an overview of the book and in finding the order of arrangement of chapters, and (4) its usefulness in locating the page numbers of specific chapters. These can be taught through actual use of the table of contents.

Several procedures may be used. For example, a teacher may ask children to find the table of contents, locate a given chapter title, give the beginning page number, and finally direct them to find the chapter in the book. The order of chapters may be checked by noting which ones come in the first part, middle part, and last part. Special attention must be given to the fact that only general or major topics are listed. At times, a teacher may ask children what specific topics they think are included in a given chapter and then have them read to see if they are right. Such a procedure is helpful in developing the ability to relate general titles to specific topics, and also to differentiate between the use of the index and the table of contents.

Another procedure to be used when a new book is introduced is to have children check the table of contents to get an overview. Illustrative questions are: What are the main topics? Which topics or titles are related to questions and problems in our unit? Do you see any new ones? In what ways does this book seem to be most helpful?

FIND THESE IN THE TABLE OF CONTENTS	CAN YOU FIND THESE IN THE TABLE OF CONTENTS?
1. Work of policemen 2. Work of firemen 3. Work of the baker 4. Work of others	1. Titles of chapters 2. Order of chapters 3. Page numbers of chapters, reference tables, glossary, and index
Chart 3	Chart 4

Probably the most basic procedure is to use the table of contents when questions and problems have arisen and children need to find chapters that deal with them. As they check the table of contents, they must read critically to select chapter titles that are pertinent. This can be done in all grades provided that the wording of the questions and problems is such that relationships to chapter titles are clear. By checking ahead of time, a teacher may plan practice materials or questions and comments that will help to clarify the relationships between problems being investigated and chapter titles.

In many textbooks for middle and upper grades, special items are listed at the end of the table of contents. A list of reference tables may be given, for example, major dates, area and population of cities, states, countries and continents, length of rivers, and height of principal mountains. The page numbers of the glossary and the index are also given. One of the most helpful features that usually is placed after the table of contents is a list of the maps included in the text. Time should be taken to check the list carefully in order to note the types that are included, where they are located, and the information that is presented on them. This should be followed by making appropriate reference to them from time to time, and by reviewing the list of maps as needed to locate those related to specific questions and problems under study. A few minutes spent in acquainting children with the listing of these special items will pay rich dividends in terms of the time saved in locating them and in getting the children to make more effective use of them.

THE INDEX

The index is the key to the topics included in a book. Some of the basic facts that children should learn about the index are these:

Names of people, places, things, events, and basic processes (farming, fishing, manufacturing, and the like) are listed in the indexes of social studies textbooks.

Topics are listed in alphabetical order, subtopics may be listed after main topics, and page numbers are given for each topic or subtopic.

Page numbers are indicated by a single numeral such as 37, which means the topic is discussed only on that page, by a hyphenated numeral such as 56–61, which means the topic is discussed on all of the pages inclusive, or by several numerals such as 9, 82, 91, which means the topic is discussed on each of the pages.

The main word is used to locate topics, for example, the last name of persons, and the first name of places and things, such as Oak Ridge and St. Lawrence Seaway.

Cross-references are included after some topics, for example, after oil, *See* petroleum, or after farming, *See also* dairy farms, orchards, ranches, and truck farms.

In developing the skills involved in using the index, a first step is to be sure that the children understand alphabetical order. Practice in alphabetizing topics and in finding topics in alphabetical order, as shown in the later section on gathering and organizing information, should be provided for those children who need it.

Instruction in the actual use of the index may be initiated by discussing the index in a social studies textbook being used by the class. Illustrative questions to guide discussion are:

What topics are listed? Can you find the names of people? Places? Things? Processes such as farming? Events?

In what order are topics listed? Why is alphabetical order used?

When are last names placed first for a topic? When are names placed in order for a topic? What names are always capitalized?

On what pages can we find information on manufacturing? Pittsburgh? The Piedmont?

What pages should be read when a hyphen appears between page numbers, as in 61–67?

What is meant by *See also* which appears after farming?

After children have become acquainted with the main features of the index, practice should be given in locating specific topics. A good beginning activity is to ask questions related to one section of the index. For example, if the M section is used, a teacher may ask: What page, or pages, contain information about Manhattan? Maryland? Missouri River? Does this book contain information on manufacturing? Matanuska Valley? Mohawk River? What minerals are listed after *mining*? After practice in locating topics in one section, many teachers later provide practice in finding topics in different sections. A short list of topics (or questions that include topics) such as the following may be used: Alaska, climate, fishing, forests, Juneau, population, rainfall, and weather. After group practice in which such topics are located, individual practice and study may be provided in clinching basic skills. As other textbooks and references are introduced, the teaching cycle may be repeated as needed, beginning with a discussion to review the features of the index, and moving to individual practice in locating topics.

Special help and practice are needed in choosing the key word or words to look for in the index. For example, what word or topics should be used in finding information related to the following?

Dr. George Washington Carver	manufacturing in different regions
Cumberland Gap	manufacturing of steel
Declaration of Independence	the first trains in America

After practice in selecting key words in sentences, questions, titles, and names, children should formulate rules that apply to the indexes they are using. Examples are: (1) Use the last name of persons. (2) Use the first name of places or things such as Cumberland Gap and Declaration of Independence. (3) If a topic such as *trains* is not listed, look for a related term such as *railroads*. (4) Use the name of the basic process *manufacturing* when information is desired on the process in different places, but use the name of the product *steel* when information is desired on how it is manufactured. Another key learning for children to make is: If there are two or more key words and you are not sure of which one to use, first check the one you think is most likely; if that is not correct, try the second one.

A desired outcome of instruction is to get children to use the index on their own as they search for information needed in discussion, reports, and other activities. Toward this end, children should have many opportunities to use the index in related textbooks, yearbooks, almanacs, encyclopedias, and other reference materials. When this is done, one may need to give special attention to differences in indexing systems. For example, the index of *The World Almanac* is in the front and a system of main topics and subtopics is used. Indexes in encyclopedias differ in certain ways as noted in the following section. Yet in all indexes there are three steps for children to follow: (1) Decide which key word or words should be used to locate a topic, (2) find the page numbers, and (3) turn to the indicated pages and locate the appropriate information.

Using References

ENCYCLOPEDIAS

Encyclopedias may be used as children search for information, pictures, diagrams, tables, charts, maps, and graphs related to questions and problems in units they are studying. In primary grades, the pictures are most helpful, although more-able children can benefit from reading selected sections related to topics under study. Beginning in Grade IV, systematic instruction is usually provided in the use of encyclopedias, with review and additional instruction in later grades as needed.

The first task is to acquaint children with the arrangement, index, and special features of the different encyclopedias that are available. If two or more are available, the differences in arrangement, indexing, and other features should be noted. The following should be given direct attention:

Arrangement of Subjects. In alphabetically arranged encyclopedias, each volume contains subjects as noted by the letters on the back, for example, Volume 1, topics beginning with *A*, Volume 2, topics beginning with *B*, and so on. Some volumes may contain subjects for two or more letters such as *D E* and *G H*, whereas large encyclopedias have split letters for certain volumes such as *A-Ant* and *Anu-Az*. In topically arranged sets, information is located by using the index and the table of contents. Subjects may be arranged alphabetically by the letter-by-letter method (New Delhi, Newfoundland, and New Guinea), or by the word method (New Delhi, New Guinea, and Newfoundland). The order of listing items that begin with the same name is usually as follows: person (Washington, George), place (Washington, D.C.), and thing (Washington Monument).

Key Words. The main or key word should be used in looking up subjects, for example, *Australia*, if information is desired on agriculture in Australia, *California*, if information is desired on products of California, and *Abraham*, if information is desired on the Plains of Abraham.

Guide Words. Words at the top of the pages indicate the subjects that are presented on each page. Compare them with the guide words in dictionaries.

Cross-references. Cross-references are given in articles, at the end of articles, and in the index.

The Index. The index may be in a separate volume or in each volume. Directions for using the index should be studied; they can be found immediately preceding the index. Some indexes include information, charts, summaries, study guides, and other material not presented in the articles. In addition to main topics and subtopics, indexes show the volume and pages for pictures, maps, charts, diagrams, graphs, tables, and other illustrative material.

Reference Outlines and Study Guides. These may be presented at the end of certain articles or in a special volume. They

USING OUR ENCYCLOPEDIAS

1. Articles beginning with *A* are in Volume 1, *B* in Volume 2, and so forth.
2. Articles are arranged in alphabetical order like words in the dictionary.
3. Guide words at the top of the pages tell what is reported on each page.
4. Places, such as New Guinea and New York, are found under the first name.
5. The names of people are found under the last name.
6. The index gives main articles and related articles. It also gives some facts not included in articles.
7. The index lists maps, charts, tables, pictures, and graphs.

Chart 5

include related articles which are helpful in studying major subjects and topics and in preparing reports. The outline for Australia, for example, may contain a list of related articles on animals, deserts, industries, plants, resources, states and territories, and other subjects in various volumes.

Bibliographies. Lists of related books may be given at the end of main articles, under the subject, and in unit guides furnished by the publisher.

Yearbooks. Yearbooks published to keep encyclopedias up to date contain a summary of major events, ideas, and developments for the past year. By referring to the index, specific topics can be found and related material can be located even though it appears in several different articles. Cross-references to main articles in the encyclopedias and to earlier yearbooks are sometimes given.

DICTIONARIES

Not to be overlooked is the fund of information contained in dictionaries. In addition to finding the spelling, pronunciation, and meaning of terms in dictionaries, children should use them to find illustrations of terms and concepts used in the social studies. Picture dictionaries contain excellent illustrations, and standard classroom dictionaries include a large number of spot maps, drawings, and sketches. Because the drawings and sketches are made simply and are uncluttered with detail, they are especially easy for children to interpret. Unabridged dic-

USING THE DICTIONARY

1. Know the alphabet.
2. Use the guide words.
3. Note the spelling.
4. Check the accent mark.
5. Check the diacritical marks.
6. Check the pronunciation key.
7. Note how plurals are formed.
8. Choose the appropriate meaning.

Chart 6

FIND SKETCHES OF
THESE SHIPS IN OUR
DICTIONARIES

Bark	Outrigger
Caravel	Sampan
Catamaran	Schooner
Frigate	Sloop
Galleon	Umiak
Junk	Yawl

Chart 7

tionaries are truly a storehouse of information on topics included in the social studies and contain drawings, pictures, sketches, maps, and colored plates which can be used to enrich and clarify terms and concepts.

The suggestions presented in standard elementary-school dictionaries on "How to Use the Dictionary" are especially helpful in teaching basic skills. Some publishers include practice materials in a graded sequence which can be used to improve dictionary skills. Many teachers use actual terms and concepts from the social studies as part of the practice. When such practice is paced with exercises provided in the children's dictionaries, the problem of transfer of skills to social studies terms and concepts is met directly and effectively.

OTHER REFERENCES

A variety of other reference materials may be used in the social studies, particularly in the upper grades and by more-able children in Grades III–V. Yearbooks and almanacs contain much information on many topics and should be used when latest facts and statistics are needed.

The World Almanac is a "book of facts" about large cities, capitals, states, countries, business, trade, exports, imports, production, transportation, sports, conservation, education, communication, organizations, political parties, population, lakes, mountains, rivers, United Nations, special days and dates for the current year, major events of the past year, and so on.

Other "information books" are *Information Please Almanac* which is similar to *The World Almanac, The Economic Almanac*, which contains facts about business, labor, and government, and *The Statesman's Yearbook*, which includes facts on countries throughout the world.

LIBRARY RESOURCES

The resources of modern libraries are especially helpful in the social studies. An increasing number of school systems are providing libraries in elementary schools so that teachers and pupils may have direct and immediate access to materials. Where this has not been done, every effort should be made to do so, for without a library in the school many excellent learning opportunities are missed. In some areas, traveling libraries, or bookmobiles, are operated for the convenience of schools and communities. Of great help are the materials in public libraries and in central school library facilities. Many teachers make a practice of checking out a varied collection of reading materials, prints, and pictures related to the unit they are planning. In some school systems, teachers may order a kit of materials related to the unit from the central school library; in others, catalogs may be provided so that specific materials may be ordered as needed.

Room libraries are organized by most teachers as convenient places to keep references and supplementary reading materials. As different units are studied, the reading materials should be changed. Materials from the school library, public libraries, and the central school library should be drawn upon freely for placement in the room library. The room library should be attractively arranged with bulletin-board space and tables and chairs for individual and small-group use.

Children should be given planned experiences in library use so that they may make full use of library resources in the social studies. Teachers should take their groups to the library to learn the location of materials, how to check out materials, rules and procedures, and the use of the card catalog. Librarians are eager to help and should be consulted before the visit so that detailed plans, appropriate to the maturity of the group, can be made.

Some of the first learnings that children make regarding the use of the library are illustrated in Charts 8, 9, and 10.

OUR LIBRARY	CHECKING OUT BOOKS	LIBRARY RULES
1. We get books.	1. Find the book you want.	1. Never bend the pages
2. We get pictures.	2. Take the book to the librarian to check out.	2. Keep books dry.
3. We hear stories.	3. Return the book on time.	3. Close books before laying them down.
4. We read magazines.		4. Sign out books with the librarian.
		5. Sign in books with the librarian.

Chart 8　　　　　　　Chart 9　　　　　　　Chart 10

Specific attention also must be given to skills involved in using reference materials. The following resources are used in connection with many different units in upper grades:

1. Card catalogs
2. City directories
3. Dictionaries
4. Encyclopedias
5. School atlases
6. Government directories
7. Guides, timetables, and folders

8. Periodicals
9. *Readers' Guide*
10. Telephone directories
11. *The Junior Book of Authors*
12. *Who's Who in America*
13. *World Almanac*
14. *Statesman's Yearbook*

Attention must be given to the skills involved in the use of each of the above. For example, children should be shown that books are classified by authors, titles, and subjects in the card catalog. Explain that the "call number" on the upper left hand corner of the card is the key to locating books; the same number is on the back of the book. When the *Readers' Guide* is first used, explain that it is an index of magazine articles by subject and by author. The abbreviations of magazine titles, months, volume, and page should be discussed. Other abbreviations such as *il* for illustrated, *por* for portrait, and those shown in Charts 11 and 12 should be noted. Planned practice should be given in using the *Readers' Guide* and the card catalog to locate material related to units being studied.

What plans might you make to encourage children to use the card catalog to look up references related to questions and problems that arise in units? *(Sybil Shelton; Courtesy of Monkmeyer)*

DO YOU KNOW THESE ABBREVIATIONS IN THE CARD CATALOG?		
Ja	S	rev
Mr	O	il
Je	Ap	por
Jl	W	pseud

Chart 11

WHAT IS THE NAME OF EACH OF THE FOLLOW-ING MAGAZINES?	
Atlan	Nat Geog Mag
Contemp	Sat Eve Post
Sci Am	UN World

Chart 12

Charts 13, 14, 15, and 16 illustrate specific ways in which other reference materials may be used. A basic point to keep in mind is that each one should be used functionally to answer questions, secure material for reports, and the like.

USE THE *STATESMAN'S* YEARBOOK TO FIND

1. Facts about British Commonwealth countries.
2. Facts about states in the United States.
3. Facts about other countries.
4. Area, population, leaders, products, religions, commerce, and other information about countries.

Chart 13

USE THE *WORLD ALMANAC* TO FIND FACTS ON

Airports	Population
Countries	Agriculture
States	Trade
Sports	Minerals
People	Education
Events	Weights
Officials	Altitudes
Rivers	Mountains
Dams	Labor

Chart 14

ENCYCLOPEDIAS IN OUR LIBRARY

Book of Knowledge
Compton's Pictured
Britannica Junior
World Book
Americana
Britannica

Chart 15

BIOGRAPHICAL REFERENCES

1. *Who's Who in America*
2. *Who's Who* (in regions)
3. *Dictionary of American Biography*
4. *Current Biography*

Chart 16

Charts 17 and 18 are illustrative of information that is essential to the use of well-organized libraries.

THE DEWEY CLASSIFICATION SYSTEM	THE CARD CATALOG
000–099 General Works —encyclopedias, references, etc.	Use the guide letters on each drawer to locate cards.
100–199 Philosophy— conduct, morals, etc.	Cards are in alphabetical order by
200–299 Religion—biblical stories, mythology, missions, etc.	a. author b. title c. subject.
300–399 Social Sciences —government, labor, capital, etc.	
400–499 Languages— English, grammar, etc.	Find the author card if you have the author's name.
500–599 Science—mathematics, nature, etc.	Find the title card if you know the title.
600–699 Useful Arts— inventions, clothing, etc.	
700–799 Fine Arts—painting, sculpture, etc.	Use the subject card if you do not know the author or title.
800–899 Literature— anthologies, poetry, etc.	
900–999 History—geography, biography, etc.	Look for cross-references which are indicated by *See* and *See also*.

Chart 17   Chart 18

Gathering and Organizing Information

ALPHABETICAL ORDER

Beginning early in the social studies program, extensive use is made of the skills involved in arranging and in locating material in alphabetical order. In fact, no way of organizing information in reference materials is more widely used. In the early grades, attention is given to the arrangement of items in picture files, picture dictionaries, scrapbooks, card boxes, and word lists of various types. The skills learned in the early grades are extended and refined in later grades as attention is given to the use of card files, outlines, reports, charts, tables, indexes, encyclopedias, dictionaries, atlases, gazeteers, glossaries, book lists, study guides, bibliographies, almanacs, and yearbooks. Without a mastery of the skills involved in handling items arranged in alphabetical order, a child is unable to use such resources effectively.

In the social studies, functional and direct instruction can be provided in a number of ways. The teaching of the names of the letters, a first task, can be done in the early grades by actually using the letters to arrange material in picture books, picture dictionaries, folders, and the like. Placing the letters in order on the border of the chalkboard or on charts is helpful. Specific practice is needed to clinch the learning of the alphabet and usually includes such activities as these:

Placing pictures of farm animals, foods, clothing, and the like under letters placed on the bulletin board or the border of the chalkboard

Arranging materials in a picture book in which a separate page is used for each letter

Direct teaching of the order of the letters with attention to those in the first, middle, and last third of the alphabet; the first, second, third . . . and other letters; the letter that comes before *f*, after *m*, and so on; and the numbering of letters

Matching letter cards with pictures and with words

Filling in the missing letters in such lists as A B __ D E __. . . .

Arranging short lists in order such as *banana, orange, apple,* and *plum*.

In later grades, review is provided as needed and use is made of such activities as these:

Arranging words in order by using the first two letters, for example, *hat, hit, hot,* . . .

Arranging words in order by using the first three letters, for example, *house, home, hope,* . . .

Arranging special word lists, making outlines, preparing bibliographies, and making card files, notebooks, and scrapbooks

Using dictionaries, indexes, encyclopedias, and other resources to refine skills

NOTE TAKING

The primary purpose of note taking is to jot down information for future use—information related to questions, problems, directions, reports, discussions, and special projects. Notes may be taken in the social studies as children read textbooks and reference materials, see films, take a study trip, interview individuals, study a map, review a picture file, or gather information from other resources. The form of the notes may vary from a short list of items to a summary of main ideas related to a topic, depending on the purpose for making the notes, the source that is used, and the capabilities of the children.

As with other writing skills that are used in the social studies, note taking must be paced with the development of basic language skills. In the early grades, note taking may be initiated after the essential writing skills are developed through such activities as (1) listing the jobs of community workers as reported in textbooks, (2) noting points about the animals mentioned in stories about farm life, (3) noting contrasts in ways of living in other communities, and (4) listing points related to other questions, problems, and activities as they arise. In later grades, the opportunities for note taking grow apace with the child's development of language skills, and can be extended to include the taking of notes in a variety of situations, as noted in the Charts 19–24.

Of crucial importance in acquiring the ability to take notes is the clarification of the purpose for note taking. The purpose guides the selection of facts and ideas; if it is not clear, the notes will include both relevant and irrelevant material. The purpose may be a simple one such as finding the answer to a question, or it may be a more involved one such as gathering ideas for a report on a topic. The purpose may be clarified through such preparatory activities as listing questions to be answered, selecting a subject for a report, skimming headings and subheadings in a reference to get an overview of main ideas, discussing the main topics to be presented in a film, and noting questions to be raised in an interview.

After the purpose is clear, notes should be taken only on those points that are related to the purpose; and only the most important points should be noted. Children should be encouraged to take notes in their own words, but care should be taken not to change the meaning. If

---

TAKE NOTES

To answer questions.
To prove points.
To get directions for making things.
To summarize ideas.
To get ideas for reports, charts, discussions, murals, and scrapbooks.

Chart 19

LISTENING TO TAKE NOTES

Watch the speaker.
Note the main topic during the introduction.
List each main point.
Put specific ideas under each main point.
Ask about ideas that are not clear.

Chart 20

TAKING NOTES AS WE READ

Read the entire selection before beginning to take notes.

Find the main ideas in each paragraph, but select only those related to your subject.

Use your own words but do not change the meaning.

Write enough so that each idea can be recalled.

Number the notes in order.

Chart 21

NOTES FOR BOOK REVIEWS

Write the author and title.

Note the main points about what happened.

Select a part you like very much and note what happened.

List the page numbers of two or three pictures you wish to show.

List the page number of a good part to read to the group.

Note two or three reasons why you think others should read it.

Chart 22

NOTES FROM INTERVIEWS

List each question to be asked on a half-sheet of paper.

Arrange the papers in order.

Jot down main points as each question is answered.

Ask questions about points that are not clear.

Take notes on new ideas that are mentioned.

Chart 23

NOTES FROM FILMS

Write the title of the film.

Note the main reasons given for seeing the film.

Get the main ideas as presented in the introductory part of the film.

Note main points as the film is shown.

Check to see if you have notes related to each reason for seeing the film.

Chart 24

a child cannot take notes in his own words without changing the meaning, he should use the words in the text. Words, phrases, or sentences may be used depending on future uses of the material and the situation in which the notes are taken. Enough detail should be included so that each note can be recalled easily and accurately. In middle and upper grades, abbreviations are used at times to facilitate note taking; for example, such terms as transportation, communication, production, and conservation can be abbreviated by using the first four letters. The numbering of each note is helpful in putting notes in order and in differentiating one point from another. Generally, each child should note the source of information so that, if necessary, it can be checked by himself or others.

OUTLINING SKILLS

Outlining skills are used in the social studies in summarizing information from textbooks and references, organizing ideas from discussions, interviews, and study trips, planning reports, making booklets, listing items needed for projects, and organizing information for future use in other activities. Outlines are especially helpful in getting ideas in sequence, clarifying main ideas and supporting details, classifying information in meaningful categories, getting a feeling for the organization of ideas related to a topic, and getting a grasp of relationships among main ideas and between main ideas and related subtopics. Outlining is truly helpful in the social studies as an aid to organize information for reference and as an aid to clear and orderly thinking.

The sequence of development of outlining skills begins with short lists of sentences or items dictated by the group and written by the teacher on the chalkboard or on charts. For example, in units on The Home or Our Community, a summary may be made of ideas noted in reading, items needed for projects, questions to be asked on a study trip, examples of uses of different modes of transportation, products that are produced locally, and the like. In the middle and upper grades, more complex outlines are made, ranging from a short numerical or alphabetical listing of items under appropriate headings to three-step outlines with main headings, subheadings, and supporting details. Use is made

---

ON OUR STUDY TRIP

1. We saw cows.
2. We saw horses.
3. We saw chickens.
4. We saw pigs.
5. We saw the farmer.
6. We saw buildings.

Chart 25

FRUITS AND VEGETABLES

Fruits	Vegetables
1. Apples	1. Beans
2. Bananas	2. Beets
3. Grapes	3. Carrots
4. Peaches	4. Lettuce
5. Pears	5. Peas

Chart 26

COMMUNITY WORKERS

I. Builders
   A. Bricklayers
   B. Carpenters
   C. Painters
   D. Plumbers
II. Businessmen

Chart 27

of both group and individual outlining activities with increasing emphasis on independent outlining ability. Charts 25–31 illustrate the skills, format, and content of outlines used in the social studies.

USES OF DIFFERENT
MEANS OF
TRANSPORTATION

I. Airplanes

  A. Transportation
    1. People
    2. Mail
    3. Goods
  B. Agriculture
    1. Crop sowing
    2. Crop dusting
  C. Defense

II. Trains

  A. Transportation

Chart 28

POINTS TO REMEMBER
WHEN MAKING
OUTLINES

1. Center the title and leave a space between it and the first topic.
2. Use Roman numerals for main topics, capital letters for subtopics, and Arabic numerals for points under each subtopic.
3. Put a period after each numeral and letter.
4. Indent subtopics under each topic, and indent each point under its subtopic.

Chart 29

MAKING AN OUTLINE

I. First main topic
  A. First subtopic indented
    1. First point indented
    2. Second point and others indented the same
  B. Second subtopic indented the same as first one
    1. First point indented the same as above
    2. Second point and others indented the same

Chart 30

OUTLINE FORM

I. _____
  A. _____
    1. _____
    2. _____

  B. _____
    1. _____
    2. _____

II. _____
  A. _____
    1. _____
    2. _____

Chart 31

Both the sentence and topic outline form are used in elementary grades. The sentence form is recommended for use in first outlining activities because it is easier for beginners to follow. Simple topic outlines are introduced as short lists of needed materials and other items are prepared for various purposes. Although topic outlines are used more frequently in later grades, children should learn that sentence outlines are helpful when the material is to be read by others, or when more complete details and ideas are needed for future reference. Special attention should be given to the point that a period is always placed after sentences in an outline, but not after topics. In addition, children should learn that topics and sentences are not mixed; one form should be used consistently throughout the outline.

USING AND PREPARING BIBLIOGRAPHIES

The skills involved in using and preparing bibliographies are used in locating and in citing sources of information on topics and problems. In the early grades, the titles of books related to questions or topics being studied may simply be listed on a chart or the chalkboard. For example, when a class is studying community workers, the titles and pages of available books that contain information about the work of the policeman, fireman, or another community worker may be listed for quick and easy reference. If books with similar titles are being used, this question should be raised: How can the difference between them be shown? Children then discover that the name of the author is helpful in finding the right book. In middle and upper grades, complete bibliographical form can be used as children prepare

---

BOOKS WITH STORIES ABOUT FIREMEN

1. *Billy's Neighbors,* pages 31–38

2. *In the Neighborhood,* pages 80–87

3. *New Friends and New Plans,* pages 79–100

4. *Visiting Our Neighbors,* pages 68–82

5. *Your Town and Mine,* pages 200–201

Chart 32

card files, use duplicated reading and study guides, find references in textbooks and other sources, use the card catalog, and include a list of references in written reports, scrapbooks, and booklets.

MAKING A BIBLIOGRAPHY

1. Follow this form: O'Meara, Walter, *The First Northwest Passage*. Boston: Houghton Mifflin Co., 1960. 184 pp.

2. Remember this order: Author, *Title*. Place of publisher: Publisher, Year published. Number of pages.

3. Arrange the list of books in alphabetical order by last name of author.

Chart 33

USING INFORMATION FROM SEVERAL SOURCES

The use of a number of textbooks, reference materials, and other resources calls for special skills in locating and pooling information from several different sources. Children need specific instruction in this, for without it, they will have difficulties that will lead to discouragement and a tendency to use a single reference. In fact, teachers also become discouraged and may thus fail to provide for the use of a variety of materials that are essential if critical thinking skills are to be developed.

A first step at all levels of instruction is a sufficiently detailed discussion of the question or problem so that each child will know just what information is needed. For a child to ramble through several references when he is not clear as to just what is needed is a waste of time. After the question or problem is clear, there are several simple procedures that are helpful in developing the necessary skills.

As an introductory step in primary grades, children can be asked to refer to two or three books in which colored slips of paper have been placed to indicate where information on certain topics can be found. For example, in a unit on The Home, a red slip may be used to show the location of a page or two on the work of the mother, a blue slip the work of the father, and a yellow slip the work of the children at home. After children have developed an adequate vocabulary, labeled slips may be used in place of colored slips. After appropriate number concepts have been developed, page numbers may be listed on the board or on a chart.

After they have gained experience in using sections on specific topics in two or three books, children themselves should be given an opportunity to locate pertinent sections on a new topic. This may be guided by having a small group check the table of contents and turn to the proper page to see if the section is related to the topic. If the section is related, a slip can be placed in the book for future reference. Other groups should then have their turn. At other times, the children can thumb through certain sections to spot pages that deal with specific topics.

After material has been located in several sources, help is needed in pooling ideas obtained from them. One effective procedure is to have children study one source carefully, and then to summarize the three or four main ideas obtained from it in oral discussion. This is followed by studying a second source and discussing similarities and differences. This is followed by checking a third source. Then the main ideas obtained from the references are summarized in oral discussion and listed on the board. The next step, after guiding children in oral work of this type, is to have children check two or three references on their own. After studying the references, each child should give a brief report on the main ideas he found in them. His findings can be compared with those of others, and individual help can be given by the teacher to help solve problems that have arisen. After several experiences of this kind, each child should work on his own in gathering material from different sources.

Many teachers guide the group in preparing outlines to use in pooling information from different sources. In the early grades, the outline may consist of only two or three items such as: (1) How Mother cleans the house, and (2) How Mother prepares food. With these two items as guides, the children select ideas from two or three references. In later grades, more detailed outlines are used, depending on the topic and the capabilities of the children in the class. After information has been gathered, the outline may be discussed point by point, with the children sharing what they have found. In subsequent experiences, individuals may complete the outline on their own. After notes are taken from several sources, each note should be related to the proper topic in the report. An effective way to do this is to have each child list the topics and write the number of each related note under them as shown in Charts 34–35. The next step is to write a paragraph on each topic and to include the related notes in the paragraph.

ARRANGING NOTES IN
OUR OUTLINES

1. List the topics in the outline.
2. Write the number of each note under the topic related to it.
3. Write a paragraph on each topic and include the notes listed under it.

Chart 34

NOTES ON
PRODUCTION OF IRON

1. Mining Iron Ore
   a. Notes 1, 2, 3, and 6
2. Transporting the Ore
   b. Notes 4, 5, 9, and 11
3. Processing the Ore
   c. Notes 7, 8, 10, and 12

Chart 35

Preparing Reports

Oral and written reports are used extensively in the social studies. They are an effective means of individualizing instruction because they provide opportunities for each child to gather and organize information on topics of special interest from reading materials and other sources of information. The following list shows the abundance of topics to be found in each unit of instruction.

ILLUSTRATIVE TOPICS FOR REPORTS

The Home: Work of Mother, Work of Father, Work of Children, How Work is Divided, Care of Pets, Taking Care of the Baby, Workers Who Come to the Home, How the Family Has Fun Together, How the Family Uses Transportation, How the Family Uses Communication

Our Community: Producers of Goods, Producers of Services, How Mail is Handled, Our Water Supply, How the Community is Kept Clean, Local Transportation Services, How Newspapers Are Printed, Our City Parks

Early Days in Our Community: Old Indian Villages, The First Settlers, What Early Homes Were Like, The First Stores, How People Traveled, The First Telephone, Early Mail Service, Our Trip to the Old Fort, How Our Community Got Its Name, The Early Fire House, The First School, The Story Behind City Park

Our State in Early Times: Where the Indians Lived, Early Explorers, The First Settlers, How the Missions Were Built, The Building of Forts, The First Town, Admission to the Union, Our First Governor, Travel Routes to Our State, How the Capital Was Chosen, How Our State Got Its Name, How Our State Got Its Nickname, The Story of Our State Flag

Our State Today: Urban Centers, Our Major Industry, Our Newest Industry, Why Agriculture Is Important, Fishing, Mining, Lumbering, Cattle Raising, What We Send to Other States, What We Get from Other States, Our Seaports, Air Transportation in Our State, How Rivers Are Used, Major Railways, Major Highways, Developing Our Water Resources, Conservation of Forests, Our Richest Resources, Our State Parks, Winter Sports

Regions of the United States: Major Industries, Resources, How Activities Are Influenced by Climate, Kinds of Farming, Manufacturing Centers, Major Rivers, Major Seaports, National Parks, How Steel Is Made, New Industries in the South, Products from Soybeans, Conservation of Land

Life in Early America: The Plymouth Colony, A Colonial Home, The Town Meeting, The First Thanksgiving, How Children Were Educated, Games Played by Children, The Erie Canal, The Tom Thumb Locomotive, Drake's Oil Well, The Saugus Ironworks, How Clothing Was Made, How the Colonists Lighted Their Homes, The Making of Candles, Contributions of William Penn

Living in Mexico: The Piñata, The Posada, Activities at a Fiesta, Contributions of Juarez, Trade with the United States, Work of the Braceros, Kinds of Farming, Mining, Major Industries, Fishing, Early People of Mexico, Why the Spanish Came, Early Explorers, How Mexico Gained Independence, Land Purchased from Mexico by the United States

Living in Other Lands: Homes and Furnishings, Fruits, Vegetables, and Other Foods, Clothing, Airports and Seaports, Highways and Railways, Main Cities, Interesting Places to Visit, Village Life, Farming, Main Products, Imports and Exports, Changes that Are Being Made, Forest and Mineral Resources. Things that We Get From Them, Things that We Send to Them, Main Occupations, Weather and Climate, Customs, What Their Schools are Like

ORAL REPORTS

Oral reports are used to share information on topics, questions, and problems of concern to the group. Informal reports based on information from textbooks, current periodicals, news reports, and other sources of information are frequently made a part of classroom discussion. Formal reports based on more detailed studies of topics are generally used as the group moves from one major topic in a unit to another, and as a part of concluding activities. Oral book reports may be used in relation to the topics under study. Individual reports are used on topics that

---

OUR ORAL REPORTS

Choose a topic from the unit.
Select ideas on the topic.
Arrange the ideas in order.
Know each idea well.
Find something to show that illustrates a main idea.
Be brief so others will have turns.

Chart 36

ASKING QUESTIONS ABOUT REPORTS

Listen carefully as the report is given.

Think of questions on parts that are not clear.

Ask questions about sources of information.

Ask questions about facts and opinions.

Chart 37

OUR BOOK REPORTS

Choose a book you like.
Learn the name of the author and the title.
Select an interesting part to tell.
Select two or three pictures to show.
Be ready to tell where others may get it.

Chart 38

GIVING BOOK REPORTS

Show the book and give the name of the author and the title.
Tell what the book is about.
Read or tell about an interesting part.
Show two or three pictures.
Tell where others may get it.

Chart 39

REPORTS ON TV AND RADIO PROGRAMS

Select a program related to our unit.

Note title of program, time, and station.

Note ideas related to topics in our unit.

Select two or three ideas to share with the group.

Chart 40

GIVING ORAL REPORTS

Stand tall and look at the group.
Talk clearly so that all can hear.
Keep the ideas in order.
Show pictures or other items as they fit into your report.
Use an expressive voice to give a feeling for different parts.

Chart 41

can be handled by a child working alone. Group reports are used on broad topics that are broken down into several related parts.

Each type of oral report calls for the use of certain basic skills. Formal reports to the group reflect a more critical application of skills than do informal reports. However, both should be viewed as opportunities to extend skills, such as those noted in Charts 36–41.

WRITTEN REPORTS

Written reports may take a variety of forms including individual papers, charts, scrapbooks, notebooks, booklets, newspapers, logs, and diaries. Individual papers and charts are helpful in organizing and sharing ideas on specific topics. Scrapbooks and notebooks are used to compile a series of reports as a unit progresses. Booklets are useful in organizing information on a topic in greater detail and depth. Class newspapers are sometimes used to organize ideas related to current events and issues and to portray historical incidents and events as if "you were there." Logs and diaries are helpful in recording information over a period of time related to events, leaders, and changes taking place in a given place. Pictures, drawings, maps, tables, and graphic charts are used in different types of reports to illustrate, highlight, and summarize key ideas.

The selection of topics for written reports is usually made a part of the group-planning discussion of the unit under study.

By selecting topics related to problems and questions that have been identified by the group, each individual's report can make a direct contribution to the development of the unit. However, this should not preclude creative thinking on the part of individual children who may, after initial planning, discover topics that are worthy of intensive independent study.

Leads to possible topics can be obtained by considering specific aspects of transportation, communication, production, conservation, education, government, recreation, and other basic social functions as they relate to the unit under study. For example, Air, Land, or Water Transportation may become the topic of a report in units on Our Community, Our State, Our Nation, and Other Lands. Other leads can be obtained by considering current events, problems, and issues related to the unit under study. For example, background reports may be prepared on leaders in Our State, Our Nation, and Other Lands, or on changes taking place in newly developing countries in such areas as education, health, and industrial development. When geographic and historical concepts are being emphasized, reports may be made on such topics as Farming in the Central States, Travel Barriers in South America, A Good Place for Rice Farming, Living in Plymouth Colony, Living in Boonesboro, The Lands Obtained from Mexico, The Purchase of Alaska, and How Hawaii First Became a Part of the United States. When basic attitudes, appreciations, and democratic ideals are being stressed, reports may be written on such topics as How to Help at Home, Being Good Neighbors, Keeping Our Parks Clean, The First Thanksgiving, Why the Pilgrims Came to America, Why Roger Williams Started a New Colony, Peter Zenger and Freedom of the Press, Democratic Ideas in the Town Meeting, and Democratic Ideas in Early Greece. Other topics for reports may be related to inventions, famous men and women, comparisons of ways of living, outstanding historical events, and the origin of holidays.

In the middle and upper grades after a topic has been selected, several steps are taken to prepare reports: *

1. Thinking of questions to be answered in the report, or possible subtopics to be included

---

* The language textbooks provided in Grades III–VIII should be used as handbooks to guide the preparation of reports. The suggestions contained in them are easily adapted to the writing of reports in the social studies.

CHOOSING A TOPIC FOR A REPORT

Is it an important topic?

Is it interesting to you and to others?

Are good sources of information available?

Is it small enough so that you can finish it on time?

Chart 42

SELECTING IDEAS FOR REPORTS

Think of the questions your report should answer.
Or, list the main topics that should be included.
Select ideas related to each topic.
Include only important ideas.

Chart 43

PLANNING REPORTS

Have a good introduction.
Put the main ideas in order.
Put the points under each main idea in order.
Have a short conclusion.
Think of a title that tells what the report is about.
Give the sources of information.

Chart 44

REVISING REPORTS

Is each idea related to the topic?
Is each idea clearly stated?
Are descriptive words used?
Are ideas in good order?
Is each statement accurate?
What changes are needed?

Chart 45

PROOFREADING REPORTS

Are capital letters used where needed?
Is the punctuation correct?
Are words used correctly?
Are words spelled correctly?
Are sentences complete?
Have you used the dictionary and the language textbooks to check questionable points?

Chart 46

FORM FOR REPORTS

Write your name at the top in the right corner.
Write the title in the middle of the page one space below your name.
Leave a space between the title and the first paragraph.
Indent the first word of each paragraph one-half inch.
Keep the margins even.

Chart 47

2. Finding sources of information and taking notes on each source

3. Making an outline of the report, in which subtopics are listed and notes are placed under the proper subtopic

4. Thinking of a clear title that is descriptive of the contents of the report

5. Writing a paragraph on each subtopic

6. Revising the paragraphs to improve the presentation of ideas

7. Proofreading each paragraph to correct errors

8. Writing the report in final and correct form

Charts 42–47 illustrate specific points to be stressed.

Effective Study Habits

A current trend in school systems throughout the country is to provide instruction to develop effective study habits. The development of good work habits begins in the early grades and progresses steadily to the refinement of study skills in the upper grades. Much can be done in the social studies to improve study habits because of the many opportunities for individual work and reports on topics included in each unit of instruction. The study habits developed in the social studies are put to use in the classroom, in the library, and in study at home.

Building on the foundation established in the primary grades, specific attention should be given in later grades to the extension and refinement of study habits such as those listed in Charts 48 and 49.

Listening Skills. Vitally important in the social studies, listening skills can be sharpened as children share reports, discuss topics and problems, note directions for activities, observe demonstrations, listen to recordings, radio, and television programs, enjoy stories and poems read by others, hear resource people report on trips to other places, and view sound films on ways of living in other communities and lands. As in reading, purposes should be set for listening in order to focus children's attention on the most significant ideas. Some of the purposes for listening in the social studies are to gain ideas on a topic, to enjoy what is being read or reported, to follow steps in a sequence, to get directions, to understand an explanation, to visualize a description, to note related ideas, to learn new terms in context, to clarify concepts, to contribute to discussion, to appreciate mood, tone, and feeling, to appraise ideas, to react to statements, and to raise questions.

GOOD STUDY HABITS	BETTER HOME STUDY
Know what to do! *Stop*—Stop other activities so that you can get the direction clear. *Look* — Watch the teacher so that you get each point. *Listen*—Get the exact details on what to do. *Ask*—Raise questions if you do not understand any part. Proceed to do it! *Organize*—Arrange the needed materials and plan the steps to take. *Concentrate*—Stick to your job and do not be distracted. *Finish*—Complete the assignment before starting other activities. *Check*—Review your work to be sure it is complete and well done.	Know exactly what you are to study. Be sure to take the necessary materials home. Plan your study time so that you will not have to stay up late. Study in a place where you will not be bothered. Arrange the study materials so that they can be used effectively. Stick to the job once you have started it. Do your own work even though others may help you with difficult parts. Review the main ideas after you have completed your work. Be ready to ask questions the next day on any parts you do not understand.

Chart 48   Chart 49

Purposes for listening and intensity of attention vary in terms of the following somewhat overlapping levels of listening:

Level 1: Getting ideas during conversation and informal discussion
Level 2: Enjoying stories, poems, and other selections
Level 3: Getting directions, questions, and problems clearly in mind
Level 4: Noting main ideas and related details
Level 5: Evaluating statements of fact and opinion

Among the habits and skills to be stressed in the social studies are setting a clear purpose, varying attention in accord with purpose, being courteous, detecting main ideas, noting details, following a sequence, interpreting terms in context, grasping the speaker's purpose, detecting bias, distinguishing fact and opinion, noting evidence to support statements, and checking one's impressions with others. A helpful procedure is to use a tape recorder so that points of disagreement can be checked, especially after a critical listening activity. Other helpful procedures are discussing points of courtesy as problems arise, considering ways to improve listening in the light of questions and problems raised by children, providing directed listening activities with immediate follow-up evaluation, and preparing standards for self-evaluation and group evaluation, as shown in Charts 50–52.

LISTENING FOR ENJOYMENT	LISTENING FOR INFORMATION	CRITICAL LISTENING
Is the mood set in the beginning? What will the climax be? Which parts can be visualized? Which parts are most exciting? Is the climax what you expected?	Have a clear purpose. Get ideas in order. Relate supporting details to main ideas. Take notes on needed items. Ask questions on parts that are not clear.	What is to be appraised? Which statements are facts? Is related evidence given? Which statements are opinions? What conclusions can be drawn?
Chart 50	Chart 51	Chart 52

Questions, Activities, Evaluation

1. Which of the study skills discussed in this chapter do you believe to be most useful in the social studies? Do you agree with the suggestion that topics and problems in the social studies provide excellent opportunities to develop study skills?

2. Select a child's textbook related to a unit you are planning and indicate ways in which instruction might be provided on (a) learning the parts of a book, (b) using the table of contents, and (c) using the index.

3. Examine one or two encyclopedias for children and note points on which instruction should be provided regarding (a) arrangement of subjects, (b) the index, (c) reference outlines and study guides, and (d) maps, diagrams, charts, and other graphic materials. List articles, pictures, maps, and other resources which you might use in a unit you are planning.

4. Examine a dictionary designed for children and note maps, sketches, or drawings that might be used to clarify terms and concepts in a unit you are planning.

5. Visit a school library or a community library and note books, references, and other materials that might be used in a

unit. Take notes on rules of procedure that should be discussed with children.

6. Indicate ways in which the following might be used in a unit of instruction: (a) note-taking skills, (b) outlining skills, (c) organizing information from several sources, (d) bibliographies, (e) oral and written reports, (f) home study, and (g) listening skills.

7. Which of the charts presented in this chapter might you use in a unit you are planning? What changes might be made in them to meet instructional needs in different units at various grade levels?

References

Anderson, Paul, *Language Skills in Elementary Education.* New York: The Macmillan Company, 1964. Sections on dictionary and reporting skills.

Burns, Paul C., and Alberta L. Lowe, *The Language Arts in Childhood Education.* Chicago: Rand McNally & Co., 1966. Sections on listening, speaking, and writing skills.

Carpenter, Helen M., ed., *Skill Development in Social Studies,* 33rd Yearbook, National Council for the Social Studies. Washington, D.C.: National Education Association, 1963. Detailed suggestions for developing skills needed in the social studies.

Conlon, Eileen, *Library and Reading Skill-Text.* New York: Scarecrow Press, 1964. Exercises for children.

Greene, Harry A., and Walter T. Petty, *Developing Language Skills in the Elementary School,* 2nd ed. New York: Allyn and Bacon, Inc., 1963. Principles and techniques for developing reporting and other skills.

Lowrie, Jean E., *Elementary School Libraries.* New York: Scarecrow Press, 1961. Section on how to find materials.

Murdoch, Faith, Elmer Pflieger, and Gertrude Whipple, "Communication Skills in the Social Studies," 32nd Yearbook, National Council for the Social Studies, pp. 176–87. Washington, D.C.: National Education Association, 1962. A grade-level summary of skills.

Preston, Ralph C., *Teaching Study Habits and Skills.* New York: Holt, Rinehart & Winston, Inc., 1962. Suggestions for improving study habits.

Tinker, Miles A., and Constance M. McCullough, *Teaching Elementary Reading,* rev. ed., Ch. IX, "Comprehension and Study Skills." New York: Appleton-Century-Crofts, 1967. Specific techniques of instruction.

Instructional
Media

Advancements and refinements continue to be made in the area
of instructional technology. Instructional systems that include
books, films, slides, transparencies, and other media for use in
a unit or course are being produced in larger numbers. Educational television and kinescoped films and video tapes of selected
programs have proven to be quite useful in the social studies.
Eight mm film loops, transparency overlays, and multimedia
kits that contain materials for a specific unit are quite useful
in improving inquiry. (And instructional materials centers are
providing a variety of services ranging from collection and distribution of essential materials to the actual handling of classroom projection by remote control.)

The emerging viewpoint is to provide the richest possible
learning environment that includes all of the needed instructional media. Instructional media are viewed as an integral part
of a teaching system, not as aids that are used if time permits.
A teaching system may include any of the following that will be
useful in attaining the objectives of a unit of instruction:

10

[1] Philip Lewis, "Instructional Technology," *New Curriculum Developments*
(Washington, D.C.: Association for Supervision and Curriculum Development, National Education Association, 1965), pp. 85–95.

Reading Materials: textbooks, references, encyclopedias, pamphlets, newspapers, diaries and other source materials, programmed material

Audio-Visual Materials: models, artifacts, pictures, film strips, slides, motion pictures, eight mm film loops, recordings, radio, television, maps, globes, charts, graphs, diagrams, transparencies

Community Resources: field trips, resource visitors, persons to interview, field studies, service projects, surveys

The current emphasis on inquiry has cast instructional media in a more helpful light. The trend is to use them as sources of data to test hypotheses, answer questions, and solve problems that have arisen in individual and group inquiry. Students are guided to approach them in a quest for useful ideas.

In this chapter, attention is given to principles and procedures essential to effective selection and utilization of instructional resources, the place of instructional materials in the social studies program, and general guidelines applicable to all types of instructional resources. In later chapters attention is given to specific techniques and procedures for the selection and utilization of reading materials, maps and globes, audio-visual materials, and community resources.

Basic Guidelines

Instructional media, like teaching strategies, should be used to achieve specific purposes. They must be selected and used in such a way that maximum learning will be possible. Only those that contribute to the solution of problems and the achievement of the purposes of a group of children are appropriate for that group. The time allotted to the social studies is too short to bring in extraneous gadgets, devices, books, or other materials that do not contribute to the purposes of the program, and, if the goals of the social studies are to be achieved, considerable attention must be given to the selection and use of instructional materials.

Questions that teachers must raise when considering an instructional resource include:

What specific purposes can be achieved by using this resource?

What concepts and main ideas can children develop through its use?

What attitudes, appreciations, and interests may be modified?

Can communicative ability, research skills, and problem-solving ability be strengthened?

What concepts of urban planning might be developed with these materials? (MATCH Box Project, Children's Museum, Boston)

All too frequently, attention is centered on facts alone; many other key learnings are overlooked. Each function of the social studies must be analyzed to determine the specific contributions that the use of selected materials may make to it.

This principle may be illustrated by considering ways in which motion pictures may contribute to the improvement of skill in critical thinking. Children should be guided to discover how questions and problems are elaborated, opened up, and clarified in the film. How are the ideas presented, organized, and summarized? Do the conclusions, suggestions, or content square with other sources of information? Propaganda effects, use of props, use of music to produce various effects, and related emotion-stimulating devices should be considered in the light of such questions as: Do they affect our judgment and stimulate an emotional reaction? Are our judgments and conclusions distorted? What ideas can we use to improve our own skill in thinking? The teacher may need to reshow the film in order to reconsider these and similar questions.

The varying levels of concreteness of experience with materials should be recognized. The following hierarchy of materials in terms of levels of abstractness, from direct experience to experiences with verbal symbols, is helpful in considering instructional resources: [2]

[2] Edgar Dale, *Audio-Visual Methods of Teaching,* rev. ed. (New York: The Dryden Press, Inc., 1954).

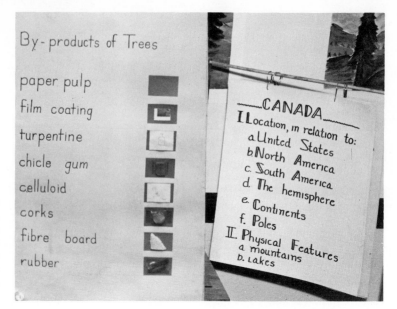

Teacher-made charts can be used to define problems, summarize key ideas, present information, and guide evaluation. Try to anticipate ways in which you can use charts in a unit. *(Los Angeles)*

1. *Direct, purposeful experience*—gardening, making something, weaving

2. *Contrived experience*—operating a working model

3. *Dramatic participation*—identification of self with others by participating in a play, tableau, or pageant (Observing a play is on the next level.)

4. *Demonstration*—observing as someone demonstrates a process or activity (A more direct type of experience if followed by doing.)

5. *Field trip*—observing people at work or processes in a natural setting (More direct if interviewing is included.)

6. *Exhibits*—seeing planned arrangements of materials (More direct if working models are used.)

7. *Motion pictures and television*—watching a planned series of pictures with action and movement involved

8. *Still pictures, radio, recordings*—seeing or hearing (These are one-dimensional aids.)

9. *Visual symbols*—charts, graphs, and maps

10. *Verbal symbols*—processes of reading, writing, speaking, listening.

This list does not necessarily refer to the best type of experience to provide; it simply suggests an order of concreteness. A teacher must determine the best for a given class on the basis of the maturity of the children, available time, problems that have arisen, availability of materials, and the unit of instruction being developed.

The classroom should be viewed as a laboratory—a planned environment—to stimulate learning. Materials should be arranged in such a way as to focus the child's attention on key problems and questions. Different types of materials should be selected and used so that the classroom environment will help to move the thinking and planning of the group in profitable directions. The overall arrangement of the room, as well as the separate sections of the room such as the reading corner or bulletin board, should receive attention. Balance, timing, selectivity, and artistic arrangement are desirable. When the classroom is viewed as an arranged environment, a laboratory for inquiry, then instructional media are used effectively.

Materials of instruction should be used to improve each phase of inquiry. The following examples are illustrative:

Recognizing and defining problems. Use pictures, maps, realia, charts, films, exhibits, and displays to stimulate questions and to direct thinking toward problems and main ideas to be considered first.

Maps and other items made by children should be used in arranging displays. Can you think of other ways to use resources made by children in a unit you are planning? (Richmond, California)

Note the arrangement of desks, easels, and other facilities in this classroom. Working out different space arrangements to provide for group work is fairly easy. Can you think of changes that might be made to suit various purposes? (Albany, California)

Recalling ideas and proposing solutions to problems. Review charts, maps, and other materials related to problems identified for study. List proposals and suggestions on the chalkboard or on charts.

Group planning. Use pictures, models, maps, charts, suggestions in textbooks, and ideas from other sources to give direction to planning. Have children experiment with different arrangements as they plan murals, graphs, scrapbooks, reports, time lines, maps, demonstrations, and other items. Discuss resources that children suggest for use in solving stated problems. Have the group assist in planning study guides, reading lists, study trips, picture files, and other resources to be used in obtaining information.

Locating and obtaining information. Use study guides, reading lists, tables of contents and indexes in textbooks, the card catalog and other library aids, interviews, study trips, maps, films, and other available resources. Develop each child's ability to identify authoritative and pertinent sources of information.

Appraising and verifying information. Compare ideas obtained from textbooks, references, maps, films, pictures, and other sources of information. Reread selected sections of reading materials and reshow films and filmstrips to "prove" points at issue. Interview experts on issues and questions for which additional information is needed.

Organizing, interpreting, and summarizing information. Use reports, outlines, charts, maps, murals, tables, graphs, diagrams, exhibits, dioramas, slides, displays, scrapbooks, booklets, movie rolls, and models.

Forming conclusions. Organize ideas and information that support conclusions on charts, on the bulletin board, in notebooks, in written reports, on the chalkboard, and in displays.

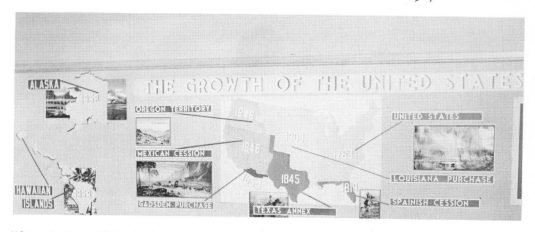

What main ideas might be developed during the making and using of such a map?
(Alameda County)

In what ways can the materials in this display be used to improve various phases of
inquiry? (Alameda County)

Evaluating individual and group work. Use charts, checklists, and tests for individual and group evaluation. Guide the group to appraise and to consider ways to improve the maps, reports, booklets, and other items they have made. Use techniques of evaluation suggested in textbooks, teacher's manuals, and units of instruction.

The use of materials of instruction should be viewed as an integral part of the sequence of experiences in the unit of instruction. A study trip, reading materials, motion pictures, and other resources should be selected as needed to develop main ideas, answer questions, and solve problems. Notice in the following example how various instructional materials and learning activities are brought together to develop the main idea that is listed first.

MAIN IDEA: MANY INDIVIDUALS AND GROUPS HAVE CONTRIBUTED TO OUR WAYS OF LIVING IN THE UNITED STATES.

1. Discuss current contributions of individuals and groups in the community, state, and nation. Summarize comments on the chalkboard.

2. Ask the group if they know about contributions of individuals and groups in earlier times. List comments, and suggest that additional points can be added as the unit progresses.

3. Prepare a large chart on which major contributions can be summarized as pupils discover them. Have each child keep a notebook in which information on contributions can be kept.

4. Provide for reading in textbooks, library materials, and other resources that deal with contributions of individuals and groups.

5. Select motion pictures and filmstrips that portray contributions.

6. Have the group assist in the preparation of a picture file of great men and women.

7. Provide for oral reading of selected poems and passages that highlight contributions.

8. Make use of radio and television programs, recordings, time lines, murals, and other resources that highlight contributions.

9. Plan a study trip to the museum to see utensils, furniture, inventions, and other items.

10. Dramatize selected events, stories, or episodes presented in textbooks.

11. Provide for individualized reading of materials that reveal the contributions of individuals and groups of differing national origin.

12. Make murals, maps, and exhibits that highlight contributions.

Children must be ready for the use of instructional materials if maximum learning is to be achieved. Several dimensions of

How can these materials be used to spur inquiry that will in turn lead to the development of insights into ways of living in early America? (San Diego County Schools)

readiness must be considered as maps, globes, references, films, study trips, and other resources are reviewed. From the learner's point of view, the instructional materials should be meaningful, related to questions and problems under study, graded in accordance with skills and conceptual backgrounds possessed by the group, and immediately useful in developing main ideas or improving various phases of problem solving. From the teacher's point of view, materials should be reviewed to determine what special preparation or instruction is needed so that readiness to use them can be developed. For example, concepts, skills, and special techniques involved in using maps, study trips, and references should be given attention as needed in order to prepare children for their use. Such preparatory instruction may be made a part of on-going classroom activities and embedded in the inquiry process.

Genuine readiness exists when teachers plan and guide instruction so that children raise questions and make such comments as the following:

Which books have ideas on this? What library materials can we find?

What do those map symbols mean? We should check the legend on the map.

Where are the pictures we saw yesterday? We have to check them against the ones in the encyclopedia.

Is there a filmstrip or motion picture on map making that will help us? Are there suggestions in our textbooks and encyclopedias?

How is this index organized? Where can we look to find information on transportation, communication, and main products?

Can we check this when we visit the museum? Or, is there someone who can give a demonstration?

Group planning, discussion, and evaluation are effective approaches to use in developing readiness for materials. Children should develop skill in the selection and use of materials and procedures as well as in getting facts and ideas from them. A persistent question is: What devices and materials can be used for this purpose? Critical thinking will be improved as children grow in their ability to make more intelligent choices of sources of information. Children should also be given opportunities to evaluate the effectiveness of the materials in communicating ideas. If this is done, there will be improvement in processes of problem solving as well as in the learning of information.

Maximum learning can be secured only if the use of materials is carefully planned. Two types of planning are essential. First, a teacher should plan a unit in which major topics or problems with related experiences and materials are sketched. This sets the use of materials in proper perspective, and enables the teacher to think through the selection, timing, and appropriateness of materials for different needs and problems. Second, attention must be given to the specific details involved in the use of different materials. The teacher must make sure that needed equipment is available, distracting elements are eliminated, purposes are clear, and necessary arrangements are made. For example, a study trip may be ruined if the guide has no knowledge of the purposes and level of understanding of the class.

Equipment and materials used in the program should not draw attention away from the main ideas to be developed. This has occurred in units on Indians and Pioneers, in which realia such as tomahawks, knives, and muskets have been used for simulated battles during a major part of the study. It has occurred in studies of Mexico in which recordings and films related to fiestas and folk dances were overemphasized. This is not a plea for the elimination of materials; it is a plea for emphasis on significant outcomes in the use of materials. Materials must contribute to learning, not detract from it! All materials should provide rich experiences and lead to the development of significant concepts and generalizations in each unit of instruction.

Follow-up activities should flow naturally and reasonably out of each experience. Artificial assignments such as a test after each film should be avoided. The intelligent thing to do next may be discussion, related reading, or some appropriate art work. What if children who took a trip to the farm had returned to take a test on animals they had seen? Would this be related to the purposes of the trip? Would this lead to the development of concepts or the solution of problems? No! It simply would have been an artificial assignment based on an outmoded conception of the use of instructional resources.

Rules of procedure cannot be followed arbitrarily in the utilization of materials. In applying general rules for the use of study trips, films, recordings, or other types of materials, a teacher must exert sound judgment and make decisions as to whether general rules of utilization can be followed. In one situation, for example, a teacher was unable to make specific plans prior to a radio program related to a Growth of Democracy unit. In spite of this, the program was used very effectively because the teacher made careful notes during the program. Although this kind of deviation from recommended procedure should be avoided, in this instance it appeared to be the intelligent thing to do. Rules for using films, manuals which accompany film strips, radio guides, and the like are suggestive only, and creative teachers use them or modify them, depending on the situation.

Materials should be organized and arranged in a systematic manner if maximum utilization is to be secured. One of the

Notice the eye-catching quality in this display. Why do you think children will find it attractive? What are some of the questions children might ask about the objects shown? *(Los Angeles)*

most effective ways to organize materials in the social studies is to place those related to a unit in a kit in the sequence in which they will most likely be used. For example, in planning a unit on Mexico, the related pictures, pamphlets, reference lists, construction plans, names of films and recordings, possible excursions, and plans for their use can easily be filed in a kit under appropriate headings. If certain items cannot be included, such as large realia and films, they should be noted in the unit plan with procedures for securing them. Each kit should be accompanied by a unit plan in which possible experiences and related materials are listed. A teacher may then use them as needs and problems arise. A variety of materials designed to meet the individual differences of the class should also be included.

A *multimedia approach to the use of instructional materials promotes learning.* The expression *multimedia* is used to indicate the use of several different instructional materials (pictures, films, books, and the like) to achieve a given objective. An extension of the multitextbook approach is to include other instructional resources, and this has been used for many years in good social studies programs. For example, in developing an appreciation of the difficulties experienced by the pioneers, use should be made of textbooks, supplementary references, stories, films, recordings, maps, and pictures. Similarly, a variety of instructional materials should be selected to develop each main idea emphasized in a unit of instruction. By using different materials that contribute to the achievement of an objective, the

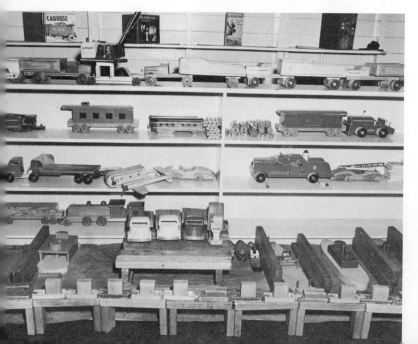

Children need a place to keep materials so that they can develop responsibility for their care and use. How might an arrangement such as this one facilitate use? (Albany, California)

chances are much greater that each child will develop broader and deeper concepts, and that individual differences will be met more effectively.

Materials of instruction should be evaluated before, during, and after use. Appraisal of materials is an essential aspect of selection and use. Only those materials that meet sound criteria should be selected for use in the program. Guidelines for selection are presented in the following section. Once materials are selected, their contribution to the program should be appraised to determine whether further use is justified. The teacher should note pupil reactions to the material they are using, giving attention to interest, level of difficulty, vocabulary, provision for individual differences, and appropriateness to the maturity level of the group. After the materials have been used, attention should be given to the types of activity stimulated by the material, and to significant outcomes such as concepts, appreciations, or changes in attitude. Continuous evaluation of this type leads to more effective utilization and to the development of a collection of instructional resources that have great value in promoting learning.

Selection of Materials

Proper selection of materials must be based on careful evaluation before use. It is folly to gamble children's time away by using materials whose values and contents are unknown. A film, study trip, recording, or book, should meet sound criteria before it is used for instructional purposes. The criteria commonly used in the selection of various types of materials are discussed in the following pages.

Purpose. The clarification of the purpose for which a film, filmstrip, recording, or radio program is to be used is a first step in its evaluation. Both the purpose for which it has been produced and the specific purpose for which it is to be used should be determined. The latter may vary, since different teachers may use the same motion picture for different purposes. For example, one teacher used a motion picture on Mexico to give an overview in connection with an initiation of a unit; another teacher used the same film to summarize key learnings. Both knew, however, that the film was designed to portray in a broad, general way, various aspects of living in Mexico. As a basic guide, then, only those materials that contribute directly and specifically to significant purposes should be selected.

Variety. Variation of materials within limits that avoid con-

Notice the many materials in this display that can be used to develop accurate and authentic concepts. How might they be used to enrich meaning as textbooks, films, and other resources are used? (Oakland City Schools)

fusion and overstimulation promotes interests and stimulates thinking. Far too many teachers fall into the rut of selecting one type of resource to the exclusion of most others. An important principle to keep in mind is to select a variety of materials, in line with changing needs and purposes, so that children learn to use many different resources in problem solving. The teacher's goal is to select the particular aid which best fits a specific purpose at a given time.

If the purpose is to show concretely how something works, a working model should be secured. If the way in which an activity is carried out by a group—weaving by Indians, for example

—needs clarification, a motion picture will portray the action and movement. Such purposes as learning about types of dwellings or homes may be met by using still pictures, which may be projected or unprojected, depending on their size and whether individual or group activity is involved. Sound motion pictures are helpful in giving realistic conceptions of activities in which both sound and motion are important elements. Eight mm film loops are helpful in developing single concepts, such as preparing meals in a Japanese family. Colored slides are helpful in studying types and colors of clothing and costumes, landscapes, and the arts and crafts of various peoples. Where sound alone is important, recordings or the radio may be used. If the purpose is to see an activity in its natural setting, a study trip may be essential. After the purpose is clearly defined, the problem of selection is well begun.

Appropriateness to Maturity of Children. The level of difficulty of instructional materials must be appropriate to the maturity of the children who are going to use them. References, films, maps, and other resources must be checked to determine concepts involved, skills needed for their effective use, and applicability to problems that the pupils are attempting to solve. Selected materials must be neither too difficult nor too simple if interest is to be held and maximum learning is to be achieved. A range of material wide enough to stimulate the gifted, less-able, and slower-learning children should be chosen.

Content. Significance and authenticity of content are essential criteria in the selection of materials. The nature of the content in a book, film, filmstrip, radio program, or recording in large measure determines its potential contribution to the program. The authenticity, clarity of presentation, timeliness, distortion, propaganda, stereotypes, difficulty of concepts, and pertinence to topics included in the unit should be checked. The content should contribute directly to a clearer understanding of problems being considered, and should stimulate critical thinking, not detract from it. Although this, of course, depends on the manner in which a resource is used, a teacher should be aware of the biases, mood, tone, and purpose of the writer or producer, so that attention may be given to these factors during and after utilization. Children should develop an awareness of bias, propaganda, and prejudice in the materials they use. A teacher's role is to guide children in the development of true impressions and accurate concepts through effective use of carefully selected materials.

Physical Qualities. Maps, motion pictures, and charts are valuable only if their format, printing, sound, photography, and organization are satisfactory. Attractiveness, clearness of presentation, and continuity or sequence of ideas are significant determinants of educational value. Obviously, these criteria should be applied to the care and repair of materials as well as to their selection.

Manuals. The teaching manuals which accompany many maps, films, filmstrips, slides, recordings, radio programs, and books should be reviewed critically. Many of them contain helpful suggestions which should be consulted before the materials are used. This is especially important if the material cannot be previewed before using it in the classroom, although material should be previewed if at all possible. When reviewing manuals, attention should be given to practicality of suggestions, pertinence to the unit, desirability in terms of past experiences in the class, and ease of use. As with all guides designed for instructional use, adaptation must be made to the needs of the children who are to use the resource. In some instances, manuals are provided which have not been tested in actual classroom situations, and their use may create difficulties instead of solving problems. This fact adds to the importance of previewing the resources and making specific plans for their use in terms of immediate needs.

Time, Effort, Expense. The time, effort, and expense involved in using instructional resources are important considerations. Some study trips that require traveling a great distance from school are highly desirable, but they may be unnecessary if other available instructional resources are adequate. On the other hand, a study trip may be more economical than other resources in terms of time, effort, and expense, because of the educational values it possesses. At times a filmstrip may be more effective than a motion picture, or a set of flat pictures more valuable than a map. Of course, such decisions are relative and must be based on the facts of the situation. A basic consideration is the value of the material to the children for whom it is being selected.

Rating Devices. Many school systems have found rating cards or checklists which include criteria such as those discussed above to be helpful. With an objective rating sheet in hand, appraising instructional materials is much easier. Checklist 1 illustrates those used to appraise films.

Selection of Free or Inexpensive Materials. Special care must be exercised in the selection of free or inexpensive materials, for example, maps, charts, diagrams, pamphlets, leaflets, booklets, maps, and pictures. Many school districts have policies for the selection and use of materials which are distributed by companies, consular offices, travel agencies, state and local groups, national organizations, and governmental agencies. In general,

FILM APPRAISAL FOR PURCHASE—FORM 7

Pasadena City Schools

Title _____

Source _____ Price _____

Running time _____ Silent   Sound   Color

   Rating: Excellent Good Fair Poor

   Remarks: (Nature and appropriateness of content, Reactions)

_____

_____

_____

School _____ Course _____

Suggested for: Grade level _____ Unit _____

Recommended adding to Library? _____ Date _____

          Signature _____

(Front Side of Card)

  Is the presentation tinged with propaganda? _____ If so, is the propaganda desirable? _____ Undesirable? _____ Directed toward advertising? _____ Directed toward upholding the American form of government? _____

Comments _____

Teaching values:	Excellent	Good	Fair	Poor	Reject
Reliability	( )	( )	( )	( )	( )
Appeals to Pupils	( )	( )	( )	( )	( )
Sustained Interest	( )	( )	( )	( )	( )
Carry-over	( )	( )	( )	( )	( )
Tempo	( )	( )	( )	( )	( )
Continuity	( )	( )	( )	( )	( )
Technical Quality:					
Photography	( )	( )	( )	( )	( )
Sound	( )	( )	( )	( )	( )
Color	( )	( )	( )	( )	( )

(Reverse Side of Card)

Checklist 1

high standards are set for the free or inexpensive materials that are distributed by reputable agencies and groups. However, to select and use such resources indiscriminately and without strict adherence to established policies is unprofessional and contrary to the best interests of children. Criteria such as the following should be applied:

   1. Is the material produced by a reputable group?

2. Are any ideas included which run counter to democratic ideals?

3. Are concepts, style of presentation, symbols, and language appropriate to the capabilities of the children who will use them?

4. Is the content related to units of instruction?

5. Are sources of information given?

6. Is the material free of bias and prejudice?

7. Is the material up to date and available from standard sources?

8. Are type size, spacing, format, and other technical qualities satisfactory?

9. Is material free of objectionable or obtrusive advertising?

10. Will the school be obliged if it uses the material?

Selection of Textbooks. Checklist 2 on the following page illustrates the criteria usually used in appraising textbooks.

Additional criteria are helpful in appraising books and other materials dealing with people in other lands. A special problem is to make sure that authentic, realistic, and up-to-date content is included. The following criteria may be used:

Is the author qualified to write about this country? Has he lived there or visited the country? Has he discussed problems with people who live there?

What is the author's purpose? How is his writing affected by his purpose?

Has the book been reviewed by a native of the country?

Is the spirit of the book in keeping with the cultural values of the people? Does the author convey a feeling for the hopes, aspirations, and problems of the people? Are clear descriptions of activities included? Are characterizations realistic?

Are facts presented accurately? Are new developments included? Are generalizations supported by facts?

Are stereotypes avoided? Are current ways of living shown along with quaint and traditional activities? Are native costumes, art, and dances portrayed in proper perspective?

An important task in rating textbooks is the development of specific procedures for applying criteria to textbooks. For example, in determining if the content is related to the program, a specific check should be made of the table of contents and sample chapters in the book. A criterion such as degree of interest and appeal to children can be checked by actually having children read comparable sections of textbooks. The degree to which pictures and drawings add meaning to the content can be determined by examining several illustrations to discover rela-

CHECKLIST FOR EVALUATING TEXTBOOKS

Directions: Rate each book on the specific points as follows: 5-Superior, 4-Good, 3-Fair, 2-Poor, 1-Unsatisfactory.

Criteria for Rating Each Textbook	Textbooks					
	A	B	C	D	E	F
As an instructional resource:						
Is it related to the content of the program?						
Is it accurate and up to date?						
Can concepts and understandings be grasped by children who will use it?						
Is level of reading difficulty—vocabulary, style of presentation, sentence structure—appropriate for children who will use it?						
Will it contribute to problem-solving skills?						
Do illustrative materials—maps, pictures, drawings—contribute to the meaningfulness of the content?						
Are study aids, suggested activities, and related references adequate?						
Physical features:						
Is it attractive and appealing to children?						
Are margins and page arrangements adequate?						
Are size, spacing, and type size adequate?						
Major emphases:						
Does the book inspire loyalty to American ideals and institutions?						
Does it contain material that can be used to develop positive attitudes?						
Are generalizations supported by facts?						
Are controversial issues handled fairly and objectively?						
Does the book emphasize movements and trends rather than isolated events?						
Does it stimulate interests that lead to further study?						
Are minority groups treated fairly and adequately?						
Total						

Checklist 2

tionships to the text. Each criterion should thus be considered with reference to the procedure that should be used in arriving at a fair rating.

Effective Use

Sound guidelines for using instructional materials are imperative if maximum values are to be achieved. Principles which teachers can use in guiding the use of materials are just as important as the materials themselves. Obviously, learning can be hindered if haphazardness and carelessness characterize the use of resources. The same painstaking care that is given to the selection of materials must also be given to their use.

Guiding Principles. Checklist 3 on the following page applies to the use of all types of instructional resources. It is based on an analysis of suggestions made regarding the use of specific types of materials and may be used as a checklist before using various materials.

Sources of Information on Instructional Materials

A first step to take in identifying sources of information on instructional materials is to review those that are available in the local school system. Although practices vary considerably among school systems, information on materials may usually be found in units of instruction, teaching guides, catalogs of materials available in the instructional materials center, supplementary lists of recently acquired materials, and special lists related to basic units of instruction. Teachers should carefully check the policies and procedures for requesting materials from the materials center, and from various lending agencies outside the school system.

In addition to local school system guides to instructional materials, the general guides listed below are helpful. Special guides to materials related to reading, maps, films, and other resources are presented in appropriate chapters that follow.

1. *Instructional Media Index.* New York: McGraw-Hill Book Company, Inc.

INSTRUCTIONAL MATERIALS CHECKLIST

Purpose
_____Does the manual suggest practical and worthwhile purposes?
_____What main ideas can be developed?
_____What questions can be answered?
_____How does it fit into individual or group inquiry with other resources?
_____What skills, attitudes, and appreciations can be improved?

Readiness
_____What concepts need development?
_____What experiences should be recalled and discussed?
_____How can it be related to problems in the unit?
_____What difficulties or understandings need explanation in advance?
_____Is a new point of view presented?
_____Does the manual suggest techniques for introducing it?

During Use
_____Should children observe? _____Take notes? _____Raise questions?
_____Should supplementary comments be made? _____Should a break be allowed during use for rest, questions, and comments?
_____Should the resource be used in its entirety without interruption?
_____Should the resource be used a second time to emphasize points, clarify questions, and make explanations?
_____Should supplementary materials be used with it?
_____Does the manual suggest activities for children?

Follow-Through
_____Is group discussion sufficient?
_____Is group planning needed to explore new questions and problems?
_____Can stated questions be answered?
_____What conclusions can be made? _____Should a summary be made?
_____Should a short test be given on key ideas?
_____Should other resources be consulted to check points at issue?
_____Are related activities suggested, such as map making, chart making, reading, committee work, construction, dramatization, processing of materials, other activities?
_____Does the manual suggest follow-through activities?

Teacher Evaluation
_____Was the resource satisfactory for the group involved?
_____How can its use be improved?
_____Should supplementary resources be available before or after its use?
_____Any special difficulties that should be noted for future reference?
_____Does the manual suggest points for evaluation?

Checklist 3

2. Catalogs and lists of resources available from the county schools office, the state department of education, state university, colleges, and other agencies from which your school district obtains materials

3. Periodicals: *Booklist, Grade Teacher, Instructor, NEA Journal, Scholastic Teacher, Social Education, Vertical File Service Media and Methods, Audiovisual Instruction, Educational Screen and Audiovisual Guide*

4. Detailed source lists in professional textbooks on audiovisual materials (See the list of references at the end of this chapter.)

5. Guides to free or inexpensive materials (also check the special section in the magazines listed above):

Catalog of Free Teaching Aids, G. S. Salisbury and R. H. Sheridan, Box 1075, Ventura, California.

Choosing Free Materials for Use in the Schools, American Association of School Administrators, National Education Association, 1201 16th St., N.W., Washington 6, D.C.

Elementary Teachers Guide to Free Curriculum Materials, Educators Progressive Service, Randolph, Wisconsin.

Free and Inexpensive Learning Materials, George Peabody College for Teachers, Nashville, Tennessee.

Free and Inexpensive Materials on World Affairs, L. S. Kenworthy, Brooklyn College, Bedford Avenue and H Avenue, Brooklyn 10, N.Y.

Inexpensive Bulletins Concerning Teaching Materials, and *Sources of Teaching Materials*, Bureau of Educational Research, Ohio State University, Columbus, Ohio.

Selected United States Government Publications, Superintendent of Documents, Government Printing Office, Washington, D.C. (Ask to be put on the mailing list.)

Sources of Free and Inexpensive Teaching Aids, Bruce Miller, Box 369, Riverside, California.

Using Free Materials in the Classroom, Association for Supervision and Curriculum Development, National Education Association, 1201 16th St., N.W., Washington 6, D.C.

Questions, Activities, Evaluation

1. Recall vivid learning experiences that you had in elementary school. Can you remember the instructional materials that were a part of them? What other factors were involved?

2. The level of concreteness of materials is one factor to

consider in selecting resources for a group. What are some other factors? Would learning in the social studies be increasingly more meaningful if only direct experiences were provided?

3. In some classrooms, a film, filmstrip, demonstration, or other resource is used merely as a side show unrelated to significant purposes of the group. What steps can be taken to prevent this?

4. Visit an instructional materials center and examine the types of resources available. Note those that might be useful in a unit you are planning to teach.

5. Examine one or more of the guides to free and inexpensive materials listed at the end of this chapter. Which materials appear to be related to a unit you are planning? Get some by writing to the publisher of each item and appraise them in terms of the criteria presented in this chapter.

6. Examine the pictures in this chapter. Would you make any changes in some of the displays shown in the pictures?

7. Select one instructional resource of your choice and make a tentative plan for using it. Use the checklist presented at the end of this chapter as a guide to planning.

8. Note ways in which the instructional resources discussed in this chapter can be used under each phase of inquiry in a unit of instruction of your choice.

References

Brown, James W., Richard B. Lewis, and Fred F. Harcleroad, A-V Instruction: Materials and Methods. New York: McGraw-Hill Book Company, Inc., 1964. Principles and procedures for using all types of instructional materials, and a listing of sources of materials.

Dale, Edgar, Audio-Visual Methods of Teaching, rev. ed. New York: The Dryden Press, Inc., 1954. A comprehensive treatment of instructional materials.

Hoffman, Howardine, and Armen Sarafian, "Instructional Resources," Social Studies in Elementary Schools, 32nd Yearbook, National Council for the Social Studies, pp. 219–33. Washington, D.C.: National Education Association, 1962. An overview of resources essential to well-rounded instruction.

Journal of Geography, LXVI (May 1967), 204–66. Entire issue on instructional media.

Joyce, Bruce R., Strategies for Elementary Social Science Education. Chicago: Science Research Associates, 1965. Suggestions for using various instructional media.

Lewis, Philip, "Instructional Technology," *New Curriculum Developments*, pp. 85–95. Washington, D.C.: Association for Supervision and Curriculum Development, National Education Association, 1965. Report on latest developments.

Community
Resources and
Audio-Visual
Materials

Community resources and audio-visual materials have a variety of uses in individual and group inquiry. Techniques of field study, mapping, interviewing, and other methods of inquiry are put to use as children gather fresh data on problems under study. Individual differences can be met by varying responsibilities for study during field trips, the viewing of films, and the use of other media. Such media are also useful in developing realistic conceptions of economic, social, and political activities as children study human activities in the community.

11

Community Resources for
Individual and Group Inquiry

The community is a laboratory for firsthand inquiry into human activities. Geographic, historical, economic, and other concepts can be developed in a realistic setting. Changing conditions and the factors that produce them can be studied as changes take place. Holidays, special events, and commemorations can be experienced with others. Field trips, interviews of experts, local publications, and historical sites can be incorporated in units of instruction. Processes of interaction can be studied directly as students observe various groups and participate in them.

A first step for teachers to take is to make a brief community survey in order to become well acquainted with the nature of the community and its history. The following model is suggestive of items to include in a survey; the items are also relevant to the planning of depth studies of Our Community and Other Communities.

Geography	Resources
History	Industry
Population	Business
Government	Transportation
Education	Communication
Religions	Conservation
Welfare Services	The Arts
Health and Safety	Recreation

An effective strategy is to involve students in the community survey if depth study of the community is included at their grade level. Observation techniques may be sharpened as students check safety hazards, type and location of residences, housing conditions, the business and industrial sections, and parks and playgrounds.

The human activities that children experience in their community provide opportunities to extend and enrich inquiry in the social studies. What activities in your community should be made a part of the instructional program? *(Hays; Courtesy of Monkmeyer)*

CHECKLIST FOR IDENTIFYING COMMUNITY RESOURCES

1. Study (or field) trips (industries, museums, etc.): _____
_____

2. Resource visitors (come to your class—panel or individuals): _____
_____

3. Radio and television (travel programs, historical plays): _____
_____

4. Published materials (newspapers, libraries, chamber of commerce bulletins): _____
_____

5. Persons to interview (travelers, policemen): _____
_____

6. Welfare and service organizations (Red Cross, service clubs): _____
_____

7. Service projects (relief programs, clean-up): _____
_____

8. Possible field studies (housing, safety): _____
_____

9. Visual resources (pictures, realia): _____
_____

10. Local current events (campaigns, drives): _____
_____

11. Resources within the school (collections of materials, teachers who have traveled): _____
_____

12. Community recreational resources (parks, camping facilities): _____
_____

13. Others: _____
_____

Checklist 1

Interviewing techniques can be improved as they put questions to old-timers, businessmen, school administrators, public officials, and other community workers. Skill in content analysis can be developed as they examine pictures, letters, newspapers, chamber of commerce reports, and other local documents.

IDENTIFYING INSTRUCTIONAL RESOURCES

One of the most useful parts of the community survey is the identification of resources that can be used to further children's learning. Children as well as the teacher should be alert to possibilities that may be used to answer questions and solve problems that arise in individual and group inquiry. Many school systems provide reports that include data on the most useful resources. Checklist 1 on page 327 may be used to guide the search for various resources in cases where a survey has not been completed.

Efforts should be made to organize information and materials in a form that will promote classroom use. This may be done by: (1) organizing a handbook of community materials and resources, (2) incorporating the material and selected references into units, (3) including materials and references in the courses of study, (4) preparing a special series of community life bulletins, (5) developing a reference volume on community information for school use, and (6) preparing kits containing materials that teachers can use in the classroom. In general, the material will be used most effectively if it is organized in a form in which its use is clearly indicated; for example, in units, in courses of study, or in teaching kits.

Using Community Resources

To achieve greatest efficiency, each type of resource and the problems incident to its use should be specifically considered. In the remainder of this section, attention is given to daily experiences, study trips, resource persons, and interviewing of resource persons.

DAILY EXPERIENCES

The day-by-day experiences of children in the community constitute one of the most valuable resources. As children see buildings under construction, watch changes in the season, see workers in action, observe holidays and celebrations, enjoy radio and television, hear and discuss current events, buy articles in stores, use the transportation system, attend churches, and engage in a host of other community activities, they discover many things and are stimulated to raise questions. Alert teachers capitalize on these experiences and use them to the fullest in the social studies. Questions are considered in discussion; current events of significance to the group are considered; ways to utilize community services and related responsibilities are discussed; comparisons are made between the child's experiences in his community and the experiences of others in different communities; misconceptions are clarified; and attention is given to an ever increasing understanding of the importance of cooperation, responsibility, and concern for others in every facet of community living.

STUDY TRIPS

Many different types of study trips are taken in dynamic social studies programs. They may be completed in a class period, a full day, or a period of several days. At times, they may be taken over the weekend, with the children's parents coming along. Children themselves may go on hikes to find the solutions to problems that have arisen. The whole class or a selected group may be involved.

The following list suggests the many opportunities in the social studies for the use of study trips.

STUDY TRIPS IN THE COMMUNITY

Aquarium	Lumbermill
Airport	Mission
Art gallery	Museum
Bakery	Newspapers
Bottling works	Observatory
Broadcasting station	Parks
Cannery	Petroleum company
Courthouse	Plant nursery
Dairy	Police station
Docks	Post office
Factories	Railroad station
Farms	River
Firehouse	Road construction
Forest service	Sawmill
Historic homes	Shipyard
Housing construction	Stores
Lake	Telephone exchange
Library	Zoo

Some of the most valuable study trips are informal walks that can be taken in the immediate neighborhood. Examples include short walks to see a house being built, changes in the season, operation of a ditch-digging machine, a special garden, soil erosion, a collection of pictures and objects, or a modern bakery. Or children may take short walking trips to gather specimens, see an old building, study architectural changes in the neighborhood, visit an expert to get answers to questions, study safety problems, and the like. Walking trips such as these are informal and easy to plan,

How do cows get their food? Who feeds them? When do they eat? Can we see them eat? These and other questions can be answered by a carefully planned study trip. (Alameda County)

require a minimum of organization, save time, and make children more critical observers of their immediate environment.

Many school systems have prepared a handbook for use with field trips. It contains a record of the study trips appropriate to units in the social studies as well as in other areas of the curriculum. Essential items regarding each trip are:

1. Name, telephone number, and address of the person to contact
2. Possible contribution to the unit—concepts, information, and so forth
3. Ages for which it is appropriate
4. Size of group that may be accommodated
5. Safety factors
6. Time, distance, mode of travel, route to follow
7. Best time to visit, length of visit
8. Eating facilities
9. Toilet facilities
10. What to see along the way
11. Resource materials available
12. Special notes or suggestions

A handbook facilitates the use of study trips and saves time for the persons with whom trips are planned, as well as for the teacher.

Planning Study Trips. The one great differentiating feature between a study trip and just going somewhere is that a real educational purpose exists for the study trip. Careful planning is essential in order to assure the achievement of learnings which will be of greatest value to the children.

Group planning through discussion is one of the most effective techniques that can be used. Attention should be given to the purpose of the trip, ways to record information, safety precautions, time schedule, travel arrangements, appropriate clothing, standards of behavior, and procedures to follow during the visit.

Health and safety precautions should be given thorough consideration. Rules for crossing the street, staying with the group, and general safety should be discussed. Hazards with reference to machinery, traffic, rivers, lakes, and the like should be mentioned. Each child should know what to do in case of an emergency on the bus or at the place to be visited.

Standards of courtesy and protection of property should be discussed. Each child has a responsibility to be courteous to the bus driver, the manager of the place being visited, and the guide. Respect for property both on the bus and at the location of the visit should be kept in mind. Children should be urged to thank the individuals who made the trip possible before they return home.

The importance of cooperating with the bus driver should be brought out in a meaningful way to each child. For example, if the children are fairly quiet, the bus driver will be able to hear signals and sirens, and thus drive the bus safely. Each child should also understand that he must stay in his seat so that the bus driver can have a full view at all times and so that no accident will occur if a quick stop is necessary.

Any parents who accompany the group on the trip should understand the major purposes to be achieved. They should be given specific instructions regarding ways they can help. If, for example, they are responsible for a group of eight children, they should learn the names of the children in their group and carry out specific directions regarding standards and regulations that have been set up. The parents should be introduced to the children for whom they are responsible, and the children should understand how they are to help on the trip.

If a bus is to be used for transportation, plans should be made for appropriate activities during the ride from the school to the destination. Quiet games which are appropriate include finding pictures on signs related to topics being studied in school, finding certain letters on signs, counting certain types of buildings, and seeing interesting bridges, factories, or other objects along the way. Those who sit next to the windows on the outgoing trip should trade places on the return trip with children who have had aisle seats, so that everyone will have an opportunity to observe important places along the way.

The teacher should plan a last-minute check just before the trip begins. The physical condition of each child should be checked, and children who are ill should be left with the school nurse or the principal. Each child should have a slip signed by his parents granting permission to take the trip. Dress and appearance should be checked, and children wearing a flowing scarf or similar item that might get caught in machinery should be asked not to wear it at the place of the visit. Individual and group assignments should be clarified. Essentials of good behavior and safety should be reviewed. Provision should be made for each child to get a drink and go to the toilet just before the trip begins.

Adequate provision should be made for any children who for some reason cannot go on the study trip. The principal should have a list of all children who are not scheduled to go and a note on plans that have been made for them—such as working in another teacher's room or working in the library.

A teacher's role at the place of the visit is that of general supervisor. Explanations should be made as needed; questions should be raised when something is not clear to the group; difficult terms should be explained; behavior problems should be met as they arise; and contact should be kept with all children. Since the group is representing the school, attention should be given as needed to any boisterousness, misconduct, or carelessness. Directions should be given as needed to any parents who are assisting with the supervision of the group. The group should be kept together, and the time schedule should be maintained. Any signs of fatigue or emotional disturbance should be noted, and steps should be taken to alleviate them. Before leaving the place of the visit, a check should be made to see that no one has left anything, and the roll should be double checked to make certain that no child has been left behind. Thanks should be expressed to everyone who assisted with the trip.

It is sound procedure to summarize specific plans on charts, on the chalkboard, or on duplicated sheets of paper so that important points are clear to each member of the group. Charts 1 and 2 show the planning done by a Grade I group who took a short walk to a grocery store.

After their walk to the store, the children engaged in dramatic play and developed the needs for materials shown in Chart 3, thus putting to use the information gained from the study trip.

An advanced type of planning for a study trip to an airport is illustrated in Charts 4, 5, and 6, which were developed by a Grade

VI group. The charts were made by the members of the class with the teacher serving as discussion leader and a child as the recorder. The class was divided into four committees, each committee being responsible for five of the questions in Chart 6.

LET'S FIND OUT

1. Where are vegetables kept?
2. How is meat kept fresh?
3. What is in the store-room?
4. Who keeps the shelves full?

Chart 1

OUR WALK TO THE STORE

1. Stay together.
2. Watch where you walk.
3. Ask questions in turn.
4. Listen to the answers.

Chart 2

WE NEED FOR OUR PLAY

A grocery store
Tables
Cash register
Vegetable stand

Counters
Delivery trucks
Shopping bags
An icebox

Chart 3

A SAFE TRIP

1. Stay in your group.
2. Keep in line.
3. Listen to directions.
4. Keep moving with the class.
5. Touch only those things the guide tells you to touch.
6. Have question ready.
7. Listen as questions are answered.

Chart 4

THINGS WE WANT TO SEE

1. Administration building
2. Control tower
3. Planes landing and taking off
4. Runways, beacons, and wind sock
5. Different types of planes
6. Weather bureau
7. Maintenance shops
8. Ticket and baggage office

Chart 5

At the airport
we can see
Hangars   Airplanes
Runways   Beacon lights
Windsocks
Office Building
A control tower

What main ideas and specific concepts might be developed as a result of a study trip to the airport? (San Bernardino)

QUESTIONS WE WANT TO ANSWER

1. How many passengers does a 727 carry? A DC-9?
2. What airlines use the airport?
3. How many planes come into the airport each day?
4. How high off the ground is the cockpit where the pilots sit?
5. How long are the runways at the airport?

6. How many runways are there at the airport?
7. At what altitude does a westbound plane travel? Eastbound? Northbound? Southbound?
8. What kinds of cargo are the planes carrying?
9. From where do the planes come?
10. How many men work in the control tower?

11. What do these men do?
12. What is a log?
13. How many instruments does the plane have on the control board?
14. What do these instruments tell the pilot?
15. How many pounds of baggage is one passenger allowed?

16. Where does the crew put the fuel in the airplane?
17. What is the runway made of?
18. How long does it take a pilot to get a commercial license?
19. What does one have to study in order to become a pilot?
20. Where is the baggage stored?

Chart 6

GUIDE FOR THE PLANNING OF STUDY TRIPS

First Considerations

_____Is it the best procedure for the purposes of the group?

_____Have adequate backgrounds, ideas, and purposes been developed?

_____Are related materials available—films, books, pictures?

_____Are there profitable follow-up activities?

_____Will it strengthen the school-community relations?

_____Others: _____

Preliminary Arrangements

_____Has administrative approval been given?

_____Has the approval of parents been secured?

_____Are eating and toilet arrangements satisfactory?

_____Has the time schedule been prepared?

_____Has the guide been advised on problems, needs, and maturity of the group?

_____Have travel arrangements and expenses been arranged?

_____Are assistants needed to help supervise the group?

_____Has a list been made of the names, telephone numbers, and addresses of those children who are going?

_____Others: _____

Teacher-Pupil Planning

_____Are questions prepared and understood?

_____Are recording procedures and assignments clear?

_____Are reporting procedures and assignments clear?

_____Have behavior standards been developed?

_____Have safety precautions been considered?

_____Have the time schedule, travel arrangements, and expenses been clarified?

_____Have significant side interests been noted?

_____Has attention been given to appropriateness of dress?

_____Are monitorial assignments clear?

_____Others: _____

Follow-Up Plans

_____Do next experiences help to develop main ideas?

_____What findings are to be reported?

_____What summaries and records should be made?

_____Is attention given to the development of charts, maps, diagrams, displays, murals, models, scrapbooks, construction, dramatic activities, and floor layouts?

_____Are procedures in mind to discover and clarify misconceptions?

_____Are interesting sidelights to be considered?

_____Are letters of appreciation and samples of follow-up work to be sent?

_____How is the children's behavior to be evaluated?

_____How are recording and reporting procedures to be evaluated?

_____Others: _____

Checklist 2

Many teachers use a checklist in order to assure effective planning of study trips. Checklist 2 on page 335 was developed by teachers in a curriculum workshop.

RESOURCE VISITORS

Community studies are enriched when firemen, policemen, newspapermen, and other workers meet with the class to discuss needs, problems, and questions that have arisen. In units on Indians, Living in South America, and Living in Japan, much help can be gained from individuals who are natives of the country or region or who have made visits there. Needs and problems which arise in units on Industrial America, Aviation, Transportation, Lumbering, and Marketing may be answered or solved by individuals who are well acquainted with them. The showing of realia, pictures, slides, and bulletins along with the discussion enhances the contributions of resource visitors.

A list of resource visitors compiled by one group of teachers in a social studies workshop included:

Does your community have resource visitors who can share authentic costumes or other materials and discuss their uses? *(San Bernardino County)*

Airport employees
Authors
Businessmen
City officials
Consuls of foreign nations
Dairymen
Ex-servicemen
Farmers
Fellow teachers
Firemen
Foreign students
Forest rangers
Gardeners
House builders
Industrial workers
Leaders of youth organizations
Librarians
Merchants

Ministers
Musicians
Newspapermen
Nurserymen
Old-time residents
Policemen
Professional men—doctors, lawyers, dentists, teachers
Representatives of service organizations
School administrators
Ship workers
Social workers
Soil conservationists
Store clerks
Traffic safety specialists
Travelers

A sound procedure is to organize a file of resource persons who can make valuable contributions to the social studies program. A simple card system can be used by noting the following information on three-by-five inch index cards:

Contribution _____

Name _____ Telephone _____

Hours available _____

Will come to school? _____

Children may visit at home or office? _____

Comments _____

_____

In building up such a file, one should interview fellow teachers and other school workers to determine which resource visitors can make a real contribution. Sending out random questionnaires is unwise because individuals who cannot make the kind of contribution that is needed by the children in the class may volunteer. Serious public relations problems can be created in this way.

Careful timing and planning are needed to obtain maximum benefits from resource visitors. As with the study trip, visitors should be invited when they can contribute to on-going class activities, and when fruitful follow-up activities may make use of their special contributions. The following guidelines are helpful:

1. Through group discussion, determine whether the use of the visitor is the best way to secure required information on existing needs and problems.

2. Clarify and list the needs and questions on which help is desired.

3. Select a resource person who can make a rich contribution.

4. Plan with the visitor, giving attention to timing and the needs, questions, interests, and age level of the group. Give special attention to vocabulary and illustrative materials that may be used.

5. Make plans with the children for reception of the visitor, introductions, expression of appreciation, behavior standards, and recording procedures.

6. Both the teacher and children should be ready to raise questions and state problems.

7. The teacher should guide the discussion and stimulate group thinking as needed.

8. Use the information to solve problems and to further expression through reporting, art, writing, dramatization, and so forth.

9. Evaluate the effectiveness of the use made of the information obtained.

10. Write a letter of appreciation including (if possible) material showing how the contribution was used.

11. Continue the unit, moving on to new needs and problems that have arisen.

Interviewing Resource Persons. An interview is a desirable procedure to use when a resource person cannot come to school, essential materials must be kept on the job, or when seeing the person in a working situation is more beneficial. Interviews may be conducted by an individual pupil or by a small group. In making plans for them, attention should be given to the same kind of planning as is carried out for the use of resource visitors. In addition, attention must be given to good interviewing technique. The following points illustrate the standards that can be set up through group planning:

1. Introduce yourself.
2. State questions clearly.
3. Listen attentively.
4. Let the other person talk.
5. Ask questions on special points.
6. Take notes on hard points.
7. Do not waste time.
8. Express thanks when finished.

Audio-Visual Materials

The list of materials in the checklist below indicates the wide range of audio-visual resources, equipment, and supplies available

Checklist 3

AUDIO-VISUAL RESOURCES CHECKLIST

Realia and Representations of Realia

___Models	___Collections	___Museums
___Objects	___Products	___Dioramas
___Specimens	___Miniatures	___Panoramas
___Samples	___Ornaments	___Mock-ups
___Exhibits	___Utensils	___Marionettes
___Textiles	___Weapons	___Puppets
___Costumes	___Facsimiles	___Dolls
___Instruments		
___Others: _____		

Sound and Film Resources

___Motion pictures	___Recordings (discs and tapes)
___Radio and television	___Sound filmstrips

Pictures and Pictorial Representations

___Photographs	___Post cards	___Montages
___Pictures	___Prints	___Murals
___Drawings	___Etchings	___Filmstrips
___Sketches	___Albums	___Silent films
___Slides	___Scrapbooks	___Opaque projections
___Transparencies		
___Others: _____		

Symbolic and Graphic Representations

___Maps	___Cartoons	___Chalkboard
___Globes	___Posters	___Bulletin board
___Atlases	___Diagrams	___Flannel board
___Charts	___Graphs	___Time lines
___Others: _____		

Projectors and Viewers   *Players and Recorders*

___Slide	___Motion picture	___Record
___Opaque	___Stereoscope	___Tape
___Overhead	___Slide viewer	___Wire

Supplies and Materials for Production

___Lettering devices	___Slide making	___Bookbinding
___Map outlines	___Chart making	___Map making
___Transparencies	___Picture mounting	___Model making
___Others: _____		

for use in the social studies. The checklist is helpful in surveying the resources available in a particular school system. It also can be used in planning a unit to answer such questions as: Which resources can be used in the initiation? Which can be used in connection with specific questions and problems as the unit develops? Which can be used to summarize key ideas? Which can be used to review and emphasize key learnings? The checklist also can be used to evaluate one's own acquaintance with resources and equipment.

Realia and Representation of Realia

REALIA

The term *realia* means real things or artifacts. In this section it is used to refer to objects, models, specimens, and items in museums, exhibits, dioramas, and panoramas. Specific materials used in the social studies that may be classified as realia include jewelry, ornaments, money, clothing, authentically dressed dolls, utensils, tools, dishes, tableware, products, manuscripts, documents, facsimiles, seals, letters, timepieces, communications devices, models of transportation equipment, musical instruments, art objects, sample foods, models of shelter, and weapons.

How can realia such as these be used to develop concepts and main ideas? What appreciations of changes in ways of living might be developed? *(Albany, California)*

Children cannot go back in time and space to early times and to the many other eras and places considered in the social studies. They can, however, have experiences with real things, or replicas of them, related to the unit. By using realia, children may identify themselves more closely with objects and persons they are studying in such units as Home and Family, The Farm, Pioneers, Indians, Mexico, China, and Aviation. For example, in a study of Colonial Living, one group made extensive use of candle molds, muskets, powder horns, cooking utensils, tableware, a spinning wheel, and clothing of the period. In a study of Mexico, another group ate tortillas, frijoles, chile, and enchiladas. In addition they had access to sombreros, serapes, rebosos, huaraches, and models of furniture and utensils. In a study of communication, one class used a simple crystal radio set, a telegraph key, drums, hollow logs, whistle, bone horn, bells, telephone, and flag signals. We should emphasize, however, that each of the foregoing was used in accordance with carefully made plans and related to important concepts and understandings.

In using realia and models, increased learning is possible if they are used in line with the following principles:

1. Use realia to initiate a unit, to enrich concepts encountered in the unit, and to culminate experiences.

2. Allow children to handle them and see how they work. If they are fragile, have their use demonstrated to the class.

3. Be alert to questions and comments made by children as they handle them; they may be vital clues to interest, needs, and misconceptions.

4. Encourage their use in dramatic activities and in construction.

5. Relate their use to pictures, reading materials, motion pictures, and experiences children have had on trips.

6. Have children see them in a complete and realistic setting— museum, restoration, displays, exhibits, dioramas, and panoramas.

7. Use them in connection with real problems that arise in the unit, not as gadgets.

Realia and models may be seen or obtained in many places. They are available in the instructional materials center in many city and county school systems. In some elementary schools, they are available in the school museum or the materials center. At times they can be obtained from individuals in the community; this is especially true of Indian and colonial realia and materials gathered on trips to various countries. Children themselves may collect and construct many different items. Other sources used by teachers include public museums, commercial and industrial organizations, and theatrical supply houses. Once individuals in a community have learned that the materials will be put to effective educational use, they are eager and willing to share them, and in some instances they will give them to the school.

EXHIBITS

Exhibits are used to display a variety of materials in the social studies. In a study of transportation by one group, models and pictures of boats, aircraft, trains, wagons, carts, and other items were arranged in a chronological sequence. The background used for the exhibit was in a time line with explanatory material and related pictures. In a study of China, another group made an exhibit of the processing of silk, starting with the cocoon and ending with a piece of cloth. In a study of industrial America, another class made several exhibits showing the processing of iron, petroleum, and soybeans, from raw material to finished product. Other examples of exhibits used successfully in the social studies are: art in the community, growth of democratic institutions, basic documents in American democracy, changes in methods of transportation, story of printing, history of records, the development of communications, intergroup contributions, weapons and utensils from different cultural groups, flags of Latin America, and products of different countries and industries.

To be most effective, such guidelines as the following should be used in planning exhibits:

1. Provide for teacher-pupil planning in the use and development of the exhibit.

2. Work out balanced-space arrangement, using tables, bulletin boards, and racks.

3. Do not clutter the exhibit with too much detail or weird color schemes.

4. Use a relatively simple background with simple labels and clear lettering to designate items.

5. Place the most important objects in strategic positions so that the eyes will naturally move to them.

6. Give attention to eye level in arranging materials; provide for effective lighting.

7. Arrange for demonstrations, discussions, and reports in order to make the exhibit more effective.

8. Use movement and sound if they add to the value of the exhibit.

9. Make plans to share the exhibit with other classes, parents, the library, or museum.

Materials for exhibits can be obtained from several sources. Parents, pupils, and individuals in the community are often happy to share hobbies and collections when they are to be put to educational use. Materials may also be obtained from governmental agencies, chambers of commerce, and industrial plants. Many audio-visual departments are developing exhibits to accompany units in the social studies.

DIORAMAS AND PANORAMAS

A diorama consists of a scene in perspective in which three-dimensional models depict the activity. They may be used to present many scenes such as life in Boonesboro, living in a log cabin in pioneer times, neighborhood helpers at work, and activities at the airport. Careful attention must be given to the setting in which the diorama is placed. Panoramas are broad scenes in which

Dioramas made by individual children have been stacked to make this exhibit depicting life in Mexico. Why must children do intensive planning and research to make such dioramas? (Richmond, California)

models are used to depict a topic; they are not necessarily in perspective. Panoramas are used to show industries, activities of the United Nations, branches of the federal government, recreational opportunities, activities in a lumber camp, and the like. Many teachers have found that children will do a great amount of research to make their dioramas and panoramas realistic.

DEMONSTRATIONS

The social studies offer many possibilities for the use of demonstrations. In a unit on the Home and Family, appropriate demonstrations include ways of growing plants and flowers, making things for the playhouse, and arranging the playhouse for different uses. In a study of the Pioneers, demonstrations may be given of carding wool, candle making, operating the spinning wheel, making soap, and processing flax. Other illustrative demonstrations which may be given at many different levels include proper use of tools, materials, utensils, musical instruments, art media, maps, globes, and models. Objects brought from home can be demonstrated by children as they relate to problems and topics in the unit.

The procedures involved in effective demonstrations may be illustrated by considering a demonstration of candle making carried out during a study of Colonial Life. The teacher's purposes were to develop increased appreciation of the processes used by the colonists to make candles, to show early methods of providing illumination in the home, and to develop readiness for candle making by the children. Need for the demonstration had arisen in a discussion of how the colonists provided light and heat in their homes. The class decided to invite a local resident (a resource visitor) who had a collection of colonial candles and candle-making equipment. The resource visitor and the teacher planned the sequence of steps in the process, giving attention to timing, space arrangements, and materials that the children should use following the demonstration. During the demonstration, the children were seated so that all could see and hear; the teacher guided the asking and answering of questions. After the demonstration, the steps in candle making were summarized on a chart. This was followed by a candle-dipping activity in which several candles were made by the class with assistance given by the resource visitor and the teacher.

Demonstrations such as the one above are planned in terms of the following:

1. Clarify the purposes to be achieved by the demonstration.
2. Decide on the person to do it—children, the teacher, a visitor.

3. Plan carefully so that the demonstration is authentic and each step is clearly understood.

4. Practice the demonstration before it is given.

5. Present only those ideas that can be grasped by the group —avoid too many ideas and overly difficult ones.

6. Be sure that necessary materials are available.

7. Check to see if each child can see and hear the demonstration.

8. Do the demonstration according to the plan.

9. Be alert to indications of misunderstanding, such as lack of interest, questioning, and grimaces.

10. Time the demonstration so that interest is maintained.

11. Use a chart or outline to summarize the steps if they are to be carried out by the class.

12. Encourage questions and comments to clarify understanding.

13. Repeat various parts as necessary to clarify understanding.

14. Have immediate follow-up activities in which the ideas of the demonstration are related to the main ideas in the unit.

Sound and Film Resources

MOTION PICTURES

Motion pictures are used extensively in the social studies because of their effectiveness in portraying action. Processes, people, the world of nature, various types of activities, and significant events can be seen in action in a realistic setting. Contemporary affairs, past events, and faraway places can be brought into the classroom. Processes that cannot be visualized in any other way can be seen in action on the screen. A broad sweep of events may be seen with various relationships highlighted, as in films showing the development of inventions, the growth of institutions, or contributions of great men and women. Time and speed can be controlled by slow-motion and time-lapse photography to show activities that are better understood when seen at varying rates of speed. Eight mm film loops can be used in individual and small-group study to develop specific concepts. In addition, motion pictures are interesting to watch, hold attention, and can exert a great impact on attitudes.

Effective use of motion pictures requires careful previewing and selection on the basis of needs and problems that arise in a unit. Selected films should be authentic, interesting, up to date, on the child's level of understanding, and mechanically satisfactory with reference to photography and sound. The following guidelines are helpful in planning for their use in units:

1. *Note concepts, main ideas, and other learnings appropriate to the group.* Increased understanding of basic human activities is a major outcome of instruction in the social studies. All films touch on one or more fundamental aspects of human living. The teacher should be alert to the possibilities inherent in each one, and guide children to discover them. No one can remember hundreds of facts, but one can organize thinking around basic concepts and generalizations. Films should contribute to this goal.

2. *Note aspects of human behavior, such as cooperativeness, acceptance of responsibility, creativeness, and concern for others.* Human behavior in many different situations is brought to children in films; examples may well be considered by the class. All too frequently significant aspects of behavior are pushed aside and attention is centered on the "number of bananas loaded on the boat," "the products raised," or a similar set of facts. While these are important, they must not rule out attention to effective human relations and group processes. This is undoubtedly one of the most neglected aspects of film utilization at the present time.

3. *Detect size, space, and time distortions, and any parts which give wrong impressions.* Time, space, and cultural concepts are telescoped in many motion pictures. Highlights given to selected activities of a cultural group may lead to stereotyped thinking. Showing the development of a nation in a thirty-minute film may lead to inaccuracies in historical perspective. Moving from border to border in a few minutes may give inadequate conceptions of size. Through discussion, reading, and the use of maps and other related materials—a cross-media approach—realistic conceptions can be developed and erroneous impressions corrected.

4. *Note difficult ideas and concepts which require further development.* Difficult concepts and terms are used in many films; for example, *steppe, latitude, prevailing westerlies,* and *conservation.* Film-makers cannot develop completely all of the concepts presented in one or two reels of film, and teachers must use related procedures, such as discussion, pictures, study trips, and research activities, to clarify concepts encountered in motion pictures and other aids to learning.

5. *During follow-up activities, give emphasis to the main ideas of greatest significance to the class.* In some instances, these may be related to social functions; in others, to human relations and group processes; in still others, to significant facts and concepts, or a combination of learnings. A reshowing of the film may be necessary to clarify issues or problems that arise during discussion.

6. *Enjoy motion pictures with the group to the extent that enjoyment is consistent with a high level of learning.* The author has

observed several teachers lose group interest during follow-up discussions of a film because of an overly zealous attempt to analyze the facts involved, and a failure to enjoy the film's interesting parts. This may occur when formally imposed and poorly understood written assignments or artificial check-up tests follow each and every film. This pitfall can be avoided by relating follow-up activities to the purposes established for the use of the film, and by guiding the group to enjoy and share its interesting features.

Nearly all of the points above also apply to television programs because many programs are in reality films which are being shown on a definite schedule. However, some programs are "live" and have added realism and interest because we are able to witness an event as it occurs. Yet difficulties arise in scheduling television programs and in finding those appropriate for a particular class. The same also applies to radio programs. Attention is given to both types of resources in the next section. The reader is urged to keep in mind points made about motion pictures as plans are made to utilize television and radio programs.

RADIO AND TELEVISION

Radio and television programs are especially valuable because real events can be shared as they occur and events of the past can be recreated. Realism is enhanced as on-the-scene reporters chronicle events in a dramatic and personal manner. Outstanding musicians, scientists, statesmen, and community leaders can be "brought into the classroom or home" to enrich and extend learning in an authentic and interesting way. Dramatized historical programs can be used to help children identify themselves with great people and events of the past. Special feature programs, such as holidays, commemorations, campaigns, and festivals, can be used to help children gain insight into their significance.

Video-tape or film may be used to record programs for future use. By building up a library of video-tapes or films, one can reuse the better programs at times that are most advantageous to teachers.

Selecting Good Programs. A major factor in the successful use of radio and television is the identification of the best programs for group use in school and the best ones for individual use at home. Information about programs can be found in local newspapers, children's news periodicals, weekly and monthly magazines, TV guides, schedules issued by local stations and national networks, and program guides issued by school systems. The last source is one of the best. Advice also should be obtained from fellow teachers and from audio-visual directors.

Some of the best programs are presented during out-of-school hours and on weekends. Children should be encouraged to watch them so that the programs can be shared and discussed in class. Some teachers successfully employ a simple forum technique in which four or five children are asked to report on a particular program. Other members of the class are urged to be ready to ask questions and make additional points about it, thus being encouraged to watch the same program. By rotating membership on the "forum group," the entire class can participate in a direct and challenging manner. As the reports and discussion are carried out in class, relationships to units of instruction and other classroom experiences can be emphasized.

Listening and Viewing Skills. Children develop and use several skills in connection with radio and television programs. Although radio programs require listening without the aid of related visual imagery, both types of program require a clear purpose as a basis for use: to learn the story behind a person or event, to get new ideas on a topic, or to note points related to a question. During the program, a child's mood should be one of critical attentiveness. Eyes should be focused on the set; extraneous movements, or noise of others should be overlooked; notes should be made as needed; and questions about the program should be kept in mind for the follow-up discussion. Critical listening and viewing as outlined in Chart 7 is the outcome which many middle- and upper-grade children can achieve.

CRITICAL LISTENERS AND VIEWERS

1. Be alert from start to finish.
2. Remember the most important points.
3. Be ready to ask questions at the end.
4. Be ready to agree or disagree.
5. Note ideas we can use in our unit.
6. Note ideas we need to learn more about.

Chart 7

RECORDINGS

Recordings of radio programs, and recordings of children's experiences have several advantages over the radio: (1) they may be used at the appropriate time in a unit, (2) they may be replayed and appraised as time permits, (3) they are inexpensive to purchase and are easy to make, (4) they may be stopped for dis-

Recorded material can be used when needed by individual students. *(San Diego City Schools)*

cussion and comments, and (5) many records are available for use in different units in the social studies.

Recordings and records are made and used for many different purposes in the social studies. They provide excellent background and sound effects for dramatization, pageants, creative work, and choral and individual readings. Recordings may be made of children's work, speeches of famous people, school visitors, travelogs, and radio programs. Growth in planning, discussion, reporting, and group evaluation may be appraised if recordings are made at various times during the year. Stories, rhythms, comments for use with slides or filmstrips, and music for folk dances and accompaniment may be recorded and used as needed.

Pictures and Pictorial Representations

STILL PICTURES

Still pictures are the most widely used of all audio-visual materials. The photographs and illustrations in textbooks, encyclopedias, and other reading materials add interest to reading and help to clarify difficult terms and understandings. Use of the opaque projector to show pictures on the screen enables the group to focus attention on specific details that have been enlarged.

Slides and filmstrips are used to present a series of related pictures in sequence. Post cards, cutouts from magazines and newspapers, and children's pictures are used in displays, bulletin board arrangements, and exhibits. Stereographs are viewed individually or projected for group viewing to give a realistic three-dimensional effect.

Carefully selected pictures can achieve many purposes. Units can be introduced in such a way as to emphasize major topics and problems. Key questions can be raised and interest can be stimulated. Reports and scrapbooks made by children can be made more meaningful. Erroneous ideas and misunderstandings can be corrected. Symbols on maps can be visualized. Realism can be portrayed and emotions can be stirred. Critical thinking can be sharpened as children use pictures to prove points at issue, for example, how tools such as the adz were used, how a serape should be adorned, or how iron ore is processed.

A child's growth in ability to get ideas from pictures proceeds from enumeration (telling about, or counting objects—"I see a cow, a barn, a farmer . . .") to description (describing colors, activities, or objects—"See the red barn. The cows are eating hay . . ."), and to the making of inferences and interpretations (saying what may happen next, or noting relationships—"The farmer is going to milk the cows. The cows are milked in the barn . . ."). The more experience children have and the greater their command of meaning, the better they can "read pictures." If children are immature, or if their backgrounds are narrow, a teacher can expect simple enumeration of pictures. As their backgrounds are enriched, the interpretation of pictures will improve.

Flat pictures. Flat pictures, such as prints, photographs, and pictures from magazines, are used in a variety of ways in the social studies. One of their most valuable uses is in the initiation of a unit in which they are used with a variety of other materials to reveal needs and problems, and to stimulate questions and interest. An especially effective use is in the clarification and development of concepts, such as *Conestoga wagon, Boonesboro,* and *Cumberland Gap* in a study of The Pioneers, or *tender, turntable,* and *roundhouse* in a study of Railroad Transportation. Many children find pictures helpful in giving reports on men at work in industry, transportation, communication, conservation, and similar activities. Art prints may be used to recreate feelings, thoughts, and hopes of people who lived in other times and places. Increasing attention is being given to the use of photographs based on life in the children's own community. Community studies in which use is made of pictures of boats, harbors, community workers, industries,

What questions might be used to interpret these photographs? What key concepts about economic activities might be developed? (MATCH Box Project, Children's Museum, Boston)

and processes have authenticity and reality which cannot be obtained from more formal approaches. Pictures showing human relations and problem situations can be used to develop higher levels of democratic behavior. Examples of cooperation, concern for others, and responsibility are easy to find in pictures: members of a family working and playing together, children doing tasks at home, nurses and other community workers on the job, pioneers building cabins, workers loading boats, or safety precautions being taken in mines and factories. Interesting and constructive discussions also can be developed around pictures showing playthings not put away, paper on the floor, and other situations in which children can detect something to be done to bring about improvement. Children's drawings can be used for the same purpose.

INTERPRETING PICTURES OF LAND SCENES	INTERPRETING PICTURES OF HUMAN ACTIVITIES
Where is the scene located?	Where is the activity located?
What items stand out? Hills? Valleys? Rivers? Others?	What are the people doing?
How high, large, or small are they?	Is individual or group work emphasized?
Is natural vegetation shown?	What tools and materials are being used?
Are crops or gardens shown? If so, what is being raised?	Are their ways of working modern or traditional?
Are there indications of the weather? Temperature? Amount of rainfall? Wind? Snow?	What kind of clothing are they wearing?
Are there roads? Canals? Railroads? Buildings? Other man-made items?	Are homes or other buildings shown?
Can you estimate the area included in the picture?	Are animals, roads, means of transportation, and other items shown?
	Can you estimate the area included in the picture?

Chart 8

Chart 9

In order to promote maximum learning, pictures should be selected and used in accordance with sound guidelines:

1. Select pictures that portray a dominant idea, are not cluttered with detail, and are artistically and technically of high quality. A few carefully chosen pictures of high quality are of greater instructional value than a random selection of many pictures of low quality. Avoid the use of pictures that contain distortions, misconceptions, and objectionable advertising material.

2. Select and arrange pictures carefully to initiate each unit so that significant questions are raised as children examine them. Use a few pictures at a time, holding back pictures related to topics that

will arise later in the unit. Such a procedure is a good way to move children from one part of the unit to another. As the unit progresses, new pictures can be used in connection with specific questions and problems.

3. Use labels and captions, colored paper for mounting, colored paper arrows and strips to highlight important items in pictures, related maps and charts, and attractive arrangements that will add to the instructional value of pictures through improved *eye appeal*. Experiment with different arrangements and with different color combinations, selecting those that are most effective; encourage children to do the same.

4. In directed picture study, guide the discussion from simple counting of objects and from brief descriptions of what is portrayed to the making of interpretations and the noting of relationships. For example, in a picture showing men building a home, children may be guided to see uses of resources such as lumber and cement, men working together cooperatively, and individual responsibilities being carried out efficiently.

5. Provide for individual and small-group use of pictures such as making scrapbooks, arranging displays and bulletin boards, making reports, planning picture-and-label matching games, proving a point in discussion, illustrating steps in construction or processing of material, and answering questions about food, clothing, shelter, transportation, and other topics in a unit. Teach children to use pictures for various purposes as shown in Charts 10 to 15.

6. Organize picture collections around main ideas or problems in the unit and place them in a kit or file for ease of handling and utilization. Mount them to add to their attractiveness and durability. Place them in labeled folders or large envelopes and make an index for easy reference. Keep the collection up to date by adding new pictures and replacing old ones. Obtain pictures from magazines, newspapers, old textbooks, travel agencies, business concerns, chambers of commerce, information offices of governments, libraries, and commercial publishers and distributors.

OPAQUE PROJECTIONS

Opaque projections used in the social studies include a variety of nontransparent materials—pictures, drawings, diagrams, pages in books and encyclopedias, maps, charts, coins and paper money, songs, illustrations from newspapers and magazines, post cards, textiles, and other items which are magnified for class discussion. Since the pictures are projected by means of reflected light, a dark room is essential. Opaque projections are valuable for several reasons. Up-to-date materials can be used in units; maps and graphs can be enlarged easily; picture interpretation can be improved;

attention can be focused on significant details in illustrations; children's work can be shared; reports can be made more interesting; and the entire class can examine an item at once instead of having it passed around the room.[1] By hinging several drawings

FIND A PICTURE THAT
SHOWS ONE OR MORE
OF THESE

plow	corral
harrow	silo
tractor	pasture
hay rack	field

Chart 10

CAN YOU DRAW A
PICTURE TO SHOW
THESE OBJECTS?

trencher	powder horn
ladle	broad axe
pewter dish	adz
Betty lamp	flail

Chart 11

USE PICTURES TO
IMPROVE ORAL
REPORTS

1. Select pictures that show the most important ideas.
2. Select large pictures so that all can see them.
3. Arrange the pictures in proper order.
4. Hold the pictures so that all can see them.
5. Point to important parts of the picture while talking.

Chart 12

WHERE TO FIND
PICTURES

1. Look in the picture file.
2. Look in magazines.
3. Look in newspapers.
4. Look in bulletins from the Chamber of Commerce.
5. Check the encyclopedia.
6. Check textbooks and references.
7. Ask the librarian.

Chart 13

together, or pasting them on a strip, children can make simulated motion pictures to illustrate stories and reports. In fact, children should have many opportunities to select pictures for showing in the opaque projector that are related to topics that are being studied.

If certain pictures, drawings, or other items are to be projected several times, mount them on chipboard with rubber cement. The

[1] A helpful leaflet, *Opaque Projection*, can be obtained from Charles Beseler Company, 60 Badger Avenue, Newark 8, N.J.

HOW WE USE PICTURES

1. To explain new words

2. To prove points

3. To make reports interesting

4. To show difficult ideas

5. To show places on maps

6. To arrange bulletin boards

Chart 14

HELPING WITH THE BULLETIN BOARD

1. Bring pictures that fit the topic.

2. Use post cards, photographs, and cutout pictures.

3. Select the very best ones.

4. Arrange them so that everybody *wants* to see them.

5. Use colored paper background.

Chart 15

chipboard should be cut to fit into the projector; leave a wide side margin so that classification information can be written on it to facilitate filing. Apply the rubber cement to the back of the picture with a flat brush and mount in the center of the chipboard. Lay waxed paper over the picture and press under books until it is dry. Wipe off excess cement after it has dried, enter classification information, and file for future use. Over a period of time, excellent sets of pictures for specific units can be built up and used to add a great deal to the program.

STEREOGRAPHS

Stereographic pictures have a realistic three-dimensional effect which ordinary photographs do not possess, and many are available on units commonly used in the social studies. Because of their realistic effect, they are a most practical aid for individual use in the social studies. Inexpensive stereoscopic reels (colored slides in a circular mounting for use in a plastic viewer) are available on states and countries throughout the world. A helpful practice is to select reels related to topics under study and to place them and a viewer in the reading center for individual use. Purposes for viewing should be clarified during discussion so that the pupils will make use of the information obtained from them in later activities.

FILMSTRIPS AND SLIDES

Filmstrips and slides are among the most popular audio-visual materials used in the social studies. They are easy to project; they are accompanied by helpful manuals; they cover a variety of topics; they are available in both colored and black and white types; they are relatively inexpensive; and their use enables a teacher to show selected materials at the time they are needed, and to discuss them as long as the situation demands. Some filmstrips are accompanied by recordings and thus require little or no commentary as they are being shown. Slides are easy to make, can be shown in any order, but cost more than filmstrips and must be handled carefully to avoid damage. Where order of showing is not a fundamental problem or the sequence of pictures in the filmstrips is satisfactory, the filmstrip is probably more desirable because of lower cost and ease of use and storage.

Making Filmstrips. Filmstrips, or 2″ x 2″ colored transparencies, can be produced to show community workers, water supply, historic places in the area, or other subjects not available from commercial producers. A 35 mm camera is used. To make a filmstrip, a negative of the script and pictures is developed first; a positive for projection is made from the negative by running it through a filmstrip printer (in photograph-processing shops). Colored transparencies are processed by the seller of the film, or by photograph-processing shops, and are returned ready to use.

In preparing a filmstrip, an outline should be made to show the step-by-step plan, and each frame that is to be photographed. Plan titles, labels, leading questions, and script for each frame, or for placement on separate frames between pictures. Use very little if any printed matter on frames for primary grades. Prepare frame cards and photograph them in proper order with the 35 mm camera, have the negative developed, and a positive printed from the negative. Assistance on technical questions such as use of a copy lens, lighting, and the like can be secured from a photographic supply store.

If a filmstrip or colored transparencies are to be made of a study trip, anticipate the "shots" that will be most effective. Include children in each picture to add personal interest, perspective, and an idea of relative size. Urge children always to look at the objects being photographed, not at the camera. Have the schedule worked out in detail so that no time is lost in taking pictures.

Making Lantern Slides. Teachers and children can learn to make lantern slides fairly easily.[2] Slides can be made of tests, songs, maps, charts, diagrams, and similar items. Photographic slides may be made of anything that can be photographed. Transparent inks and water colors, slide-making crayons, India ink,

---

[2] See John U. Michaelis and Enoch Dumas, *The Student Teacher in the Elementary School* (Englewood Cliffs, N.J.: Prentice-Hall, Inc., 1960).

pencils, pens, brushes, glass, and materials for silhouettes are the essential working tools and materials for handmade slides. Many teachers have found slide making an excellent activity for children to use in organizing, summarizing, and presenting information.

OVERHEAD PROJECTIONS

Teachers may use overhead projectors to project material while facing the class. A teacher can write on transparent plastic, or point to diagrams, sketches, and pictures on slides, and guide discussion while the material is being projected. A most effective technique is the preparation of overlays (laying one drawing over another) to show relationships. For example, one drawing may show the topography of the United States; on this is placed a second one showing forests or some other item. By showing the sketch of topography and then laying the sketch of forests over it, pupils can grasp relationships quickly. By taping one drawing to another along one edge to achieve a hinge-like effect, the second drawing can be folded over the first easily so that borders line up effectively. By choosing colors carefully, one can obtain dramatic and realistic effects. The technique of making overlays is similar to that of placing sketches made on clear plastic over a relief map to show relationships.

DRAWINGS

Simple drawings and sketches are used in a variety of ways. Examples are: making a sketch to use in designing floor layouts, posters, murals, backgrounds for plays; using drawings in planning for construction of boats, looms, utensils, and model buildings; showing sketches or drawings in making reports, clarifying points in discussions, and giving demonstrations; using simple drawings to help carry out processes such as dipping candles; sketching a map to show travel routes, ports, airways, or physical barriers; and drawing the route that is to be taken on a study trip.

Sketches or drawings may be made on the chalkboard or on paper, depending on difficulty, the need for future reference, and the purpose for which they are to be used. Their unique value results from the fact that they are a fast, easy means of illustrating key ideas and relationships.

Symbolic and Graphic Illustrations

THE BULLETIN BOARD

The bulletin board is useful in initiating units, stimulating new interests and clarifying problems, posting children's work, and

Simplicity in design is a characteristic of effective bulletin board displays. Notice the use of realia in the foreground. (Los Angeles)

displaying maps, charts, and similar materials. In initiating units, one should display materials that will evoke interests and stimulate questions related to those problems in the unit that are to be considered first. By changing and rearranging materials to stimulate

BULLETIN BOARD PLANNING	
Color	Cloth
Lines	Posters
Pictures	Graphs
Letters	Yarn
Rhythm	Contrast
Paper	Circles
Charts	Models
Maps	Symbols
Tape	Symmetry
Space	Textiles
Blocks	Clippings
Objects	Diagrams
Signs	Strips

Chart 16

TRYING DIFFERENT ARRANGEMENTS

Arrange materials on a table or on the floor.

Try different arrangements.

Try different background material.

Try different ways of placing the title and lettering.

Try lines, circles, arrows, and colors to accent ideas.

Try different mountings for pictures.

Chart 17

new interests, the development of the unit can be guided in sound directions. Related materials, such as posters, drawings, charts, maps, or graphs, should be posted as they are needed to solve problems that arise in the unit. Children's work may be displayed for purposes of sharing and summarizing the various learning experiences that have been undertaken.

Bulletin boards require care in the selection of materials, arrangement, and timing of displays. The following guidelines are necessary for effective use:

1. Material should be interesting and understandable.

2. Material should be related to the topics being considered in the unit.

3. Material should be changed as purposes and problems change, and used to move the unit forward in profitable directions.

4. Balanced, artistic arrangements should be made with appropriate headings, titles, explanatory information, mountings, colors, and similar artistic elements.

5. Children should have opportunities to assist in arranging and rearranging materials that they have made or brought from home.

6. Children should have ample opportunity to explore and discuss the material.

FLANNEL BOARD AND MAGNETIC BOARD

Although the flannel (or felt) board is not used as extensively in the social studies as in other subjects, it does have certain uses that should not be overlooked. It is especially helpful in presenting events or ideas in sequence as a story unfolds, a report is given, a demonstration is performed, steps in a process are given, or basic concepts are presented in a definite order. It can also be used to show the layout of a farm, to experiment with different arrangements of items for a display or floor layout, to show, by placing cutouts that represent areas on a map that has been sketched on the flannel board how territory was added, to assemble jigsaw maps, to show how a bill becomes a law, and to make circle and bar graphs. One of the main advantages of flannel boards is the extreme flexibility that permits various arrangements to be tried experimentally.

The magnetic board is similar to the flannel board in its uses. Small magnets are attached to objects, pictures, maps, map cutouts, and other items so that they will be drawn to the thin iron sheeting that is used to make the board. The magnetic board is used primarily to demonstrate or illustrate key concepts, although it may occasionally be used as a bulletin board. Some schools have installed magnetic chalkboards which serve the same purpose.

THE CHALKBOARD

The chalkboard serves many purposes in the social studies. It may be used for listing suggestions during group planning, sketching illustrations, listing reading materials, noting assignments, copying suggestions for charts, noting facts under main ideas, summarizing a discussion, recording group-dictated stories or letters, and so on. Many teachers increase the effectiveness of chalkboard use by adding simple stick figures to illustrate points, using colored chalk to emphasize key ideas, and using rulers, compasses, and stencils to obtain neat, artistic effects. Care must be given to the selection of materials to place on the chalkboard, since slides, charts, and duplicated materials are more effective when large amounts of information or detailed data are to be presented.

Several points in chalkboard use should be kept in mind in order to avoid certain errors and to achieve maximum effectiveness: (1) write legibly and organize material neatly; (2) keep the chalkboard clean and uncluttered; (3) adjust room lighting to prevent glare and eye strain; (4) write high enough so that all can see; (5) keep the amount of writing small (distribute duplicated materials if a large amount of information is to be presented); and (6) stand to one side so that each child can read what is placed on the chalkboard. Careful planning before writing on the chalkboard, practice in writing legibly, and systematic evaluation of one's use of the chalkboard are important considerations. Many teachers check material on the chalkboard from the back of the room or from a child's seat in order to see it from the child's point of view.

Questions, Activities, Evaluation

1. Conduct a brief survey of resources in your community. Use the "Checklist For Studying Community Resources," noting resources you can use in a unit.

2. Outline a plan for using one of the following in a unit: a clipping from a local newspaper, a report from the local historical association, a study trip, a resource person.

3. Discuss the "Guide for the Planning of Study Trips." Is each point clear? Should other points be added because of conditions or regulations in your area?

4. Use the "Audio-Visual Resources Checklist" to analyze a unit of instruction. Note the ones that are used most frequently, least frequently, and not at all. Make a check by the ones you might include in a unit.

5. Obtain some old magazines, pamphlets, and bulletins that

contain pictures related to a unit you plan to teach. Cut out and mount the best pictures and organize a picture file. Select pictures that can be used to stimulate questions, build concepts, and enrich discussion.

6. Study the radio and television schedules in a local newspaper. Select two or three programs, watch or listen to them, and appraise them. See if you can locate some that can be used in the social studies program.

7. Arrange to preview a filmstrip or motion picture. Analyze it in terms of the criteria presented in this section. What are its strengths and weaknesses? How can it be used in the social studies?

8. Reread the section on realia. Can you construct any? Can you get any from a local audio-visual department or museum? Can any be shared in the school by resource persons in the community? How can they be used in a unit you plan to teach?

References

Brown, James W., Richard B. Lewis, and Fred F. Harcleroad, *A-V Instruction: Materials and Methods*. New York: McGraw-Hill Book Company, Inc., 1964. Procedures for using all types of materials with examples of their use in elementary schools.

East, Marjorie, and Edgar Dale, *Display for Learning: Making and Using Visual Materials*. New York: Dryden, 1952. A handbook on the making of materials.

Educational Media Index. New York: The Educational Media Council, 1963. A new index of over 60,000 items including charts, graphs, maps, multimedia kits, films and kinescopes, filmstrips, flat pictures, models, mock-ups, phonodiscs, phonotapes, programed materials, slides, transparencies, and videotapes.

Lord, Clifford L., *Teaching History with Community Resources*. New York: Teachers College, Columbia University, 1964. Suggestions for enriching history units.

Michaelis, John U., and Enoch Dumas, *The Student Teacher in the Elementary School*. Englewood Cliffs, N.J.: Prentice-Hall, Inc., 1960. Sections on community resources, audio-visual materials, and construction of materials.

Minor, Ed, *Preparing Visual Instructional Materials*. New York: McGraw-Hill Book Company, Inc., 1962. Techniques for making visual media.

Olsen, Edward G., *et al.*, *School and Community*. Englewood Cliffs, N.J.: Prentice-Hall, Inc., 1954. Principles and procedures for studying the community and for using community resources.

Pflieger, Elmer F., "Use of Television," *Social Studies in Elemen-*

tary Schools, 32nd Yearbook, National Council for the Social Studies, pp. 234–43. Washington, D.C.: National Education Association, 1962. Procedures for using television in the classroom.

Wittich, Walter A., and Charles F. Schuller, *Audio-Visual Materials: Their Nature and Use*. New York: Harper & Row, Publishers, 1967. A comprehensive treatment of materials and an up-to-date list of sources.

Reading Materials, Reading Skills

12

Reading materials can be used to open a gateway to many vital learnings in the social studies. Family and community living, people and places near and far, ways of living at home and in other lands, contributions of others, activities of great men and women, events of historic significance, places in the news, holidays and special events, life in early and modern America, changes stemming from scientific developments, emergence of new nations, human progress through the ages, and a host of other topics are included in social studies reading materials. As a result of reading experiences, a child can identify himself with others, develop richer appreciations of their ways of living, and gain new concepts and understandings. His reading and study skills are strengthened as he engages in critical reading to solve problems and gathers information on questions that have come up in units of instruction. Recreational and independent reading are stimulated as stories, novels, poems, and biographies are introduced in connection with units. For most children, no materials contribute more to learning in the social studies than do reading materials.

Types of Reading Materials

Many different kinds of reading materials are needed to meet individual differences in reading ability, to present different points of view, and to provide adequate backgrounds of understanding of people, processes, and places considered in the social studies. Included in a well-planned program are the following:

Textbooks in geography, history, civics, or those that contain some combination of geography, history, civics, and other content

Unit booklets on a variety of topics ranging from family life and neighborhood workers to other lands and famous people

Reference materials, including almanacs, anthologies, atlases, dictionaries, directories, encyclopedias, gazetteers, government bulletins, scrapbooks, and yearbooks

Fugitive materials, including bulletins, clippings, folders, leaflets, pamphlets, and other free or inexpensive materials

Current materials, including children's weekly news publications, children's magazines, daily newspapers, and adults' magazines

Literary materials, including biography, fiction, folklore, short stories, and travel books

Source materials, including ballots, diaries, directions, logs, maps, minutes of meetings, recipes, and timetables

Programmed materials, including geographic, historical and other content arranged in a step-by-step sequence

Self-help materials, including charts, checklists, directions, outlines, study guides, teacher-prepared practice materials, and workbooks

Display materials, including titles, captions, signs, and labels

Graphic materials, including charts, diagrams, tables, and maps

In planning a unit of instruction, a teacher should select from each of these kinds of reading materials. Availability, pertinence to the problems in the unit, and appropriateness to the maturity of children are guiding considerations in determining which materials to use. By using a variety of reading resources along with other instructional materials, the problem-solving process can be improved, thinking skills can be sharpened, and individual differences among children can be met.

REWRITTEN MATERIALS

Some teachers provide easy-to-read, rewritten materials for those children who have not developed levels of reading ability that are adequate for handling standard reading materials. Teacher-prepared materials are also helpful when material on a topic is unavailable. Rewritten materials should be organized in a file so that children can refer to them as they attack problems in the unit being studied. Many teachers prepare one or more rewrites related to each major problem in the unit; these may be related to food, shelter, clothing, transportation, communication, or other

We heard a good story.

Can you plan an attractive center of interest such as this one which includes a variety of reading materials? (Los Angeles)

social functions, as well as to specific topics in a unit. Adding illustrative material such as pictures, charts, photographs, and post cards is also helpful. A simple style of writing should be used. The best approach is to imagine that you are writing a letter to a child in which you wish to tell him about a certain topic. Simple sentences and nontechnical vocabulary should be used. The two examples below are illustrative of both language and sentence structure.

The pilot boat [1]

The busy pilot boat is the leader for all the foreign boats which come into San Francisco Harbor.

The pilot has his office in the pilot house on the wharf. He knows exactly what day and what hour any ship is going to arrive at the Harbor. He receives the messages by telegraph and by radio. He reads the time schedule which many ships follow.

When a foreign boat is due to arrive, the pilot captain climbs into his boat. He chugs the little boat out toward the lighthouse to meet the boat. On the big boat is a captain who knows how to steer

[1] Prepared by Ruth Sarson, second grade teacher, Summer Demonstration School, University of California, Berkeley, California.

and guide his ship all over the deep, wide oceans. He needs help when coming into narrow harbors.

He needs a pilot captain to climb upon his boat to help steer it safely to the dock.

He needs to know how to go safely out of the harbor when he is ready to return home.

PEDRO MAKES HIS HOUSE [2]

Pedro lives in a house made of bricks. In Mexico, these bricks are made of clay. This clay is called adobe. Pedro's father will put hay or straw with the clay. It makes adobe stick together. He then makes the adobe into bricks.

The bricks are very big. They are about twenty-four inches long. They are about twelve inches wide. They are about six inches tall. There is much adobe in Mexico. There is so much adobe that most houses in Mexico are made of adobe brick.

Adobe houses can have a roof of palm leaves. They sometimes have a roof of wood. Many times they have a roof of tile. Tile is red. Have you ever seen a house with a tile roof? Pedro's father made his roof of wood. He used the wood he saw near the house. He made the roof flat and put adobe in the cracks. Can you tell why?

PRACTICE MATERIALS FOR IMPROVING SKILLS

Practice materials for use in developing reading and other skills in the social studies should be selected and used in accordance with sound principles of learning and teaching. A widely accepted principle is to provide practice materials for individuals and small groups in the light of specific difficulties that have arisen. A second principle is to provide practice at the time it can be used to strengthen skills that will be put to use in the on-going program of instruction. A third principle is to provide multilevel practice materials so that each child can work at his level and make the greatest progress to higher levels. A fourth principle is to relate practice closely to the reading materials, maps, and other resources that children use most frequently. A fifth principle is to provide for immediate feedback to the child so that he is aware of his progress and his needs for further improvement. In short, the same care should be taken to provide for individualized practice in the social studies as is taken in reading, arithmetic, and other areas of the curriculum.

Many different materials are available for use in the social studies. The major problem for teachers is to make a critical selec-

[2] Prepared by Mrs. Jerome F. Harrington, Oakland Public Schools, California.

tion from them. The following is a list of practice materials available on social studies reading skills, independent study skills, map-reading skills, and the interpretation of tables, graphs, charts, pictures, diagrams, and cartoons:

1. *The teacher's manual that accompanies social studies textbooks.* Individual activities for pupils, questions to guide the organization of information, test items, vocabulary-building techniques, and other activities that are based on the text are provided. In addition, helpful suggestions for teachers to use in meeting the needs of more-able, average, and less-able children are usually included.

2. *End-of-chapter activities in children's textbooks.* Summarizing activities, map-making activities, vocabulary extension activities, study skill suggestions, and other suggested activities are directly related to the text and are worded in children's language.

3. *Children's weekly news periodicals for all grades.* Practice materials and tests are provided on reading and study skills, interpreting graphs, tables, diagrams, pictures and cartoons, and map-reading concepts and skills. Editions on different reading levels are available. (See Chapter 6 for a complete list.)

4. *Supplementary practice materials on different skills and concepts.* The examples below are illustrative:

   a. Booklets on study and map skills from publishers of children's periodicals, for example, Education Center, 1250 Fairwood Ave., Columbus, Ohio, and Scholastic Magazines, New York.

   b. *Study Skills Workbook, Elementary Edition, Social Studies Skills Workbook* (Grade V and up), Scholastic Magazines, 50 West 44th St., N.Y. 36, N.Y. Subscriber booklets.

   c. SRA *Basic Skills Series,* Science Research Associates, 259 East Erie St., Chicago, Ill. Multilevel kits on (1) Graph and Picture Study Skills, (2) Organizing and Reporting Skills, (3) Map and Globe Skills.

   d. *The Grade Teacher,* and *Instructor,* magazines for teachers. A variety of practice materials are included on different skills; suggestions are given for all grades in the elementary school.

5. *Social studies units of instruction.* Resource units contain many specific examples of ways in which basic skills may be developed as an inherent part of specific units of instruction.

6. *Social studies workbooks that accompany children's textbooks.* Some publishers provide workbooks, others do not. Ordinarily, one can find adequate practice materials in the teacher's manual and in children's textbooks because most publishers recognize that many schools do not provide workbooks. Some teachers select practice materials from workbooks for different grades, cut them apart, mount

them on tagboard, use them for individualized practice, have children write the responses on sheets of paper, and thus use them over and over again.

PLANNING FOR DIFFERENCES IN ABILITY

A wide range of reading ability may be found in any class. It is not unusual to find a five-to-seven year range of achievement in a class of middle-grade children. The following reading achievement levels for a fifth-grade class are illustrative: between second- and fourth-grade level of achievement—five children; between fourth- and sixth-grade achievement—22 children; between sixth- and eighth-grade achievement—four children; and above eighth-grade achievement—two children.

Should a single textbook be used in such a class? No. Should the pace of the class be set by the middle group, the low group, the high group? None of these. Differentiated planning is necessary so that each child can learn as much as possible. This does not mean that no group activity is possible, but it does mean that a variety of reading materials and activities should be provided.

In planning for the diversity of reading ability that is always present in a class, the steps discussed below should be taken.

Gather Information on Each Child's Reading Abilities. A teacher may obtain information from standardized tests, from tests of his own making, tests and exercises provided in workbooks, and by observing the children as they read selected paragraphs. This last source of information—observing a child as he reads—is especially helpful in getting clues to a child's ability to read social studies materials. Tests and exercises in recently published workbooks that accompany social studies textbooks are helpful in getting specific information on such abilities as finding main ideas, noting details, using maps, and reading charts, graphs, and tables. Analysis of reading and study-skills tests provide clues on children's specific needs and problems.

After information is gathered, it should be summarized on a class sheet or on an individual card for each child (see page 369) and should include the items shown. With such information in hand, a teacher can select reading materials and plan instruction that is appropriate to each child's capabilities.

Locate and Select Appropriate Reading Materials. One of the best sources of information is the list of materials in resource units for each grade. This usually includes materials that are available in the local school system. In some school systems, kits of materials on varying readability levels have been assembled for different units and may be requisitioned by the teacher. In others,

Child's name _____ Age _____ Grade _____ Mental
age _____ Reading group _____ Scores on reading tests _____
Scores on study skills test _____ Reading level for individual
reading _____ Reading level for group instruction _____
Ability to use: Table of Contents _____ Index _____ Glossary _____
Ability to read: Maps _____ Graphs _____ Tables _____ Charts _____
Diagrams _____
Ability to use: Encyclopedias _____ Atlas _____ Dictionary _____
Card catalog _____
Comments: (Special notes on reading difficulties, interests, etc.)
_____
_____
_____
_____

materials may be requisitioned by the teacher from the instructional materials center. In schools where teachers must find materials on their own, the list of materials in resource units is especially helpful in finding those resources directly related to the units for a given grade.

Another good source is the list of additional reading materials included in basic social studies textbooks and teacher's manuals that accompany them. Poems, stories, biographies, and other related materials may be included.

The room library, school library, and neighborhood or community library are excellent sources. Pupils as well as teachers should search for materials in them. Not to be overlooked is cooperation among teachers in sharing books contained in room libraries. For example, when such units as Our Community, Our State, Life in Early America, or Other Lands are being studied, one can be sure that reading materials on various grade levels may be found in different classrooms. Some schools maintain a central card file which facilitates the sharing of classroom reading materials among teachers.

Guides to children's books and free or inexpensive materials should be used to build up a basic collection of reading materials related to different units of instruction. (See references at the end of the chapter.) Some may be placed in the classroom library while more general materials may be placed in the school library. Free or inexpensive materials may be placed in the classroom resource file so that children can have direct access to them. By making careful selections over a period of time, the teacher can provide reading materials on varying levels of difficulty related to the many different topics and problems included in the units of instruction for any given grade.

Provide for Individual, Small-group and Whole-class Reading Activities. An individualized reading program is especially helpful in the social studies because it permits each child to investigate questions and problems as deeply and broadly as his capabilities permit. Textbooks, library materials, paperbacks, free or inexpensive materials, clippings, teacher-prepared materials, children's weekly newspapers, and other resources may become a part of the child's individualized program. Use also may be made of practice materials from workbooks, duplicated materials, questions on the chalkboard or charts, games and exercises in folders or large envelopes, scrapbooks and notebooks on special topics, past issues of children's newspapers and magazines on different readability levels, and periodicals such as *National Geographic, Holiday, American Heritage* and various news magazines. Also helpful are the varied materials offered through reading clubs for children such as *Arrow Book Club,* Scholastic Magazines, New York, and *Weekly Reader Children's Book Club,* Columbus, Ohio, and others listed in the reference by Spache cited at the end of this chapter.

Small-group instruction is helpful in developing needed reading skills, building vocabulary, interpreting material, providing practice, meeting needs that several children have in common, and providing for depth studies of selected topics and problems. Groups may be organized on the basis of (1) *achievement level,* in which children who read on approximately the same level are grouped together and materials on the appropriate level are provided for them; (2) *special needs,* in which children are given instruction in using the index, interpreting material, or other basic skills; (3) *assigned topics,* in which children are given a topic or problem to investigate in depth; (4) *common interest,* in which children who have chosen a topic or problem read materials related to it; (5) *partner study or group-leader study* in which one child assists a partner, or two or three children, in reading selected materials.

Reading materials must be selected to meet the purposes and needs of the children in each group that is organized. In *achievement* and *special needs* groups, materials are selected in accordance with the children's level of reading ability and reading difficulties. In *assigned topic* and *common interest* grouping, materials on varying levels of readability are provided in accordance with the differing levels of reading ability of the children in the groups. In *partner* and *group-leader* study grouping, materials on which less-able children need assistance are provided.

Definite questions and problems should be set for small-group reading activities. Precise and specific questions are in general most helpful to guide the reading of less-able children. More general questions may be used with average and superior readers, but care must be taken to balance specific and general questions so that each child has clear purposes to guide his reading and searches for the most significant ideas related to topics and problems in the unit of instruction under study.

Reading activities that include the whole class are provided when skills, concepts, and problems of common concern are given attention. The following examples are illustrative: providing an introduction to questions and problems at the beginning of a unit, identifying questions for further study, interpreting pictures, maps, diagrams, and other graphic aids, reviewing selected passages to highlight key concepts, oral reading of selected paragraphs by the teacher, audience reading of selected sections by pupils, reviewing key ideas presented in tables, charts, or graphs, providing instruction in the use of the glossary, index, or other parts of a book, using the index to find selected topics, and using maps and reference tables. Such activities may be followed by individual and small-group work in which the concepts and skills developed in whole-class activities are applied and refined. Other suggestions for whole-class activities are presented in the sections that follow.

USING TEXTBOOKS EFFECTIVELY

Textbooks are used in several different ways by teachers in the social studies program. In some schools, a series of textbooks is used as the basis for the instructional program. Children in each grade are helped to learn as much as they can from the text, related audio-visual materials are used to enrich the text, the reading of supplementary materials is encouraged for more-able children, and special help is given individually or in small groups to less-able children.

Some teachers use a basic textbook as a general guide and provide for the reading of other materials in conjunction with various chapters of the basic textbook. This approach is a step beyond reliance on a single textbook, gives children planned opportunities to use materials on differing readability levels, obtains different points of view, and develops the skills involved in pooling information from various sources. Many teachers use this approach when they undertake new areas of study, when they are trying to build up their backgrounds of understanding, and when they wish to become acquainted with the large number of reading materials that are appropriate for the children in their classes. The basic textbook provides for a core of learning for the group, and related materials are used to meet individual differences in reading ability.

In schools in which units of instruction are used, reading or study guides which include references to several textbooks and other reading materials are helpful. For example, one or more questions or problems followed by related readings may be duplicated, or listed on the chalkboard. Certain readings may be noted for the entire group, while others are included for children with high and low reading ability. Each child proceeds to gather information from the listed references, which include textbooks and materials on varying levels of reading difficulty. Teacher guidance is given as needed in the selection of references that are appropriate for individual children, for groups within the class, and for the entire class.

No matter which of these approaches is used in the social studies, social studies textbooks may be used for a variety of purposes:

1. To provide an introduction to, or an overview of, a unit as children check appropriate sections of the table of contents, consider headings and subheadings as main topics for further study, read and discuss introductory paragraphs, discuss pictures, recall previous experiences related to ideas presented in the text, discuss possible use of maps in the text, and get a feeling for main points to be stressed in the unit

2. To develop new terms and concepts related to the unit as children use picture clues, context clues, structural analysis, phonetic analysis, other word recognition techniques, and the glossary

3. To provide descriptions of homes, clothing, food, modes of transportation, and other ways of living as children read selected sections, discuss them, make comparisons, and attempt to identify themselves with others

4. To provide an initial background of ideas that children can use as a springboard in making comparisons, and to gain further information as they read other materials and use audio-visual materials which present different ideas, descriptions, and points of view

5. To find specific facts and ideas as children seek answers to such questions as these: What food do we get from truck farms? What different kinds of material are used to make clothing? How was lighting provided in colonial homes? What are the main products of Brazil?

6. To provide for audience reading of selected sections by the teacher or superior reader

7. To "prove" specific points as children skim to note details or main ideas related to disagreements that have arisen

8. To find main ideas related to a topic, question, or problem as children locate the key idea in each of several related paragraphs

9. To provide instruction in basic study skills as children use the table of contents, headings and subheadings, index, glossary, and end-of-chapter study aids

10. To provide experience in reading and interpreting maps, charts, diagrams, graphs, tables, and pictures as children use them to answer questions and find key ideas presented in them

11. To summarize and bring together key ideas and basic concepts at certain points during the unit and at the end of the unit as children read summaries, note and discuss generalizations and conclusions, carry out selected end-of-chapter activities, and answer test items taken from the text, related workbooks, or the teacher's manual

Skills

BUILDING VOCABULARY

To read social studies material, children must be able to identify and grasp the meaning of the words that are used, and use the meaning to interpret what is written. Each unit of instruction calls for the development of new terms and concepts. A twofold task of the teacher is to identify the specific terms and concepts that should be developed, and to make plans for developing them at appropriate times as the unit progresses.

Identifying Concepts. Among the procedures to use in finding terms and concepts to be developed in each unit are the following:

1. Check the word lists in units. In many units, new terms are listed in the introductory section, or in different sections of the unit in which they will be used.

2. Check the vocabulary list in the back of the teacher's edition of social studies textbooks for primary grades. The pages on which new terms are introduced are given in many basic textbooks.

3. Check the teacher's manual that accompanies social studies textbooks. Specific terms to be taught before the reading of different chapters are presented along with techniques to use to develop them.

4. Skim new materials to note words that have not been used in class. By skimming materials ahead of time, a teacher can make note of new terms and concepts and make plans to develop them.

5. Keep a list of words that are difficult for children. As different materials are used, a teacher should note any terms that should be clarified.

Vocabulary-building Techniques. In the social studies, the teacher utilizes the full range of vocabulary-building techniques.

Those developed in the reading program are supplemented by techniques and procedures suggested in units and in teacher's manuals that accompany social studies textbooks. Among the most helpful are the following:

1. *Use of independent word-recognition skills developed in the reading program.* The use of context clues is perhaps the most helpful aid to word recognition in the social studies because the meaning of many terms is determined by their use. For example, the specific meaning of such terms as *bank, range, lock, set, run,* and *strike,* and the basic meaning of such terms as *humid, prevailing, swampland, fertile, soil robber, growing season, yield,* and *crop rotation* are developed in context in recently published textbooks for children.

Structural analysis is helpful in unlocking the meaning of words that are made up of common roots, prefixes, suffixes, and inflectional endings. Examples are *play, playmate, player, replay, playground; way, byway, expressway, highway, superhighway; large, larger, largest; impossible, improbable, impolite; disarm, disband, disclose, displace, disqualify, dissolve; colony, colonial, colonist, colonize, colonization, precolonial;* and *depend, dependent, independent, dependence, interdependence.*

Phonetic analysis may be used in deriving the pronunciation of certain common terms such as *run, sun, fun, hat, hut, home, parade, provide, travel,* and *transportation,* but should not be used when such names as *Belem, Chile,* and *Spokane* are encountered. Fortunately, many textbooks contain pronunciation guides and glossaries which can be used to obtain the pronunciation of such names.

2. *Picture clues.* Social studies materials contain pictures, sketches, pictorial maps, and drawings which illustrate a variety of terms and concepts. Children's attention should be directed to them through questions and comments so that they develop the habit in the early grades of using picture clues to unlock the meaning of words. The many illustrations in dictionaries and encyclopedias should also be used to clarify word meanings.

3. *Firsthand experiences.* Certain concepts can be developed through such firsthand experiences as study trips, demonstrations, construction, processing of materials, and dramatic play. For example, a study trip to a dairy farm can be used to clarify such terms as *silo, corral, milking parlor, stanchion,* and *milking machine.* Or, the processing of wool can be used to develop the meaning of *washing, carding, spinning,* and *weaving,* as was done in early America.

4. *Related audio-visual materials.* Films, filmstrips, slides, and pictures may be used to enrich concepts presented in reading materials. For example, *broad grassy plains, towering redwoods, tundra, steppes, jungle, plateau,* and *glacier* may be visualized as films and other pictorial materials are shown.

5. *Group discussion.* Group discussion may be used to define

terms, give explanations, correct misconceptions, list difficult words, consider descriptive phrases, point out changes in word meanings, use roots to build new terms, and consider specific questions raised by children.

6. *Directed listening activities.* Oral reading and story-telling by the teacher may be used to introduce or enrich selected terms and concepts. Materials on an advanced reading level may be used with special explanation of selected words and phrases.

7. *Pupil-prepared vocabulary aids.* Card files of new words, word lists kept in notebooks, picture dictionaries made by the class, scrapbooks arranged in alphabetical order, illustrated cards classified under such headings as transportation, communication, housing, and so forth, and pictures collected to illustrate terms and concepts may be used in connection with each unit of instruction.

8. *Glossaries and dictionaries.* These are two of the most valuable aids in the social studies. Each child should develop skill in using them to select the meaning that fits the context in which a word is used.

9. *Direct word study.* Because of the heavy vocabulary load in the social studies, considerable attention must be given to the direct study of terms and concepts. Practice materials, charts, phrase cards, workbook exercises, synonyms and antonyms, classification of related terms, word parts, use of new words in oral and written expression, and vocabulary testing are illustrative of word study materials and activities frequently used in the social studies.

10. *Wide reading.* No substitute exists for the provision of wide reading of supplementary materials in connection with each unit. Concepts are deepened and broadened, new terms are learned in context, independent word-recognition skills are put to use, and familiar terms are encountered in new and novel situations. Most important of all, children develop meanings and concepts on their own—this definitely is a desired outcome of the instructional program.

READING TO INTERPRET MEANING

Comprehension and interpretation of the meaning intended by an author calls for a variety of basic reading skills *plus* an understanding of special concepts, aids to reading, and patterns of organization used in social studies materials. Getting an author's intended meaning is prerequisite to more complex reading-thinking abilities, such as drawing implications, making inferences, discovering relationships, making appreciative responses, and making critical evaluations. Procedures to use in helping children to interpret an author's meaning are presented in this section, from preparation for reading to the critical reading of a selection.

Preparation for Reading a Selection. The first step is to be sure that the group is ready for the selection whether it is a pamphlet, section of a chapter, a story, or some other material. When literary or descriptive materials are being used, children should be sensitized to the mood or setting through teacher-guided recall of related experiences, viewing of a related film, discussion of pictures, or similar activities. Specific questions may be asked to focus children's attention on aspects of their own experience which are related to the selection; both similarities and differences may be brought out. New terms and background concepts which are to be encountered in the reading material should be presented so that they will be interpreted meaningfully. The reading selection also should be related to questions and problems currently under study with specific attention to ways in which this selection will be of greatest help. As this is done, clear purposes may be set for reading the selection, as noted in the following section, and the direction of the child's thinking is oriented toward the reading task.

Clear Purposes for Reading. Many teachers develop purposes for reading as a part of preparation for reading a given selection. As questions and problems in a unit are discussed, the teacher clarifies specific purposes that may be achieved through the reading of the selected material. Such questions and comments as the following may be used: What can you find out about how families have fun? Let's find out how the work of the mailman is different from the work of other community workers. Check the questions listed on the chart before you read. How are the ideas in this selection like those in our basic textbook? How are they different? Do you agree with the conclusions that are stated? As some selections are read, more specific questions may be used, such as: Why did Dick want to help Father? What did he do? Was it helpful? Why was Father happy after they finished? By checking the selection ahead of time, a teacher can be prepared to guide the setting of purposes that will be most helpful to the group in solving problems and answering questions that may come up in the unit.

Children themselves should develop skill in clarifying purposes for reading. Since the development of independent reading-study skills is very important, procedures such as the following should be used to help children grow in the ability to set purposes for their reading. As the title of a story, chapter, pamphlet, or special reference is discussed, the teacher may ask: What questions do you think we can answer by reading this? What do you expect to find in this chapter? What should be included in a reference with this title? Which questions on the chart are related? Do you have any questions about it? A child may uncover other clues to purposes by checking headings in the selection, noting questions and purposes presented in the introduction to the selection, and skimming the selection to get an overview. Sometimes the purpose of an author is determined through the use of such comments as: Find the author's reasons for writing this selection; check the preface; notice the statements in the beginning paragraphs. After having guided experiences in setting one's own purposes for reading, children should summarize different procedures that may be used, as shown in Chart 1.

FINDING PURPOSES FOR READING

Does the title suggest a purpose?
Do main headings suggest questions to be answered?
Do you have questions of your own?
Are questions to guide reading given in the first part of the selection you are reading?
Can questions listed during group discussion be answered?
Can you find purposes by skimming the material?
Do you know something about the author that suggests a purpose for reading?

Chart 1

Concentrating on the Reading Task. After children have been prepared to read a selection, and clear purposes have been set, the next job for a child is to complete the reading task. Concentration —that is, sticking to the job—is now of utmost importance. If clear, strong purposes for reading have been developed, most children will proceed to read the selection without letting other activities interfere. However, certain study habits should be given attention, as noted in Chart 2.

CONCENTRATING AS YOU READ

Focus your thinking on what you are reading.
Have note-taking and other needed materials ready for use.
Keep the purpose or question in mind and search for related ideas.
Use headings for clues as to what is coming next.
Do not let noise or activity of others distract you.

Chart 2

Using Clues to Meaning. A desire to figure out the intended meaning as one reads needs continuing emphasis in the social studies. The following procedures are examples of those that are most helpful in the reading of different social studies materials:

1. The meaning of terms and shifts in meaning may be determined in a variety of ways:

Shifts in word meaning may be determined in context. For example; they went to the *bank* to get money for the trip. They made their camp on the *bank* of the river.

Definitions may be given directly. For example, *natural resources* are useful things provided by nature. Examples are soil, water, plants, animals, and minerals.

Definitions may be developed in context. For example, Bob, Betty, and Jim all lived near the school. They were *neighbors.* Dick lived in another part of town. He lived in another *neighborhood.*

Comparisons may be made with familiar things. For example, *sorghum* is used to feed animals. The sorghum plant is like a corn plant. But, it does not have ears with kernels. Instead, it has a head of small seeds at the top. Or: The *canal* was like a huge ditch dug out of the land.

Summary terms or phrases may be used following the presentation of several related ideas. For example, after a description of the leader, scouts, families, animals, and wagons that make up a wagon train, a summary may be found in such sentences as: This was the *wagon train* that Jed's family had joined.

Differences between similar words may be clarified. For example, the *Capitol* is the building in which our state legislature meets. The *capital* of our state is Sacramento. The main offices of the state government are located there.

Visual images may be stimulated to add meaning. For example, the dark heavy clouds moved closer and the sky became dark. Then the rain began to fall. Soon it was falling in torrents. The *monsoons* had arrived!

Feelings may be stimulated to extend meaning. For example, Jed was left alone in the cabin. When night fell he heard the hooting of an owl and the howl of a strange animal. Jed called his dog, Rover, and put his arm around him.

Synonyms may be used. For example, the first settlers believed that this was an *injustice.* The new settlers agreed that the governor's action was *unfair* and *harmful* to them. They said, "This is wrong! It is unlawful!"

Antonyms may be used. For example, he believed in *liberty* for all. He asked, "Can we have liberty when there is *slavery*? When there is *oppression*? When there is a *denial* of freedom of speech?"

GOVERN		EMINENT		JUSTICE	
Synonyms	Antonyms	Synonyms	Antonyms	Synonyms	Antonyms
command	accept	famous	common	fairness	favoritism
control	be ruled	notable	inferior	fair-play	injustice
direct	comply	noted	low	lawfulness	partiality
manage	obey	outstanding	ordinary	right	untruth
rule	submit	prominent	unknown	truth	wrong

Chart 3

Synonyms and *antonyms* may be used to sharpen contrasts. For example, the captain called his men to attention and said: "*Allegiance* means *devotion* and *loyalty* to our country. We cannot tolerate *treason, mutiny,* or *sedition.*" (See Chart 3.)

Prefixes, roots, or *suffixes* may be defined. For example, these regions are interdependent. Interdependence means depending on each other. Whenever you see *inter,* remember that it means *between, among,* or *together.*

Appositives may be used. For example, the Appalachian Uplands were a barrier, a great wall, between the colonies and the inland plains.

Figures of speech may be used. For example, straight as an arrow, as the crow flies, brave as a lion, muscles like steel.

2. Using punctuation marks as clues to meaning may be done as children learn that:

Commas are used to set off items in a series, terms and phrases in apposition, dependent clauses, adverbial phrases containing a verb form, and parenthetical expressions.

The apostrophe is used to show a contraction or to indicate possession.

Exclamation points are used to show surprise, joy, anger, or danger.

The colon is used before an expression that explains or gives examples of what has gone before, or means *as follows.*

The semicolon is used to separate clauses in compound sentences, and to separate parts of a sentence that includes commas.

3. Interpreting expressions and figures of speech is called for when children meet such phrases as *booming metropolis, hovering helicopter, muscles of steel, long arm of the sea stretching inland,* and *lush tropical foliage.* A major teaching problem here is to identify those that are not developed in context in children's reading materials and to clarify them before reading.

4. Distinguishing between the real and fanciful, fact and opin-

ion, and informational and emotional statements is essential to comprehension. In many social studies materials, direct clues are given, such as: "This is a story that is told by *old-timers*," or, "Here is a *legend* that has been told down through the years," or, "One of the *myths* that children like begins on the next page." Sometimes, however, a teacher must prepare his group by pointing out that this selection is a story that is not based on facts, or that fact and opinion are mixed, as in some materials dealing with current issues and problems. Some expressions may be written deliberately to create a mood or feeling which is related to the intended meaning. For example:

> Warm and balmy breezes keep them warm throughout the year.
> The cold sleet and rain made travel difficult.
> The hot, sticky climate kept pressing in on them.
> The strong and fearless leader had a plan that would surprise the Tories.

5. Grasping the relationships among words and phrases in sentences is necessary in interpreting what one reads, as may be noticed in the following example:

> At last, the day came for the people who had registered to decide if a new school should be built.

Questions used by one teacher to help children clarify relationships in the above sentence were as follows: "What does *at last* refer to? Which people could vote? What was to be decided?"

In response to the question, "How might we rephrase the sentence?" replies were made as follows:

> "After the issues had been discussed, the registered voters cast their ballots for and against the school bonds."
> "After much discussion, the day to vote on the school bonds arrived. The only people who could vote were those who had registered."

6. Grasping relationships among sentences in a paragraph is essential to relate supporting details to the main idea or topic sentence of the paragraph. If the topic sentence comes first in a paragraph, a child should note what ideas are added or elaborated by each following sentence. If the topic sentence comes last, a child must gather the ideas as he reads the paragraph and relate them to the summary statement, or think back to the details that

support it. Illustrative questions to focus attention on relationships are: What is the main idea? What does the first sentence add to it? The second sentence? The third sentence? The remaining sentences? Are any details unrelated to the main idea?

Using Pictorial, Graphic, and Other Aids. The many headings, pictures, graphs, charts, and other graphic devices used in social studies materials have a definite contribution to make to the comprehension and interpretation of the text. The tendency of some children to skip over them can only lead to problems and difficulties in getting a clear understanding of the ideas that are presented. A helpful practice in many classrooms is to direct children's attention to headings and graphic aids, and to raise questions about them during discussion. Chart 4 is illustrative.

USING READING AIDS IN BOOKS

Do you check headings to get a general idea?
Do you use pictures to clarify words and ideas in the text?
Do you get the main ideas from graphs and tables?
Do you follow the steps in charts and diagrams?

Chart 4

Understanding the Organization. The organization of reading materials in the social studies should be explored carefully as selected materials are used. With children in the middle and upper grades, for example, the group should discuss the major headings, subheadings, and minor headings in a text, giving attention to ways they can be used by the class, the way the ideas are arranged, the reason why the material has been organized in this particular way, and the relationship of the headings to topics and problems in the unit. If clear purposes for reading are developed, children may be guided to discover that topical headings are especially helpful in locating key ideas and information related to stated purposes. Furthermore, the problem of reorganizing the material to meet various needs becomes easier if purposes are clear and meaningful to the class. Other items related to organization of materials are format, use of pictures, charts and diagrams, chronological presentation, logical development of topics, cross-references, references to maps and charts on distant pages, sequence of topics, and use of italics. These should be considered in connection with the specific materials which a group is using, and attention should be given to their helpfulness in locating key ideas, explaining selected sections, and summarizing basic data.

HOW IS IT ORGANIZED?

Is the organization explained in the first paragraphs?
Do the headings give clues to the organization?
Are steps given for a sequence of activities?
Is the order of major events given?
Is a timeline or a series of pictures included to show the order?
Do other clues reveal the way ideas are organized?

Chart 5

Speed of Reading. Some children may need special help in varying their speed of reading according to the purpose for reading and the nature of the material being read. A rapid rate of reading is possible when the purpose is to form a general impression, and when descriptive or literary materials on an easy reading level are being read. On the other hand, when the purpose for reading is to gather details related to main ideas, or to evaluate statements critically in materials on a difficult reading level, a slower rate of reading is to be used. Sometimes, the teacher may need to provide special practice by having children read materials on different levels of difficulty and for different purposes, as noted in Chart 6.

CHANGING OUR SPEED OF READING

How does your speed of reading vary when reading:

To get the main ideas?	Easy material?
To form an impression?	Hard material?
To get specific details?	Timelines?
To follow directions?	Graphs and tables?
To select a definition?	Charts and diagrams?
To prove a point?	Maps and atlases?
To find a statement?	Stories?

Chart 6

SKIMMING

Skimming is helpful in getting an overview and in locating specific items in social studies reading materials, as shown in Chart 7.

Skimming is put to use as children check titles of references on a book shelf, the table of contents for chapter headings, the index for topics, and sections of a textbook or reference for a particular item. Skimming in a textbook or reference can be aided by using headings and subheadings. In addition, topic sentences in paragraphs should be used as clues to location of the specific item that is desired. When a date or other quantitative information is desired, the reader should skim to locate figures. Sometimes, the needed information may be on a map, diagram, chart, or in a table. Not to be overlooked are pictures, illustrations, and sketches that contain information related to particular topics and questions. Practice should be given on all of these types of skimming and related to topics and questions in units of instruction in the social studies.

SKIMMING IS USEFUL

1. To get an overview
2. To verify a statement
3. To answer a question
4. To check a date
5. To check location
6. To find definitions
7. To find main ideas
8. To find a reference
9. To find a map or chart
10. To find a graph or table
11. To find illustrations
12. To find other items

Chart 7

READING TO FORM SENSORY IMPRESSIONS

Much reading in the social studies involves the forming of sensory impressions as various terms, phrases, and sentences are encountered. Examples are: "The swirling snowflakes covered the city with a soft blanket" and "They listened to the tooting of the boats in the harbor."

Descriptive terms, phrases, sentences, and paragraphs are used to create a host of impressions and feelings, for example, *the room cluttered with paper, the noisy traffic, the color of the leaves in autumn, the cold barren landscape, the grassy plains, the rolling hills, the roaring river, the steaming jungle, the dense tropical foliage, the jagged shoreline, the gay fiesta, the busy vendors at the bazaar.* Unless a child can form accurate sensory impressions, he will not grasp the meaning or appreciate the full flavor of the ideas portrayed by an author. The goal is to help the child become sensitive to the use of descriptive and figurative expressions so that he will make meaningful associations with them and thus be able to gather the intended meaning.

Procedures, activities, and resources that may be used to help the child form clear sensory impressions are as follows:

1. Raising questions such as these: Have you ever seen a roaring river? What was it like? Where was it? How large was the river? Was it like the one we are reading about?

2. Discussing the feelings, images, sounds, and other impressions stimulated by the text

3. Recalling the children's past experiences and comparing them with those in the text

4. Comparing words or phrases, such as *a gushing spring* and *a trickling spring, a windswept plateau* and a *tree-covered mesa, the grassy plains* and *the golden wheat fields*

5. Drawing pictures and making murals to illustrate descriptions

6. Comparing descriptions of mountains, rivers, historical events, and other items as presented in different textbooks, films, pictures, and other materials

7. Comparing children's descriptions of various items with descriptions of the same items as given in textbooks, films, and other materials

8. Using films, pictures, slides, filmstrips, and other visual materials to illustrate verbal descriptions given in the text

9. Discussing the feelings evoked by such statements as:
The cunning Indian chief sent the fiercest braves to fight the poor settlers.
The wise Indian chief knew that his brave warriors could not withstand the hordes of gold-seekers.
The brave Indian chief sent his best warriors to stop the Spanish conquerors.

READING TO DISCOVER RELATIONSHIPS

Reading materials in the social studies are replete with relationships, some directly stated, some implied, in the text. The social studies abound with human relationships in situations ranging from the home and neighborhood to the state, nation, and other lands. Specific attention to the discovery and understanding of relationships enhances the development of basic concepts and understandings, and, at the same time, contributes to children's growth in reading ability. The following examples may be found in both basic textbooks and supplementary materials. Each set of examples is followed by illustrative questions that may be used to guide children's reading to discover relationships.

Cause-effect relationships may be found in materials dealing with such questions and problems as how the behavior of some members of the family affects the behavior of others, how adjustments are made to changing weather conditions, why traffic problems are greater at certain times, how people in different places adjust to climatic conditions, how resources limit production of goods, how inventions change ways of living, how certain historical events led to others, how cultural exchange has improved ways of living, and how cultural values and customs affect individual behavior. Examples of questions used to help children find cause-effect relationships are: What happened after Tom told his father what he had done? Why did that happen in the story? What caused them to do that? What reasons can you find for that event? How are houses built to withstand the heavy rains? What did the rain force them to do? How do they plan for winter? What kind of houses do they build in that climate? Why do they wear light clothing in the tropics? How did the invention of the reaper change the work of farmers? Why did they leave to start a new colony? How do the people of Mexico enjoy the Piñata?

Sequential relationships are presented in materials dealing with daily routines at home and in school, activities of community workers and farmers, seasonal changes, processing of milk and other foods, making of clothing, production of lumber and other building materials, steps in manufacturing steel and other products, growth of the community, history of the state, chains of events in the development of the nation, growth of democracy, emergence of new nations, and events leading to current issues and problems. Illustrative questions and directions related to sequential relationships are: In what order did Dick do his jobs at home? How are vegetables prepared for market? What are the steps in baking bread in a modern bakery? Tell how the Indians made clothing from deerskins. Trace the steps followed by the pioneers in building log cabins. What are the steps in manufacturing steel? What were the major periods in the development of our state? What events led to the decision to write the Declaration of Independence? What steps did people in that country take to win their freedom? Why was that event called the "turning point" in their fight for freedom?

Part-whole relationships are to be found in materials dealing with individuals as members of the family, families as a part of the neighborhood, neighborhoods and shopping centers as a part of the community, communities and states as a part of regions; the nation, telephones, and other devices as a part of networks of communication; different means of transportation as a part of networks of transportation; labor, capital, and resources as a part of industry; events and periods of time as a part of the development of our nation; and historical events as a part of movements and trends. Illustrative questions are: What do we mean by a family? What do we mean by a neighborhood? Why does a large community have several shopping centers? What different means of transportation are used by people in the community? Our state is a part of what region? Why is that region of the United States important to us? How is that period related to the one preceding it? How did that event contribute to the "opening of the West"? What individuals worked together to bring our state into the United States?

Place relationships are highlighted in materials dealing with the relative location of homes, schools, neighborhoods within the community, farms, communities, industries, resources, states, regions, countries, historical events, distance from the Equator, altitude and nearness to water bodies, mountains, and other surface features. Sample questions are: Where was the school located in Tom's neighborhood? Why was this a good place? Why was Mr. Jones' farm located in the valley? Why was the factory located near the river? How do they transport the raw materials to the factory? What travel problems do the people have in the highlands? How do distance from the Equator and elevation affect the climate? What effect do the mountains have on weather conditions? Why is that a good place to raise wheat? Why did the steel industry develop in that region?

Quantitative relationships presented in social studies materials include relative time and distance to various places, size or area of states and nations, density of population, speed of travel by different modes of transportation, temperature and humidity, and value of resources and products. Illustrative questions are: Is Tom's family larger or smaller than yours? Is Dick's community larger or smaller than ours? How do these states compare in area? Which regions are most densely populated? What is the distance by train? How much time is saved if you travel there by airplane? Why are mineral resources of greatest value to them?

Analogous relationships may be found in materials that highlight likenesses or similarities in different objects, activities, or events, such as steps in baking bread at home and in bakeries, problems of adjusting to the weather in different places, ways of processing basic resources to produce different goods, modes of travel used by early settlers and Indians, activities of children in different lands, and means of transporting goods in different countries. Illustrative questions are: How are these items alike? Are they used for the same purpose? Are the same steps taken to carry out the activity? Are similar problems involved in each situation? What similarities can you find in these activities? Special attention must be given to correcting erroneous interpretation of analogies and to checking the development of the mistaken idea that if two things are alike in certain characteristics they are alike in all characteristics. Questions that may be used to prevent such errors are:

What idea is the author trying to convey? Why do you think he pointed out this likeness? Did he mean that there are other likenesses? Can you think of other likenesses? Can you also think of differences? Why must differences as well as likenesses be kept in mind?

Other ways in which reading to discover relationships can be promoted are shown in Charts 8–11.

FIND OUT HOW THESE ARE RELATED

Time, speed, distance
Place, elevation, distance
Resources, products, industries
Exports, imports, trade
Transportation and surface features
Beliefs, customs, and ways of living
Food, clothing, shelter, and climate

Chart 8

FINDING RELATED IDEAS

Relate what you read to things that you have done.
Relate what you read to ideas in pictures and films.
Relate information to questions and problems discussed by the group.
Bring ideas together from several different sources.
Relate facts to main ideas.
Use facts to form conclusions.

Chart 9

FIND INFORMATION RELATED TO THESE MAIN IDEAS

People process resources for food, shelter, and clothing.
People in all communities depend on each other in many ways.
Where a person lives has much to do with how he acts.
People form groups and work together to get many jobs done.

Chart 10

GROUPING RELATED IDEAS

Put ideas gained from reading under the following headings:

Transportation	Communication
Production	Conservation
Education	Recreation
Exports	Imports
Land forms	Water bodies
Villages	Provinces
Countries	Continents

Chart 11

CRITICAL, CREATIVE, AND APPRECIATIVE READING

When a reader goes beyond word identification, casual reading, and reading to get the author's intended meaning, he enters what may be referred to as creative reading: [3]

1. reading for implied or inferred meanings
2. reading for appreciative reactions
3. reading for critical evaluations

These three overlapping types of reading may be put to extensive use in the social studies. For example, as children read about the hot, moist summer climate of Iowa, they may make inferences about the kind of crops that will grow there. Or, as children read about people in other lands and identify themselves with them, they may respond with new feelings to their hopes, aspirations, and problems. Or, as children distinguish between fact and opinion, relevant and irrelevant information, and right and wrong, they use standards to evaluate statements in reading materials. Thus, each of the three types of reading is a step beyond literal interpretation of the material.

The following are illustrative of critical reading skills and are suggestive of activities to employ in the social studies to develop critical reading abilities:

Making inferences, judgments, and decisions in the light of facts, ideas, and values

Evaluating the author's purpose, organization of ideas, clarity of expression, appropriateness of ideas, relevancy of information, relation of content to generalizations

Grasping relationships, comparisons, contrasts, cause and effect, sequence of ideas, and order and structure of content

Classifying terms, facts, ideas, concepts, principles, generalizations, motives, moods, feelings, dates, places, events, people, objects, products, resources, surface features, cities, states, regions, countries

Distinguishing fact and fancy, fact and opinion, relevant and irrelevant, implied and stated ideas, evidence and hearsay, warranted and unwarranted assertions

Predicting or anticipating outcomes, next steps, order of events, future trends

Selecting main ideas and related details to make generalizations, proving statements, preparing directions, constructing objects, processing materials, making charts, preparing reports, planning programs, making maps

[3] David Russell, *Children Learn to Read*, rev. ed. (Boston: Ginn & Company, 1961), Ch. xiv.

Reorganizing information in outlines, summaries, reports, charts, graphs, diagrams, tables, maps, murals, drawings

Forming conclusions, sensory impressions, associations, concepts, generalizations, reasoned opinions

Identifying elements of style, issues, problems, differences of opinion, purpose of the author, character traits, values, cultural factors

Interpreting figurative and idiomatic expressions, mood, tone, elements of style, humor, motives, emotional reactions

Judging ideas and outcomes in terms of author's purpose, standards, evidence, reasonableness of arguments, relevancy of facts

Appreciating contributions of members of the family, community workers, current leaders, famous men and women, resources provided by nature, use of resources in improving ways of living, conservation of resources, creative ways of meeting problems, factors that contribute to change, growth of democracy, increasing interdependence

CRITICAL EVALUATION

Critical evaluation of the ideas obtained through reading is essential. Controversial issues, prejudices, biases, opinions versus facts, varied interpretations, irrelevant ideas, generalizations, inaccuracies, mood and interest of the author, usefulness of ideas, and the like should be noted and discussed thoroughly by the group. Ideas should be checked against other references and sources of data as needs arise. Misconceptions and biases of the reader should also be considered. In addition, children should be helped to detect the difference between informational and fictional material.

In evaluating ideas obtained through reading, several key questions may be considered by the group; the choice of questions for consideration will depend on their appropriateness to the selection, and on the maturity of the class with which they will be used. The following are illustrative:

Is the writer's purpose clear?
Are facts presented clearly and differentiated from opinion?
What type of proof is given?
Does the author appeal to emotion?
Are generalizations supported by ample evidence?
Do the ideas square with other sources of information?
How are figures of speech used? Analogies? Similes? Metaphors?
Are differing views presented on controversial issues?
Are cause and effect relationships clear?
Are conclusions clearly established?
Is the material pertinent to class problems?

Charts 14 and 15 illustrate ways in which two different classes handled certain phases of critical evaluation of reading materials. Such charts also can be used in situations other than reading, and thus have double value because they are clearly related to the problem-solving process.

CRITICAL READERS	CRITICAL THINKERS
1. Check the facts.	Use these steps:
2. Compare ideas.	1. State problems.
3. Raise questions.	2. Find facts.
4. Find out about the author.	3. Filter facts.
5. Notice general statements.	4. Organize facts.
6. Look for proof.	5. Base conclusions on facts.
7. Check conclusions.	6. Act on conclusions.
	7. Change conclusions on basis of new facts.

Chart 12   Chart 13

Questions, Activities, Evaluation

1. Which of the types of reading materials would you consider most useful in a unit you are planning?

2. Examine a unit of instruction and note ways in which multiple textbooks are suggested for use in answering questions and solving problems.

3. Get a textbook for children from the library and analyze it in terms of the criteria presented in this chapter. Note strengths and weaknesses.

4. Observe a group of children reading social studies material. Note techniques used by the teacher to develop readiness, set purposes, and improve reading skills. Which of those skills mentioned in this chapter are being put to use? Note ways in which you can utilize and improve reading skills in a unit you are planning.

5. Prepare a rewrite of some material related to a problem or question in a unit you are planning. Write it on the level of the children with whom you are (or will be) working. If possible, try it out to note ways in which it may be improved. Can you find a picture or sketch to illustrate it?

6. Make a list of poems, stories, or biographies that are re-

lated to a unit you plan to teach. Note different ways in which they can be shared and enjoyed by the group.

7. List several terms that should be developed in a unit you are planning. How might you use the vocabulary-building techniques suggested in this chapter to develop them?

8. How might you make use of some of the charts presented in this chapter in a unit of instruction? What modifications might be made in them to meet reading problems at different grade levels?

9. How might you provide for creative and critical reading in a unit you are planning?

References

Best Books for Children. New York, R. R. Bowker Co., annual. Includes social studies books.

Bond, Guy L., and Eva B. Wagner, *Teaching the Child to Read.* New York: The Macmillan Company, 1966. Sections on vocabulary building, special skills, and social studies materials.

Chase, Linwood, *A Guide for the Elementary Social Studies Teacher.* Boston: Allyn & Bacon, Inc., 1966. Section on meeting individual differences.

Fay, Leo, Thomas Horn, and Constance M. McCullough, *Improving Reading in the Elementary Social Studies*, Bulletin No. 33, National Council for the Social Studies. Washington, D.C.: National Education Association, 1961. Skills needed to read social studies materials.

Harris, Albert J., *How to Increase Reading Ability*, Ch. xvi, "Developing Understanding in Reading." New York: Longmans, Green & Co., Inc., 1961.

Huus, Helen, *Children's Books to Enrich the Social Studies.* Washington, D.C.: National Council for the Social Studies, 1966. Annotated list.

————, "Reading," *Skill Development in the Social Studies*, 33rd Yearbook. Washington, D.C.: National Council for the Social Studies, 1963. Problems, difficulties, and procedures for handling them.

Jarolimek, John, *Social Studies in Elementary Education.* New York: The Macmillan Company, 1967. Section on reading of social studies materials.

McKee, Paul, *Reading, A Program of Instruction for the Elementary School.* Boston: Houghton Mifflin Company, 1966. Specific techniques and illustrative lessons on reading graphs, critical reading, and literature; list of guides to children's books.

Preston, Ralph C., *Teaching Social Studies in the Elementary Schools*, rev. ed., Ch. 4, "Improving Reading in Social Studies." New York: Holt, Rinehart & Winston, Inc., 1958.

Resnick, Lauren B., "Programed Instruction and the Teaching of Social Studies Skills," *Skill Development in the Social Studies*, 33rd Yearbook. Washington, D.C.: National Council for the Social Studies, 1963. Types of programing, examples, and evaluation.

Russell, David, *Children Learn to Read*, rev. ed., Ch. ix, "Building Meaning Vocabularies," Ch. xi, "Work-Type Reading," Ch. xix, "Creative Reading Abilities." Boston: Ginn & Company, 1961.

Spache, George D. *Good Reading for Poor Readers*. Champaign, Ill.: Garrard Publishing Co., 1966. Detailed list of materials and sources.

Tinker, Miles A., and Constance M. McCullough, *Teaching Elementary Reading*, 2nd ed., Ch. vi, "Acquiring Concepts and Skills," Ch. xii, "Reading in the Content Fields." New York: Appleton-Century-Crofts, Inc., 1962.

Graphic
Materials

Graphic materials are designed to present information or main ideas clearly, concisely, and convincingly. Some are created to stir feelings; others are designed to present facts and show relationships in an objective manner. As with other instructional resources, one must be alert to symbols, meanings, background factors, distortions, inaccuracies, and erroneous interpretations. Critical thinking skills must be put to use as different graphic materials are used and as they are prepared by pupils.

Greater use has been made of graphic materials in children's instructional resources in recent years. Textbooks, films, reference materials, and encyclopedias contain excellent examples. Children's weekly news periodicals present graphs, posters, cartoons, and diagrams especially designed to be meaningful to children. Practice materials have been produced to develop the skills and concepts children need to interpret graphic materials.[1] The variety of materials currently available presents both a challenge and an opportunity to teachers to develop the skills and concepts needed to get meaning from graphic materials, and to guide children in the production of them in the classroom.

13

[1] Robert A. Naslund and Jack McClelland, *Graph and Picture Study Skills* (Chicago: Science Research Associates, 1966).

393

A large diagram such as this one may be used for reference when needed in discussion, reporting, and individual study. *(Alameda County)*

Posters

Posters are designed to convey an idea that can be grasped at a glance. They are used to sway people to a course of action in such activities as conservation, safety, politics, health, sports, recreation, welfare, citizenship, travel, and business. The primary purpose in using posters is to give a quick and lasting impression of an idea, topic, or activity.

Effective posters, whether they are made by children or adults, possess the following characteristics:

1. A single idea or purpose is highlighted.
2. The idea is presented dramatically, clearly, forcefully.

3. The use of space, color, lines, and pictures is planned to focus attention on the key idea.

4. Cluttering detail is avoided.

5. The poster is large enough to assure quick and easy viewing in the place where it is to be located.

6. Those who will see the poster are familiar with the idea it portrays.

The making of posters by children may be a profitable learning activity in the social studies. Children's creative thinking can be brought to high levels as they consider ideas to be portrayed and design posters that possess the characteristics noted above. Experimentation with different materials and arrangements should be encouraged. Photographs, pictures from magazines, and children's sketches and drawings should be considered. Large show cards, heavy wrapping paper, pieces cut from old window shades, the back of old posters, and tagboard can be used. Three-dimensional posters can be made by using a cardboard base and attaching textiles, models, specimens, and other objects. Titles, labels, or captions can be prepared to highlight the key idea. Plans can be made to use posters separately or as a part of larger displays and classroom arrangements.

Commercially prepared posters may be obtained from business firms, airlines, railways, bus companies, shipping companies, travel bureaus, governmental agencies, and national associations such as the National Dairy Council. When commercial posters are used,

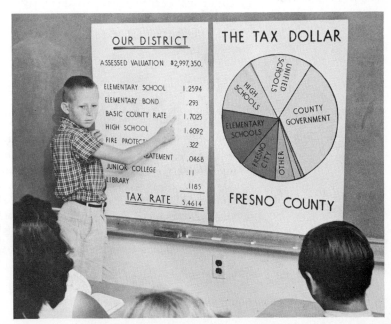

This group is considering information gathered through a study of the county budget for various services. What other topics might be investigated? (Fresno County)

care must be taken to (1) clarify the purpose, (2) discuss the title, (3) note special appeals and points of view, (4) rewrite the title if needed to relate the poster to current activities, and (5) edit or delete obtrusive or objectionable advertising. After the poster has served its purpose, it should be removed.

Cartoons

Cartoons are designed to convey an idea by means of caricature, humor, oversimplification, emotional appeal, symbols, exaggeration, satire, or stereotype. The cartoonist's purpose is to present a person, event, or activity by emphasizing a feature that will quickly convey the meaning. Use is made of such well-known symbols as Uncle Sam, John Bull, the English bull dog, the golden eagle, the dove of peace, the vulture of disease or death, the hobnailed boot of the oppressor, the cigar-smoking lobbyist, the Republican's elephant, and the Democrat's donkey.

To get the meaning of a cartoon, a reader must know the meaning of the symbol and understand the situation in which it is used. This is why so many political cartoons that amuse adults have little or no effect on children. Without a knowledge of the symbols that are used and the situations that are depicted, children cannot be expected to interpret cartoons effectively. Each symbol must be clarified, and an understanding of the issues, conditions, events, or problems must be developed. An effective approach is to make use of those cartoons that are related to current affairs and units of instruction being studied by the group. The cartoons presented in children's weekly news periodicals are designed to be used in this way.

Guidelines to be followed in using cartoons in the social studies are as follows:

1. Collect cartoons and introduce them as a part of units of instruction. Relate them to current events and issues. Be sure to include cartoons that present different points of view on selected issues.

2. Encourage children to bring to class cartoons that are related to topics under study. Again, cartoons that present different points of view are needed.

3. Take time to analyze selected cartoons in detail with attention to symbols that are used, the purpose of the cartoonist, and the points that are exaggerated. Illustrative questions to raise are: What is the title? Why was it chosen? What is the cartoonist's purpose? (To explain something? To make a joke of a situation? To arouse

people? To reveal an injustice? To influence voters?) Why was this symbol used? What is the cartoonist's point of view? What are other points of view? What ideas are distorted? In what other ways might ideas be expressed?

4. Have children make cartoons related to current affairs and to topics in units of instruction. Have them use stick figures, simple sketches, and drawings that depict situations, problems, and events which are significant in terms of purposes of the social studies. Do not waste time on problems and issues that are trivial.

Charts

An especially valuable resource, charts are needed to record and classify information that is to be used or referred to several times. Their most common use in the elementary school social studies program is to record work standards, plans, responsibilities, membership of committees, directions, creative expression, terms and concepts, information needed in construction and dramatic play, and instructions for working with materials. They may be developed by the group, or made by the teacher to present information, introduce topics, raise questions, provide directions, and direct attention to specific needs. The most common types are as follows:

Experience charts for reading and discussion based on study trips, experiments, constructions, and other firsthand experiences

Group standards charts for use in work periods, discussion, dramatic play, reports, committee and other cooperative work

Sequential charts such as time lines, flow charts, records and logs of activities, calendars of events, sequences of activities, and records of progress

Direction charts for guiding construction projects, field trips, map making, processing of materials, use of references or tools and materials, and other activities

Creative expression charts to record songs, poems, and stories

Tabulation charts for summarizing information about cities, states, countries, continents, resources, products, and other items

Vocabulary charts for listing frequently used terms and concepts related to the unit

Organization charts to summarize committee organization, organization for a trip, or organization of various institutions or groups studied in units

Classification charts to record such items as types of boats, dwellings, food, shelter, clothing, weapons, utensils, and arts and crafts

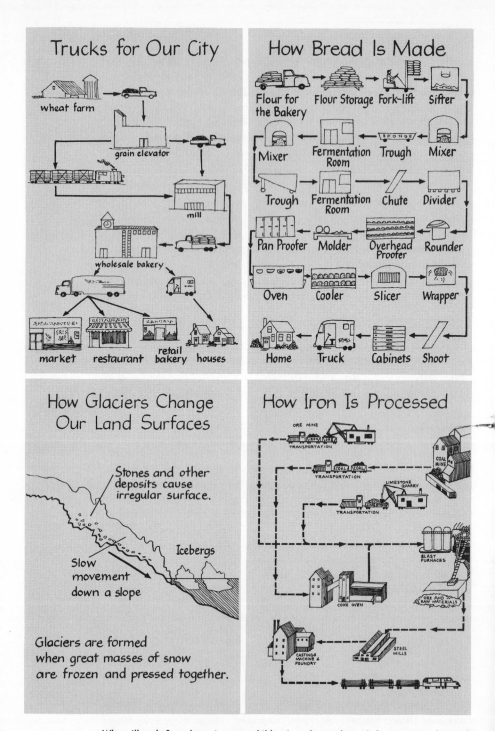

Trucks for Our City

wheat farm

grain elevator

mill

wholesale bakery

market   restaurant   retail bakery   houses

How Bread Is Made

Flour for the Bakery   Flour Storage   Fork-lift   Sifter

Mixer   Fermentation Room   Trough   Mixer

Trough   Fermentation Room   Chute   Divider

Pan Proofer   Molder   Overhead Proofer   Rounder

Oven   Cooler   Slicer   Wrapper

Home   Truck   Cabinets   Shoot

How Glaciers Change Our Land Surfaces

Stones and other deposits cause irregular surface.

Icebergs

Slow movement down a slope

Glaciers are formed when great masses of snow are frozen and pressed together.

How Iron Is Processed

ORE MINE

TRANSPORTATION

COAL   COAL

TRANSPORTATION

COAL MINE

LIMESTONE QUARRY

LIME STONE

TRANSPORTATION

BLAST FURNACES

COKE OVEN

ORE AND RAW MATERIALS

CASTINGS MACHINE & FOUNDRY

STEEL MILLS

Why will such flow charts increase children's understanding of the processes depicted? (San Bernardino County Schools)

The content of charts should be based on the experiences of the class and directly related to activities in the unit. Vocabulary and sentence patterns should be appropriate to the level of maturity of the group. The language in the chart should be simple, and use should be made of descriptive phrases and sentences dictated by the group. Illustrations should be attractive and add to the meaningfulness of charts. Correct punctuation, capitalization, spelling, and language usage are essential.

The format and composition of charts should be similar to that of the printed page in a well-made textbook. Lettering should be legible and easy to read. Sharp contrast between lettering and paper, standard paragraph form, balanced placement of illustrations, adequate spacing of words and lines, consistent use of standard letter forms, and margins similar to those on picture mats are other essential considerations. Specific attention should be given to the points that follow:

Paper. Oak tagboard, 22½″ × 28½″ or 24″ × 36″, 80 lb. weight, is durable, has a smooth surface, takes ink well, can be obtained unlined or lined ½″ or ¾″, and is excellent for long-term use.

White chart paper, 24″ × 36″, ¾″ ruling, has a smooth surface, takes ink well, is fairly durable, and is good for both temporary and long-term use.

Wrapping paper, 24″ to 36″ wide, 40 to 60 lb. weight, takes ink or crayon well, is fairly durable and smooth, can be cut into any size, and is less expensive than tagboard.

Newsprint, ruled or unruled, in sheets cut to size or in rolls (unruled), is inexpensive, takes black crayon or pencil well, and is good for temporary use; it is not durable and tears easily.

Chart Liners. Masonite, 15″ × 25″, with slits ¾″ apart, is easy to make and use. Or, ¾″ strips of wood or metal can be nailed ¾″ apart on a frame 18″ × 25″.

Writing Materials. Black crayon, China marking pencil, or soft black pencil may be used on newsprint or wrapping paper. Pencils make sharper lines than do crayons.

Speedball pens 2, 3, and 4 are fairly large, decreasing in size as the number increases; Esterbrook 4, 5, and 6 are large, increasing in size as the number increases. Use black India ink with pens.

Felt-tip pens are easy to use but do not make lines as black as pens dipped in India ink.

Lettering. Manuscript writing is preferred. In Grades I and II, make small letters ¾″ to 1″, capitals and tall letters 1½″ to 2″;

WHY THE SEASONS?

How might this chart be used to develop concepts related to changes in the seasons? How might a globe and flashlight be used to demonstrate ideas presented on the chart? (Berkeley)

if small groups are to use the chart use ½″ for small letters, 1″ for capitals; in Grade III and above, make small letters ½″, capitals 1″, larger letters for special purposes; both upper and lower case should be used.

Spacing. Margins should be similar to the mat of a picture; leave 1½″ to 3″ at sides and bottom of chart, place title three spaces (2½″ to 3″) above first line; distance between lines should be one to two ruled spaces; space between words should be equal to width of *w* in Grade I, *o* in Grades II and up; sentences over one line should be divided by phrases; use regular paragraph form with the first line indented.

Correct Usage. Correct sentence structure, spelling, usage, punctuation, and capitalization are essential.

Illustrations. Illustrations add to the interest, meaningfulness, and attractiveness of charts; they may be made by children or the teacher; or magazine pictures and photographs may be used.

Picture

The trucks haul food to the store.

Chart 1

Picture

The trucks haul food to the store.

Chart 2

Charts 1 and 2 illustrate format. Chart 1 is properly indented; Chart 2 has the hanging paragraph, which is not so desirable in the primary grades.

The following charts illustrate types used successfully by elementary school teachers. Charts 3, 4, 5, and 6 show differences at various stages of development, even though the content is similar.

Not to be overlooked are the many charts and diagrams in textbooks, encyclopedias, and other materials. A sampling of those in encyclopedias is listed in Chart 7.

TELLING STORIES

1. Look at the class.

2. Speak so all can hear.

3. Have a good start.

4. Have a good ending.

GRADE II

Chart 3

TELLING STORIES

1. Have a plan for your story.
2. Relate your story to previous discussions.
3. Speak clearly and directly to the audience.
4. Make the characters seem real.
5. Have a good climax and then stop quickly.

GRADE VI

Chart 4

DISCUSSION

1. Talk about one thing at a time.

2. Listen without making noise.

3. Tell something new.

4. Ask questions.

5. Take turns.

GRADE III

Chart 5

DISCUSSION

1. Keep the purpose and topic clearly in mind.
2. Be considerate of others.
3. Be careful not to repeat ideas already presented.
4. Raise questions and make suggestions related to the topic.
5. Share discussion by being brief and to the point.

GRADE VI

Chart 6

DIAGRAMS AND FLOW CHARTS IN
OUR ENCYCLOPEDIAS

Baking bread

Milk production

Processing foods

Lumber production

Building houses

Making paper

Drilling for oil

Refining petroleum

Mining coal

Mining salt

Hydroelectric power

Making electricity from coal

Electric power from atomic
energy

Transmission of electricity

Laying ocean cables

How the telephone works

How television works

Automation systems

Branches of government

Chart 7

Time Charts and Time Lines

Time charts and time lines have been used with increasing frequency in recent years to clarify time relationships, to relate events to major time periods, and to relate events in one country to those in another. In the early grades, charts may be made to show events of the day, major events during the week, events related to the growth of the community, changes in transportation, changes in farming, and changing ways of providing food, shelter, and clothing. In later grades, charts and time lines may be used to show events during major periods of the history of the state, nation, other lands, transportation, communication, and the like. Throughout all grades, emphasis is given to the use of units of time that children comprehend and that can be used as a basis for making comparisons.

Time charts and time lines take many different forms. A commonly used form is simply a list of events in order with space provided between the events to show elapsed time. Another is to string a wire across the room and to space dated events written on cards at proper intervals. A third is to place large envelopes under time periods so that children can place pictures or names of events in them. A fourth is to place events in two or more regions or countries in parallel form, one under or beside the other, to show what occurred in different places at the same time.

Tables

Tables are a concise way of presenting related quantitative information. Facts or figures are arranged in columns or rows for fast reading and for making comparisons. In the social studies, tables are used to present comparative information on products, crops, value of commodities, exports, imports, elections, population, distances, time to various places, length of rivers, height of mountains, elevations, sea depths, area, and many other items. Tables may be presented along with related graphs thus providing children with opportunities to compare two different ways of presenting information. Tables are also used as the basis for making graphs, hence children should clearly understand how to make them as well as how to interpret them.

The first tables made or interpreted by children may simply be a short list of figures headed by a title, for example, daily classroom attendance for a week, temperature readings over a period of time, distances to nearby places, travel time to various places, value of state products, and the like. The next step is to make and interpret tables that contain two or more columns, thus moving from single-topic to multiple-topic tables. Charts 8–11 are illustrative of single- and multiple-topic tables and the kinds of questions children may answer in order to develop the skills needed to interpret them. Charts 12 and 15 summarize questions and pointers which can be used to direct attention to the construction and interpretation of tables so that different skills and concepts are put to use.

ANIMALS ON PAUL'S FARM

Animals	Number
Cows	14
Pigs	31
Sheep	6
Horses	4

How many cows are there?

How many pigs are there?

How many more sheep are there than horses?

Chart 8

DAILY WEATHER

Day	Weather
Monday	Fog
Tuesday	Sunshine
Wednesday	Sunshine
Thursday	Fog
Friday	Sunshine

How many days of sunshine were there during the week?
How many days of fog were there?
Were there more days of sunshine than days of fog?

Chart 9

POPULATION GROWTH AND PERCENTAGE OF INCREASE IN THE FIVE LARGEST STATES

State	Population		Per Cent of Increase
	1950	1960	
New York	14,830,192	16,782,304	13.2
California	10,586,223	15,717,204	48.5
Pennsylvania	10,498,012	11,319,366	7.8
Illinois	8,712,176	10,081,158	15.7
Texas	7,711,194	9,579,677	24.2

Which state had the largest population in 1950? In 1960?
Which state showed the largest per cent of increase?
Which state showed the smallest per cent of increase?
Which state has since become the largest?

Chart 10

WEATHER AND TEMPERATURE DURING THE WEEK

Day	Weather	Temperature
Monday	Fog	57
Tuesday	Rain	52
Wednesday	Rain	54
Thursday	Cloudy	66
Friday	Sunshine	72

How many days of rain did we have?
How many days of sunshine?
On how many days was it cloudy?
On what days was it coldest?
On what day was it warmest?
What was the temperature on the foggy day?
What was the temperature on the sunny day?

Chart 11

UNDERSTANDING TABLES

Is one topic presented?

Are two or more topics presented?

Is the title clear?

Are column headings clear?

What do the numerals mean? Units? Hundreds? Thousands? Millions? Others?

What measures are used? Pounds? Tons? Bushels? Miles? Dollars? Others?

Chart 12

GETTING IDEAS FROM TABLES

What questions can be answered by using information from the table?
What does the title indicate?
What comparisons can be made?
Are changes or trends shown?
Can you find the greatest, average, and least amount shown?
Can any conclusions be made?
Can you think of a similar table which you might make?
What kind of table could we make for the unit we are studying?

Chart 13

MAKING A TABLE

What information is to be given?

How many columns are needed?

What heading is needed for each column?

Place the information in each column.

Plan a complete title.

Chart 14

IDEAS FOR TABLES

Growth of school enrollment
Yearly construction of new homes
Growth of population
Agricultural products
Manufactured products
Distance to places
Travel time to places
Area of places
Can you think of others?

Chart 15

Graphs

Graphs designed for use in the social studies are a combination of quantitative concepts and factual information that have social significance. Well-made graphs are easy to read, concise, attractive, and limited to the most significant facts. They are designed to show main ideas or relationships clearly so that they can be read quickly. The major types of graphs are pictorial, bar, circle or pie, and line. In general, pictorial and one-dimensional bar graphs are the easiest to make and to interpret, and line graphs, which are two-dimensional, are the most difficult. Circle graphs are usually the best to show relationships of parts to the whole.

In the early grades, limited use is made of simple pictorial and bar graphs to show such information as daily temperature, collection of money, enrollment, books read, products and animals on farms, and simple time, distance, and speed relationships. In the middle and upper grades, graphs may be used to show such information as population growth, production of goods, extent of resources, comparison of exports and imports, relative size of cities, states, countries and continents, relative distances between places, relative speed of travel by different modes of transportation, increase in number of cars, telephones, and other items, sources of revenue, and expenditure of funds. In all grades, the interpretation and construction of graphs must be paced with the children's grasp of the related mathematical terms, concepts, and skills. Many teachers, therefore, relate the work provided in arithmetic very closely to the use of graphs in the social studies. In fact, the suggestions presented in arithmetic textbooks for interpreting and making graphs are excellent for adaptation and application to the use of graphs in the social studies.

PICTORIAL GRAPHS

Pictorial graphs are designed to show clearly the approximate amount or number of an item. They are effective for making comparisons and are used more extensively than other types in the elementary school. In reading or interpreting them, special attention must be given to the meaning of the symbols and the specific amounts that they represent. In making them, pictures or symbols of the same size should be used and a quantitative value that children understand should be assigned to them. Easily recognized symbols of uniform size must be used so that erroneous impressions and distortions can be avoided. At first, one symbol or picture should be used to represent one item; later it may be used to represent two, five, ten, and larger numbers. Such an approach is helpful in developing the concept that the picture or symbol stands

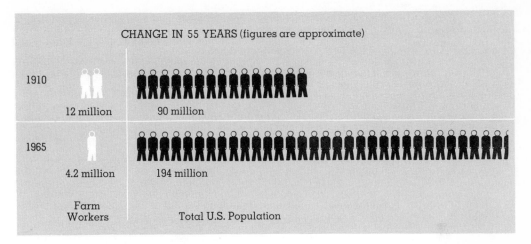

CHANGE IN 55 YEARS (figures are approximate)

1910   12 million   90 million

1965   4.2 million   194 million

Farm Workers   Total U.S. Population

As the need for agricultural laborers declined, many Americans left the farms to seek jobs in the cities. *(Civic Education Press)*

for a given number or quantity, and in improving accuracy of reading. Of course, when such large multiples as hundreds and thousands are taken, the exactness of reading decreases, as is true of any situation in which the rounding of numbers is involved. In cases where exact numbers are needed, they may be written on the graph or placed on an accompanying list or table.

BAR GRAPHS

Bar graphs are relatively easy to make and are useful in comparing the size or amount of different items. A helpful procedure in introducing bar graphs is to compare them with pictorial graphs. This may be done by taking a pictorial graph and a bar graph based on the same information and having children make comparisons row by row or column by column. If this is followed by making comparable picture and bar graphs, children get a clearer grasp of the similarities and differences and move toward a more abstract way of summarizing basic information. Among the key points to stress in interpreting bar graphs are clarifying the meaning of the title or heading, checking the scale, and determining exactly how much is shown by each bar. In making bar graphs, a good initial approach is to use strips of paper or tape which have been cut to show the proper amount for each bar. A decision must be made whether to place the bars horizontally or vertically.

READING PICTURE GRAPHS

What does the title tell us to look for?
What does each picture or symbol stand for?
What does each row or column show?
What questions can be answered?

Chart 16

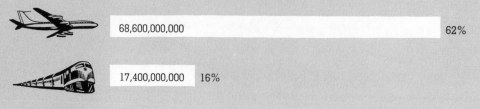

PASSENGER MILES TRAVELED ON COMMERCIAL CARRIERS IN U.S.

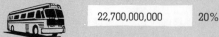

68,600,000,000   62%

17,400,000,000   16%

22,700,000,000   20%

The big three in transportation handle 97 per cent of the passenger business. Boats and interurban railways get the rest. (*Civic Education Press*)

CHECKING OUR BAR GRAPHS

Is it of proper size to show the facts clearly?
Is the title complete and easy to read?
Is each bar labeled and drawn correctly?
Are the bars the same width and evenly spaced?
Is the lettering clear and easy to read?
Is the source of information given?

Chart 17

The width of the bars and the spacing between them should be planned so that the graph can be seen clearly and is easy to read. If pieces of tape or strips of paper are used for the bars, children should be encouraged to try different arrangements until they arrive at one that is satisfactory. A clear title or heading should be placed on the graph so that the content included in it is clear. This is related to the basic point of always checking the title when reading a graph, to determine just what is presented in it.

CIRCLE GRAPHS

Circle or pie graphs are used most frequently to show the relationships of parts to the whole, for example, per cents, proportions, or various common fractional parts of specific items such as how the tax dollar is spent, agricultural products in relation to total production, imports, and exports. In interpreting these graphs, one must check the heading to find just what is shown by the whole

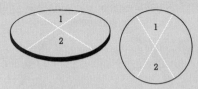

Does portion 1 equal portion 2 in both circles? Yes.

How does perspective affect the impression in the circle on the left?

OUR BOOK DRIVE

15
10
5
0
Mon. Tues. Wed. Thurs. Fri.

Notice the impressions given by symbols that vary in size?

Why is it a good general rule to use pictorial symbols of the same size?

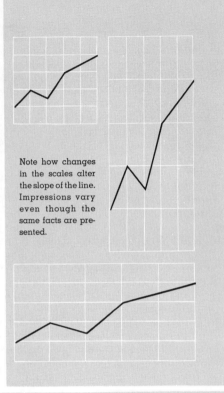

Note how changes in the scales alter the slope of the line. Impressions vary even though the same facts are presented.

GROWTH IN SCHOOL ENROLLMENT
SHOWN ON DIFFERENT GRAPHS

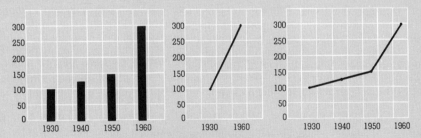

Which graph is easiest to read? Which one fails to show the period of most rapid growth?

How do the differences in intervals change the impression given in the one in the center?

Interpretation of graphs.

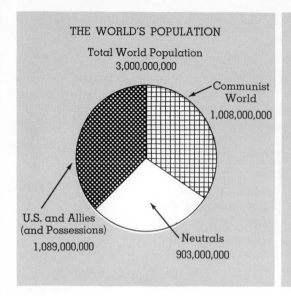

THE WORLD'S POPULATION

Total World Population
3,000,000,000

Communist World
1,008,000,000

U.S. and Allies
(and Possessions)
1,089,000,000

Neutrals
903,000,000

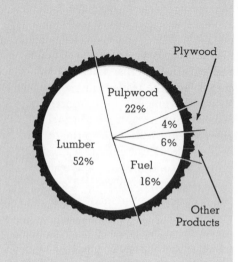

Plywood

Pulpwood
22%

4%

Lumber
52%

6%

Fuel
16%

Other
Products

Circle graphs.

circle and compare the parts with each other and with the whole. Before children have learned *per cent* as a concept, only known fractional terms such as *one-half* and *one-quarter* can be used. In making circle graphs, a first step is to list data for each part and then to find what proportion each part is of the whole. This is followed by measuring each part or sector of the circle, drawing the radius of the circle at the proper places, and labeling each part. Before children have developed the concepts and skills needed to handle *per cent* and *degrees*, simple instructional approaches must be used. For example, circles of construction paper can be cut into halves, thirds, fourths, and so on, to represent different parts. These can be mounted and labeled, and, in cases where needed, the fractional amount may be written on each part to show how much of the whole it represents. In upper grades, children can measure the degrees in a circle by means of a protractor.

MAKING CIRCLE GRAPHS

List the facts to be shown and find the total.
Figure the amount that each part is of the total.
Measure each part or sector on the circle.
Draw lines for different portions and label them.
Select a title and put it on the graph.
Put the source of information on the graph.

Chart 18

LINE GRAPHS

Line graphs are especially useful in showing changes, trends, and growth patterns. They are two-dimensional, as are many bar graphs, and the reader must check the vertical scale which usually shows the amount or number, and the horizontal scale which usually shows time or another related factor. In interpreting them, attention must be given to the scale and to the degree of gradation of the scale. Because many scales are in multiples such as hundreds, thousands, and millions, the reader must learn to estimate the distance between each point that is read, and the lines that show the units of measurement. This can be facilitated by placing the corner of a piece of paper on the point to be read and reading the scales at the points where the edges of the paper cross the side and the bottom of the graph.

Other key learnings in the interpretation of line graphs are the direction and steepness of the slope of the line. As children use line graphs, they should discover upward trends, downward trends, and speed of change as indicated by steepness of slope. Special attention must be given to the scale so that a distorted view will not be obtained. For example, if the horizontal scale is greater than the vertical scale the steepness of the line is reduced, as shown in the illustration on this page. The best way to teach such a point is through the actual analysis and discussion of graphs that chil-

(Adapted from *Study Skills in the Elementary School*. Copyright © 1960 by Scholastic Magazines, Inc., by permission.)

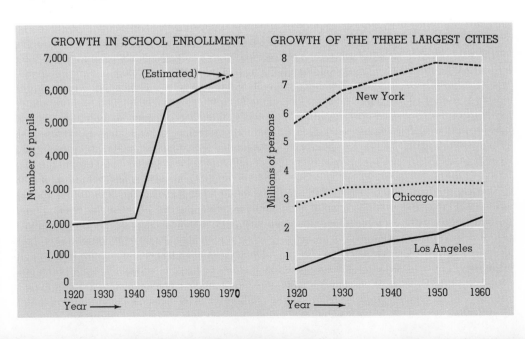

GROWTH IN SCHOOL ENROLLMENT   GROWTH OF THE THREE LARGEST CITIES

dren are using. Teachers can find excellent examples in children's weekly newspapers, local newspapers, encyclopedias, and textbooks.

In making line graphs, one should first construct simple ones based on information related to daily temperature, growth in school enrollment over a period of years, or other familiar data. Special care must be given to the selection of the vertical and horizontal scales so that distorted impressions are not given. The actual trying out of various scales followed by critical discussion is helpful in this. Another helpful procedure is to compare bar and line graphs based on the same information. The plotting of points on the grid should be double checked before the lines are drawn from point to point. As with other graphs, a clear descriptive title should be placed on them, and the source of information should be given.

BASIC GUIDELINES

In summary, specific instruction is needed on the following points when graphs are used in the social studies:

1. Read the title or heading carefully to determine exactly what is presented and note key terms such as *growth, decline, change, size, trends, average, square miles, value, predicted,* and the like.

2. Note what each picture or symbol represents on picture graphs, and the size of scales on bar and line graphs.

3. Note the source of information and check the original source if questions arise.

4. Look out for distortions, breaks in the scale, changes in size of symbols, and graphs drawn in perspectives which may give false impressions.

5. Make graphs that summarize information being used in units.

6. Develop the terms and concepts needed to discuss graphs: *key, symbol, bar, grid, grid lines, scale, horizontal, vertical, row, column, portion,* and *sector.*

7. Compare graphs of different types that are based on the same data.

8. Avoid the making of erroneous and inaccurate interpretations, such as inferring that one thing causes another because the two are presented together on a graph.

Questions, Activities, Evaluation

1. Examine the following to find other examples of graphic materials appropriate for use in the social studies program: (a) children's textbooks and reference materials, (b) children's weekly

news periodicals, (c) children's encyclopedias, and (d) local news-papers.

2. Which of the following might be suggested for children to make as a part of activities in a unit of instruction you are plan-ning: (a) posters, (b) cartoons, (c) charts of various types, (d) diagrams, (e) time charts or timelines, (f) tables, (g) graphs of various types? Sketch examples that you think would be appro-priate.

3. Which of the different types of charts presented in this chapter do you believe to be most useful in Grades I–III? Grades IV–VI? Grades VII–VIII? What changes or adaptations might be made in them?

4. Which of the different types of graphs do you believe to be most useful in the same grades listed above?

5. Which skills and concepts involved in making graphs ap-pear to you to be most difficult for children to learn? Make a brief plan showing how each step in making a graph might be taught.

6. Check an arithmetic textbook and see how arithmetical concepts involved in making and interpreting graphs are developed.

References

Arnsdorf, Val E., "An Investigation of the Teaching of Chronology in the Sixth Grade," *Journal of Experimental Education*, XXIX (March 1961), 307–13. A report of a study indicating that in-struction on time relationships helps sixth graders understand chronology, a finding contrary to that reported by others.

Brown, James W., Richard B. Lewis, and Fred F. Harcleroad, A-V *Instruction: Materials and Methods*. New York: McGraw-Hill Book Company, Inc., 1964. Section on graphic materials.

East, Marjorie, *Display for Learning: Making and Using Visuals*. New York: The Dryden Press, Inc., 1952. A handbook on mak-ing displays, drawings, graphs, charts, and posters.

Fraser, Dorothy M., and Edith West, *Social Studies in Secondary Schools*, Ch. xi. New York: The Ronald Press Company, 1961. Section on time concepts.

Glenn, William H., and Donovan A. Johnson, *Adventures in Graph-ing*. St. Louis: Webster Publishing, 1961. Graphing activities for children.

Jarolimek, John, *Social Studies in Elementary Education*. New York: The Macmillan Company, 1967. Section on graphic materials.

McCune, George H., and Neville Pearson, "Interpreting Material Presented in Graphic Form," *Skill Development in the Social*

Studies, 33rd Yearbook. Washington, D.C.: National Council for the Social Studies, 1963. Guidelines, techniques, and illustrative activities.

McKee, Paul, *Reading, A Program of Instruction for the Elementary School*, pp. 366–75. Boston: Houghton Mifflin Company, 1966. Sample lessons for teaching interpretation of graphs.

Minor, Ed, *Simplified Techniques for Preparing Instructional Materials*. New York: McGraw-Hill Book Company, Inc., 1962. Illustrated procedures.

Naslund, Robert A., and Jack McClellan, *Graph and Picture Study Skills*. Chicago: Science Research Associates, Inc., 1966. This is a kit of study materials similar to the SRA reading labs.

Thomas, R. Murray, and Sherwin G. Swartout, *Integrated Teaching Materials*, Ch. xii–xiv, "Drawn and Printed Graphic Materials." New York: Longmans, Green & Co., Inc., 1960.

Wittich, Walter A., and Charles F. Schuler, *Audio-Visual Materials: Their Nature and Use*, Ch. v, "Graphics." New York: Harper & Row, Publishers, 1962.

Maps
and
Globes

Maps and globes are used in units at all levels of instruction as an integral part of individual and group inquiry. Both commercial maps and maps made by the teacher and children have a place in the instructional program. The following summary includes the major uses of maps and globes in the social studies:

14

1. Determining distance between places; finding shortest travel routes; comparing early travel time and routes with travel time and routes today; discovering how concepts of time, distance, and travel have changed because of technological advances

2. Locating places in the neighborhood, community, state, nation, other lands; locating parks, recreational areas, resources, products, seaports, water bodies, mountain ranges, historical and current events, and centers of population

3. Comparing selected regions, countries, and continents with reference to area, resources, population, climate, surface features, transportation networks, distance from the equator, elevation, crops, products, and occupations of people

4. Making maps of study trips taken by the class; making maps of the neighborhood and community, transportation networks, routes of explorers, resources, products, current events, and other items being studied in units

5. Using pictorial maps to find out about food, shelter, clothing, resources, products, plant and animal life, famous persons, and historical events

6. Using maps in textbooks, weekly news periodicals, atlases, encyclopedias, and other materials to answer questions, clarify concepts, and prepare reports

7. Using maps from newspapers and magazines to report on places being studied and to locate places in current events

8. Using maps in scrapbooks and reports to summarize data obtained from various sources of information

9. Studying maps to discover relationships and to make inferences regarding climate and living conditions, industries and resources, terrain and travel routes, amount of rainfall and vegetation, location of cities in relation to harbors, and latitude and altitude as related to climate

10. Making outline and relief maps to illustrate significant relationships and to summarize information related to questions raised in class

11. Using maps on transparent material as overlays to show relationships between selected features, and as projectuals for use in the discussion and analysis of distributions, associations, and interconnections within and between regions

Maps and globes should be used as an integral part of the inquiry process. While problems and questions are being defined and set up in the initiation of a unit, they can be used to give an overview of places being studied and to stimulate questions about ways of living, products, travel ways, and uses of resources. And as plans are made to solve problems, attention can be given to possible uses of globes, maps, and atlases to secure information. The use of outline maps, slated globes, and slated maps to summarize and organize information should be considered. Attention should also be given to the use of maps and the globe in giving reports and sharing information gathered by individuals and com-

GET INFORMATION FROM MAPS		USING THE GLOBE AND MAPS TO ANSWER QUESTIONS
Locate places.	Find major cities.	Where is it?
Find distances.	Note waterways.	How far is it?
Find elevation.	Find air routes.	In what direction is it?
Note directions.	Note highways.	How large is it?
Find water bodies.	Note railways.	What is the climate?
Note rainfall.	Compare areas.	What is produced?
Note products.	Note products.	Where do people live?

Chart 1   Chart 2

mittees. If a special effort is made to have children use maps and the globe along with pictures, films, and other resources, they will grow in their ability to use many sources of information to solve problems and answer questions.

Criteria for Selection

In selecting maps and globes for use in elementary schools, special care must be taken to obtain those which children can and will use. Too often, children are asked to use maps designed for advanced students—maps loaded with fine print, and cluttered with concepts and detail far beyond their maturity. The use of such maps has probably done more to create a poor attitude toward map use than any other single factor. Simple, clear, easy-to-use maps and globes are essential for elementary school children. The following criteria are helpful in selecting *globes*:

1. Large globes, from twelve to sixteen inches in diameter, are desirable for most purposes in the elementary school; eight inch globes are satisfactory for desk use.

2. They must be well constructed in order to withstand the wear and tear of frequent use by children.

3. They should be mounted in such a way as to encourage use; cradle and stand mountings are preferred by many elementary school teachers.

4. Simplified material should be presented, such as major continents, bodies of water, countries, and cities.

5. Colors should be clear and easy to distinguish: blue for water, green for lowlands, and so forth.

6. Lettering should be clear and easy to read.

The markable globe is used for a variety of purposes in the social studies. (College Elementary School, Chico, California)

Points to keep in mind in selecting *maps* are:

1. Content should be simple, authentic, and related to the program.
2. The title should be meaningful.
3. Sources of information should be given.
4. Form of presentation of content should be appropriate to the maturity of the group that will use the map.
5. Colors should be clear and easy to distinguish: blue for water, green for lowlands, and so forth.
6. Symbols should be easy to see and clearly explained in the legend.
7. Lettering should be clear, large, uncluttered, and easy to read.
8. Projection should be satisfactory.
9. Size should be large enough for classroom use.
10. Scale should be clear and easy to follow.
11. Mounting should be durable and facilitate use.

The Globe

The globe is the most accurate representation of the earth's surface; it should be referred to whenever problems come up about relative location, size, distance, direction, and shape of land masses and water bodies. Because the globe is a sphere like the earth, it has properties that cannot all be found on any one flat map: (1) distance between places in correct proportion, (2) correct shape of land masses and water bodies, (3) areas in correct proportion, and (4) true directions. When a sphere is transferred to a flat surface, some distortion is inevitable; in many flat maps it is greatest at the outer edges. No world map is as true a representation of earth's surface as is the globe.

The globe should be used in conjunction with maps whenever there are problems of distortion, and when misconceptions need to be corrected. Such a misconception as the belief that Greenland is larger than South America (it is about one-eighth as large), or that the shortest distance from San Francisco to Moscow is across the Pacific (a polar route is shorter), can be avoided by referring to the globe. The relative position of continents, the shapes of land masses, and the size of various regions should be checked in a similar manner.

The globe should also be used to develop fundamental concepts about the earth and its surface features. In the early grades, the

Maps and globes should be simple and uncluttered with detail. Use them together to teach relationships. *(Education Workshop, University of California, Berkeley)*

globe is used to develop concepts of the roundness of the earth, directions, the extent water covers the earth's surface (about three-fourths), differences in surface features from place to place, and size differences among major land masses and water bodies. In later grades, the globe is used to develop concepts related to night and day, time zones, changes in seasons, rotation and revolution, and high, middle, and low latitudes. Concept development of this kind is essential to the development of map-reading skills and is closely related to the development of major geographic concepts. (See Charts 3–8.)

SHOW THESE ON THE PROJECT GLOBE

Main land masses and water bodies
Names of the oceans, the continents, and islands
North Pole, South Pole, Equator
Tropic of Cancer, Tropic of Capricorn
Arctic Circle and Antarctic Circle
Prime Meridian and International Date Line

Chart 3

FIND THESE ON THE GLOBE

Northern hemisphere

Southern hemisphere

Western hemisphere

Eastern hemisphere

Land hemisphere

Water hemisphere

Daylight hemisphere

Darkness hemisphere

Chart 4

SHOW DIRECTIONS ON THE GLOBE

North toward the North Pole

South toward the South Pole

North along the meridians

South along the meridians

East along the parallels

West along the parallels

Chart 5

ROTATION AND TIME

Demonstrate the cause of day and night.

Show how to find time in different places.

Locate the hour circles or meridians and compare them with time zones.

Show noon and midnight by finding opposite meridians.

Show how the calendar is adjusted when crossing the International Date Line.

Chart 6

GREAT CIRCLES ON THE GLOBE

Show that a great circle divides the earth into two equal parts.

Show that the equator is a great circle.

Show that the meridians are great circles.

Show that parallels north and south of the equator are not great circles.

Show a great circle route from New York to Bangkok.

Chart 7

REVOLUTION AND SEASONS

Show how the earth's axis is tilted.

Show the orbit of the earth as it goes around the sun.
Show the sun's rays during the summer and the winter solstices.
Show the sun's rays during the spring and the fall equinoxes.
Show the northern limit of the sun's vertical rays.
Show the southern limit of the sun's vertical rays.

Chart 8

Because the globe is such a useful teaching device, at least one should be provided in each classroom. In the primary grades, a raised relief globe that clearly shows land and water features is

helpful in giving children the "feel" of the earth's surface. Raised
relief globes are available in lightweight plastic that can be marked
with crayon or chalk. These globes, which children can handle
easily, can be used to develop initial concepts of the roundness of
the earth, main land and water areas, and general nature of surface features. A good globe for the next stage of instruction is

How might a markable
raised-relief globe such as
this one be used to de-
velop basic concepts of
the earth's surface? (Rand
McNally)

the simplified, merged color, beginner's globe. By comparing it
with the raised-relief globe, children quickly grasp the meaning
of the colors that are used to show relief. Also helpful is the
markable project globe that simply shows major features in outline form with land clearly differentiated from water. This globe
can be used in different grades to develop concepts of direction,
to mark the location of places and special features, and to outline
countries, regions, travel routes, and other items. For middle and
upper grades, a physical-political globe that clearly shows main
surface features, yet is not cluttered with detailed printing, should
be available in each classroom. A physical-political globe with a

horizontal mounting that can be used to develop concepts of motion, time, distance, seasonal sun position, and the like is helpful in Grades VII and VIII, and for advanced children in Grades V and VI. Small desk globes (eight inches in diameter) for individual projects can be used to develop concepts and skills in all grades. In some schools, a classroom set of desk globes is kept in a central storage place so that teachers in different classrooms may check them out.

Flat Maps

Flat maps are needed to show areas in large perspective. The globe is too small to show distributions of items so that they can be studied in detail. The wide range of content shown on maps enables one to see at a glance many surface conditions and relationships that cannot otherwise be portrayed as clearly and as efficiently.

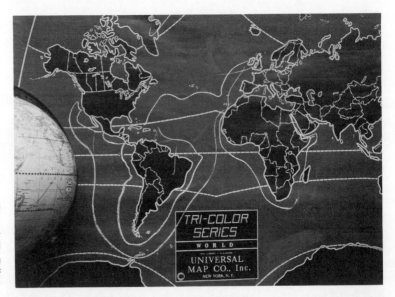

Slated maps and globes can be used by children to show travel routes, location of resources, and many other items being considered in the unit of instruction. (Berkeley)

CONTENT

Maps may be classified according to content into such types as political, physical, physical-political, economic, historical, and special feature. The following list illustrates the diversity of content shown on maps:

Political—boundaries, cities, states, countries, blocs
Physical—mountains, lowlands, rivers, lakes, oceans
Climate—rainfall, temperature, winds
Population—density, relation to surface features
Economic—resources, crops, occupations, products
Physical-political—combinations of the above
Historical—explorations, events, territorial changes
Travel—trade routes, roads, railroads, air routes
Community—streets, buildings, agencies, harbors
Special—parks, monuments, literary works, religion

USING OUR WORLD ATLAS

Basic Maps

World Maps	Asia
North America	Africa
South America	Australia
Europe	Polar Regions

Other Maps

Climate	Population
Temperature	Resources
Vegetation	Products

Tables

Rivers	Population
Mountains	Sea depths

Glossary

Places	Map terms

Chart 9

USING MAPS IN OUR ENCYCLOPEDIAS

Location of cities, states, countries, continents, and water bodies

Physical relief maps that show surface features

Political maps showing cities, states, provinces, and countries

Regional maps of the United States, Central America, and other places

Historical maps of notable events

Interesting places such as parks, monuments

Comparison maps that show relative size of states and countries

Pictorial maps that show plants, animals, products, and resources

Chart 10

TYPES

Flat maps of various types are needed in the elementary school. Frequently used maps should be placed in each classroom; those used less frequently may be kept in a central location for checking out as needed. In the early grades, occasional reference may be made to simplified maps of the state, United States, and world, in addition to using the globe to develop basic concepts. Neighborhood and community maps made by the teacher, or by the teacher and the children, also are used, for example, to show the block around the school, where pupils' homes and other important places are located, or the routes of study trips. Beginning in Grade III, increased use is made of state, United States, and world maps as communities in other places are studied. Markable maps should also be available in addition to the project globe. A geographical-terms chart that illustrates such features as *bay, hills, valley, mountains, plateau,* and *valley* is helpful in clarifying and differentiating surface features.

In Grades IV through VIII, the following should be available as needed in relation to topics that are studied in each grade:

1. Markable maps of the United States and the world
2. Physical-political maps of the state, United States, Canada, the continents, and the world
3. Outline maps for desk use and for making large wall maps
4. Raised relief (three-dimensional) maps of the United States and the continents
5. Special maps that show such items as voyages and discoveries of early explorers, exploration of America, territorial expansion of the United States, and distribution of population, resources, and products
6. Air-age map centered on the North Pole
7. A desk atlas and a reference atlas
8. A geographical-terms chart.

Map Reading

Maps are a combination of lines, symbols, colors, and terms. Symbols may be pictorial, semipictorial, or nonpictorial. The nonpictorial are most difficult for children to interpret—points, solid lines, broken lines, circles, letters, colors, shading, hachures, and others. The grid consists of lines which are used as points of reference. Cities may be shown by dots, circles, triangles, squares, or crosses. Terms are used to designate various features such as mountains, cities, water bodies, political divisions, and regions. Colors or shading are used to show land and water, and to distinguish one area from another in relation to such factors as elevation, density of population, rainfall, vegetation, temperature, or fertility of soil. Drawings and symbolic characters are sometimes used to represent such items as products, animal life, railroads, or mountain ranges.

THE GRID

Maps and globes are made on grids which include reference lines, for example, east-west lines or parallels, and north-south lines or meridians. The importance of these grid lines can be brought home to children in several ways. One widely used technique is to use a large ball in place of a globe and ask children to show the location of their community or another well known place on it. Immediately the question of reference points and lines will arise: Where should we mark the North Pole, the South Pole, and the Equator? Do we need other lines? After checking the classroom globe, they should proceed to mark reference lines on the ball with chalk and to locate the given place on it. A similar procedure can be used to locate surface features on a piece of paper. For example, when children are asked to locate places in the neighborhood, they must mark lines to show the different streets and then proceed to locate homes, the school, and other important places. In later grades, the same procedure can be used for locating states, countries, and other places by first drawing squares on the paper to serve as a grid and then sketching the places to be shown. Other helpful procedures are to review the grid lines on road maps, state maps, maps of the nation, wall maps of various continents, and the globe.

GUIDING PRINCIPLES

Because maps are symbolic representations, attention must be given to the gradual development of map language. First of all, simple maps with very little detail should be selected for use in the primary grades. In later grades, more detailed maps may be used to meet the various problems that arise. The symbols, colors, and terms on the maps should be identified, learned, and used in reading maps and in making maps. In general, a new symbol should be taught when needed for functional use. The legend should be analyzed and the symbols and colors contained in it should be located on the map and interpreted. Important terms should be learned and located on the map. Children should have opportunities to use the terms as they write on slated globes and maps and complete desk and wall outline maps. Directions north and south, and east and west should be pointed out and reviewed as children change rooms, as new maps are introduced, and as questions arise. The scale of miles should be learned and used in measuring distances between places being studied in the unit. The different colors relating to elevation should be considered and related to places of varying elevation visited by chil-

Our Growing Vocabulary

mountains

grassland

desert

forest

tropics

plateau

swamp

Map reading requires systematic attention to concepts and symbols. (*Education Workshop, University of California, Berkeley*)

dren in the class. Sizes of cities, distances between places, and types of climate should be associated with cities children already know, places they have visited, and places in which they have lived. In short, the use of maps must be related to children's backgrounds and experience, concepts and symbols must be developed gradually, and map-reading skills must be put to use in solving problems.

Maps and map symbols can have meaning to children only if many concrete experiences are provided, such as observing and discussing surface features, and seeing pictures, films, and filmstrips of places and features being studied. Each child must develop sufficient background to visualize what is represented on the map and to translate symbols into realities that exist on the landscape. For example, the dot that represents a city should bring to mind a picture the child has seen or an actual trip taken to the city. After a period of meaning-building, attention may be given to specific skills involved in map reading.

The development of map-reading skills requires specific instruction in the symbols, colors, scale, and network of lines used to represent specific information. Such instruction should be related to specific needs for the use of maps so that children can make immediate applications of what they learn. Maps should be used

426

in a setting of meaningful content developed in current units; isolated, encyclopedic dissection of maps in a formal manner leads to a negative attitude toward map use. Map-reading skills should be graded in difficulty, reviewed as needed at succeeding grade levels, and put to actual use in each unit. Never assume that children can read maps simply because maps are in their books, or because maps are on the walls of the classroom.

As with skills taught in other areas of the curriculum, grade placement of map-reading skills must be flexible. The ability of each child, his previous learning, and the richness of his present learning determine what should be taught next. The suggested placement of topics made in various places throughout the following sections should be viewed as a tentative guide subject to changes as needed in a particular class, with topics shifted upward or downward so that each child continues to progress satisfactorily.

PREPARATION FOR MAP READING

Before children can use maps meaningfully, certain skills and understandings should be taught. Most important among these are directions, surface features, and concepts of the earth.

Cardinal Directions. The directions—north, south, east, and west—can be taught in terms of specific locations known to the child. For example, in what direction does his house face? The school? What is the direction from home to school? To the grocery store? To other familiar places? What buildings are north? South? East? West?

Arrange layouts and maps of the community together so that children can visualize the symbols on the map. (Berkeley)

Another technique is to have a group of children stand with their backs to the sun at noon. Explain that they are facing north, that south is in back of them, that east is to their right, and that west is to their left. Have them locate the same directions in the classroom. Cards with the directions written on them can be shown later with the suggestion that individual children point in the direction shown. Some teachers place labels showing directions on the appropriate walls of the classroom.

Directions should be discussed after study trips and short walks, and after trips taken to nearby towns with parents. The directions to important cities from a child's home town also should be considered. Specific attention should be given to the fact that east is the direction of the earth's rotation; therefore, it seems that the *sun rises in the east and sets in the west.* Encourage children to look for the North Star at night; explain that this method has been used for a long time by sailors to determine direction. Many teachers find it helpful to summarize key learnings about directions on the chalkboard, or on charts as shown in Charts 11–12.

DIRECTIONS AT NOON	THE SUN AND DIRECTIONS
Stand with your back to the sun. You are facing north. East is to your right. South is in back of you. West is to your left.	The sun rises in the east. The sun sets in the west. At noon the sun is south. Our shadows are toward the north at noon.
Chart 11	Chart 12

Children can also use a simple box compass to find directions. Have them associate the direction the needle points with familiar places and with the direction of their shadows at noon. A simple compass can be made by suspending a bar magnet by a string and letting it hang until it comes to rest in a north-south line. Or, a magnetized needle (one stroked against a magnet) may be floated on a thin slice of cork in a glass of water. In the upper grades children should check the magnetic declination in *The World Almanac* and make a correction to determine the true geographic north.

Surface Features. Children need specific experiences to develop an understanding of surface features shown on maps, and the terms used to express them. Both natural features (landforms, water bodies and other concept clusters listed in Chapter 4) and man-made features (highways, canals, dams, and the like) should be given attention. A teacher's purpose should be to provide sufficient experience for each child to develop a clear concept of the land-scape features represented by symbols used on maps. Then children can bring meaning to map reading, as they should bring meaning to other kinds of reading.

On short walks and on study trips, different surface features should be pointed out and discussed. Children's ability to observe should be sharpened; they should be encouraged to ask questions about what they see. Films, pictures, terrain models, and charts showing map terms should be discussed to clarify specific concepts such as *plateau, bay, gulf, harbor*. Commercial or teacher-made charts, and pictures of surface features with appropriate labels attached to them are especially helpful. Children should report on trips they have taken to mountains, beaches, lakes, valleys, canyons, parks, dams, and other places where various surface features could be seen; they should share and discuss post cards and photographs which show the features they are discussing. Maps with raised relief should be used to help them visualize *mountains, valleys, winding rivers*, and other surface features. Sketches and drawings made by children as well as those in textbooks also should be used in discussion. When textbooks are used, teachers should be alert to new concepts that are introduced, being sure to clarify them through discussion, showing of pictures, or viewing of films and filmstrips. Another helpful technique, illustrated in Chart 14, is to have children in intermediate grades locate pictures or sketches that illustrate specific features. The next step, of course, is to have them locate the same features on a map.

Concepts of the Earth. Specific concepts of the earth can be

CAN YOU FIND EXAMPLES OF THESE CONCEPT CLUSTERS ON MAPS?		
RESOURCES	MAJOR LANDFORMS	WATER BODIES
Soil	Plains	Rivers
Water	Hills	Lakes
Minerals	Plateaus	Gulfs
Wildlife	Mountains	Oceans

Chart 13

effectively developed through showing and discussing a simplified globe. Begin by discussing the fact that the globe is a good representation (not a picture) of the earth. The surface is land and water, and where we live is one small part of the earth. Explain that the earth is shaped like a ball and that the globe shows the main land and water features. Introduce the term *sphere* and have children tell about objects they know which are shaped like a sphere or ball. Explain that the earth is a sphere, too. Teach the meaning of the term *hemisphere* by cutting an orange or ball of clay in half; point out that hemisphere means half of a ball. Hold the globe so that they can see the hemisphere on which they live.

The North Pole should be located; explain that this is the farthest point north. Next locate the South Pole and point out that we are farther from the South Pole than we are from the North Pole. Explain the term *equator*; locate it and point out that it is midway between the poles. Show the northern and southern hemispheres and have the group tell in which hemisphere we live.

FIND PICTURES TO SHOW EACH OF THESE FEATURES

1. The rugged coastline of a fiord
2. Mountainous land
3. A broad plateau
4. The hub of the highways
5. A long, winding river
6. A network of railways
7. Area of dense population
8. Desert as far as the eye can see

Chart 14

DO YOU USE THESE TERMS CORRECTLY?

North—toward the North Pole
South—toward the South Pole
Up—away from the earth, higher
Down—toward the *center of the earth*, lower

Chart 15

DIRECTIONS ON THE GLOBE

North—along meridians, toward the North Pole
South—along meridians, toward the South Pole
East—along parallels, toward the rising sun
West—along parallels, toward the setting sun

Chart 16

Directions on the globe should be clarified. North is toward the North Pole; south is toward the South Pole. Never use the terms *up* and *down* to indicate north and south. Explain that *up* is away from the earth, and that *down* is toward the center of the earth. The diagrams in geography texts are helpful in this connection. Show east and west to the group; have them identify known places to the east and west of their state.

The major land and water bodies should be discussed. Begin with North America, explaining that this is the continent on which we live. Show the location of the Atlantic and Pacific Oceans, pointing out that our country is between them. Name the other continents, beginning with ones that have been mentioned in class. Mention one or two places on each continent that are familiar to children. Show the Indian Ocean, pointing out that it is south of the equator and between the Atlantic and Pacific Oceans.

THE CONTINENTS

1. How many major continents are there?
2. On which continent is the United States?
3. In what direction is each continent from our continent?
4. Which continent is largest?

Chart 17

USE THE GLOBE

1. To find distance
2. To find directions
3. To find location
4. To note distortion in flat maps
5. To compare places
6. To find shortest travel routes

Chart 18

Some teachers have children take a ball of clay and mark the equator, the North and South Poles, and the continents. Another technique that has been used successfully is to build up a simple globe by pasting strips of paper on a balloon. In some schools small globes for individual desk use are available.

MAP SYMBOLS

Clear perception and meaningful association are involved in learning map symbols. A primary goal is to help each child visualize the feature for which the symbol stands. Bear in mind that good map readers can recreate in their mind's eye what is shown on maps. Toward this end the following should be done:

1. Each map symbol should be visualized, and pictorial and semipictorial symbols should be introduced before nonpictorial symbols.

2. After a symbol has been taught, provide for some review without any label or caption so that children will learn the symbol and not rely on the label.

3. Be sure each child checks the legend before using a map. Discuss any new symbols or new uses of color. Review any symbols about which there is a question. Do this for textbook maps as well as for wall maps. Points to consider at different times are shown in Charts 19 through 23.

CHECK THE LEGEND

1. What is the scale of miles?
2. What do the colors mean?
3. What do the symbols mean?
4. Are other facts given?

Chart 19

CHECK THE KEY
TO THE MAP

1. What do the colors mean?
2. What do shadings mean?
3. Can you figure elevation?

Chart 20

CAN YOU FIND THESE ON OUR MAPS?

Plain	Hill	Island
Desert	Mountain	Isthmus
Tundra	Valley	Peninsula
Forest	Volcano	Continent

Chart 21

HOW ARE THESE
SHOWN ON OUR MAPS?

Capitals	Lowlands
Cities	Plains
Seaports	Plateaus
Roads	Mountains
Boundaries	Products
Railways	Rainfall
Airways	Population
Rivers	Resources

Chart 22

SYMBOLS ON MAPS
IN OUR BOOKS

1. Straight lines show roads on level land.
2. Curved lines show roads on hilly land.
3. Black squares show houses.
4. A cluster of squares shows a town.
5. Lines winding between hills show rivers.
6. The winding line by the ocean is the coastline.

Chart 23

4. Compare the symbols on a new map with those used on a familiar map; be alert to questions, or misconceptions, that children have about symbols.

5. Give specific attention to symbols for cities of different size, rivers, coastline, boundaries, canals, dams and the like.

6. Explain and illustrate the uses of color to show elevation, countries or states, and vegetation (see Chart 24). Point out that various shadings of black and white, lines, or dots may be used to show some of the same features (see Chart 25). Have the group summarize what the colors and shadings represent.

WHICH ARE SHOWN BY
COLORS ON OUR
MAPS?

1. Elevation of lands?
2. States and countries?
3. Distribution of
   resources?
4. Density of population?
5. Other information?

Chart 24

RAINFALL PER YEAR AS
SHOWN ON OUR MAP

less than 5 inches
5 to 10 inches
10 to 20 inches
20 to 50 inches
over 50 inches

Chart 25

7. Discuss the key on a map showing elevation. Explain that elevation is measured from sea level and that the colors show the elevation. Discuss profiles of mountains as illustrated in textbooks, and have the class make profiles showing elevation. Relate these to color maps showing elevation, explaining that the colors enable us to determine elevation; summarize the colors and elevation represented by them as shown in Charts 26 and 27.

WHAT HEIGHTS OR
DEPTHS DO THESE
COLORS SHOW?

Shades of red
Shades of brown
Shades of yellow
Shades of green
Shades of blue

Chart 26

ELEVATION ON OUR WALL MAPS

Red	10,000 and up
Dark brown	5,000–10,000
Light brown	2,000– 5,000
Yellow	1,000– 2,000
Light green	500– 1,000
Dark green	0– 500
Grayish green	Below sea level

Chart 27

8. Be sure that children use their growing knowledge of map symbols in many different situations. Keep charts, chalkboard notes, and pupil-made materials available for continuous reference in map use and map making.

WHERE IS IT?

1. What direction is it?
2. How many miles away?
3. How many hours by air?
4. What is the latitude?
5. Check the globe and atlas.

Chart 28

HOW BIG IS IT?

1. Compare it to our state.
2. Compare it to our country.
3. See it on the globe.
4. Check equal-area maps.
5. Use maps with same scale.

Chart 29

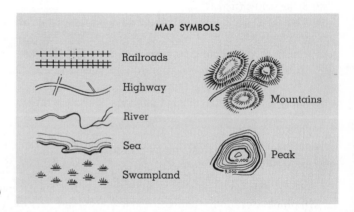

MAP SYMBOLS

Railroads

Highway

River

Sea

Swampland

Mountains

Peak

Chart 30

Teachers can add to the meaningfulness of maps by using them in conjunction with related study trips, pictures, filmstrips, motion pictures, the globe, reading, and discussion. For example, pictures of vegetation, landscapes, products, and types of shelter create in a child's mind impressions of the actual conditions in the area being studied. Aerial photographs should be compared with related sections of the map. Symbols such as those used for canals and other cultural or man-made features become more meaningful after a child sees them in picture form. Similarly, the differences between the jungles along the Amazon and the forests in Oregon can be clearly distinguished through the use of pictures. Study trips are helpful where the landscape can be studied first-hand and then checked against available maps. Motion pictures and filmstrips that show canals, seaports, animal and plant life, examples of clothing and shelter, and people at work contribute other important meanings. Reading and discussion help in giving adequate backgrounds of understanding and in correcting misconceptions. As mentioned earlier, frequent comparison should be made between the map and globe to develop true conceptions of space relationships, size, direction, distance, and relative location.

LOCATING PLACES ON THE MAP

Special attention must be given to teaching children how to locate significant places. First experiences in the locating of places should be carried out on floor layouts and maps of the community. The school, children's homes, and main buildings in the neighborhood should be given first attention. As the broader environment is studied in Grade II, other places can be located, such as the airport, railroad yards, nearby farms and dairies, and other places visited on study trips.

In Grades III and IV, experiences may be provided in locating significant places on road maps. The grid on road maps—numbers and letters to designate east-west and north-south lines—is fairly easy to use. Call children's attention to the index of places and guide them to find the point on the map where the given numbered and lettered lines meet. For practice use several places that are familiar to children; for example, shown in Chart 31 are places in Wisconsin as listed in the index of a road map.

The mileage chart on road maps also may be checked to determine the distance between places. Have the children use two narrow strips of paper to find the point of intersection which gives the mileage between two places. They can also find the mileage between starred cities on the map itself. Points of interest (national parks, monuments, historical places) listed on road maps may be noted, too. Incidentally, the map inserts which show major cities can be projected easily by means of an opaque projector in order to make simple maps of the community. This is an excellent procedure if the desired community is shown, because one can eliminate unnecessary detail and thereby secure a large map which can be used for many different purposes.

FIND THESE PLACES ON OUR ROAD MAPS

Green Bay	3-O
La Crosse	3-S
Madison	4-E
Milwaukee	4-G
Superior	2-B

Chart 31

When maps of the children's state or the United States are introduced, they should be placed on the floor, or on a table, so that they can be oriented properly and directions can be noted realistically. Have the children find where they live, and then point out neighboring cities and states. This may be followed by

A simple outline map can be used to show the location of important places in a state or region. *(Alameda County)*

locating places they have visited or read about. Discuss places being studied in the unit with attention to direction and distance (time as well as miles) from where they live. This will create a real need for learning how to use the scale of miles and how to compute distance. (The scale of miles is discussed in a later section.)

The problem of relative location—location of a place in relation to other places or surface features—should not be overlooked. Not just distance but such factors as accessibility, transportation facilities, and terrain need to be considered in this regard. Some places may be nearby "as the crow flies," but difficult to reach because of some barrier such as a mountain range, or lack of transportation facilities such as an airport or natural waterways.

In the primary grades, children begin to grasp concepts of relative location as different places in the community are studied, such as home and school in relation to stores, the library, parks, and playgrounds. Later, their concepts will be extended as attention is given to nearby towns, places in mountains and valleys, transportation facilities, and the location of cities near markets and resources.

In the middle grades, specific attention should be given to the

436

effect of mountain ranges, rivers, lakes, oceans, deserts, swamps, and jungles on accessibility to given places. Ways in which man changes the environment and overcomes barriers—roads, canals, railways, airports—should be discussed too. After all, relative distance and location change as improvements are made in transportation facilities. Modern air routes which follow great circles can be considered to bring home the importance of the area around the North Pole as related to travel between our country and Europe. The location of many cities near natural waterways and the availability of markets and resources to industrial centers also should be discussed. In addition, some children in the upper grades may discover that political and economic barriers, such as the Iron Curtain, are also factors to be considered.

A clear understanding of direction on maps and globes will help children grow in their ability to find and describe the location of places significant to them. Most fifth graders, and many fourth graders, can grasp the idea that lines of latitude are true east-west lines, and that meridians are true north-south lines. At first the terms *east-west lines* and *north-south lines* may be used; later the terms *latitude, parallels, meridians,* and *longitude* can be introduced. *Degrees* as a concept of measure should be taught in relation to latitude and longitude, and the location of main places. Guide children in their use of lines of latitude to note places north or south of their city or state, and places nearer to, or farther from, the equator. Also show them that places on the same line of latitude, or parallel, are east or west of each other because parallels are true east-west lines.

By checking meridians, children can be guided to note places to the east or west of their city or state. For example, Los Angeles is to the east of San Francisco (even east of Reno), and South America is located to the east of most of the United States. They also should be shown that places on the same meridian are directly north or south of each other because meridians are true north-south lines. Much review and practice should be given on these uses of parallels and meridians in the upper grades and in high school.

In all work of this type, emphasis should be given to the location of places being studied, or places being discussed in current events. The location of places should be tied in with significant questions regarding distance, products, climate, relationships between key factors, or some other problem that has arisen in class. To be avoided is the outmoded practice of having children engage in routine, meaningless location of places as busywork.

The phrases *middle latitudes, high latitudes,* and *low latitudes* should be substituted for *temperate, frigid,* and *torrid zones.* The latter are climatic rather than locational terms, and are not accurate descriptions of climatic conditions in the particular zones which they are used to designate. However, since some writers do use the terms, children should become acquainted with them and understand the inaccuracies and limitations that exist in their usage. An example of how one group of children in Grade VI handled this problem is shown in Chart 32. The children should learn about the differences in seasons, and the varying lengths of night and day and their causes.

LOW, MIDDLE, AND HIGH LATITUDES

1. Low latitudes are between 23½ degrees north and south of the equator; this area is sometimes called the torrid zone.
2. Middle latitudes are between 23½ and 66½ degrees north, and between the same degrees south; these areas are sometimes called temperate zones.
3. High latitudes are between 66½ degrees north and the North Pole, and the same degrees south and the South Pole; these areas are sometimes called frigid zones.

Chart 32

In the middle and upper grades, after degrees of latitude and longitude have been introduced, children can make more exact location of places. For example, they may locate their own city and other well-known places being studied, such as New York, approximately 40° north latitude and 74° west longitude; Columbus, approximately 40° north latitude and 83° west longitude; and Denver, approximately 40° north latitude and 105° west longitude. The fact that places such as these are along approximately the same line of latitude and, therefore, are east or west of each other, should be reviewed. Latitude and longitude of major cities of the United States also may be checked in *The World Almanac.*

Great-circle routes, longitude, and an acquaintance with a few of the commonly used map projections can be learned and used by many students in the upper grades. A great circle around the globe forms two hemispheres, and the shortest distance between any two points is along a great circle. The meridians and the equator are great circles; others can be shown by stretching a tape measure or string tightly along the surface of the globe. A simple global ruler can be made for measuring great-circle distances as

Use global projections to help children see relationships between continents, travel routes, time, and distance more clearly. *(Education Workshop, University of California, Berkeley)*

follows: measure the circumference of the globe, divide 25,000 by the circumference, and you then know the number of miles per inch. Have students use a global ruler to find great-circle distances between places.

Longitude is not used so much as is latitude, but it can be taught in connection with the location of specific places and time zones. The Prime Meridian, the International Date Line, and how Greenwich came to be used as the main point of reference for longitude should be discussed. Specific location of familiar places may be considered first, followed by places being discussed in current events or in units. Consideration of time zones should begin with those in the United States, followed by a consideration of time in Europe, beginning with time at the Prime Meridian and moving toward the United States and then on across Eurasia. A globe should be available for the discussion, and students should discover that meridians (on most globes) are spaced 15° apart, showing one hour of time ($360° \div 24 = 15°$). They should also check time zones in the United States to find out whether they coincide with meridians on the globe.

SCALE OF MILES

Several points should be kept in mind in teaching the scale of miles. The scale of miles on maps may be expressed graphically (0   200   400), as a statement (one inch equals 500 miles), or as a ratio (1: 1,000,000). The graphic scale is relatively easy to use to compute distances between places. Use of the inch-to-mile scale requires a child to measure accurately in inches and then to convert to miles. Both the graphic and inch-to-mile scale should be taught in the intermediate grades and reviewed in the upper grades. The ratio scale is the most difficult to understand because its use requires an understanding of fractions and ratio, and conversion to miles requires the use of simple algebra. It is difficult for pupils to visualize 1: 1,000,000 or to convert such a ratio to an inch-to-mile scale. However, since the scale on most maps and globes is expressed graphically or in terms of inches to miles, the ratio scale need not cause undue difficulty in the elementary school. The teaching of the ratio scale and conversion to miles should be carried out in junior high school as the necessary understandings and skills are taught in arithmetic and algebra. This, of course, should not prevent gifted children from learning to use this scale if situations arise in which functional use of it is warranted.

Several practical techniques can be used to help children understand distance as expressed by a scale. First, specific concepts of distance should be built up by considering familiar distances such as home to school, school to downtown, and to neighboring towns and cities. This should be followed by noting the same places on community maps and road maps. In this connection, community maps used in the primary grades should be drawn to scale by the teacher, or use should be made of simple community maps furnished by business concerns. Road maps can be used effectively by many third and fourth graders if emphasis is given to distance between known places. Another good technique is to consider the distance traveled on study trips. The group should take a map or sketch of the route on the trip and check key points along the way. Travel time on study trips, to and from school, to and from places in the community, and between familiar places, or places being studied, also should be considered because distance becomes more meaningful if travel time is considered.

Many intermediate-grade teachers have found the following activities helpful in teaching scale: drawing a sketch of the classroom to scale; making neighborhood or community maps; comparing two places shown on maps of different scale; discussing distance and travel time between places the children have visited; making maps of their state, or region, to scales of varying size; discussing the use of small-scale maps to show a large area; comparing outline maps (used by the children) with wall maps and noting the difference in scale; discussing the scale used on textbook maps; comparing distances between places being studied and familiar places (such as between New York and Chicago) and noting the scale; and comparing cities, states, and countries with respect to size. Of vital importance is the actual use of the scale on maps to answer questions that come up in daily classwork.

Discovering Associations and Making Inferences

The discovery of associations is a major objective of units in which geographic understandings are emphasized. Proper use of maps and the globe will contribute to this end. However, their use should be combined with reading, viewing of materials, and plenty of guided discussion so that any stated association has a basis in fact. Caution also must be exercised in discussing cause and effect relationships; have children double check first conclusions by making reference to other sources of information.

Among the important associations that children can be guided to discover are the following: (1) elevation and growing season, (2) elevation and density of population, (3) highlands and grazing, (4) lowlands and farming, (5) soil and farming, (6) mountains and rainfall, (7) growing season in relation to altitude and latitude, (8) natural vegetation in relation to rainfall, soil, and growing season, and (9) industry and natural resources.

Each unit should be checked to determine if a contribution can be made to the development of one or more of the understandings listed above. Each understanding must grow out of experiences in the unit; it cannot be imparted by simply telling the children that they exist. Through reading, seeing pictures and films, discussing problems of people in different environments, and similar activities, children come to realize that certain relationships exist between the environment and ways of living. Understanding among the children in any group will differ widely. Some will know only a few facts about a particular group, while others will generalize findings and be able to apply generalizations to peoples living in similar places. Through questioning and discussion, a teacher should try to get higher levels of generalization on the part of each child.

Systematic use should be made of globes and maps to help children discover associations such as those listed above. One technique is to have children compare two maps showing different facts about the same area. For example, after comparing a map showing population of the United States with one showing topography, children can discover that few people live in high mountainous areas; they can later find out if this relationship exists in other places. Or, by comparing a physical relief map and a map showing crops, children may discover that much farming is done in lowlands. Another technique is to have children study a map and make inferences about conditions there on the basis of information they already have. For example, if a desert is shown, have them infer living conditions they might expect to find. Or, if a rainfall map is being used, can they make inferences regarding areas where crops may be grown and areas which are too arid to support crops? (In this connection, they also may discover something about soil in relation to rain and crops.) Or, if a place of relatively low elevation is near the equator, what inferences can they make about climate? Or, as shown in Chart 33, can they make inferences about the effect of the ocean currents, winds, the Gulf Stream, and other factors on climate in various areas? Still other inferences can be made after a careful study of symbols which represent resources, industries, and similar items. (Guiding questions are shown in Charts 33 and 34.)

HOW DO THESE INFLUENCE CLIMATE?		HOW ARE THESE RESOURCES USED?	
Gulf Stream		Coal	Titanium
California Current		Iron	Petroleum
Japan Current		Lead	Forests
Prevailing winds		Tin	Water
Mountain ranges		Silver	Soil
Latitude and altitude		Gold	Animals
		Uranium	Fish

Chart 33

Chart 34

In discussing man-land relationships and making inferences about ways of living, teachers should avoid the erroneous idea that "human behavior is caused by the environment," or that people must always do what they are doing at the present time. Rather, the idea should be kept in mind that custom, tradition, education, and the desires of the people living in a particular area are also involved in the choices they make. As new ideas are accepted, changes take place in ways of living, and resources may be used differently. In short, maps and other resources should be shown in a study of regions and countries from the standpoint of the people living there. Their ways of living, education, customs, and beliefs should not be overlooked as attention is given to climate, surface features, and other aspects of the physical environment.

Summary of Map and Globe Concepts and Skills

The summary which follows is based on recently published courses of study, manuals that accompany social studies textbooks, handbooks on map and globe use, professional books for teachers, and recent studies of map-reading ability of children.* The grade designations are illustrative of the levels at which the concepts and skills are introduced and put to use in units of instruction. Grade placement for instructional purposes should be viewed in relation to the background and capabilities of children in a class, with each child moving ahead in terms of his ability and background of experience.

KINDERGARTEN–GRADE II

The following are introduced by the end of Grade II:

Directions. Left, right; up, down; north, south, east, west; how to find directions by using a shadow stick, compass, the sun

Orientation. Within the classroom, on the playground, and in the neighborhood

Distance. Blocks from school to the home, to the store and other places; relative distance to places on neighborhood and community maps; using distance between two well-known places as a basis for comparison

Time. In relation to distance from home to school and to main places in the community

Symbols. Pictorial and semipictorial symbols; lines to show streets, roads, and boundaries; use of color for land and water

Key. How used on simple maps to represent items meaningful to children, for example, houses, school, stores in neighborhood

Globe. A model of the earth—it is round to represent the earth; how land and water are shown; how the earth makes one complete turn every day—cause of day and night; measuring the distance around the globe to show that it is the same in every direction

* Grateful acknowledgement is made to Dr. Val Arnsdorf, University of Delaware, and to Dr. Haig Rushdoony, Stanislaus State College, for their comments and suggestions on this section.

Compare. Distance and time between familiar places; map symbols with what they actually represent and with pictures; large-scale maps with what they represent—classroom, school, neighborhood, community

Locate. Principal's office, nurse's office, library, and other places in the school; lakes, parks, main streets, and other features on simple maps; land, water, community, state, nation, and continent on a globe

Make. Floor layouts and floor maps; sand-table maps; pictorial symbols to show places on neighborhood community maps; simple maps related to study trips; floor plan of the classroom; legend for own maps

Infer. Time and distance to places in the community; directions to places; check inferences

Terms. Those related to uses of maps and the globe, for example, land, highway, road, street, freeway, hill, river, lake, ocean, mountain, county, city, town, bridge, tunnel, north, south, east, and west.

Physical surface features are clearly shown on raised relief maps. How might this map be used to develop concepts of physical features? *(Aero Service Corporation)*

The following are illustrative of the concepts and skills introduced by the end of Grade IV:

Review. Concepts and skills introduced in earlier grades

Directions. Relation to poles and equator; intermediate directions—northeast, northwest, southeast, southwest; grid lines on the globe and on maps as direction lines; direction of flow of rivers; upstream, downstream; use of compass

Orientation. Of textbook, outline, highway, wall and other maps; identification and use of north arrow on maps

Distance. Blocks in a mile; miles to places studied; miles to places discussed in current events

Time. In relation to distance to places; time of rotation and time of revolution of the earth

Symbols. Identifying towns, cities, capitals; color; coastline; roads; boundaries; relating pictures and symbols; recognizing relief shown by shading; using the map symbols chart; noting how symbols may vary on different maps

Legend. Checking before and while using maps

Scale. Used in making maps, for example, one inch to a foot, one inch to a block, one inch to a mile; measuring distance to places studied; checking scale on textbook and classroom maps

Globe. A sphere that represents the earth; axis of the earth; poles; equator; Arctic and Antarctic Circles; orbits of the moon and man-made satellites

Compare. Distances to places studied; relative size of oceans, lakes, rivers, cities, counties, states, countries, continents; length of rivers; height of mountains; natural conditions and distance from the equator; natural conditions and elevation; photographs and symbols; shapes of continents and countries

Locate. Land and water masses on the globe; boundaries; coastline; products; industries; resources, travel routes; rivers, canals; airports; cities; states; countries; continents; places by using grid lines; places on outline maps, wall maps, and the globe; the North Star; places in relation to the poles, equator, and Arctic and Antarctic Circles

Make. Pictorial maps; relief model maps; special maps on desk, outline maps, outline wall maps, and slated maps; legends for own maps

Infer. General type of climate in relation to location and elevation; centers of population; major products

Terms. Those related to textbook and classroom maps; for example, dam, reservoir, sea, island, forest, bay, delta, tributary,

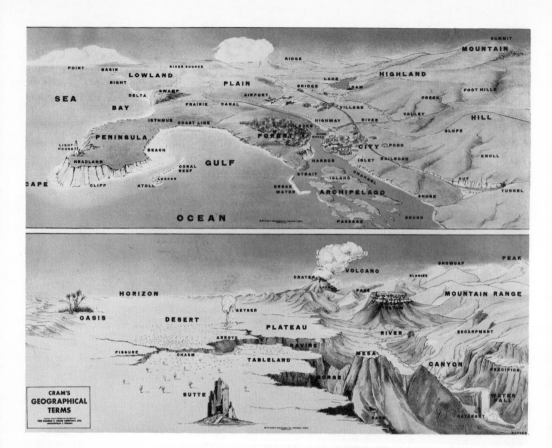

A geographical terms chart should be available for frequent reference use. How might this chart be used to improve map-reading skills? *(George F. Cram Company)*

desert, oasis, plateau, canyon, soil, climate, irrigation, basin, harbor, continent, country, state, province, city, town, village, capital, capitol, hemisphere, region, poles, equator, coast, fiord, glacier, iceberg.

GRADES V AND VI

The following are illustrative of concepts and skills introduced by the end of Grade VI:

Review. Concepts and skills presented in earlier grades

Directions. Using lines of latitude and longitude to determine directions; east-west lines as lines of latitude or parallels; north-south lines as lines of longitude or meridians; latitude and longitude expressed in degrees; noting directions on different map projections and directions to places studied

Orientation. Habit of orienting maps before using them; orienting the globe to show position of the earth in relation to the sun at different seasons of the year

Distance. Using great circles to find the distance between places on the globe; measuring distances north or south of the equator in degrees and miles

Time. Time needed to travel by various means to places studied; time zones; time in relation to rotation of the earth; time in relation to longitude; Prime Meridian and International Date Line

Area. Square miles; comparison of area of home state and other places; comparison of area of the United States and other places; distortion of area on flat maps; variations in amount of area distortion on different projections used in class

Symbols. Reading charts of map symbols; interpreting relief as shown by colors; visualizing steepness of slope from change in colors; interpreting contour lines

Legend. Habit of checking before and while using maps

Scale. Comparing maps of differing scales; using the scale to compare and to determine distances, for example, between places, and to places by different routes

Globe. Tropic of Cancer as a line of latitude 23½° north of the equator (the sun is directly over it about June 21); the Tropic of Capricorn as a line of latitude 23½° south of the equator (the sun is directly over it about December 22); area between them referred to as the low latitudes

The Arctic Circle as a line of latitude 66½° north of the equator; the Antarctic Circle as a line of latitude 66½° south of the equator; the area between each circle and its corresponding pole as a polar region; these areas referred to as high latitudes

Lines of longitude, or meridians, as great circles that pass through the poles; the prime meridian (zero degrees) at Greenwich near London; longitude measured from 0° to 180° east or west of the Prime Meridian; longitude used to determine time; 15° equal one hour (360° divided by 24); twenty-four time zones of 15° each; setting the clock ahead when traveling eastward through time zones; setting it back when traveling westward

Compare. Size, elevation, surface features, products, climate, and other characteristics of places studied; distances; early and modern maps; size of other places in relation to home state and the United States; surface features in areas studied—mountain ranges such as the Appalachians, Rockies and Sierras, lakes, oceans, rivers; shipping routes via the St. Lawrence Waterway and others to Europe

PICTORIAL EXPLANATION OF MAP SYMBOLS

Notice the pictorial explanation of map symbols at the bottom of the map. How might these be used to improve map-reading skills? *(Rand McNally)*

Locate. Places studied by noting direction and distance from the United States; by using latitude and longitude; states, regions, and countries in relation to others; changes in boundaries, for example, expansion of the United States, formation of new nations

Make. Maps to organize information related to questions in units of instruction or current events; special feature maps on desk outline maps, outline wall maps, and slated wall maps, overlays on clear plastic for placement on physical, climatic, and other maps to show relationships to travel routes, population, products, and other features

Infer. Temperature at places near the equator and at high and low elevations; location of population centers and travel routes; types of industry in relation to resources and level of technology; climate in relation to location, elevation, ocean currents and other factors; checking inferences by gathering and organizing related data

COMPARING SOUTH AMERICA AND AFRICA

Where: Distance and direction from the United States? In relation to each other? In relation to other continents? In relation to oceans? In which hemisphere? Latitude and longitude?

Size: In relation to the United States? In relation to North America and to other continents?

Equator: Where continents crossed? Distance north and south of the equator each extends?

Tropic of Capricorn: Where continents crossed? Extent each in the low latitudes?

Antarctic Circle: Distance from Cape Horn? Distance from Cape of Good Hope? Which the larger area in the middle latitudes?

Elevation: Major regions? Cities?

Surface features: Lowlands? Highlands? Mountains? Deserts? Plains? Coast line? Harbors? Lakes? River systems—Amazon, Orinoco, LaPlata, and Nile, Niger, Congo? Tributaries? Navigable rivers? Highways? Railroads? Airports?

Climate: In different regions? Seasons? Relation to location, elevation, oceans, and other factors? Relation to living conditions and products?

Countries: Location? Size? Population? Religions? Languages? Capitals and other major cities? Government? Distances between cities? Disputed boundaries? New nations? Places of historical and current interest? Scenic wonders? Soils? Farming? Grazing? Mining? Products?

Chart 35

What concepts of the earth can be clarified with a globe such as this one? *(Rand McNally)*

Terms. Understanding and using those related to maps in textbooks, the classroom, and other materials utilized in the program; for example, mesa, peninsula, isthmus, reef, ocean currents, prevailing winds, wind currents, canal, strait, cape, gulf, upland, lowland, rapids, swamps, watershed, timber line, rotation, revolution, latitude, longitude, altitude, elevation, degrees.

GRADES VII–VIII

Considerable review and additional instruction are provided in these grades. A better understanding of map projections and how they are made, finding information on historical maps, using reference atlases, making more precise inferences, using the analemma (the "figure 8" on the globe) and ecliptic (the circle on the globe showing the apparent yearly path of the sun), using different scales, and related concepts and skills are given direct attention. Mathematical aspects of map making are considered by more-able children. By the end of Grade VIII, attention is given to such specific concepts and skills as the following:

Review. Concepts and skills introduced in earlier grades

Directions. Reading directions on different map projections; noting changes in directions on great circle routes

Orientation. Systematic orientation of maps as they are used

Distance. Using both statute and nautical miles; changing degrees of latitude and longitude to miles

Time. International Date Line—from pole to pole along the 180° meridian for much of the distance; showing where calendar time is changed and the new calendar day begins; associating longitude and time; determining time in major cities around the world; finding the difference in clock and sun time during the year; using the globe as a sun dial; checking time of sunrise and sunset during the year

Area. Square miles; acres; hectares; distortion on maps; relative size of countries, continents; water bodies; use of ratio in comparing relative size of states, countries, and other areas

Symbols. Contour lines to show relief and elevation; hachures and layers of color to show elevation and slope; International Color Scheme; isobars and isotherms; new symbols on textbook, atlas, and classroom maps

Legend. Independence in determining the meaning of symbols by checking the legend

Scale. Understanding of ratio scale, graduated scales on air-age maps, and selection of scale in relation to intended use

POSITIONS IN ORBIT

Aphelion—point of a planet's orbit farthest from the sun

Apogee—point of a satellite's orbit farthest from the earth

Perihelion—point of a planet's orbit nearest the sun

Perigee—point of a satellite's orbit nearest the earth

Chart 36

MEASURES OF DISTANCE

Statute mile—5,280 feet

Nautical mile—6,080 feet, about one minute of latitude

Latitude—degrees north or south of the equator; one degree equals about 70 statute miles

Chart 37

LINES ON MAPS

Contour—connects points of the same altitude

Isobar—connects places of equal atmospheric pressure

Isotherm—connects places of equal temperature at a given time

Hachures—show elevations and slope

Others—boundaries, rivers, roads, railroads, pipelines, and the like

Chart 38

SOLSTICE AND EQUINOX

Solstice—time when the sun is overhead above the point marking its greatest distance north or south of the equator—about June 21 at Tropic of Cancer and December 22 at Tropic of Capricorn

Equinox—time when center of the sun crosses the equator; day and night are equal; about March 21 and September 23

Chart 39

CONNECTING STRIPS

Isthmus—a strip of land with water on both sides that connects two larger bodies of land

Strait—a strip of water that connects two larger bodies of water

Chart 40

ROTATION AND REVOLUTION

Rotation—turning of the earth on its axis from west to east

Revolution—movement of the earth around the sun each year

Chart 41

451

Globe. Using the analemma to find the latitude at which the sun's rays are vertical at noon at a given time; using the ecliptic to find where the vertical rays of the sun strike the earth on any day during the year; understanding the equinoxes

Compare. Size and location of lands claimed in early North America by English, French, Spanish, Russians; changing frontiers; travel routes westward; early and modern routes; mountain ranges, great river valleys, and other surface features; metropolitan areas; map projections; old and modern world trade routes; ocean currents and their affects on countries; climates, soils, and vegetation; products and altitudes; continental land forms and water bodies

Locate. Relative position of countries and continents in high, middle, and low latitudes; places by latitude and longitude; places along major travel routes; the ecliptic—apparent path of sun during the year; historical and current events; natural and cultural surface features

Make. Desk outline, wall outline, slated, relief, and special-purpose maps

Infer. Climate; type of vegetation; products; population centers; travel routes; farming areas; industrial centers; double checking inferences by using authoritative references

Terms. Understanding those used with globe, maps, and atlases, for example, analemma, ecliptic, globe, gore, horizon ring, midnight meridian, contour line, isobar, isotherm, circle of illumination, continental shelf, zenith, nadir, aphelion, perihelion, apogee, perigee, equinox, solstice, degrees, minutes, seconds.

Questions, Activities, Evaluation

1. Which of the examples of map- and globe-use presented in this chapter might you incorporate in a unit you are planning? Can you think of additional uses of maps and globes in the social studies?

2. Appraise a map or globe in terms of the suggested criteria. Note strengths and weaknesses.

3. Study a recently published map and check the legend, the use of colors, and the information that is presented. Can you find related pictures for use in illustrating items on the map?

4. Prepare a list of questions that you can use with children to direct their attention to items on the map. Review the "Summary of Map and Globe Concepts and Skills" to identify specific points to include in your questions.

5. Study the charts presented in this chapter and note ways in which you can adapt them for use in a unit. Can you prepare additional charts for the unit?

6. Which of the map-reading concepts and skills do you believe to be most difficult to teach to children? List specific ways in which you might present them.

7. Examine two or three social studies textbooks which contain maps and notice how they are discussed in the text. Note questions that can be answered by children as they use the maps. Refer to the accompanying teacher's manual for suggestions.

References

Brown, James W., Richard B. Lewis, and Fred F. Harcleroad, *A-V Instruction: Materials and Methods.* New York: McGraw-Hill Book Company, Inc., 1964. Section on maps and globes; list of sources in Appendix.

Forsyth, Elaine, *Map Reading.* Normal, Ill.: National Council for Geographic Education, 1964. Detailed suggestions.

Gabler, Robert E., ed., *A Handbook for Geography Teachers.* Normal, Ill.: National Council for Geographic Education, 1966. Section on equipment, materials, and sources.

Hanna, Paul R., Rose E. Sabaroff, Gordon F. Davies, and Charles R. Farrar, *Geography in the Teaching of the Social Studies.* Boston: Houghton Mifflin Company, 1966. Basic concepts and skills; list of sources of materials in Appendix A; map and globe symbols in Appendix B.

Harris, Ruby M., *Map and Globe Usage.* Chicago: Rand McNally & Co., 1959. A handbook of teaching suggestions for all grades.

Hill, Wilhelmina, ed., *Curriculum Guide to Geographic Education.* Normal, Ill.: National Council for Geographic Education, 1964. Section on skills and techniques.

Joyce, Bruce, *Strategies for Elementary Social Science Education.* Chicago: Science Research Associates, Inc., 1965. Techniques for map making and map reading.

Kennamer, Lorrin, "Developing a Sense of Place and Space," *Skill Development in the Social Studies*, 33rd Yearbook, National Council for the Social Studies, pp. 148–70. Washington, D.C.: National Education Association, 1963. Concepts and skills involved in using maps and globes.

Kohn, Clyde F., *et al.*, "Interpreting Maps and Globes," *Skills in Social Studies*, 24th Yearbook, National Council for the Social Studies, pp. 146–77. Washington, D.C.: National Education

Association, 1953. Principles and procedures for teaching concepts and skills.

McAulay, J. D., "Some Map Abilities of Second Grade Children," *Journal of Geography*, LXI (January 1962), 3–9. Report of a map concept study.

McFall, Christie, *Maps Mean Adventure*. New York: Dodd, Mead & Co., 1961. A description of map making and map projections.

Sabaroff, Rose, *Journal of Geography*, LVII (September 1958), 300–306; LVII (October 1958), 364–70; LVII (November 1958), 410–15; LVIII (October 1959), 350–54; LVIII (December 1959), 451–55; LIX (February 1960), 85–87. A series of articles on concepts and skills in the early grades.

Thralls, Zoe A., *The Teaching of Geography*. New York: Appleton-Century-Crofts, Inc., 1958. Guidelines for improving instruction in geography.

Witucki, Lillian G., "Map Reading Skills," *Social Studies in Elementary Schools*, 32nd Yearbook, National Council for the Social Studies, pp. 196–205. Washington, D.C.: National Education Association, 1962. A summary of skills to be developed in primary, middle, and upper grades.

Making
Maps

In addition to using maps, children should have many opportunities to make maps. Careful attention should be given to accuracy so that correct impressions rather than erroneous ideas of geographic conditions in places being studied will be learned. A sound procedure is to have children check their maps against comparable commercial and textbook maps as well as against information secured from reading and from audio-visual materials. A good supply of outline maps should be available for use in both individual and group map-making activities. Where possible, standard practices should be observed in the use of colors and map symbols. As with other activities in the social studies, map making should be directly related to specific problems in the unit, not carried on as busywork or as something isolated from a study of major human activities. The following list suggests types of maps that children can make.

15

1. Floor maps using blocks, boxes, and models, or chalk, tempera, and crayon on linoleum, paper, or oilcloth; simple line maps in the schoolyard
2. Pictorial maps of community buildings, harbors, products, types of housing, food, clothing, plant and animal life, minerals and other resources, birthplaces of famous people, arts and crafts, modes of travel, methods of communication, raw materials

3. Specimen maps using real items such as wheat, corn, cotton, and rocks

4. Relief maps of papier-mâché, salt and flour, plaster of paris, clay, or moistened sand; large relief maps on a section of the schoolyard

5. Mural maps with strips of paper for streets, pictures or silhouettes for buildings, and so forth

6. Wall outline maps made by using an opaque projector or a pantograph

7. Jigsaw puzzle maps of states and countries

8. Slated maps and globes, or individual and wall outline maps to show air routes, famous flights, early explorations, trade routes, physical features, boundaries, rivers, and so forth

9. Simple political and physical maps using colors to show various features

10. Transportation maps using various line and dot patterns to show railroad lines, airplane routes, steamship lines, and major highways

11. Progressive or developmental maps of a region or topic such as the westward movement, colonization, or industrial America

12. Communication maps using symbols to show telephone lines, cable crossings, radio networks, and television networks

13. Maps of features of special interest, such as national parks, state parks, major imports, major cities, seaports, and river systems

14. Historical maps of the colonies, early travel routes, and early settlements

15. Transparent maps of resources, transportation networks, and other distributions to project and to place over other maps in order to show relationships

These examples illustrate the many opportunities for making maps in the social studies. When a teacher is planning a unit, he should think through the possibilities for map making that are related to problems and topics in the unit. With adequate preplanning and guidance by a teacher, children can make maps of considerable accuracy and artistry.

Growth in map-making skills begins with simple sketches on the school grounds and simple floor layouts in the classroom. After a short study trip, children in the primary grades may sketch the route on the ground showing where they started, where they went, and two or three important places they passed. Simple floor layouts may be made with blocks and boxes to show a study trip, important buildings around the school, or a few important places along a street in the community. Simple line sketches may be made on large sheets of paper on the floor. The school map and neighborhood may may be made on the floor or sketched on the chalkboard. Picture maps that are large

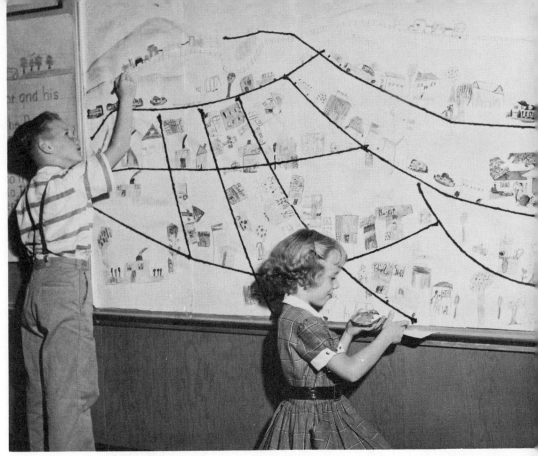

After a study trip and after making a floor layout to show important places in the neighborhood, a group of children made this pictorial map. *(Alameda County)*

in size and contain a few items are also appropriate in the primary grades. A combination of simple lines and pictures is also used effectively by some teachers. Later, as the community is more widely studied, simple community maps may be made and used to show water reservoirs, the railroad center, the post office, and similar places and things. Care must be taken, however, to keep the maps uncluttered with detail. As larger areas are studied, such as the country, state, region, nation, and other countries, a variety of maps can be made, their scope depending on the topics being studied and the maturity of the group.

Map-Making Techniques

Certain techniques can be used to improve map making. Teachers should select, from the suggestions that follow, those that are most appropriate for children in their classrooms in terms of maturity, available materials, and important needs that have arisen for map making.

457

FIRST EXPERIENCES

First map-making experiences should be realistic and concrete; they must be related to the children's immediate environment and based on concepts that they understand. The following experiences are illustrative of those used by primary-grade teachers.

Use blocks, or boxes, to make a simple floor layout of the neighborhood around the school. Begin with the school and the main street in front of the school; add other items known to the children. Do not get involved in a long drawn-out and detailed modeling project, since blocks can be used satisfactorily.

Black tape can be used to show streets on the community maps. If a change is needed, the tape can be lifted and placed where it should be. *(Washington School, Oakland)*

Make a simple drawing of the school and nearby places on a large strip of wrapping paper placed on the floor. A good time for such a project is after a study trip. Begin with the school, trace the route, put in key places seen, and mark the main streets clearly. Use colored paper cutouts, or crayon drawings, to show important places.

A floor map of a farm can be made by using objects made by children—barn, fences, trees, animals, trucks, silo, other buildings. Similarly, a layout can be made of the airport, harbor, or railroad yards.

On a map of the school district on which the school and streets are shown, have children locate the school, their homes,

Notice how this floor layout is arranged on a large outline map. The next step is to use the outline map by placing semi-pictorial symbols on it to represent the buildings. (Fresno City Schools)

and the more important buildings. Small pieces of colored paper can be used to show the children's homes; have each child write his initials, or name, on the paper that represents his home before it is pasted or pinned to the map. Use larger pieces of paper to show the school, stores, and other buildings.

Sand-table maps can be made to show many different features: farm layout, airport or harbor layout, a well-known park, a section of the community, the community, the child's community, and neighboring towns. Line up the table so that it parallels a major street or road; discuss the direction the road runs and where the sun rises and sets in relation to the table. Consider space between places, and locate major features accurately. Streets and roads should be laid out after a discussion of distances between places, thus providing readiness for later use of the scale. Use blocks, cutouts, or miniature buildings to locate places. Color hills, valleys, and bodies of water.

A flannel board can be used effectively to show different space arrangements. The layout of the school grounds, neighborhood, or a farm are illustrative of possible uses.

Airplane view maps can be made of a farm, airport, or the community. They may be made on a large piece of paper on

MAKING MAPS

What is to be shown?
What facts are needed?
What size should the grid lines be?
What symbols should be used?
What colors should be used?
What would be a good title?
What should be in the legend?

Chart 1

USING OUR MAPS

Displays

Reports

Scrapbooks

Programs
Discussion
Testing

Reviewing

Chart 2

MAP-MAKING MATERIALS

Chalk or pencil for sketching outline
Ink or pencil for details, terms, and symbols
Wax crayons on muslin, window shades, paper, back of oilcloth, tagboard, cardboard
Tempera and calcimine on cardboard, drawing paper, oilcloth, wrapping paper

Chart 3

COMMUNITY MAPS

Way to school
Around the school
The city park
The dairy farm
The harbor
The airport
The business section
Historic buildings
Expressways
Neighborhood libraries
Water reservoirs

Chart 4

STATE MAPS

Where Indians lived
Historic events
First settlements
Early travel routes
Agricultural areas
Lumbering areas
Industrial areas
Parks and monuments
Harbors and airports
Capital and main cities
Major highways

Chart 5

MAPS OF OUR COUNTRY

Trails of explorers
The first settlements
Lands claimed by countries
The first colonies
Territorial expansion
Trails westward
The first railroads
Canals and waterways
Mountain ranges
Main river basins

Chart 6

CURRENT EVENTS MAPS

Select important events.
Find a news report for each event.
Make a dot to locate each event on the map.
Mount the reports around the map.
Run a string from each report to the map.

Chart 7

TRANSPORTATION MAPS

Main highways in our state
Railroads across the United States
Main seaports
International airports
Pipelines to main cities

Chart 8

A MAP OF BRIDGES

Golden Gate—California
Brooklyn—New York
George Washington—New York
Verrazano—New York
Ends Bridge—Missouri
Huey P. Long—Louisiana
Mackinac—Michigan

Chart 9

460

How might you use such a layout in a unit you may be planning? *(San Diego City Schools)*

the floor. One group, for example, after seeing an airport from the control tower, laid out the runways, hangars, beacons, nearby roads, and buildings as seen from above. Another group made a view map of a section of their city after viewing it from a tall building. They also compared their map with aerial photos of the same section of the city.

Freehand drawing or sketching of maps is done in many classrooms after a trip, film, or discussion in which the purpose is to make a map of a small area, and when a map of the area is not available. If time permits, a helpful method is to lay out the area first with blocks, or in sand, so that the children get a realistic impression of the surface features. In the primary grades, sketches may be made of the neighborhood, farm, harbor, airport, or other places being studied.

MAKING MAP OUTLINES

As children gain in experience and maturity, many needs will arise for both large and small map outlines; both individual and group projects should be provided. The techniques most frequently used to make outline maps follow.

Use the opaque projector to make map enlargements; project maps from textbooks, newspapers, magazines, or references. Another method is to use slides in the 3¼" x 4" projector; these may be made by tracing on a frosted glass placed over the desired map, or they may be purchased. A third technique is to project and trace maps contained in filmstrips or slides that present geographic content.

Inquiry in depth and care in planning are essential to the completion of enlarged maps such as this one. (San Diego City Schools)

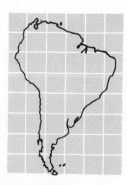

Proportional squares may be used to make enlargements of maps.

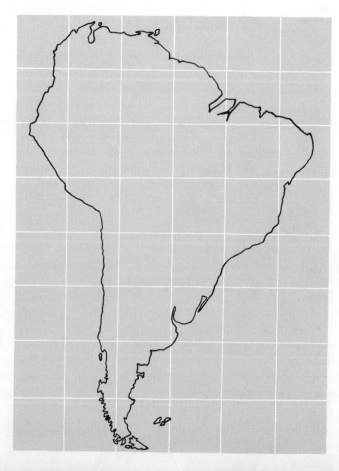

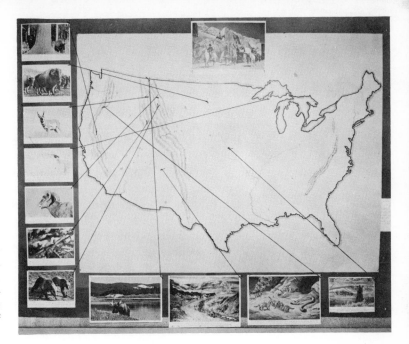

How might you plan for the use of a large outline map in combination with pictures to show specific locations? *(Education Workshop, University of California, Berkeley)*

Maps made in the classroom should be used in reports and in discussions. Note the vocabulary chart to the right of the map. In what ways might both be used in discussion? *(Cleveland)*

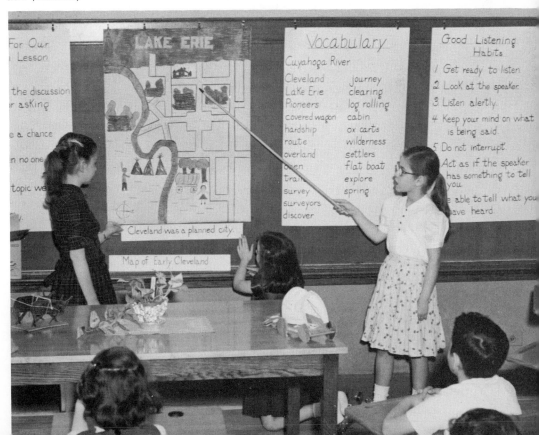

Use proportional squares to make enlargements. Draw small squares over the map to be enlarged, or trace a copy on tissue and then draw the squares. Draw the same number of large squares on butcher roll or tagboard. Mark the outline shown in each small square on the matching large square.

Make chalkboard map stencils by punching small holes one inch apart on a large map outline. Hold this against the chalkboard and pat over the holes with an eraser containing chalk dust. Mark a heavy line over the dots to show the outline clearly. Another procedure used by some teachers is the tracing of maps on the chalkboard utilizing cardboard outlines as a pattern.

Small outline maps can be prepared by teachers on stencils for reproduction on duplicating machines; some audio-visual departments in school systems furnish such outline maps on request. Printed desk maps can be secured inexpensively from commercial publishers.

Tracing paper or onion-skin paper can be used to make maps if no projectors are available. If a large map is to be traced, use Scotch tape to fasten individual sheets of tracing paper together. Place the tracing paper over the map to be copied and outline the desired features. Place carbon paper on the sheet to which the map is to be transferred, lay the tracing paper on it, use weights (books or blocks) to prevent slipping, and go over the map outline. Remove the tracing paper and carbons carefully to prevent smearing.

COMPLETING OUTLINE MAPS

Several points should be kept in mind as children are guided to make accurate and attractive maps. A major emphasis throughout should be on accuracy in presenting a *few* key ideas rather than a myriad of detail. It is better for children to make several simple maps that are clear and usable than to make one which is of little value because it is cluttered and difficult to read.

Materials for use in making flat maps should be selected with care. If tagboard or other slick-surfaced materials are used, India ink and pens for printing and sketching are better than wax crayons or calcimine type paint. Colored drawing pencils also may be used. On softer papers such as bogus, newsprint, construction, mimeograph, manila, chipboard, and certain types of wrapping paper, wax crayons and tempera paint can be used successfully. Crayons and tempera also can be used effectively on window shades, muslin, percale, and the rough side of oil-

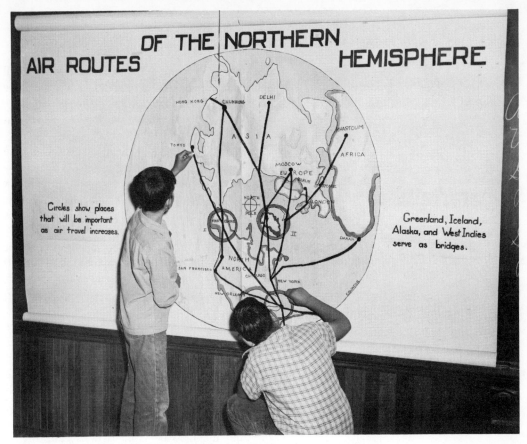

New perspectives of time and distances are gained when children make and use maps showing polar air routes. The globe should be referred to frequently when a map of this type is being made or used. *(Alameda County)*

cloth. An effective technique is to use a hot iron to press the muslin between blotters after wax crayon has been applied. This technique is most effective when the crayon strokes are in the same direction and the right amount has been applied; if too much is applied the wax will run. Try a few samples on small pieces of cloth before the map is made.

In using colors for making physical maps, the standard, international color plan should be used—blue for water, green for lowlands, and yellow, orange, and brown for higher altitudes. In using colors to show other features—states, countries, historical changes such as the frontiers during different periods—be sure to use colors that contrast well and that do not decrease visibility of lettering. The end product should be a map that is clear, sharp in color contrast, and easy to read.

If lines, dots, or shaded areas are used, be sure to plan for

465

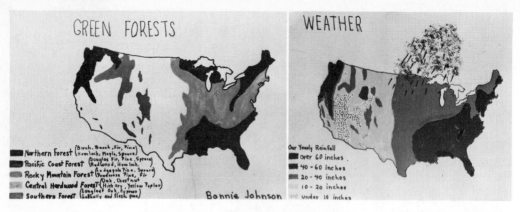

GREEN FORESTS

WEATHER

Northern Forest (Birch, Beech, Fir, Pine)
(Hemlock, Maple, Spruce)
Pacific Coast Forest (Douglas Fir, Pine, Spruce)
(Redwood, Hemlock)
Rocky Mountain Forest (Lodgepole Pine, Spruce)
(Ponderosa Pine, Fir)
Central Hardwood Forest (Hickory, Chestnut)
(Oak, Chestnut)
(Longleaf Oak, Cypress)
Southern Forest (Loblolly and Slash, pine)

Bonnie Johnson

Our Yearly Rainfall
over 60 inches
40 - 60 inches
20 - 40 inches
10 - 20 inches
under 10 inches

What association might be developed through the use of such maps? *(Contra Costa County and Alameda City Schools)*

contrast and clear lettering. Some teachers have pupils print the lettering on white strips which can be placed over shaded area and thus stand out.

All lettering on maps should be done clearly and neatly. Have children print difficult terms first on a piece of practice paper. Give attention to spacing, spelling, and proper use of abbreviations. Wherever possible, have all words printed parallel to each other. Guide children in close examination of wall and textbook maps in order to discover ways to line up lettering effectively on their maps.

Encourage the use of pictures and specimens to highlight ideas portrayed on maps. Use ribbon, yarn, or tape running from the picture (or specimen) to its location on the map.

Guide the group to select symbols that effectively portray what is shown. Have them check other maps and suggest symbols that seem to them to be appropriate. Consider the use of paper cutouts, hand-drawn symbols, colored symbols, pins and varied colored bead heads, symbols carved in pencil eraser heads, or stick-prints, which can be reproduced easily by pressing on an ink pad and stamping on the map. Movable symbols also may be used.

The legend, or key to the map, can be planned for placement in a corner of the map. The title, symbols, colors, shading, scale, and other pertinent data should be shown clearly. A neat border around the legend will set it off clearly and add to its appearance. Make the legend on a separate piece of paper so that the map will not be ruined if a change or correction must be made in the legend.

Give attention to directions on the map. Use arrows where necessary to show the flow of a river, wind currents, or ocean currents. Orientation of the map may be shown by using arrows in one corner to show the cardinal directions.

Puzzle maps (jigsaw maps) can be made from plywood, beaverboard, or heavy chipboard. Outline the map, trace in major features to be shown (states, regions, produce areas), and color in rivers, lakes, and other significant features. Saw into reasonable and logical sections by means of a jigsaw or coping saw. Fasten the border that remains to a whole piece of plywood; this can be used as a holder into which the cutout pieces can be placed. If it is a map of the United States, the border can be labeled to show relative location of the Atlantic and Pacific Oceans, and Canada and Mexico. Encourage children to make puzzle maps of their own out of chipboard.

Another type of puzzle map can be made of felt. Secure a large piece of green felt for the base and several smaller pieces of different colored felt to use as sections. Make a paper pattern of the desired region, for example, the United States. Lay the pattern on the large piece of green felt and cut around the edges. Glue the whole map to a piece of plywood, cardboard, or chipboard; this is the base map on which the smaller sections can be placed. Next, mark sections on the paper pattern (New England states, Pacific states, and so forth); cut the pattern into marked sections; place each section on a colored piece of felt and cut around the edges of the section. The cutouts will adhere to the base map when placed on it. Make other cutouts to represent different regions and thus vary the use of the puzzle map. Transparent maps for projection can be made by using special pencils and inks on plastic, by placing colored plastic

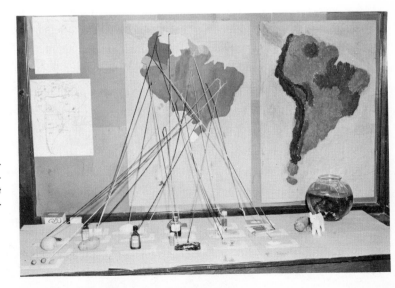

How might you use this device to show the distribution of products in a unit you are planning? (Richmond, California)

cutouts on a plastic base map, and by making copies of maps in copying machines.

Hooked rug maps are decorative and not difficult to make. Outline the map on a piece of burlap with chalk and tack it to a box or wooden frame. Use a hooked rug needle to sew in heavy yarn. Select colors to show boundaries, states, provinces, or other features. Have children practice using the needle before they work on the map.

MAKING OUTLINE MAPS

Project the slide on the mapping material.
Trace the boundaries and main features.
Locate other important items.
Mark basic symbols on it.
Label important places.
Color the parts according to plan.
Make a complete legend.
Print a clear title.

Chart 10

MAKING FLANNEL MAPS

Use outing flannel cut to the proper size.
Draw the outline on it.
Locate items to be shown.
Cut pieces of flannel of different colors to represent the items.
Put each piece on the flannel in its place.
Cut other pieces to show different items.

Chart 11

MAKING MUSLIN MAPS

Cut the muslin to the desired size.
Trace or project map outline on the muslin.
Mark other important items.
Mark basic symbols.
Color with crayon as planned.
Label main places.
Make a legend.
Print a title.

Chart 12

CLAY RELIEF MAPS

Have a map to guide modeling.
Mix clay or use ready mixed clay.
Spread the clay over outline map.
Build up mountains, hills, and valleys.
Trace rivers with a pencil.
Use tiny sticks to show trees and other items.

Chart 13

PAPIER-MACHE MAPS

Have a map to guide modeling.
Put one layer of papier-mâché on outline map.
Add other layers as needed for hills and mountains.
Form valleys and river channels.
Allow the map to dry.
Paint with enamel or water paints.

Chart 14

SALT AND FLOUR MAPS

Mix ¼ cup of salt, ¼ cup of flour, and ¼ cup of water.

Pour mixture on center of outline map.

Build up high areas and then shape other areas.

Paint after it is dry.

Chart 15

Modeled Relief Maps

Modeled relief maps can be used in discussing such problems as why people settle in certain places, why highways are built in certain places, where mountain passes are located, how mountain ranges cause certain areas to be dry and other areas to receive much rainfall, how climate is affected by terrain, how areas are drained by rivers, and a host of other questions related to distance, travel, elevation, and topography. The use of relief maps enables children to visualize surface features and conditions in the area being studied.

Remember that the vertical scale on relief maps is different from the horizontal scale. For example, Pike's Peak, which may be prominent on a relief map, is only a tiny pin point on the earth's surface when its elevation (under three miles) is considered in relation to the circumference of the earth (25,000 miles). However, one child, who had seen it, said, "It was no pin point from where I saw it," thus indicating that relief on smaller areas stands out dramatically and realistically. By mapping a smaller area, less distortion is introduced. However, when large areas are mapped, considerable distortion will be introduced and should be considered as children grow in their understanding of map scale. One technique is to draw a long line on the chalkboard to represent the distance across the area being mapped.

Arrange flat maps and modeled relief maps so that children can make comparisons. *(Los Angeles)*

Then draw vertical lines to show the relative height of mountains, plateaus, and other features to be shown. Thus, if a mountain approximately three miles high is located in an area 300 miles long, the vertical line would be three inches while the base line would be 300 inches, one inch to 100, or half an inch to 50 inches. After such a demonstration, one fifth grader said, "Gee, that mountain isn't so high when you think of how long the ground is." When distortion exists, the teacher should explain that features are relatively higher than they should be to show them more clearly.

The outline on which the relief map is made should be prepared carefully. In fact, a wise procedure is to make two outline maps and to use the second one as a working guide while the modeling material is being placed on the relief map. Then, when one area is covered or one layer is on, the second outline map is available for easy reference. Make a list of the features that are to be shown; show pictures illustrating them (the jagged Rockies, long flat prairies, great valleys) and guide children to find them on physical maps, either wall maps or maps in atlases. Make the map outline by means of a projector or one of the other methods discussed earlier in this chapter. Sketch in rivers, mountains, other features, and contour lines where needed. Use colors to note changes in elevation; check wall maps or a school atlas to insure accuracy. After the outline is mounted on a base board, drive brads and small nails to show relative height and position of peaks, mountain ranges, and hills; these serve as guides during the modeling process. Anticipate and discuss common errors that arise, such as gross distortion of features (hills and mountains too large), omission of significant features (lakes, valleys, dams), inaccuracy of slope (rivers running uphill), errors in relative location of features (mountains extending into plains), and mistakes in relative size of features (Appalachians and Rockies same height). Plan for gradual upslopes from plains to hills to mountains where appropriate. Some teachers also find it helpful during the making of the outline to show and discuss relief maps made by classes of preceding years; attention is given to good points and to points needing improvement, and the outline is modified accordingly.

Many relief maps can be made and used without coloring them in any way. The features will stand out clearly and the surface will speak for itself as children use the map. In other instances, the surface can be painted to highlight features and to show contrasts. Tempera-type water paint works very well; the surface can be protected by shellacking after it has dried. Enamel

Relief and outline maps may be used together. *(Oakland and Fresno City Schools)*

also can be used if the surface is shellacked first. Another effective technique is to place sawdust in a can or jar of powered paint and to shake thoroughly. After coating the areas to be colored with glue, sprinkle the sawdust on and allow the glue to dry. Brush off any loose particles. Clean sand can be used in a similar manner. Be sure to plan carefully for the use of different colors on appropriate sections of the map so that they will be clear in contrast, and consistent with standard uses of color on maps.

RECIPES FOR MODELING MATERIAL

Several different recipes can be used to model relief maps. If the maps are to be used for a short period of time, simple and inexpensive recipes should be used, and the finishing of the surface with paint and shellac will be unnecessary. If the maps are to be used often, they should be well made and shellacked to protect the surface.

Paste and Paper. Tear paper towels or newspapers into 1½-inch pieces. Put paste on one piece at a time, wad it or shape it with your fingers, and stick it on the map outline. Build up hills and mountains as desired. Paint with tempera paint after the paste has dried.

471

Paper Strips and Paste. Use crumpled paper to build up terrain; use string or masking tape to hold paper in place. Dip half-inch strips of toweling into wheat paste and place them on the crumpled paper form. After two layers have been placed on the map, coat the entire surface with paste and allow to dry; secure the base of the map so that it cannot buckle. After the map is dry, paint with calcimine-type paint.

Sawdust and Paste. Mix any sawdust, except redwood or cedar, with wheat paste (from wallpaper store); spoon paste into sawdust until it is well moistened and of good modeling consistency. Good proportions are five cups of sawdust to one cup of wheat paste. The mixture may be applied directly to wood or cardboard. Paint it after it is dry.

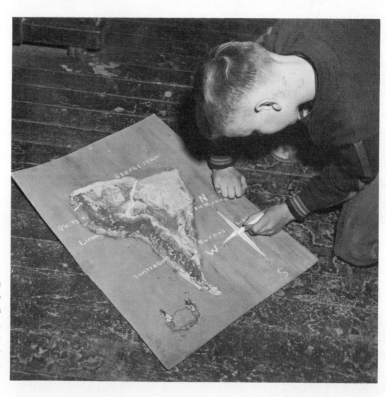

Children should be given an opportunity to make individual relief maps as well as group outline maps. Notice how directions are shown on the corner of the map. *(Washington School, Oakland)*

Papier-mâché. This is one of the most popular modeling materials. Tear twenty to twenty-five newspaper sheets (or paper towels) into fine shreds and soak them for twenty-four hours. Pulverize the soaked paper by rubbing it over a washboard, or by kneading it. Add wheat paste (or 4 cups of flour and 2 cups of salt) until mixture is of the same consistency as modeling clay.

Build up mountains, plateaus, and hills by applying papier-mâché mixture to the surface. After three to six days of drying, paint elevations, water, and other features.

Salt and Flour. Mix equal parts of salt and flour, using only enough water to hold the ingredients together. Apply to map outline, modeling the terrain according to plan. Keep out of humid places because salt attracts moisture.

Asbestos Pulp. Excellent large or small relief maps can be made of asbestos pulp (from plumbing and heating shop). Mix five pounds of asbestos pulp with two handfuls of wheat paste; add water to secure a consistency similar to clay that is ready for use in modeling. Use the mixture on a plywood, chipboard, or beaverboard base. Build up one layer at a time. Smooth the joining sections (around mountains, lakes and hills) carefully to prevent cracking. After three to six days of drying, paint with poster or powder paint. Shellac if map is to be handled much.

Burlap and Patching Plaster. Finished results can be obtained by immersing burlap in patching plaster. Build terrain on outline by using crumpled paper and masking tape. Lay a piece of burlap (or towel) over the outline and cut along edges to get a good fit. Remove burlap and soak it thoroughly in Spackle, or other patching plaster mix, which has been mixed to consistency of pancake batter; knead the plaster mix in so that the burlap is well-soaked. Lay the soaked burlap over the outline, fitting it into hills, valleys, and other features. After about thirty minutes and *before* the plaster is completely dry, paint with calcimine-type paint. If it is completely dry, the paint may flake and crack.

Plaster. Because maps made of plaster are heavy, many teachers use plaster only for small maps. Mix five pounds of plaster with two handfuls of wheat paste. Add water to get consistency of modeling clay. Build up layers, let dry for three to six days, and paint.

Plaster and Sawdust. Mix one pint of plaster, one pint of sawdust and a quarter pint of paste that has been dissolved in water. Knead and apply to map outline. Paint after the mixture has set for fifteen to thirty minutes.

Plaster and Paper-mâché. Add two pints of plaster, a quarter tablespoon of LePage's glue, and a half pint of water to prepared papier-mâché. Be sure that the mixture is of modeling consistency. Paint after mixture has set thirty to forty-five minutes.

Plastic Starch and Detergent. Mix one part plastic starch with four parts detergent. Beat mixture until it is fluffy and apply to map outline. Be careful of the surface because it crumbles easily.

Questions, Activities, Evaluation

1. Which of the map-making activities suggested in this chapter are appropriate for use in a unit you are planning?

2. How can you make map-making activities an important part of the problem-solving process?

3. How can map making be used to develop main ideas or concepts in the social studies?

4. Try the different techniques suggested for making outline maps. Which can you use in a unit you are planning?

5. Complete a large outline map which you can use in a unit. Use the techniques suggested in this chapter. Note tips and suggestions that will be of help in guiding children to complete outline maps.

6. Try the various recipes for modeling material. Which do you think would be easiest for children to use to make a relief map?

References

See the references at the end of the preceding chapter and past and current issues of *Journal of Geography, Instructor,* and *Grade Teacher.*

Greenwood, David, *Mapping.* Chicago: University of Chicago Press, 1964. Techniques and examples.

Merritt, Edith P., *Working with Children in Social Studies,* Ch. X. "Making Maps, Charts, and Graphs." Belmont, Calif.: Wadsworth, 1961.

Raisz, Erwin, *Principles of Cartography.* New York: McGraw-Hill Book Company, Inc., 1962. Background information for teachers to use in making and interpreting maps.

Expressive
Experiences

A stimulating and dynamic social studies program includes expressive experiences designed to enrich children's learning. Expressive experiences go beyond the use of factual materials to include (1) activities that give insights into the hopes, feelings, and aspirations of people at home and in other lands, (2) activities that develop the "doing side" of thinking, and (3) opportunities for children to identify themselves creatively and effectively with others. Expressive experiences are essential to the development of feelings and shades of meaning, which are an inseparable part of well-rounded inquiry into our own and other cultures.

Expressive experiences are helpful in meeting individual differences. The able, disadvantaged, less-able, and average child can express himself in ways that are truly his own. Responses and reactions to the arts of others should be divergent, not convergent, in the true spirit of artistic expression. Children's own creative expression through dramatic activities, language, and rhythms springs from within and is attuned to each child's level of esthetic development. Construction and processing of materials bring into play a combination of intellectual and manual skills that can be geared to each child's capabilities.

Expressive experiences are included in the social studies in two main ways. The first is to include material on the characteristic

16

475

literature, art, music, industrial arts, dramatic activities, and rhythmic expression of the people under study. For example, in such units as Indians of the Southwest, Living in Japan, and South America, the rich storehouse of materials dealing with "the arts" should be drawn on and used. The second is to provide opportunities for children's own creative expression and interpretation of thoughts and feelings gleaned from experiences in each unit. For example, poems, stories, descriptions, pictures, murals, skits, plays, and songs may be created by children to highlight main ideas and feelings for others as they are developed in units. In short, both "impression" and "expression" are essential to well-rounded learning.

Five types of experience have been selected for discussion in this chapter: literature, dramatic representation, music, arts and crafts, and industrial or practical arts. All five types have one element in common: the *esthetic expression* of thoughts and feelings. Esthetic expression has always been a basic human activity and has contributed much to man's cultural heritage. Poems, stories, biographies, dramas, paintings, crafts, textiles, sculpture, pottery, basketry, songs, and rhythms all reflect man's urge to express himself creatively and to interpret human activities.

Literature

LITERARY SELECTIONS

Literature makes rich contributions to social learning in the elementary school. As stated many years ago: "Of all the subjects not traditionally included under the social studies, none is more intimately affiliated with them than literature." [1] Literary selections are used in the social studies to heighten interest, deepen understanding, create moods and atmosphere, portray the diversity of ways of living and thinking among people in various cultures, stimulate imagination, give colorful backgrounds, promote more complete identification with others, give a warm feeling for the problems of others, improve attitudes toward others, build appreciations for the contributions of others, provoke creativity, and give vivid impressions of ways of living being studied in various units. A feeling for the joys, sorrows, and problems of others can rarely be kindled through the use of factual material alone; hence, the importance of poetry, stories, biography, fiction, letters, legends, and travel literature to take

---

[1] Ernest Horn, *Methods of Instruction in the Social Studies* (New York: Charles Scribner's Sons, 1937), p. 265.

children beyond facts to the spiritual and the esthetic qualities and values involved in human relationships. The development of wholesome attitudes toward others and appreciation for the problems, needs, and contributions of others require that literary selections be used in the social studies.

The following examples of the uses of literary selections in various units may serve to clarify the specific contributions that can be made to the enrichment of the social studies program.

In studying pets as a part of a unit on the Home, one group was thrilled by the teacher's reading of Hill and Maxwell's *Charlie and His Puppy Bingo*, and Gemmill's *Joan Wanted a Kitty*; selected poems were also enjoyed from *Sung Under the Silver Umbrella* (Association for Childhood Education).

A primary group learning about the community enjoyed Field's *General Store*, Medary's *The Store at Criss-Cross Corners*, and Chute's *Rhymes About the City*; another group studying the farm liked Chute's *Farmers* and Nast's *A Farm Story*; a group studying trains liked Tippett's poem "Trains," and Lenski's *The Little Train*.

In a study of Life in the United States several children read Gate's *Blue Willow* and expressed keenly felt sympathy for the problems of the itinerant worker's child. Others read Buffler's *Rodrigo and Rosalita*, and Lenski's *Blue Ridge Sally*, *Bayou Suzette*, and *Strawberry Girl*, which enriched their understanding of life in different sections of the country. Several were sensitized to the needs and problems of minority groups by reading Jackson's *Call Me Charley*, De Angeli's *Bright April*, Davis' *Americans Everyone*, Eberle's *Very Good Neighbors*, Jones' *Small Rain*, and Beim's *Two Is a Team*. These books were also helpful in showing how individuals and groups can work and play together even though differences exist.

A study of Growth of Democracy was greatly enriched for upper-grade children who read D'Aulaires' *George Washington*, Daugherty's *Abraham Lincoln*, Forbes' *Johnny Tremain* and *America's Paul Revere*, and Barksdale's *The First Thanksgiving*, and who listened to recordings such as "Ballad for Americans," "The Lonesome Train," and "Mine Eyes Have Seen the Glory" and radio programs such as "Cavalcade of America." A greater appreciation of the contributions of famous Americans was developed by those who read Franklin's *Autobiography*, Meadowcraft's *The Boy's Life of Edison*, Pace's *Clara Barton*, Gray's *William Penn*, and Holt's *George Washington Carver*.

In using literary selections, attention must be given to authenticity of material, explanations of deviations from reality, comparisons between factual and fictional materials, distortions because of author's point of view, setting, and inaccuracies in content. The attitude of the group should be one of delight and enjoyment. In general, when using a literary selection, the teacher should keep the following points in mind:

1. Enjoy it, do not dissect it; analyze it only if analysis increases enjoyment.
2. Share it, do not ask questions; do not give tests on it or evaluate it, as is done with factual materials.
3. Approach it to have fun, not to study it, as is done in work-type materials.
4. Be aware of fiction and fantasy; do not teach them as facts.
5. Let the children discover values, moods, and meanings; do not moralize or struggle to develop certain points of real interest to yourself.
6. Let children memorize their favorites.
7. Use varied techniques and activities to share and enjoy literary selections in the social studies, such as those in the following list:

Book reports	Motion pictures
Card files of favorite poems and stories	Oral reading by children
	Oral reading by the teacher
Choral reading	Programs and pageants
Creative writing	Puppets and marionettes
Dramatization	Radio and TV programs
Filmstrips	Recordings
Independent reading	Storytelling

CREATIVE WRITING

In addition to enjoying literature written by others, children should have opportunities to create and to share poems, stories, and descriptions. After backgrounds of understanding have been built up in a unit of instruction, the teacher should encourage the children to express their thoughts and feelings in written form. In the early grades, a sound procedure is to have the group dictate their ideas to the teacher for recording on the chalkboard and on charts. As children develop independent writing skills in later grades, they may express their thoughts and feelings in written form and share them with the group. The writing of poetry as done by people in other lands is a rewarding experience, for example, haiku as Japan is studied. Related art and music activities may be coordinated with creative writing.

Over a period of time, collections may be made and kept in individual or class scrapbooks, posted on the bulletin boards, and used in culminating activities in units of instruction. Charts 1–4 are illustrative of items to consider in group planning, discussion, and the evaluation of creative written work.

IDEAS FOR CREATIVE WRITING

1. Stories and poems—topics, events, travel, people, activities
2. Descriptions—persons, places, things, events, and activities
3. Dramatization—sketches, playlets, plays, and pantomimes
4. Booklets, scrapbooks, leaflets, charts
5. Quiz programs
6. Radio and TV programs
7. Movie box rolls

Chart 1

FINDING EXPRESSIVE TERMS

1. Check the vocabulary chart.
2. Use the picture dictionary.
3. Listen as others discuss topics.
4. Look for them in our books.
5. Use the classroom dictionary.
6. Get ideas from pictures.
7. Get ideas from films.
8. Think of feelings as well as facts.

Chart 2

USING TERMS CLEARLY

1. Know the group or class to which it belongs—person, place, event, mineral, time, and the like.
2. Know how it is different from others in its group.
3. Know how it is used, or what it does.
4. Use it in a sentence.
5. Be ready to answer questions about it.

Chart 3

PLEASANT OR UNPLEASANT?

warm balmy breeze	strong and fearless
cold driving wind	loyal soldier
soft and warm	cowardly deserter
hot and sticky	glowing ember
smooth as silk	raging fire
rough as sandpaper	roaring flood
brave and loyal	soft rain
cunning and sly	soft wind

Chart 4

Dramatic Representation

Dramatic representation is used in the social studies to enable children to identify themselves with persons, activities, and situations that are being studied. It is *simulated* activity in which children are guided to portray and interpret human relationships in the home, community, and places far removed in time and space. At its best, dramatic representation is a sincere, authentic, and dynamic reconstruction of vital and significant experiences.

Dramatic representation is an excellent substitute for firsthand experience with people, events and situations far removed from the classroom. For example, children cannot direct activities in a control tower at the airport, a railway classification yard, or a wagon train, but they can participate in dramatic representation to gain insight into their direction. They cannot be firemen, post office workers, pilots, colonists, pioneers, scouts, or early settlers, but they can identify themselves with others through dramatic activities. They cannot take study trips to distant lands or go back in history to early times, but they can realistically recreate and interpret distant events, activities, and situations.

Dramatic representation is a mode of expression that children have used before entering school as they engaged in make-believe and imaginary play, for example, "being" Mother, Father, a teacher, bus driver, fireman, or airplane pilot. On entering school, children are eager to "act out" activities they are studying and to portray their impressions of people, events, and situations. Their interest and skill in dramatic representation may be capitalized on and used to steer learning in worthwhile directions.

A point to be kept in mind, however, is that dramatic representation in school is different from make-believe play at home. At home, children engage in dramatic play on their own; in school, they are guided and supervised so that significant outcomes may be achieved. At home, children base their dramatic play on ideas and impressions they have gathered in an incidental fashion; in school, background information is gathered and used as the basis for dramatic representation of social studies experiences. At home, make-believe play is a means of keeping children occupied; in school, dramatic representation is a means of developing definite concepts, skills, attitudes, and appreciations.

Dramatic representation offers excellent opportunities for the evaluation of children's learning. As a teacher observes children in dramatic activities, he or she can appraise children's use of concepts, grasp of main ideas, expression of attitudes, ability to

Dramatic representation of the roles of producers and consumers enables children to develop rich understandings and concepts. What planning do you think was necessary for this activity? What clues for evaluation and future planning might the teacher obtain by observing the children as they act out various roles? (Alameda County)

identify themselves with others, and their ability to express themselves creatively. Children spontaneously reveal the ideas, feelings, and impressions they have gained. In addition, teachers may detect and use misconceptions and erroneous ideas to plan and guide subsequent study.

FORMS OF DRAMATIC REPRESENTATION

Dramatic representation takes a variety of forms in the social studies:

Dramatic play is used frequently in the early grades to portray activities in units on the Home, School, Neighborhood, and Community. Dramatic play is an informal and creative portrayal of experiences without a set pattern, refined staging, costumes, or memorization of parts.

Dramatic rhythms involve the interpretation of activities and events by means of rhythmic bodily movement. Dramatic rhythms differ from dramatic play in that rhythmic movement is emphasized. Dramatic rhythms differ from creative dance in that the child is interpreting something learned in the social studies. They are similar to creative dance in that the child gives his own interpretation, not that of another.

Dramatic skits are more formal than dramatic play; they involve the enactment of a selected event or activity in which assigned roles are taken and lines are learned to portray an incident of importance such as the signing of the Mayflower Compact, or the landing at Plymouth Rock.

Pageants are used to portray a sequence of incidents or activities related to such unit topics as The History of Our Community, The Development of Our State, The Growth of America, and

481

How might you arrange an attractive center of interest like the one above to stimulate children to engage in dramatic activities? (Oakland)

Living in Mexico. Dramatic skits prepared by small groups within the class are easily arranged as a pageant.

Pantomimes may be used to portray simply and briefly such an activity as a plane landing, the movement of a boat into the harbor, or a scout on the lookout for Indians.

Dramatization may be employed to present a playlet or play in which a script, costumes, and stage setting are used.

Marionettes and puppets may be used for both creative dramatics and formal dramatization. Children may construct them, plan for their use, use them to present skits and plays, and use them in new situations by preparing new lines, staging, and costumes. Some teachers use them to build confidence in shy children as well as to provide a different form of dramatic expression for typical children.

Mock meetings may be planned and conducted in the upper grades to simulate New England town meetings, city council meetings, and legislative sessions.

Unfinished stories or *reaction stories* may be used to stimulate the enactment of situations in which children show what they would do if they were involved. After hearing a story which may deal with such problems as fair-play, helping others, carrying out one's responsibilities, respecting property, or minority group relations, children act out a solution and evaluate the enactment.

Role-playing or *sociodrama* may be used to develop insight into human relations, problems of others, a main idea, or the feelings of individuals in a critical situation. After the role is portrayed in different ways, such questions as these may be discussed: Which role did you prefer? Why? Which role was least desirable? Why? How did each role make you feel? How might individuals feel in the actual situation? What might be done to improve the situation?

Each one of the above dramatic activities should be critically selected for use in the social studies. If not, the activity may not contribute to the achievement of basic purposes. In some instances, for example, attention is diverted to the "putting on of a show," "the preparation of elaborate props and costumes," or "extended rehearsals." Sometimes the activity may make such demands on the time and energy of the teacher and pupils that significant social studies learnings are neglected. The trend is clearly toward the selection of dramatic activities that are simple, and directly related to main ideas being emphasized in units.

In the following sections, major attention is given to creative and informal dramatic activities. This has been done because they are more difficult to plan and guide than are formal dramatics in which a script is followed. A teacher who has not observed or guided creative dramatic activities might well start with a play that has been written for children. After experimentation with it, a good next step is to plan with the class short skits that are related to topics under study. This may be followed by longer dramatic activities until finally the group has moved to a creative approach to dramatization.

Sometimes, a teacher may decide that a play written for children is more appropriate than creative dramatics, for example, a program for a special occasion or a dramatic activity related to the commemoration of a special event. If this is the case, an appropriate play should be selected, rehearsed, and presented with full attention to the development of backgrounds of understanding, pupil planning and evaluation, and the attainment of other educational values.

EXAMPLES OF DRAMATIC ACTIVITIES

The following examples of activities to dramatize have been taken from different types of units of instruction. As you read them, note examples that you might use in a unit you are planning.

The home. Cleaning, gardening, washing and ironing; taking care of the baby, taking care of pets; preparing and serving meals, having a tea party; enjoying leisure activities, telephoning friends

The supermarket. Being the groceryman, butcher, cashier, fruit and vegetable man, a customer; stocking shelves, making signs and price tags, weighing items, sweeping

Community workers. Being a fireman; working in the post office, receiving, sorting, and delivering mail; operating a filling station, cleaning trucks; broadcasting news; running the airport; being other community workers

The farm. Pitching hay, feeding and watering animals, herding cows, milking cows; fixing the corral, plowing land, planting seeds, irrigating, harvesting; picking, washing, and bunching vegetables; loading, hauling, and distributing produce in trucks

Trains. Operating the trains, being engineers, firemen, brakemen, dispatchers; using the classification yard, loading and unloading freight, checking the freight; operating signals and switches; operating sand towers, water towers, and turntables; making repairs in the shops and the yards

Our state. Early ways of transporting goods and communicating with others; hunting, trading, other life activities; outstanding episodes and personalities in the growth of the state; modern ways of transporting goods, earning a living, and communicating with others

China. Travel in sampans, junks, and rickshas; preparing and serving Chinese meals and eating with chopsticks; house-building ceremony, visiting fortune-teller to determine lucky day, placing poles, frightening away evil spirits, group ceremony and feast, decoration of ridgepole, scattering of prosperity dumplings, dividing money, and so forth; using an abacus in buying and selling; engaging in festivals such as New Year's, Festival of the Lanterns, Festival of the Dragon Boats, and the Mid-Autumn or Moon Festival

Colonial life. Pilgrims leaving Holland, the trip in the Mayflower, the Mayflower Pact, landing at Plymouth Rock, the first Thanksgiving; starting the first community, meeting Indians, getting food, cutting logs, planning the houses, planting and hunting, spinning and carding wool, making soap and candles; playing games such as leap frog, wood tag, spinning tag; a town meeting, a day in the colonial home, a visit with Indians, a quilting bee.

Notice the objects and costumes these children are using in their dramatization of life in early America. What research activities were necessary? What inquiry techniques might be used to check authenticity of costumes? *(Alameda County)*

GUIDING DRAMATIC ACTIVITIES

An essential first step is to develop adequate backgrounds of understanding so that children will dramatize events and activities authentically and creatively. Much planning, discussion, and study are necessary as shown in the following list of steps taken by a group of ten year olds who dramatized the journey of pioneer families into Kentucky.

1. Discuss the stories read about the journey and make a list of important points to incorporate in the play:
   a. Welcoming Daniel Boone home
   b. Talking things over with the settlers
   c. Preparation for the trip
   d. Problems of travel over the trail
   e. The departure for Russell Camp
   f. The Indians' attack, which was damaging to the settlers
   g. The returning home of many settlers.
2. Find out what the settlers took with them.
3. Find out the ways in which the pioneers traveled. Decide which trail they took and find out about the dangers. Locate the trail and rivers on a map.
4. Read material about early settlers, hear stories read by the teacher, and write a creative story about them.
5. Find out how to mark trees, how to cut down obstacles, and how to stay on the trail.
6. Plan and incorporate these ideas in dramatic activities.
7. Carry out the plan and evaluate the effectiveness of individual and group activities.

After rich backgrounds of understanding have been developed, group planning may be employed effectively. Attention should be given to such questions as these:

What shall we dramatize?
What space do we need?
What materials are needed?
What characters are needed?
Who should take each part?

By beginning with *what* to do, the children can open up many possibilities without undue concern about *who* will take each part. Decisions on who will take each part may well be left until the last stage of planning after what is to be included in the dramatic activity is clear.

After plans are made, the group should try out the different suggestions, discuss them, and make changes as needed. During dramatic activity, the teacher should look for needs, problems, and suggestions for improvement that may be used during follow-up discussion. Taking notes so that specific guidance can be given during evaluation is a good idea.

After a group has dramatized an episode, time should be taken to share and evaluate problems, questions, needs for materials, needs for additional information, and ways to make improvements. The teacher should guide the discussion so that appropriate points that have been noted during the activity will be considered. Group standards should be set up when needed to improve the value of the activity. For example, during a unit on The Harbor, one group developed the standards in Chart 5 after a dramatic activity in which difficulties arose because of "wrong boat sounds," "boats clogging the harbor," and "fireboats tugging liners in." Following a skit involving life in Boonesboro, another group listed the standards in Chart 6 because several children had failed to dramatize their roles authentically.

RUNNING THE HARBOR

1. Share the boats with others.
2. Remember how each boat sounds.
3. Keep the harbor open for liners.
4. Let the tugs pull the liner in.
5. Listen to the captain's signals.

Chart 5

PROTECTING BOONESBORO

1. Sentinels should keep a sharp lookout.
2. The gates should be closed on the signal.
3. Gun loaders should load guns and not shoot.
4. Scouts should sneak out through the little gate.
5. Get gun powder out of the powder horns.

Chart 6

Special care should be taken to see that dramatic activities stimulate further learning in the social studies. The following examples show how this may be done:

1. A group was dramatizing activities in a harbor. A liner was signaling to enter the harbor. One child with a fire boat and a child with a tug boat went out to guide it in. The boy with the tug protested, saying, "This is for tugs, not fire boats." The child with the

first boat said, "I got here first, so I can bring her in." During the evaluation period, attention was given to using boats for the right job and to helping others to carry out their roles.

2. Several children were re-enacting life on the Oregon Trail. They had gathered around the campfire and were discussing the day's journey. One child suggested that they should sing some songs while sitting around the fire. When asked to sing, several children suggested contemporary songs. One child said they should learn "real ones sung by the pioneers." Later they learned *Dan Tucker*, *O Susannah*, and other songs, along with folk dances typical of pioneer times.

Continuous planning is needed to utilize dramatic activities effectively. Checklist 1 is a summary of specific factors that may be used for planning, guiding, and evaluating dramatic activities.

DRAMATIC ACTIVITIES CHECKLIST

Teacher Preplanning

_____What needs have arisen for dramatic activities?

_____Are materials available and accessible?

_____Are space arrangements adequate?

_____Are new ideas and information needed? How should they be introduced?

_____Which children probably will wish to participate first? Which should?

_____What will others do?

Group Planning

_____Is attention given first to what to dramatize?

_____Do the children select important aspects of living to portray?

_____Are needs for materials considered?

_____Do individuals suggest roles that are essential?

_____Does each child who is to participate know his role and the materials to use?

_____Are new ideas and materials introduced to enrich the activity?

During the Activity

Children:

_____Are the children identifying themselves with the person and objects involved?

_____Are important aspects of living portrayed?

_____Are space and materials used effectively?

_____Are suggestions made during planning carried out in the activity?

_____Are concepts being used accurately?

Checklist 1

Teacher:

_____Are new needs emerging for:

a. clarification of ideas? _____

b. authentic information? _____

c. group standards? _____

d. language expression? _____

_____Are concepts being expressed accurately in language and in action?

_____Are any individuals confused or uncertain as to purpose, use of materials, or role?

_____Are changes needed in space arrangements or materials?

Group Evaluation

_____Does the group appraise the activity in terms of the purposes set during planning?

_____Are newly discovered needs and problems considered?

_____Are inaccuracies and misconceptions clarified?

_____Have leads developed to other group and individual activities that will extend and broaden interests and keep the unit moving forward?

Checklist 1 continued

DRAMATIC RHYTHMS

Children are quick to respond to the rhythm in life around them. Grain swaying in the field, waves rolling in to shore, birds flying from tree to tree, men at work in the community, trains starting and stopping: all these will stimulate rhythmical expression that is natural and spontaneous. Similarly, rich experiences in the social studies lead to dramatic rhythms that are meaningful demonstrations of the children's impressions.

"I'll show you how the liner comes in," said a boy demonstrating the slow, even movement of a large ocean liner.

"Out goes the pilot boat," said a girl moving gracefully and speedily as she gave her interpretation of the pilot she had seen on a trip to the harbor.

"Here comes a tug to help," said another child moving slowly but powerfully to assist the liner.

"Here comes another tug. Chug! Chug! Chug!" said a boy who had seen a tug work in the harbor nearby. With considerable realism, he moved over to help bring the liner in.

Thus do children spontaneously and eagerly use rhythmic expression through bodily movement to interpret experiences they have had.

Dramatic rhythms may be used in many different situations in the social studies. The following examples have been taken from selected units developed by successful elementary school teachers. As you read them, note ways in which you can use dramatic rhythms in a unit you may be planning.

1. *The Home.* Home activities such as washing and ironing clothes; digging, raking, and working in the garden; play activities such as swinging, sliding, climbing, seesawing; using fundamental rhythms, such as marching, skipping, running, galloping, hopping, and sliding to express thoughts and feelings; using rhythm instruments to accompany bodily movement

2. *Community.* Rhythms related to growing things such as the trees, flowers, and shrubs; community work activities such as loading and unloading trucks, building and painting houses; movement of trucks and trains; rain, snow, and wind; using fundamental rhythms and rhythm instruments creatively to express ideas grasped in the social studies

3. *The Farm.* Activities of the farmer such as working in the field, milking, riding horses, driving tractors, loading and unloading trucks; movements of farm animals; swaying wheat fields

4. *Freight Trains.* Movements of trains starting, gaining speed, speeding along, slowing down, stopping, putting cars on a siding, backing up, coupling and uncoupling cars, loading and unloading; wigwag signals, signalling trains to start and stop

5. *Mexico.* Carrying baskets to market, weaving, dancing at the fiesta, loading and unloading burros, hammering silver, working in the fields

6. *Pioneers.* Bodily expression of movements in such processes as making candles, quilting, and weaving; building, cutting trees, digging, planting, hunting, making log canoes; movements of animals in the forest

In addition to interpretation through dramatic rhythms, there is a real place for folk games and folk dances in the social studies. Many units would be incomplete if folk dances were omitted. For example, the *Fandango, La Cucaracha,* and *St. Michael's Wheel* in units on Mexico, and *Old Dan Tucker, Virginia Reel,* and *Captain Jenks* in units on Pioneer Life are most appropriate. Other examples can be found in the selected references at the end of this chapter.

Growth in dramatic rhythms progresses from simple interpretation of single episodes to more complete patterns of expression centered in a unifying theme. At first, children's responses to rhythm are short and simple. A single phrase of an activity, such as the train starting, may be interpreted with real satisfaction. Other phases, such as gaining speed, slowing down, or going up a steep hill, may be added later. Still later, several phases are brought together in a pattern of rhythm that is the child's portrayal of the complete activity. Finally, several children co-operate in rhythmic bodily expression of related activities, such as the train backing up to couple cars, starting up, traveling along, leaving cars at different places, and arriving at its destination. In this final stage, the group develops a unifying pattern that is more satisfying and meaningful than individual interpretations.

Guiding Rhythmic Expression. In developing rhythmic experiences with children, the first consideration is to build a rich background of experience. Study trips taken so that children can actually see that which is to be interpreted are helpful. Films, pictures, and recordings add to the meaningfulness of the experience. Rich literary experiences and follow-up discussion give additional insights.

After backgrounds of experience have been developed, the group should discuss the rhythms involved and witness individual demonstrations voluntarily given by different children. Children should experiment by trying one form and then another, thereby inventing new modes of bodily expression. Each child's contributions should be well received and commended by the teacher and the group.

At first a few children may give their own interpretations. Others may join later and add new movements or carry out rhythms that have been learned earlier yet are adapted to the new situation.

Following the first rhythmic expression, the group should share ideas and consider outstanding movements. This may lead to the selection of one or more rhythms that express the group's ideas in an effective and satisfying manner.

Later the selected rhythms may be tried again, new ideas being added as they develop. Group planning and evaluation should produce new ideas and lead to a pattern of expression that is more unified and complete than first trials. Needs may arise for more experiences to enrich backgrounds, such as a study trip, a film, or stories related to the activity. These should be provided so that the cycle of planning, engaging in rhythmical expression, and evaluation may be carried on to higher and more meaningful levels.

The guidelines presented in Checklist 2 will help the group to obtain maximum value from the use of rhythmic expression in the social studies.

DRAMATIC RHYTHMS CHECKLIST

Teacher Preplanning

_____Have experiences been provided for development of activities which may be expressed meaningfully through rhythmic expression?

_____How can previous experiences with rhythms be used in planning, enriching, and evaluating this experience?

_____Does the selected activity lend itself to rhythmic expression?

_____How many children can be accommodated in available space?

_____Is satisfactory musical accompaniment available?

Group Planning

_____Do the children see relationships between the rhythms and ideas to be expressed?

_____Do they draw on previous experiences in discussing and demonstrating rhythmic movements?

_____Do they sense the rhythmic patterns involved?

_____Are suggestions made regarding the use of space and materials?

_____What types of rhythmic responses are suggested?

_____Is guidance given in helping the group select music to fit the rhythms?

_____Are suggestions made regarding group organization and individual roles?

_____Are suggestions made regarding a unifying pattern appropriate to the group's level of development?

During Rhythmical Activity

_____Are the responses individualized and spontaneous?

_____Is the expression guided by suggestions made during planning?

_____Are fundamental rhythms, such as walking, running, skipping, hopping, and galloping, being woven into a unified pattern?

_____Are materials and space being used so that they contribute to creative expression?

_____Is increased understanding of the ideas, objects, or persons involved being revealed?

_____Does the accompaniment contribute to effective expression or detract from it?

_____Is the group revealing increased sensitivity to changing moods by varying rhythmical expression accordingly?

_____Are the children growing in confidence, poise, and control?

Group Evaluation

_____Are each child's suggestions and comments considered?

_____Are individual demonstrations voluntarily given to clarify points?

_____Are questions and comments raised about use of space?

_____Is group discussion leading toward a more unified pattern?

_____Does the group consider the accompaniment appropriate?

_____Are more effective and satisfying modes of expression considered?

_____Are related activities and needs for further background experience considered, such as a study trip to clarify ideas?

_____Do the children express pleasure and satisfaction as a result of the experience?

Checklist 2

What terms and concepts might be developed in this type of activity? What kind of planning and investigation should precede it? (Osburn Schools, Arizona)

Music Activities

Man's musical heritage is a rich source of content and activities for use in gaining an understanding of people and their ways of living. In societies at home and around the world, people have expressed their customs, traditions, and ideals in music. Patriotic music has been written to stir feelings of loyalty, to highlight great events, and for use in festivals, ceremonies, and religious activities. Poems, stories, legends, and other literary works have been set to music. Folk songs and dances have evolved from everyday activities of people. Musical instruments have been invented to provide unique modes of expression. In addition, cultural interdependence has been increased as the music created in one part of the world has had an impact on people in other parts of the world.

The following six types of music activity are used in social studies units of instruction:

Singing activities	Instrumental activities
Listening activities	Creative expression
Rhythmic activities	Research activities

By directing children's participation in each type of activity, a teacher can guide children to make meaningful cross-cultural comparisons. (This is one of the main reasons for giving attention to music in the social studies.) If the program is limited to singing and listening activities, as is the case in some classrooms, children's learning will be greatly limited. But if all six types of activity are carefully planned and carried out, then children's study of music as a part of human activities will be broader and more fully grounded in its cultural setting.

SINGING ACTIVITIES

Singing is the most extensively used music activity in the social studies. Many songs related to topics in each unit of instruction may be found in children's music books. Children's identification with others is increased as they sing songs which portray human experience and activities, for example, Mother's work at home, activities of community workers, working on the farm, living in a hogan, trekking westward across the plains, and living in other lands. Sensitivity to the effects of natural conditions on human activities may be developed as children learn songs about nature and get a feeling for the icy winds of the northern steppes, the hot dry desert, the steaming jungle, the grandeur of high mountains, the vastness of the prairies, and changes in the seasons. Feelings of patriotism and loyalty are aroused as children sing *The Star-Spangled Banner, America the Beautiful, Battle Hymn of the Republic*, and *Columbia, the Gem of the Ocean.* A feeling of kinship with others may be kindled as children sing the folk songs of different regions of America and of other lands.

In the social studies, special attention is given to the development of backgrounds of understanding of the songs included in each unit. The questions in Chart 7 may be used to guide children's study and discussion.

UNDERSTAND THE SONGS WE SING
IN OUR UNIT

What thoughts and feelings are being expressed?
What is the mood, the rhythmic pattern, and the melody?
Is this a song of work, play, worship, adventure, nature, fantasy, or patriotism?
Is this song sung at home, at festivals, or at ceremonies?
What type of accompaniment is appropriate?
What instruments might be used to play the melody?

Chart 7

LISTENING ACTIVITIES

Through directed listening experiences, children can learn much about the folk songs, dances, instruments, festivals, holidays, patriotic events, composers, and performing artists of greatest importance in each unit. Recordings are available of different types of music and may be used to give realism and authenticity to children's learning. In addition, use is made of radio and TV programs, community concerts and folk festivals, individuals invited to school, and children's own recordings. Courses of study, units of instruction, and children's music textbooks all have many suggestions on listening experiences to include in the social studies.

How might a listening center such as this be used by small groups of children to enrich learning in a unit? *(San Bernardino County)*

Examples of questions that may be used to guide listening experiences in the social studies are listed in Chart 8.

LISTENING TO MUSIC FROM OTHER LANDS

How is it like ours? How is it different?
What rhythmic patterns are used?
What tonal patterns are used?
What instruments are used?
What types of songs do they enjoy?
What moods are portrayed?
How is their music related to customs and traditions?

Chart 8

RHYTHMIC ACTIVITIES

Four types of rhythmic activity that may be provided in the social studies are *informal rhythms* in which children express rhythmic patterns without direction from the teacher, *formal rhythms* in which the teacher directs children to move to the rhythm (skip, gallop, and the like) as music is played, *creative rhythms* in which children express their responses in original ways, and *dramatic rhythms* which were discussed in the preceding section. As these activities are used in the social studies, special attention is given to the rhythmic patterns that are characteristic of the music, folk dances, and activities included in units of instruction. (See Charts 9–12.) Rhythm instruments, recordings, native instruments, the piano, and the autoharp are used to accompany rhythmic activities and to play rhythmic patterns.

RHYTHMS AROUND US

People working
Horses trotting
Trees swaying
Motors humming
Hammers pounding
Bells ringing
Horns tooting

Chart 9

RHYTHMIC PATTERNS

Walk	March
Trot	Waltz
Hop	Polka
Skip	Gavotte
Gallop	Minuet
Slide	Schottische
Swing	Tango

Chart 10

FINDING RHYTHMS

Songs and poems
Folk dances
Recordings
Radio and TV
Activities of people
Animals moving
Trains, planes

Chart 11

EXPRESSING RHYTHMS

Tapping
Clapping
Humming
Strumming
Drumming
Chanting
Moving

Chart 12

INSTRUMENTAL ACTIVITIES

Musical instruments of various types may be used in the social studies to extend children's learning. Rhythm instruments such as drums, sticks, blocks, bells, triangles, cymbals, gongs, rattles, and tambourines may be used to accompany rhythmic and singing activities, produce sound effects, and play rhythmic patterns. Chording instruments such as the autoharp and harmolin may be used to accompany various activities and to demonstrate harmonic and rhythmic patterns. Simple melody instruments such as melody bells, tuned bottles or glasses, song flutes, and recorders may be used to play tunes created by children as well as melodies discovered in the songs and recordings presented in units. Native instruments may be examined and played to give authenticity to music activities. Examples of these are the claves, guiro, maracas, cabaca, bongo, conga, antara or pipes of Pan, quena or flute, and chocalho in units on South America, and the bamboo xylophone, gong, temple block, and finger cymbals in units on Oriental Countries. In addition, some simple folk instruments may be made by children.

HOW CAN WE USE THESE INSTRUMENTS IN OUR UNIT?

Percussion

Drums	Woodblocks	Triangles
Shakers	Tambourines	Cymbals
Gong	Castanets	Scrapers
Sticks	Jangles	Maracas

Melody

Bells	Recorder	Water glasses
Songflute	Psaltery	Harmolette
Tonette	Harmonica	Xylophone

Harmony

Autoharp	Harmolin	Marimba

Chart 13

CREATIVE EXPRESSION

Creative expression through music may be brought to high levels in the social studies as children develop insights and appreciations through activities in units of instruction. Poems and verse created by children may be set to music as children hum tunes or play them on simple melody instruments while the teacher records them on the chalkboard, a chart, or a tape recorder.

How can the composing of a song such as this be related to the processing of materials? How might it be related to other experiences? *(San Bernardino County)*

Accompaniments for songs, rhythmic movement, choral reading, and dramatic activities may be created by children as they catch the mood and rhythm of thoughts and feelings to be expressed. Special sound effects may be created and background music may be selected for skits, plays, and pageants. Simple instruments may be made of gourds, bamboo, bottles, glasses, and

COMPOSING A SONG FOR OUR UNIT

What moods or feelings shall we try to express?
What words and phrases shall we use?
Shall we hum, whistle, play, or sing to create the melody?
What rhythm shall we use?
Shall we record the lyric and the melody?
What key shall we use?

Chart 14

other materials. Creative expression through art, writing, dramatics, and rhythmic movement may be stimulated as children listen to recordings. A range of creative processes may be brought into play as children plan and develop culminating activities that include a script, lyrics and melodies, costumes, staging, musical accompaniments, and their own special effects.

RESEARCH ACTIVITIES

Individual and group research activities may be undertaken to find background information on the music emphasized in units of instruction. A trip may be taken to a nearby museum to examine instruments and to see costumes that are used in folk dances. Experts may be interviewed or invited to come to the classroom to give demonstrations and to tell about experiences they have had. Encyclopedias, library resources, and supplementary music books may be reviewed. Notebooks and scrapbooks may be compiled to summarize information. Of utmost importance is the actual use of the information that children gather in their music activities.

Illustrative questions that may be used to guide children's research activities are listed in Chart 15.

The diversity of the musical heritage to be found among people in different cultural settings should be explored by the class. For example, in units on South America, Africa, Europe, Canada, and the United States, many different types of music may be found and the influences of diverse cultural backgrounds may be discovered. Folk music, adaptations of music from other lands, music created by native composers, and famous performing artists may be made a part of units. The following examples drawn from units on countries in South America are illustrative:

FINDING OUT ABOUT THE MUSIC IN OTHER LANDS

What are some of their best-known folk songs?
What folk dances do they have? How are they related to festivals?
What costumes do they wear?
What music do they play at ceremonies and other activities?
What folk instruments do they have? How are they made?
What composers and artists live there?
What influences have others had on their music? How has their music influenced ours?
What customs, traditions, and beliefs are expressed through music?
What events, deeds, and activities have been set to music?

Chart 15

Argentina. Influences of the Italians, Indians, and Spaniards are evident. *El Estilo*, a melancholy and nostalgic song of the pampas, shows the Italian influence. The Tango shows Spanish influence. The rich folk music shows the Indian influence. The compositions of Alberto Ginastera and Juan José Castro, and the folk music recordings and publications of Carlos Vega show the richness of Argentina's musical heritage. Well-known songs which may be found in children's music books are *Sí Señor, Palapala, Adiós Te Digo, Chacarera, Song of the Pampas, The Gaucho, Vidalita,* and *Ay, Zamba.*

Brazil. Influences of the Indians, Portuguese, and Negroes are evident. Tender and sentimental ballads show the influence of the Portuguese who sang the *Modinha* to drive away homesickness. The *Chôros* is a rhythmically rich musical form that includes improvised variations; it originated during the Second Empire. The samba, one of the most sophisticated of the carioca dances, shows the Negro influence. Among the famous Brazilian singers are Bidú Sayão, Elsie Houston, and Olga Coelho. Two renowned composers are Heitor Villa-Lobos and Francisco Mignone. Illustrative of the Brazilian songs included in children's music books are *The Painter of Cannahay, My Pretty Cabacla, Tutu Maramba, Cantilena, Sambalele, Bambamulele, In Bahia Town, O Gato,* and *Come Here, Vitu.*

Chile. The gay mood of the folk and popular music of Chile shows a strong Spanish influence. The scarf dances (danzas de panuelo) in which couples dance separately have been brought to a high level of artistic development. The cueca or zamacueca is the most popular dance. A new cueca may be created to commemorate special events ranging from the winning of a football game to an outstanding historical event. Among the renowned musical figures in Chile are Claudio Arrau (pianist), Domingo Santa Cruz (composer), and Ramon Vinay (tenor). Illustrative songs are *San Severino, The Lovely Chilean Maid, Buy a Dozen, El Marinero, Pol Perica, Dance Song,* and *Bom Bom Bom.*

ARRANGING A CLASSROOM MUSIC CENTER

A classroom music center may be arranged and changed as different units of instruction are developed. Song books, instruments, other music materials, and pictures showing musical activities may be placed in the music center. If headphones are available for listening to recordings, children may go to the center at different times for individual listening. The following are examples of items that may be placed in the center from time to time:

Bulletin Board: Current events about musicians in places being studied, announcements of related programs on TV and radio, a list of recordings for individual listening, charts containing information on songs, rhythms, dances and instruments, and pictures showing native musical activities

Books: Textbooks and references containing folk songs, rhythms, stories of musicians, descriptions of instruments, and accounts of musical activities

Instruments: A collection of instruments used by the people being studied

Other Resources: A listening post (phonograph and headphones) for individual and small-group listening, maps showing the locale of songs and musicians, an autoharp and rhythm instruments for musical accompaniment, and a flannel board for showing rhythm and tonal patterns

Arts and Crafts

From ancient times to the present, people have expressed their thoughts and feelings through various art forms. Artists and artisans of each generation have selected ideas and created forms that clarify, simplify, and interpret the ideals, beliefs, and customs characteristic of the times in which they lived. Line, form, color, texture, space, and other elements have been unified in ways that are expressive of the artist's intentions. Touches of beauty have been added to dwellings, clothing, utensils, festivals, ceremonies, and other objects and activities. Folk crafts have been developed to meet everyday needs and have provided opportunities for creative expression in homes and villages throughout the world.

HOW ARE THESE PORTRAYED IN ARTS AND CRAFTS?		WHICH OF THESE ITEMS DO THEY MAKE?		CAN YOU DISCOVER CREATIVE USES OF THE FOLLOWING?	
Ideas	Aspirations	Pottery	Baskets	Line	Design
Ideals	Superstitions	Tiles	Rugs	Form	Integration
Hopes	Traditions	Figurines	Blankets	Color	Movement
Fears	Customs	Mosaics	Shawls	Texture	Variation
Feelings	Nature	Copperware	Instruments	Space	Repetition
Beliefs	Religion	Silverware	Containers	Balance	Perspective
Freedom	Recreation	Jewelry	Featherwork	Rhythm	Emphasis
Events	Heroes	Leather work	Bead work	Unity	Subordination

Chart 16   Chart 17   Chart 18

In many ways, the study of art contributes to children's learning in each unit of instruction. For example, deeper insights and appreciations are developed as children discover the impact of art on homes, furnishings, cars, trains, airplanes, buildings, bridges, and other man-made objects. Appreciation of the beauty in nature may be increased as children study The Community, Our State, Our Nation, and Other Lands. Subtle shades of meaning may be developed as children consider the work of artists who have portrayed great events, heroes, landscapes, poems, songs, everyday activities, ceremonies, festivals, and holidays. Basic concepts may be enriched as children see and discuss pictures that simplify and clarify changes in the seasons, the dense jungles, storms lashing a seacoast, a ship being tossed by the stormy sea, a lagoon by a tropical isle, earth-moving machines cutting a road through mountains, and workers toiling in the fields. A feeling for modes of expression enjoyed by others may be kindled as children discover the concepts of nature in sand paintings of the Navajos, the simple beauty of the Puritan church, the delicate patterns in Japanese paintings, the search for harmony between man and nature in Chinese art, the recurring themes and patterns in Egyptian art, the stateliness of Roman architecture, and the desire for freedom boldly revealed in Rivera's murals. Cultural interdependence may be highlighted as the thunderbird, the

What elements of design might be discovered as children examine these items? What appreciations might be extended? (Berkeley)

cross, geometric forms, and other designs are discovered in the art of peoples in different lands.

Creative and appreciative experiences may be intertwined as children engage in art activities. For example, the sand paintings of the Navajos may be considered in terms of the concepts of nature, human activities, myths, and ideas that they portray. Paralleling such study may be activities in which children engage in sand painting to portray their impressions of selected activities. In a study of Mexico, pictures of the murals of Diego Rivera may be explored to discover the ideas, hopes, and feelings that are expressed. This may be paralleled or followed by an activity in which children create a mural to portray their own impressions of life in Mexico. When such parallel activities are provided, care must be taken to be sure that children's expression is truly creative, truly their own, and not a copy of that of others.

As a general guideline, creativeness should be emphasized in

FIND OUT HOW PEOPLE EXPRESS THEMSELVES THROUGH ART

Study pictures in our textbooks.
Look at reproductions of pictures and art objects.
See films, filmstrips, and slides.
Visit a museum or art gallery.
Examine textiles, pottery, jewelry, and other objects.
Interview people who have visited other cultures or studied their art.
Read art books, reference materials, and current periodicals.
Collect pictures from magazines, newspapers, and travel folders.

Chart 19

WHICH OF THESE HANDICRAFTS ARE USED IN OTHER CULTURES?

Weaving mats, tapestries, cloth, rugs, wall hangings
Basket making from reeds and raffia
Creating designs on cloth, bark, woven raffia, parchment, skins, metal, stone, clay, wood
Embroidering or appliqueing on clothing, costumes, and textiles
Carving in wood, stone, ivory, and bone
Modeling and constructing objects out of clay
Making objects out of metal
Dyeing cloth, leather, bark, and other materials
Making masks, costumes, and objects for use in ceremonies and festivals

Chart 20

both appreciative and creative activities. As the artwork of other people is studied, each individual, whether a child or an adult, will respond in ways that are his own. To be sure, children may have similar understandings of background ideas about the culture in which the art product was created and certain common understandings regarding the processes that were involved. But the individual's reaction, his response, and the feelings that are evoked are always highly individualized. Similarly, as children engage in art activities, every effort should be made to assure creative expression on the part of each child. What is desired is his interpretation of what he has learned in the unit of instruction, his own expression of thoughts and feelings.

HOW CAN WE USE THESE TO SHOW MAIN IDEAS?	MAKING A MURAL
Drawing, painting, sketching, illustrating Making items out of paper, cardboard, metal, wire, wood Weaving, sewing, stitching, embroidering, appliqueing Modeling, carving, sculpturing, whittling Making dioramas, panoramas, shadow boxes	What main idea shall we show? What related ideas are needed? How shall the ideas be arranged? What materials shall we use? What colors will be most effective? What contributions can each person make?
Chart 21	Chart 22

Some teachers ask: But what if a child has misconceptions and erroneous ideas about the people or activities that are being portrayed? The way to correct misconceptions is to provide for additional study; simply telling or showing a child how to draw something is not a substitute for developing backgrounds of understanding of people and their ways of living. The ideas to be expressed and the media and processes that are used in an art activity may be enriched through directed study. But when a child proceeds to express the ideas, he must use his own techniques if the experience is to be called an art activity. Otherwise it is merely copying, illustrating, or reproducing the technique of another person. It is not art.

TYPES OF ART ACTIVITY

Checklist 3 includes the main types of art activity used in the social studies. Each major type is followed by examples of items that may be made, designed, or arranged by children.

Drawing and Painting: _____Pictures _____Murals _____Friezes _____Posters _____Cartoons _____Illustrations _____Sketches _____Designs _____Backgrounds _____Landscapes _____Decorations _____Borders _____Greeting cards

Modeling, Sculpturing, and Carving: _____Animals _____Utensils _____Dishes _____Bowls _____Pots _____Vases _____Jugs _____Jars _____Trays _____Tiles _____Candlesticks _____Jewelry _____Beads _____Figurines _____Plaques

Designing: _____Booklets _____Programs _____Announcements _____Greeting cards _____Fans _____Mats _____Markers _____Borders _____Wrappers _____Containers _____Stage scenery _____Prints _____Backgrounds for collages _____Mosaics

Arranging: _____Displays _____Exhibits _____Flowers _____Gourds _____Driftwood _____Fruits _____Cornucopias _____Textiles

Paper and Cardboard Construction: _____Mats _____Wall hangings _____Table covers _____Designs _____Puppets _____Marionettes _____Notebooks _____Scrapbooks _____Booklets _____Posters _____Montages _____Collages _____Mosaics _____Masks _____Mobiles _____Stabiles _____Buildings _____Ornaments _____Furniture _____Decorations _____Containers _____Dioramas _____Panoramas _____Shadow boxes

Weaving, Sewing, and Stitching: _____Bags _____Mats _____Wall hangings _____Caps _____Head bands _____Belts _____Rugs _____Scarves _____Curtains _____Stuffed animals _____Costumes

Using Mixed Media: _____Paint and Yarn _____Chalk and paper sculpture _____Cut paper and tempera _____Chalk, crayon, and paint _____Water color and chalk _____Paper, cork, and wire _____Combinations of discarded materials

Printing and Stenciling: _____Designs _____Borders _____Textiles _____Decorations _____Programs _____Announcements _____Greeting cards

Checklist 3

THE CLASSROOM ART CENTER

A work center for the arrangement of art materials facilitates pupils' work and makes possible more effective utilization of art activities in the social studies. Materials in the work center should be changed as new topics are studied in the unit of instruction. Related pictures may be displayed on the bulletin board, and selected art objects may be exhibited on nearby shelves, window sills, or tables. Space should be provided for the displaying of

How might the making of a mural contribute to the development of main ideas in a unit? What steps are taken to plan to complete a mural such as this? *(Alameda County)*

Paper: _____Newsprint _____Drawing _____Water color _____Construction _____Poster _____Bogus _____Wrapping _____Tagboard _____Poster board _____Tissue _____Crepe

Paint: _____Powdered _____Finger _____Water color _____Enamel _____Textile _____Silk screen _____Poster

Brushes: _____Easel _____Enamel _____Water color _____Paste _____Wash brush

Crayons: _____Large primary size _____Large colored _____Standard size

Chalk: _____White for sketching _____Large colored _____Standard size colored

Clay: _____Plastic modeling _____Wedged _____Dextrine _____Slip _____Glaze _____Underglaze paints _____Plastic to keep clay from drying _____Kiln _____Sponges _____Workboards _____Crocks _____Rollers _____Wire tools

Crafts: _____Soap _____Papier-mâché _____Raffia _____Reeds _____Carpet warp _____Cloth _____Wood _____Cardboard _____Tin _____Cooper _____Tools _____String _____Yarn _____Looms _____Cloth _____Beads _____Buttons _____Jute _____Needles _____Scrap materials

Printing and Stenciling: _____Pens _____India ink _____Spray guns _____Brayers _____Cutting tools _____Sheet glass _____Water-base inks _____Sticks _____Carrots _____Potatoes _____Sponges _____Linoleum blocks _____Inner tubes _____Gum erasers _____Silk-screen materials

Other: _____Charcoal _____Scissors _____Knives _____Paste _____Rubber cement _____Fixative _____Tape _____Pins

Checklist 4

children's completed art work and for storing unfinished work. Materials such as those noted in Checklist 4 may be selected and placed in the work center as needed to carry out art activities.

Industrial or Practical Arts

Two types of industrial or practical arts are included in this section. The first is construction of objects for use in various social studies activities. The second is the processing or changing of raw materials to usable forms. Both types of activity are provided to help children develop realistic and authentic concepts and understandings related to people's use of objects and resources to meet basic needs.

CONSTRUCTION

Construction as used in the social studies may be defined as the use of tools and materials to make authentic objects needed to promote growth of social concepts and understanding of social processes. Construction involves the development of purposes, group planning, selection of materials, appropriate use of tools, manipulative skills, group evaluation, and planning for use in related social studies activities. Examples include the making and using of airplanes, trucks, boats, looms, furniture, weapons, utensils, and various models. The value of construction lies in

How might the construction and use of objects such as these be used to further inquiry in a unit you are planning? *(Education Workshop, University of California, Berkeley)*

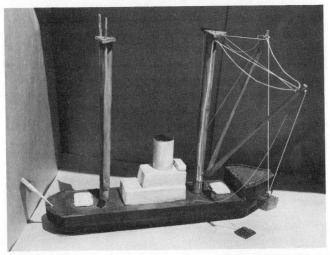

its contribution to inquiry, not in the products that are made. Lasting values can be achieved only if construction serves significant purposes, involves careful planning, is authentic, and is used to stimulate learning in the unit of instruction.

Construction may be closely related to dramatic activities in the social studies program. Dramatic representation of activities in units on The Home, The Farm, The Harbor, The Airport, Colonial Life, Mexico, and Other Lands creates needs for objects, models, props, and scenery. Children can plan and make essential items and thus relate the making of objects to significant purposes.

Notice the roles of these "producers." What might be produced with these resources? (Alameda County)

Precision and authenticity in construction grows steadily as children gain in maturity. In the primary grades, children are satisfied with blocks, boxes, boards, and simply made items. A box may be used as a truck to haul things, two boards nailed crosswise can serve as an airplane, blocks may be arranged to serve as a corral, and a can fastened to a board is used as a tank car or oil truck. Older children require more detail and precision in materials used in dramatic play. The freight car has sliding doors, the covered wagon can be pulled and is authentic in detail, the airplane is complete from "prop to tail assembly," and the airport is an authentic copy of one that has been visited.

Criteria. If the educational values are to be achieved, criteria such as the following must be used to select activities involving construction.

1. Does this activity meet a need that is significant to the group?

2. Is it practical in terms of available time, tools, and materials?

3. Is it more effective than other experiences that can be provided?

4. Will it help to develop accurate concepts?

5. Does it bear a direct relationship to other experiences in the unit?

6. Do children have readiness for it in terms of backgrounds and construction skills?

7. Will it promote critical thinking, cooperative planning, and group problem-solving skills?

Uses of Construction. The following examples of objects that children may make are taken from units of instruction frequently taught in the elementary schools. As you read them, note specific activities that you may carry out in a unit for some group you may have in mind.

The home. Playhouse furnishings, including chairs, tables, cupboards, flower boxes, rugs, curtains, wall paper, borders, and dishes

Community life. Simply made houses, stores, schools, churches, and other community buildings; various types of trucks, such as oil, lumber, pick-up, milk, mail, and delivery; crates, boxes, bags, fruits and vegetables, hand trucks, and sheds for use in the market

The farm. Farmhouse, barn, fences, chicken coops, pens, corrals, silo, trucks; milking and feed barns, nursery for the calves, bottling plant, stanchions, feeding troughs, grain sacks, and milk trucks for a dairy farm

Boats. Different types of boats: for example, an oil tanker, tug, liner, freighter, lumber boat, fireboat, speedboat, rowboat, fishing boat, and pilot boat; items for a harbor, such as piers, breakwater, buoys, drydock, and drawbridge

Trains. Classification yard on the floor; various types of cars, such as freight, refrigerator, flatcar, boxcar, gondola, hopper, stock, poultry, tank; engines of various types, such as passenger, freight, switch; caboose; other items to use in the unit, such as truck farm,

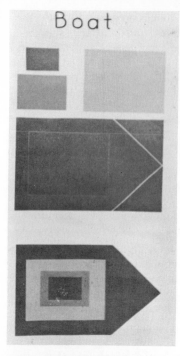

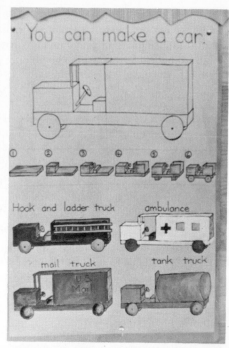

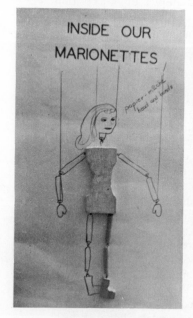

These charts were designed to show or tell how various objects could be constructed. (*Burbank and Oakland*)

wholesale market, stockyard, lumber yard, animals to haul, fruit to haul, sacks for produce, trucks, tractors, dollies, and land trucks to load and unload freight; signals and switches; sand towers and water towers; roundhouse and turntable

Colonial life. Colonial kitchen, fireplace, bed, table, rag rugs, chair, benches, cupboard, lamps, candles; spoons, ladles, brooms; horn books, powder horns, bullet pouches, rifles; tape and box looms

Aviation. Model planes, gliders, wind sock, control tower, hangars, maintenance shops, runways, model airport

Tools and Materials. Only simple tools are used in construction in the social studies. Saws, C-clamps, hammers, T-squares, brace and bit, mallet, chisels, and a hand drill are adequate for most activities. Proper use of tools, safety measures, and care of tools are taught systematically so that accidents and injuries can be avoided. Portable tool racks permit many groups to use the same tools and also provide a good storage place for tools and materials.

Materials for construction may be obtained in the community. Boxes made of soft pine wood are especially useful. Orange crates

Such a tool rack facilitates construction. Notice that it is designed so that children can help themselves. *(Ventura County and Los Angeles)*

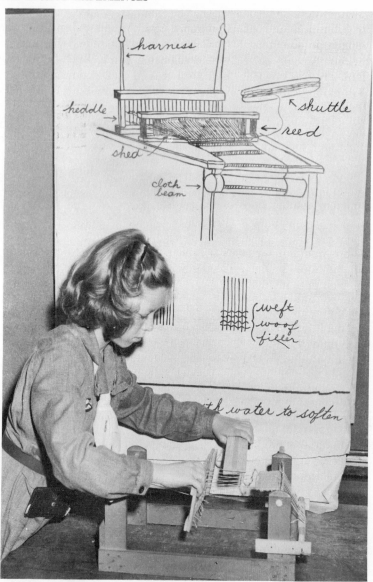

harness

heddle

shed

shuttle

reed

cloth beam

weft
woof
filler

...th water to soften

Can you think of a better way to inquire into processes of weaving? (Los Angeles)

and apple boxes can be used for buildings such as houses, barns, stores, hangars, and depots. Boards from wooden boxes make excellent scrap lumber which can be used to make boats, trucks, looms, airplanes, and the like. Doweling ranging in size from a quarter inch to 1″ can be used to make masts, steering shafts on trucks, derricks, funnels, smokestacks, and any other item that is cylindrical and of appropriate size. Wooden button molds ranging in size from 1″ to 2½″ in diameter should be used for wheels. Awning pole, 2½″ in diameter, is excellent for making tank cars, tanks for milk and oil trucks, and locomotive boilers. Tin roofing caps make excellent headlights or hub caps on trucks. Tops of cans, scraps of tin, bottle tops, spools, screws, screweyes for hooking railroad cars and trailer-trucks, sandpaper, nails, brads, brushes, and paints round out the list of supplies used most frequently. Once materials such as these are assembled, children under the guidance of a creative teacher will think of innumerable objects to construct; real ingenuity will be shown in using different combinations of materials.

PROCESSING MATERIALS

Processing of materials is similar in many ways to construction as described in the foregoing pages. Similar values, techniques of planning, instructional procedures, and skills are involved.

Processing materials in the social studies may be defined as the changing of raw materials, or semiprocessed materials (yarn, for example), into products that can be used. Typical examples are: making cottage cheese, processing wool and flax, dyeing fabrics, weaving, drying fruit, and making soap. As children engage in such processes, emphasis should be given to the development of concepts and understandings regarding simple ways in which people have met their needs without benefit of technological developments.

In early times, children had many firsthand experiences with processes in their everyday life in home and community. Typical experiences were planting wheat, harvesting it, grinding it into flour, and making bread; shearing sheep, and washing, carding, spinning, and weaving wool; catching, cleaning, and salting fish; processing of meat; felling and sawing trees, and using the lumber for buildings; cleaning and tanning hides to make shoes and clothing; collecting berries and dyeing clothes; using tallow to make candles; watching the blacksmith as he forged implements from iron; and seeing flour ground at the mill. Today, children see finished products in the store and have little opportunity to learn about the processes involved in making them.

Outlined below are a few examples of processes that have been used successfully in units carried out at various grade levels. Steps to take to carry out several processing activities are shown in Charts 23–28, and additional suggestions may be found in the references at the end of this chapter.

MAKING BUTTER

Materials: ½ pint of whipping cream, ¼ teaspoon salt, a pint jar
Pour cream into jar and seal it.
Shake until butter appears.
Pour off bluish milk.
Place butter in a bowl and add salt.
Add a few ice cubes and water; work with spoon to remove milk.
Pour off water and mold butter into a block.

Chart 23

WASHING, CARDING, AND SPINNING WOOL

Materials: wool sheared from a sheep, soap, pair of cards for carding
Wash wool in soapy lukewarm water, rinse it, and dry it.
Place a small amount of wool on one card and draw other card over it.
Continue carding until fibers are separated into slivers.
Shape slivers into a fluffy roll by rolling them between back of cards.
Stretch and twist the roll into yarn for weaving.

Chart 24

DIPPING CANDLES

Materials: 3 lbs. tallow, candle wick cut into 7" lengths, 2 tall cans

Chop tallow into small pieces and fry out grease.

Pour grease into one can and keep it hot.

Pour water into other can.

Dip wicking into grease and then into water.

Repeat dipping until the candle is the desired size.

Chart 25

MAKING APPLE LEATHER

Peel some apples and cook them in water.
After apples are cooked to a mush, spread them on a cloth to dry.
Let them stand for a day or two.

Chart 26

MAKING PUMPKIN RINGS

Cut a pumpkin crosswise into halves.
Remove seeds and cut rings ½ inch thick.
Place rings on a pole to dry.
Put small ends and pieces on a string to dry.

Chart 27

MAKING PUMPKIN LEATHER

Peel small pieces from the pumpkin.
Cook the pieces in water.
Stir until water is cooked out and mixture is thick.
Spread the cooked peelings on a board to dry.

Chart 28

The home. Making popcorn, applesauce, and cornstarch pudding; decorations and clay dishes

The dairy farm. Churning butter and making cottage cheese

Mexico. Drying corn and peppers, grinding corn with a metate, making candles, carding and spinning wool, making pottery, weaving, preparing and using natural dyes, cooking Mexican foods, making adobe bricks, making sombreros, serapes, and rebosos

CONSTRUCTION AND PROCESSING ACTIVITIES CHECKLIST

Teacher Preplanning

_____What needs for construction and processing activities have arisen in the unit of instruction?

_____Are working space and storage facilities available?

_____Are tools and materials in easily accessible places and arranged to avoid congestion and to promote effective utilization?

_____Are models, pictures, illustrations, and charts available for use in clarifying procedures?

_____What work standards are needed to guide the use of tools, materials, and space?

_____What activities should be provided for those who will not be involved in construction or processing activities?

_____What activities can be carried out successfully at home? Which should be completed in the classroom?

Group Planning

_____Are purposes clarified so that each child knows what to do?

_____Are plans made regarding use of space?

_____Is help given on individual problems and questions?

_____Is attention given to needed materials and where to obtain them?

_____Are questions answered regarding the correct use of tools and materials?

_____Are responsibilities discussed and assigned regarding the clean-up period?

During the Activity

_____Is each child proceeding with his work?

_____Are tools being used safely and correctly?

_____Are materials being used wisely?

_____Do the children's informal conversations and comments show that related concepts are being used accurately?

_____Is initiative shown in raising questions, giving and asking for assistance, and helping others?

_____Are effective work habits being used?

_____Is the teacher moving about and giving assistance?

_____Is the teacher making notes for use in evaluation?

_____Do the children stop promptly when the signal is given for clean-up time?

_____Is the clean-up period handled efficiently?

Group Evaluation

_____Is evaluation concerned with the children's purposes and problems?

_____Are teacher-noted needs injected at appropriate points and related to children's comments and questions?

_____Is help given on individual questions?

_____Are needs established as to next steps, needed information, and related number and communication skills?

_____Are sources of needed information considered?

_____Is consideration given to authenticity, and to deviations from authenticity?

_____Are charts or other records made of needs for materials, tools, work standards, or directions?

Checklist 5

China. Cooking rice, Chinese cabbage, and bean curd, making tea, raising silkworms, reeling silk from cocoons, making paper, ink, and block prints

Colonial and pioneer life. Weaving and quilting, dipping and molding candles, tanning hides, making soap, rippling, retting, curing, breaking, scutching, heckling, and spinning flax; carding and spinning wool, knitting, making a quilt, making dyes; drying apples, making salt, making brooms and brushes, making clothing

Communication. Making and using ink, paper, parchment, clay tablets, papyrus, and simple books

The planning and guiding of construction and processing activities are similar in many ways to the planning and guiding of study trips, dramatic activities, and other "doing" activities in the social studies. Four basic steps are involved: (1) preplanning by the teacher, (2) planning with the class, (3) providing guidance during the activity, and (4) evaluating progress after the activity. Checklist 5 on page 515 includes specific points to check during each step.

Questions, Activities, Evaluation

1. Locate and list poems, stories, and other literary selections that you might use in a unit of instruction you are planing.

2. Which forms of dramatic representation discussed in this chapter do you believe most useful in the social studies? Indicate specific ways in which you might use each form.

3. Review two or three music books for children and note songs, rhythms, listening activities, and instrumental activities that you might use in a unit. Make a brief plan to show how you might provide for creative expression and for investigative activities in a unit.

4. Review the checklist of art activities and indicate specific ways in which you might use each major type in a unit. Note the materials that should be provided for each activity.

5. Select two construction activities and note how you might use them in a unit.

6. Select two processing activities and note how you might use them in a unit.

7. Review the charts presented in this chapter and modify them for use in a unit you are planning.

References

Andrews, Gladys, *Creative Rhythmic Movement for Children.* Englewood Cliffs, N.J.: Prentice-Hall, Inc., 1954. Practical suggestions on rhythmic expression in the elementary school.

Brown, James W., Richard B. Lewis, and Fred F. Harcleroad, *A-V Instruction.* New York: McGraw-Hill Book Company, Inc., 1964. Sections on constructing and dramatizing.

Brown, Ralph A., "Biography in the Social Studies," *Social Studies in Elementary Schools*, 32nd Yearbook, National Council for the Social Studies, pp. 243–55. Washington, D.C.: National Education Association, 1962. Principles and procedures for enriching instruction by using biography.

Erdt, Margaret H., *Teaching Art in the Elementary School*, rev. ed. New York: Holt, Rinehart & Winston, Inc., 1962. Suggestions for use in providing a variety of art activities.

Garretson, Robert L., *Music in Childhood Education.* New York: Appleton-Century-Crofts, Inc., 1966. Techniques for different musical experiences.

Hanna, Lavone A., Gladys L. Potter, and Neva Hagaman, *Unit Teaching in the Elementary School.* New York: Holt, Rinehart & Winston, Inc., 1963. Examples of dramatization, construction, and esthetic expression in units.

Horn, Ernest, *Methods of Instruction in the Social Studies.* New York: Charles Scribner's Sons, 1937. A classic statement of fundamental principles and procedures.

Jarolimek, John, *Social Studies in Elementary Education*, Ch. XV, "Extending Social Studies Understandings Through Activities." New York: The Macmillan Company, 1967. Suggested enrichment activities.

Krone, Beatrice, and Kurt Miller, *Help Yourselves to Music.* San Francisco: Chandler Publishing Co., 1959. A handbook of procedures for teaching music activities.

McFee, June K., *Preparation for Art.* Belmont, Calif.: Wadsworth Publishing Co., Inc., 1961. A discussion of art in anthropological perspective and a presentation of teaching techniques.

McKee, Paul, *Reading: A Program of Instruction for the Elementary School.* Boston: Houghton Mifflin Company, 1966. Guidelines of experiences in literature.

Nye, Vernice T., R.E. Nye, and H.V. Nye. *Toward World Understanding with Song.* Belmont, Calif.: Wadsworth, 1967. Songs for use in units of study.

Preston, Ralph C., *Teaching Social Studies in the Elementary Schools*, rev. ed., Ch. XII, "Planning Creative Experiences." New York: Holt, Rinehart & Winston, Inc., 1958.

Rosen, Martha O., *Elementary School Economics Game.* Cambridge, Mass.: Abt Associates, 1966. Market game and economy game.

Russell, David H., *Children Learn to Read*, rev. ed., Ch. XIII, "Personal Growth through Reading and Literature." Boston: Ginn & Company, 1961.

Sagl, Helen L., "Dramatic Play: A Tool of Learning in Social Studies," *Social Studies in Elementary Schools*, 32nd Yearbook,

National Council for the Social Studies, pp. 205–12. Washington, D.C.: National Education Association, 1962. Suggestions for using dramatic play to improve learning in the social studies.

Shaftel, Fannie R., "Industrial Arts in the Social Studies Program," *Social Studies in Elementary Schools*, 32nd Yearbook, National Council for the Social Studies, pp. 212–18. Washington, D.C.: National Education Association, 1962. A discussion of the place of industrial arts in the social studies with emphasis on anthropological considerations.

————, and George Shaftel, *Role-Playing for Social Values*. Englewood Cliffs, N.J.: Prentice-Hall, Inc., 1967. Guidelines for expressing values through role-playing.

Taba, Hilda, and Deborah Elkins, *Teaching Strategies for the Culturally Disadvantaged*. Chicago: Rand McNally & Co., 1966. Suggestions for creative as well as other learning experiences.

Tiegs, Ernest W., and Fay Adams, *Teaching the Social Studies*, Ch. XIV, "Contributions of Other Curriculum Areas." Boston: Ginn & Company, 1959.

Tooze, Ruth, *Storytelling*. Englewood Cliffs, N.J.: Prentice-Hall, Inc., 1959. Techniques for storytelling, and a bibliography that includes stories about peoples in different lands.

————, and Beatrice P. Krone, *Literature and Music as Resources for Social Studies*. Englewood Cliffs, N.J.: Prentice-Hall, Inc., 1955. Examples of literature and music in units of instruction.

Torrance, E. Paul, *Guiding Creative Talent*, Ch. VIII, "Goals for Guiding Creative Talent." Englewood Cliffs, N.J.: Prentice-Hall, Inc., 1962.

Evaluation

Evaluation is the process of determining the extent to which objectives have been achieved. It includes all of the procedures used by the teacher, children, principal, and other school personnel to appraise outcomes of instruction, and it involves such steps as (1) formulating goals as behaviors, (2) securing evidence on the achievement of goals in selected situations, (3) summarizing and recording evidence, (4) interpreting evidence, and (5) using interpretations to improve instruction.

Evaluation has many functions as a part of the social studies program. Objectives can be clarified and redefined as a result of the appraisal of children's learning. Through evaluation, teachers gain insights into children's progress, problems, strengths, and weaknesses. Evaluative evidence is helpful in planning units, guiding learning activities, selecting materials of instruction, appraising methods of teaching, and revising the instructional program. Feelings of security for both the teacher and children can be enhanced if results are used constructively to strengthen the program. Finally, evaluation is essential in gathering evidence needed to interpret and report the child's progress to parents, and in carrying out the community public relations program.

Guidelines to Effective Evaluation

Evaluation should be based on several guiding principles, which serve as a framework for effective development and use of evaluative devices in all aspects of appraisal. They may be used in

519

guiding self-evaluation, in teacher appraisal of classroom experiences, and in appraising the overall effectiveness of the program.

Evaluation should be based on a cooperatively developed point of view. Teachers occupy a key position in evaluation, since their point of view, methods of teaching, knowledge of children's growth characteristics, selection of materials, and ability to make intelligent judgments in the light of democratic values determine the quality of evaluation.

Teachers must be aware of the point of view that they use in evaluation, since values determine the emphasis given to appraisal of learning experiences. Consider the case of two teachers attempting to foster self-evaluation in children. Both of them used charts, examples of which follow, to guide the evaluation of discussion.

One teacher developed Chart 2 cooperatively with the class on the basis of needs that had arisen; the other imposed Chart 1 on the class, using it as an admonition to work harder. One teacher conceived evaluation as being part of the instructional program; the other saw it as a tool to secure obedience. One viewed it as being cooperative, the other as teacher-dominated. Thus, each teacher's point of view brought about a vastly different type of evaluation.

GOOD WORKERS
Answer all questions.
Check work for errors.
Hand in work on time.

Chart 1

WORKING TOGETHER
1. Help in group planning.
2. Carry out group plans.
3. Use many sources of ideas.

Chart 2

Evaluation is an integral part of instruction. Appraisal cannot be separated from instruction in the classroom. The alert teacher observes and notes children's needs, and makes changes to improve the program as it is being developed in the classroom. Some of the most valuable evaluative procedures, such as group discussion, observation by the teacher, making charts on group standards, and using checklists, are part of instructional procedures.

Evaluation is a continuing process. This principle flows from the one immediately preceding and suggests that effective evaluation is always going on in the classroom. This means simply that throughout the day, from day to day, and from week to week throughout the year, constant and continuous appraisals must be made, both by the children and the teacher. This guideline clearly implies that evaluation is not something that is done just before the report cards are given out.

This principle does not imply that periodic summaries and scheduled testing have no place in evaluation. As a comprehensive picture of a child's development is being built up, many different devices should be used at stated intervals. For example, checklists and tests are used in some school systems at stated intervals to evaluate growth in concepts and attitudes. Periodic summaries are used in reporting to parents, in summarizing the work of a term or year, and in counseling and guiding students.

Evaluation is a cooperative process. Evaluation must be cooperatively done with other teachers, the children, parents, supervisors, and administrators. All have a stake in the program. The teacher and the children share in the clarification of purposes and in the use of various techniques of evaluation. Group evaluation and many types of self-evaluation are based on group-made standards and goals. Parents should be involved in the discussion of goals, the clarification of goals in terms of the hopes they have for their children, and the interpretation of information gleaned through the use of evaluative instruments. Supervisors and administrative officers cooperate in the program in order to give it balance, direction, and systematic consideration.

Evaluation is made in terms of the purposes of the program. The central function of evaluation is to determine the extent to which established goals are achieved. In appraisal by the teacher and in self-evaluation by children, goals must be clearly defined. Attention must be given to attitudes, concepts, methods of inquiry, utilization of skills, and growth in interests, and not solely to facts and information. All outcomes—cognitive and affective —must be evaluated.

Evaluation is facilitated if goals are defined behaviorally. Theoretical and lofty statements of purposes provide little direction for sound evaluation. By stating purposes in terms of behavior, one obtains a clear grasp of the meaning involved. For example, *responsibility* may be appraised specifically and concretely when defined as follows:

1. Helps in planning ways to investigate problems.
2. Engages in both individual and group inquiry.

3. Uses a variety of sources of information.
4. Organizes ideas for presentation to others.
5. Participates in individual and group evaluation.

Such a statement enables a teacher to do down-to-earth appraisal in getting at such questions as: What experiences are most effective in developing this type of behavior? Which children are developing these aspects of behavior? Which children need help? What situations should be provided?

Evaluation is made in a variety of situations. Children's growth in attitudes, interests, concepts, and group action skill can be appraised in group planning, discussion, sharing, reporting, and evaluation. Behavior in dramatic activities, construction, rhythms, and dancing reveals many evidences of growth. The ways in which children use materials, share materials with others, take and give suggestions, accept newcomers, and work together are of special importance. These and other situations should be used to determine whether key learnings are carrying through into a variety of situations.

Creative efforts of children also reveal evidence of learning. A teacher should be alert to new ideas, new ways of doing things, originality in construction, dramatic play, and artistic expression, and suggestions that arise in group discussion. These are excellent clues to intellectual development.

Use is made of a variety of devices and procedures. If all outcomes are to be appraised, then many different instruments and techniques are needed. For example, checklists can be designed to appraise cooperation, discussion, and use of materials. Tests are available for measuring concepts, information, and study skills. Anecdotal records, charts, rating scales, and other devices can be used as special needs arise. The following list contains the devices in use in many school systems at the present time.

Directed observation	Logs	Case studies
Informal observation	Diaries	Activity records
Group discussion	Autobiographies	Tape recordings
Small-group interview	Scrapbooks	Cumulative records
Individual interview	Collections	Pupil graphs
Case conference	Samples of work	Profiles
Checklists	Teacher-made tests	Sociograms
Rating scales	Group-made tests	Flow-of-discussion
Inventories	Standardized tests	charts
Questionnaires	Sociometric tests	Behavior journals
Charts	Anecdotal records	Evaluative criteria

The selection of evaluative devices depends on the goal being evaluated, the conditions under which children are working, and the type of behavior involved. If appraisals are needed on the behavioral level, direct observation may be used. Thus, if a teacher desires insight into the use of concepts, attitudes, or group processes, the children should be observed in discussion, dramatic play, construction, or similar situations in which concepts and attitudes are being used. The ways in which children use concepts and attitudes may be recorded in anecdotal records, a behavior journal, or a specially prepared recording form. If, on the other hand, a teacher must determine the accuracy of concepts or the attitudes of children toward certain objects or persons, he may use a simple concept test or attitude questionnaire.

This is not to imply that a single device should be used exclusively to evaluate a given purpose. Observation may be used continuously even though checklists, ratings, or tests are employed. A combination of devices is generally better than a single device. The important point is to decide on the kind of evidence needed, and then to select and use those devices that will secure it. For example, in a social studies workshop directed by the author, one group proposed the following for evaluating various outcomes, recognizing that others might be added to each category as special needs arose:

Critical Thinking. Tests, observation, group discussion, checklists, charts

Attitudes. Questionnaires, checklists, scale of beliefs, observation, anecdotal records, recordings, discussion, individual interviews

Interests. Observation, diaries and logs, interest inventories and checklists, questionnaires, records of activities and use of leisure time

Concepts and Generalizations. Observation of use, group discussion, tests, samples of written work

Work-Study Skills. Samples of work, tests, observation of use, checklists, charts, group discussion, interviews

Functional Information. Tests, charts, discussion, observation, samples of work

Group Processes. Observation, group discussion, charts, checklists, sociograms

As far as possible, evaluative instruments selected for use in the social studies should meet the following criteria:

Validity. Measure what they purport to measure.

Reliability. Measure consistently and accurately.

Objectivity. Give similar results even though used by different persons.

Practicality. Easy to administer and do not require the expenditure of unreasonable amounts of time and money.

Relatedness. Related to the social studies program (sometimes referred to as curricular validity).

Usefulness. Contribute evidence which can be put to use.

Appropriateness. Related to the level of development of the group with which they will be used and fit into the overall program of evaluation.

Descriptiveness. Give evidence that describes the behavior of children.

Self-evaluation by children is essential. Self-evaluation leading to increasing self-direction is an essential aspect of evaluation in the social studies. It is a mode of appraisal used throughout life. Through self-evaluation, children gain increasing ability in analyzing their own skills, attitudes, behavior, strengths, needs, and success in achieving purposes. They develop feelings of personal responsibility as they appraise the effectiveness of individual and group efforts. They learn how to face squarely the competences needed in various tasks and to assess their own potentialities and contributions. Their role in group processes can be clarified as they check themselves on cooperatively made criteria. Social learning is sharpened and enriched through self-evaluation because the child himself is participating more extensively in the learning process.

If children are to be capable of self-evaluation, they must be guided in the development of a clear conception of purposes to guide their evaluative efforts. This may be done through group discussion based on needs that are significant to the group. Attention also must be given to the preparation of checklists, charts, and rating devices that children can use. This is an essential aspect of self-evaluation, because children must understand the evaluation devices they use, or little value will be derived from their use.

Types of devices commonly used to promote self-evaluation by children include the following:

Group discussions and interviews
Samples of the child's work gathered through the term
Standards developed by the group and placed on charts
Checklists made by the individual or group
Scrapbooks made by each child

Diaries or logs containing examples of ways in which the child
has been cooperative, shown concern for others, and so forth

Recordings of discussion, reporting, singing, and so forth

Graphs kept by each child

Evaluative data are organized to facilitate interpretation. Considerable care must be given to the interpretation of data gathered
through evaluation. A large number of factors must be considered,
since single measures have little meaning. For example, data
obtained by means of anecdotal records and checklists have much
greater value when the child's mental status, level of achievement,
previous difficulties, and home background are known. Because
no one measure is adequate to appraise social learning, each bit
of data should become a part of a more complete picture of the
child's development.

Information should be summarized in a form that can be most
easily interpreted; the form, depending on its purpose, may vary.
If a picture of the status of children in a class is needed, a list
may be prepared giving each pupil's name with related data
summarized in tabular form. If information on attitudes or interests is needed on a child, a simple profile may be developed.
In other instances, graphs, charts, summaries of anecdotes, sociograms, or a complete case study may be used. In addition, a
cumulative record should be kept for each child in order to develop a composite picture of his growth.

Included in the cumulative record should be space to record
information about units of instruction the child has completed,
growth in problem-solving ability, social attitudes, democratic
behavior, skill in group work, interest in the social studies, and
types of activity in which he shows strengths and types in
which he needs help. When such information is included, subsequent teachers can make more effective plans for the child's
continuous growth.

*Interpretation of evaluative data is made in terms of each
child's development.* Each child has his own rate of growth and
development. His uniqueness, personality, background, level of
achievement, interests, problems, and needs must be reckoned
with in all phases of evaluation. A child's growth to increasingly
higher levels of behavior (not merely his status in the group
or his position with reference to national norms) should be the
concern of each teacher. Arbitrary standards for all children are
unrealistic and impractical.

Norms are helpful, however, as a frame of reference for considering the achievement of an individual or of a group. If a bright child falls far below the average, the reason for the deviation should be studied. If a group "deviates from the norm," the reasons for the deviation should be investigated. In all instances, the first question is, Why do deviations exist? not, What shall we do to get them up to the norm? After the reasons for the deviations are determined and needs of the child, or group, are established, steps can be taken to provide those learning experiences most significant to the individual or the group.

Evaluative data are put to use. Data gathered by the teacher or by the children through self-evaluation should be used to improve learning experiences. Group evaluation in the classroom should reveal next steps, needs for materials, new sources of ideas, and improved standards of work. Overall evaluation of the effectiveness of the program should lead to clarification of goals and improved use of methods, materials, and evaluative techniques. Conferences with parents and interpretation of the program are other illustrative uses of evaluative data. Evaluation that does not lead to improvement is of little value. It is just another form of busywork.

Techniques of Evaluation

OBSERVATION BY THE TEACHER

No technique of evaluation is more common in the elementary school than observation by the teacher. Day-to-day observation of children gives a developmental picture of growth that cannot be obtained in any other way. It is especially effective in the social studies because of the varied types of experiences provided in the program. Children themselves create new and different situations (such as forming groups, meeting new problems, and locating new sources of information) in which learning may be observed. A teacher may create other situations in which specific concepts, attitudes, and skills may be observed; their carryover to out-of-school enterprises also may be noted. The actual behavior of children in new situations—the goal of the experienced evaluator—thus becomes the focal point of evaluation.

Possible uses of observation for evaluative purposes are as varied and numerous as the types of experiences provided in the social studies. A teacher may obtain evaluative data by listening to discussions, oral reading, dramatic play, comments about objects or persons, questions, and spontaneous expression during construction or on study trips. By watching children at work and at play, data may be obtained regarding interests, attitudes, concern for others, group processes, use of time and materials, use of skills, physical ability, emotional adjustment, attentiveness, persistence, ability to carry out directions, and acceptance of responsibility. No evaluative technique offers as many immediate and practical applications as does directed observation.

In using observation as an evaluative device, teachers must recognize the fact that similar types of behavior may reveal different kinds of learning. Different purposes, needs, and backgrounds produce different responses. One child may work industriously when a problem arises because he grasps its significance, whereas another may do so because he fears the consequences of not working industriously. Some children offer to help others because they are growing in cooperative skills, while others offer help because they want to "move in on" another's activity. Some children may accept one responsibility eagerly to avoid another more important one, whereas some accept it because it is in line with significant purposes. A teacher can gain competence in meeting these problems by knowing each child's background and by becoming a skillful observer.

Checklists are helpful guides to observation. They should be specific, descriptive of desirable behavior, and easy to use. They may be used as an overall guide in many situations, or they may be applied specifically to the child's behavior in planning, discussion, research, or construction. Checklists 1 and 2 are illustrative; others are presented in later sections of this chapter.

Needs for charts, rating devices, and other evaluative instruments which children can use in self-evaluation may be discovered through teacher observation. For example, after noting specific needs and problems in a discussion, one teacher guided the class in the development of a chart that listed these points:

1. Stick to the topic.
2. Be brief so that others may have a turn.
3. Speak so all can hear.
4. Give turns to others.
5. Listen to others.

The effectiveness of observation as an evaluative device may be improved by the use of the following guidelines. Others should be added as skill is gained in observational techniques.

1. Notice little things that may have great value in understanding the child's behavior.
2. Be alert to the uniqueness of each child and to his creative contributions.

APPRAISAL OF STUDY HABITS AND ATTITUDES DURING RESEARCH PERIODS								
	Names of Children							
Behavior to Be Observed								
Locates sources of information								
Uses the table of contents								
Uses the index								
Gets information from study aids— charts, tables, maps								
Uses encyclopedias effectively								
Uses dictionaries effectively								
Uses library facilities								
Takes notes related to topics under study								
Uses correct form in outlines								
Organizes information from several sources								
Arranges ideas in good order								
Selects illustrative material for reports								

Checklist 1

3. Look for constructive, improved behavior; avoid fault-finding.

4. Do not assume that similar expressions of behavior indicate the same learning for all children.

5. Be aware of your own feelings and prejudices.

6. Be sensitive to the halo effect, since some characteristics may not be related to others.

7. Develop and use specific observational guides to appraise specific aspects of behavior.

8. Make necessary records while the data is fresh in mind.

CONCERN FOR OTHERS								
Note: Check each child two or three times during the term to determine if growth has taken place.		School _____ Date _____						
Behavior to Be Observed	Names of Children							
Is sensitive to needs and problems of others								
Helps others meet needs and solve problems								
Willingly shares ideas and materials								
Accepts suggestions and help								
Makes constructive suggestions								
Sticks to group plans and decisions								
Works courteously and happily with others								
Gives encouragement to others								
Respects the property of others								
Enjoys group work								
Thanks others for help								
Commends others for contributions								

Checklist 2

9. Record what actually happened, not your reaction to it.

10. Use observation to secure evidence on many different types of learning, not on conduct alone.

GROUP DISCUSSION

In social studies programs, extensive use is made of group discussions in which children evaluate work periods, study skills, research activities, and specific problems as they arise. Each member of the group can participate, charts and checklists can be developed, attention can be given to problems as they arise, specific instances of behavior can be considered, and cooperative and continuous appraisal can be carried on. The essence of group evaluative discussion is constructive consideration of needs and problems of the group. Emphasis should be given to contributions of individuals and committees. Negative comments should be tactfully redirected toward constructive suggestions for improvement. Attention should be focused on the job to be done, ways to help each other, and next steps that should be taken to achieve stated goals. (For specific techniques, see Chapter 8.)

Many teachers raise specific questions during discussion when various learnings are being evaluated. Clues as to types of questions to raise may be noted as children engage in research activities, use the library, work in committees, use audio-visual resources, engage in dramatic play and construction, or participate in other activities. *How* and *why* questions, which bring children's thinking to bear on causes, effects, and reasons involved in various situations should be used as well as *what, when,* and *where* questions. Questions should be directly related to major purposes of the unit currently underway. In the primary grades, for example, questions related to home, school, and community might include the following: How do we share at home? What jobs (responsibilities) do children, parents, and community workers have? Who helps us get library books? Or, in later grades when appraising skills in problem solving: Where can we find out about this? How shall we share what we find out? Why must all ideas be considered? How shall we put our ideas to use? Or, when evaluating map-reading skills: How can we use the scale of miles? How can we find rivers, lakes, and highlands? Questions such as these reveal quickly and easily which children are grasping key ideas; they also indicate points of emphasis for the teacher. They make evaluation a part of the instructional program—*as it should be.*

Also helpful, particularly in small-group discussions, are questions involving what comes next and what is missing. Questions of this type may be used to assess a child's ability to grasp the wholeness of a situation, to predict outcomes, to use ideas to solve problems, and to identify himself with others. For example:

1. Cover part of a mural, map, picture, exhibit, chart, diagram, or collection and ask, What is covered? or, What is missing?

2. Remove an object from an exhibit, a part of a jigsaw map, or a part of a model and ask, What is missing?

3. Give incomplete directions for making something, going somewhere, using something, conducting a meeting, or introducing someone, and ask, What is missing?

4. Cover part of a time line, or do part of a demonstration and ask, What comes next?

5. Tell part of an incident or a story and ask, What comes next?

6. Show several pictures in sequence and ask, What comes next?

Another technique which may be used as a part of discussion, or at least may be introduced during discussion, involves the arranging of objects or ideas in sequence or in proper order. For, example, consider the following activities:

1. Show a set of pictures, or cards with phrases or sentences, and have children arrange them in order.

2. Show pictures that belong in a scene (for example, airport, farm, stockade) and have children arrange them in relative position.

3. Have children put together, in proper position, parts of maps or large pictures which have been cut to show key ideas, such as relative location, relative size, and distance.

4. Have children arrange a floor layout of the community, a farm, or airport.

The discussion that follows such activities is often as revealing of what children have learned as is the manner in which they carry out the activities.

Not to be overlooked as a good source of evaluative data are unstructured or free discussions in which children talk over problems and questions of individual and group concern which come up with a minimum of teacher guidance. In such discussion, children usually reveal attitudes toward others, concepts, erroneous ideas, reasoning ability, individual needs, and the ability to participate in group work. Clues gained through careful observation of children in informal discussions can be put to use in planning experiences to improve attitudes, to clarify concepts, or to meet other needs.

CHARTS AND CHECKLISTS

Charts are especially helpful in individual and group self-evaluation. They should be cooperatively developed by the group so that clear understanding of their meaning and use will be had by each member of the class. They can be referred to by individuals in the group or used in group discussions in which specific items are being evaluated. (Because many examples of charts are given throughout the text, it is unnecessary to include any here.)

Checklists are very helpful in evaluating many aspects of social learning. Specific behavior, interests, skills, and concepts have been appraised by means of checklists. Some are designed for use by teachers; others are used by the children themselves for self-evaluation. Some are used in group work; others are

---

Name: _____   Date: _____

School: _____   City: _____

WORKING WELL WITH OTHERS

How do you work with other students in making plans, discussing problems, making things, looking up ideas, and using materials? All of us need to check ourselves to see if we are doing those things that improve the work of the group. By checking ourselves, we can learn things to do to improve group work. Each person needs to know his good points and shortcomings and to consider things to do to improve himself. Read the statements below and place a check in the square that tells how often you do each item in the list.

How Often Do You Do Each Item Listed Below?	Always	Usually	Sometimes	Never	?
1. I stick to the job until it is finished.					
2. I take part in many different activities.					
3. I work with everyone in the class.					
4. I am eager to try out new ideas and to work on new problems.					
5. I share materials with others.					
6. I help set up plans and directions and follow them.					
7. I work happily without grumbling or losing my temper.					
8. I give in if my ideas conflict with the best interests of the group.					
9. I consider the rights of others.					
10. I am courteous and use good manners.					

Checklist 3

used by each individual in the group. Many checklists are made by the teacher to meet specific needs of the group, whereas others are planned cooperatively by the class.

Checklists 3–5 included in this section provide practical illustrations of devices that can be developed in social studies classes.

HOW DO I WORK?		
1. Do my own job?	Yes	No
2. Finish each job?	Yes	No
3. Follow directions?	Yes	No
4. Listen attentively?	Yes	No
5. Return materials?	Yes	No
6. Clean up properly?	Yes	No

Checklist 4

AM I COURTEOUS?		
1. Listen to others?	Yes	No
2. Take turns?	Yes	No
3. Share materials?	Yes	No
4. Express thanks?	Yes	No
5. Return materials?	Yes	No
6. Work quietly?	Yes	No

Checklist 5

INTERVIEWS

Both formal and informal interviews are helpful in appraising learning. Informal interviews are helpful in talking over immediate problems, determining difficulties, and clarifying group standards and procedures. Formal interviews ordinarily involve the use of checklists, lists of questions, or rating scales, and are carefully planned ahead of time. In either type of interview, the teacher should aim to achieve and maintain rapport, be a good listener, guide the interview so that the purpose is achieved, and maintain a sympathetic attitude so that tensions are not created. Written records of interviews are helpful because they can be added to the child's cumulative record, and thus give a more descriptive picture of his growth.

LOGS AND DIARIES

Both individual and group diaries or logs can be used for evaluation of learning. The group-made log contains material dictated by the class, much of it growing out of group planning and evaluation. The individual log is kept by each child and is a record of his activities, such as cooperation, acceptance of responsibility, work completed, or books read. Many teachers have group discussions regarding the items to be kept in individual logs; also helpful is the sharing of ideas as the logs are being written. Pictorial logs are usually made in primary grades in order to avoid the use of writing, spelling, and composition skills that have not yet been developed.

QUESTIONNAIRES AND INVENTORIES

Questionnaires and inventories are helpful in determining interests, hobbies, attitudes, home background, and other items about individual children. Many teachers make and use informal inventories and questionnaires to meet specific needs as they arise in class.

PEOPLE FROM MEXICO			
Check Each of the Following:	Agree	Disagree	Not Sure
1. People from Mexico are hard workers.			
2. It is fun to listen to Mexican music.			
3. Drawings and paintings from Mexico are beautiful.			
4. Many intelligent people live in Mexico.			

Checklist 6

INTERESTS IN TRANSPORTATION			
Do You Like to Do the Following?	Like	Do Not Like	Not Sure
1. To make model planes?			
2. To play with planes?			
3. To talk about planes with friends?			
4. To read stories about pilots			
5. To visit the airport?			
6. To ride on planes?			
7. To make boats?			
8. To read stories about seamen?			
9. To visit the railroad yards?			

Checklist 7

Checklists 6 and 7 illustrate types that can be made by teachers themselves.

ANECDOTAL RECORDS

Anecdotal records are brief sketches of specific instances of behavior. Figure 17-8 is an excerpt from a behavioral journal; it concerns a child who was being given help in working with others.

Because anecdotal records are time consuming to make, every effort should be made to simplify the procedures involved in making them. Some teachers simply keep a page headed by each child's name, making entries during the day or after school. Others simply make brief notes as incidents arise, and drop them in a folder which has been prepared for each child. Records should be limited to three or four aspects of behavior on which evidence of growth is needed and that cannot be recorded in other ways. Anecdotes are most valuable when specific instances, such as those listed above, are recorded. Of little value are such general comments as, "Paul cooperated with Mary," or "Peter was unkind in his manner."

BEHAVIOR JOURNAL

Name: Walter Doe   Class: Miss Smith   Grade: IV

Date	Incidents	Comments
9–21 10–2 10–19 11–2	Did not share the picture with others. Helped to make rules for using materials; shared only a few tools. Discussed need for sharing with others. Worked with David in preparing a report.	Needs help in carrying out standards. Group chart may help. Seems to understand reason for sharing; needs to work with one or two children. Growth in evidence; must place in a group of three or four as a next step.

Checklist 8

CASE STUDIES AND CASE CONFERENCES

Some teachers make a simplified case study of one or two children each year. Pertinent information on such items as home background and previous school experience, and health records, anecdotal records, and data from tests are brought together and analyzed. Such a procedure gives a more complete understanding of a child's growth and has great value for the improvement of guidance and teaching. However, a teacher can make only one or two each year because of the time required.

Case conferences are helpful in analyzing and interpreting the information regarding a child's development. In a case conference, all available evidence is considered by the child's teacher, former teacher or teachers, the principal, and guidance workers. The pooled judgment of several individuals is thereby brought to bear on specific questions and problems. To be successful, all data about the child should be carefully organized in a form that is easy to use. Descriptive information such as that secured by means of interviews and anecdotal records is needed in addition to test scores.

Making and Using Tests

Three kinds of tests are used in social studies programs. These are teacher-made tests, teacher-pupil made tests, and standardized tests. All of them have a place in a complete program of evaluation, provided that they are selected or constructed in accordance with the needs of the children and the purposes of the program.

TEACHER-MADE TESTS

Teacher-made tests are commonly used to determine a child's skills, needs, strengths, background of information, and grasp of concepts. The tests facilitate planning, grouping, and specific evaluation of various topics in the program. If they are geared to the ideas and problems that arise in a unit, they become an integral part of instruction. Tests made by a teacher are meaningful from a child's point of view and valuable from a teacher's point of view because they are designed to fit a particular program.

The forms of test items commonly used in informal objective tests are *multiple choice, matching, simple recall, completion,* and *alternative response.* Each of these forms is discussed in detail in the next section in this chapter.

Essay tests are also used in the social studies, particularly in the upper grades when children are mature enough to express themselves by writing responses to essay questions. Essay tests are helpful in obtaining evidence on attitudes, controversial issues, ability to interpret data, ability to organize and summarize ideas, application of principles, and ability to describe events, persons, and places. The element of free response in them frequently gives clues not secured by objective devices. They should not be too broad in scope nor used to test information alone. Each question should be phrased so that children will know exactly what is expected of them. For example, the question: How did the Pioneers live in Boonesboro? is too general. A better question is: How did the Pioneers in Boonesboro obtain food? In general, essay questions should only be used when children will not experience undue difficulty in handling the writing, spelling, and composition skills involved in answering them. If they will experience great difficulty in writing out the answers, then the essay form of questions should be used in small-group discussion, or the essay question should be broken down into small units and objective test items prepared.

A valuable new type of test that can be prepared to measure children's ability to apply ideas and draw conclusions is the interpretive, situational, or problem-solving test. A situation, problem, or body of information is presented, and children are asked to indicate what they would do, to choose a proposed solution, or to make an interpretation. A sentence, paragraph, short selection, map, chart, or current event may be presented and followed by questions or statements in true-false, multiple-choice, or one of the other test item forms. Or, a teacher may present a problem orally, or read part of a story, and have the children respond to test items related to it. The following are illustrative:

1. A class was having a discussion on the duties of a committee chairman. Listed below are suggestions as made by different children. Make a + mark beside the suggestions which you think are good ones for the chairman to follow:

_____Get ideas from all members.
_____Tell each person what to do.
_____Ask others to accept his plan.
_____Urge everyone to do his best.
_____Ask members to stick to the topic.
_____Do most of the talking.

2. Children can be asked to study the scale of miles on a map in one of their textbooks, or in a desk atlas. This may be followed by such questions as:

How far is it in a straight line from New York to San Francisco? _____

How far is it from the northern boundary of California to the southern boundary? _____

If the ability to interpret and use the legend on a map is to be measured, test items can be made on different map symbols and colors. Or, if other phases of map reading are to be appraised, items can be made involving directions, size of states, location of cities, physical features, and other facts shown on maps.

When making situational or interpretive tests, teachers should be careful to present problems that are realistic and challenging to the group. The kind of situation that could be used as a topic for a discussion is usually satisfactory. In fact, some teachers base situational tests on topics which have been discussed by the group. By making notes on comments made by children during discussion, the teacher can obtain leads to plausible answers or responses to include in the test. A variety of item forms should be used. A discussion of different types and how to prepare them is presented in the following section.

WRITING TEST ITEMS

Teachers should keep several basic guidelines in mind when they prepare test items. Only the most significant learnings should be appraised. Trivial details, obvious answers, and material of little value should be avoided. Each item should be clearly worded and written on a level of difficulty appropriate to the group. Textbook wording should be avoided; if not, children will engage in rote memorization, and their ability to apply ideas and principles will not be measured. Items which provide an answer to other items should not be included. Also to be avoided are tricky questions and any item which does not have a definite answer. No clues or suggestions which can be used to figure out the correct answer to an item should be given. Directions should be clearly written, and space for responses should be arranged to facilitate the writing of answers and scoring. Items of each type should be grouped together in separate sections (*completion, true-false,* and the like), and an adequate range of difficulty should be included in each section.

In addition to the foregoing guidelines, specific points must be kept in mind for each form of item. A consideration is given next to the item forms most frequently used in the social studies.

Simple-recall items. Simple-recall items should be used to measure a child's ability to recall a specific name, place, concept, or date which is of sufficient importance to be memorized. A child must recall the appropriate response rather than identify it from a list of possible answers. Questions or statements involving *who, when, where, what, how many,* and *how much* can be presented in oral or written form to measure a variety of specific learnings as shown in the following examples:

What should we say when someone helps us? _____

Who helps us check out library books? _____

Which airport worker tells plans when to land? _____

What are the four major landforms?

_____   _____

_____   _____

Simple-recall items should be kept short. Questions are usually easier than statements to prepare and are more meaningful to a child. Adequate space should be provided at the right for the answers. The items should be written in such a way that there is only one correct response.

Completion Tests. The completion test is another form of recall; it may be either a sentence or a paragraph in which blanks are provided for children to fill with words, numbers, or phrases that complete the meaning. For example:

The president during the War of 1812 was (1)   1. _____

from the state of (2).   2. _____

Several points must be kept in mind if this type of item is to be used effectively in appraising learning in the social studies:

1. Omit only key words, phrases, or dates; avoid the omission of minor details, common words, or everyday expressions.
For example, "The pioneers ate much _____." Many different common words could be used here (food, meat, berries, and the like).

2. Use blanks of uniform size for all responses since children use variations as clues to answers.

3. Avoid textbook phrases and sentences. Use definite statements with omissions which call for only one correct response; if another response is found to be acceptable, give credit for it.

4. Avoid the use of *a* and *an* before a blank so that no clues will be given, for example, "Bill took an _____ from the fruit basket." Apple or orange are possibilities, but banana, pears, plum, or other fruit beginning with a consonant can be eliminated.

5. Avoid the omission of several words in any one statement; if too many words are omitted, one cannot get the meaning, for example, "Jamestown was _____ in the year _____ by _____." If used at all, this item should be written: "Jamestown was settled in the year _____."

6. Arrange the test so that answers can be written in spaces at the right as shown in the example at the beginning of this section.

Multiple-choice Tests. This type of item is used more frequently than any other type by professional test-makers. It consists of a question or incomplete statement (called the stem) followed by two or more responses. (The correct or best one is the answer, the others are distractors.) The usual procedure is to have children select the correct response from three to five choices. Variations on this procedure are: (1) select the best answer, (2) select the incorrect answer, and (3) select two or more correct answers.

In the primary grades, children should be asked to underline the correct or best answer so that no difficulty will arise in marking letters or numbers which designate answers.

Directions: Draw a line under the one word that makes the sentence true. Look at all four words and choose the best one. (A variation on this is: Draw a line through the incorrect words.)
1. Workers in sawmills make
   nails   bricks   plaster   lumber

In later grades, numbers or letters may be marked, or machine-scorable answer sheets may be used successfully with most children.

Directions: After each question are listed four words which might be used to answer the question. Only one of the words is correct or better than any of the others. Make a circle around the letter in front of the word you think is best.
1. From which country did the United States purchase the Louisiana Territory?
   A. England   B. Russia   C. Spain   D. France

If an answer column is provided at the right, the directions should indicate the marking procedure as follows:

Directions: One of the four numbered answers is the best for each exercise. Choose the one you think is best and write its number in the space at the left.
_____1. Which reference would you use to find the number of people born in Illinois last year?
   (1) an atlas
   (2) an encyclopedia

(3) an almanac
(4) a geography

The following suggestions have been found to be helpful in making multiple choice items:

1. Use them to check recognition and discrimination. Use the simple-recall form if the children should be expected to remember a given fact. Use the alternative-response form if there are only two possible answers.

2. Place the major portion of the statement in the introduction or stem, not in the possible answers. Make the stem clear and complete so that the nature of the answer will be known to the pupil. Avoid negative statements in the stem whenever possible; they tend to be confusing.

3. Be sure all possible answers are plausible; absurd options are quickly eliminated by children. Word the incorrect responses as carefully as the correct; make some of them about the same length as the correct response if more than one word is involved.

4. Avoid clues such as words or phrases in the introduction which also appear in the correct answer, or the placing of *a* or *an* at the end of the introduction when the options do not all begin with a vowel or consonant. For example, "A pictogram is an A. illustration B. narrative C. tool D. mural" can easily be answered by associating *an* with the option which begins with a vowel.

5. Phrase all choices so that they are grammatically correct when joined to the introduction; avoid choices that overlap or include each other, for example: Last year air travel increased A. less than 10%, B. less than 20%, C. more than 30%, D. more than 50%; place choices at the end of the item; distribute them evenly among answer positions; include at least four choices whenever possible; and keep all choices in the same category—that is, do not mix persons, places, or things.

6. Arrange the items in groups of five with a double space between groups. Group together items with the same number of choices, that is, do not mix three-choice and four-choice items.

Matching. Matching items are used to measure the ability to associate events and dates, events and persons, terms and definitions, principles and applications, tools and their uses, pictures and concepts, causes and effects, and the like. They should be used only when several pairs of items are sufficiently homogeneous to require a child to think critically in order to make proper associations.

Fairly simple matchings are used in the primary grades. For example, pictures of household objects such as a refrigerator, stove, or sweeper may be matched with words or phrases that describe each picture. Or parts of sentences or pairs of words may be matched as shown in the two following examples:

1. Draw a line between the two parts in each sentence that belong together.

The farmer keeps baby chickens	in a corral.
The farmer keeps horses	in a pen.
The farmer keeps pigs	in a brooder.

2. Draw a line from each worker to the word which tells what he uses.

carpenter	cement
electrician	lumber
mason	pipe
plumber	wire

Two basic varieties of matching used in later grades involve simple matching as shown in the first example and classification into categories as shown in the second example.

1. On the space before each of the duties, write the letter of the official responsible for it.

Duties	*Officials*
_____1. Collects taxes	A. Assessor
_____2. Determines the value of property	B. Clerk
	C. Judge
_____3. Keeps records	D. Sheriff
	E. Treasurer

2. On the space before each of the responsibilities, write the letter of the branch of government which carries it out.

Responsibilities	*Branches*
_____1. Makes laws	A. Executive
_____2. Interprets laws	B. Judicial
_____3. Enforces laws	C. Legislative
_____4. Appropriates money	
_____5. Prepares the budget	

Guessing is minimized in the first example above by providing a surplus of names in the second column; it is minimized in the second example by providing for the use of some responses more than once.

Another form of matching involves the use of maps, diagrams, or pictures, which have been lettered to show significant features.

For example, a map of the United States may be marked with large letters to show regions in which different types of production are carried on. The map is placed in the front of the room and children are asked to study it and then write the letters on spaces before matching questions such as the following:

_____1. Which area is noted for steel production?
_____2. Which area is noted for cotton production?

The following suggestions should be used when matching items are prepared:

1. Place related material in each matching exercise; do not mix men and events with other associations such as causes and effects.

2. Keep the number of items small (three to five); provide extra responses (two to three) in the second column, or permit certain responses to be used more than once in order to minimize guessing.

3. Arrange the items in the first column in random order; arrange those in the second column in alphabetical, chronological, or some other reasonable order.

4. Keep the columns close together and on the same page so that children will not become confused looking back and forth or turning the page to check matching pairs.

5. Use consistent form so that items in each column can be associated without difficulty. If parts of sentences are to be matched, be sure that no grammatical clues are introduced.

Alternative-response Tests. Items in this category may be written in several forms: true-false, yes-no, right-wrong, correct-incorrect, and two-option multiple choice. They may be dictated or presented in written form. Carefully constructed alternative-response items can be used to appraise interests, attitudes, misconceptions, superstitions, and understanding of principles and generalizations. They should be used when only two logical responses are possible, such as north or south, right or left, larger or smaller, and the like. Examples of several different forms follow:

1. (The true-false variety is simply a statement.)
   The area of Brazil is greater than the area of
   the United States.   T   F
2. (The yes-no variety consists of a question.) Do
   you have the right to break a rule made by

your class if you did not vote for it?   Y   N

3. (The cluster variety is a statement with several
completions.) Agriculture is profitable in the
south because:
1. many workers are available.   T   F
2. the land is mountainous.   T   F
3. there are many forests.   T   F
4. there is a long growing season.   T   F

Avoid items for which more than two plausible responses may be made, such as:

The pioneers came to Sutter's Fort on the Wilderness Trail.

The multiple choice form should be used in this instance since the Oregon Trail, Mohawk Trail, and California Trail could be used as other choices.

Alternative-response items may be used in a variety of ways. Places on a map can be marked by letters or numbers and children can be asked to write T or F in response to statements regarding what is grown, what conditions exist, and the like. Comprehension of a topic can be appraised in a similar way after children have read a selection, heard a report, or seen a film. More than mere knowledge can be tested by making items which require application of concepts, such as:

If Iowa were in a mountainous region, its corn crop would be larger.   T   F

The ability to make comparisons can be tested by such an item as:

Make a + beside each of the items found in Mexico and California:
_____oil   _____forests
_____gold   _____(and so forth)

The ability to read and interpret maps can be measured by preparing items based on textbook or wall maps.

New York is farther from San Francisco than from Shannon.   T   F

The ability to describe conditions or activities can be measured by such an item as:

Make a + beside each of the objects listed below which pioneers took on hunting trips:

____blankets   ____canned food

____kettles   ____(and so forth)

The following suggestions are recommended for use in making alternative-response items:

1. Include an equal number of true and false statements; be sure the true statements are not consistently longer than the false statements; arrange true and false items in random order.

2. Avoid the use of specific determiners, for example, items containing *alone, all, no, none, never, always* and the like are usually false, whereas items containing *generally, should, may* and the like are usually true.

3. Be sure each statement is definitely true or false; avoid ambiguous terms such as *few, many,* and *important.* Place the crucial element in the statement in the main part of the sentence, not in a phrase or subordinate clause. Avoid the use of double negatives.

4. Make each item short and specific. Avoid the use of unfamiliar or figurative language.

5. Simplify the marking of correct responses (and scoring) by placing T and F (or Y and N for *yes-no*) in a column at the right as shown in the examples above. For scoring, make a stencil (with holes punched in the position for correct responses) which can be placed over the answer column. If the items are dictated, or no answer column has been provided, instruct the children to write + for true and O for false, which are easier to score than T and F or + and −.

TEACHER-PUPIL MADE TESTS

Tests cooperatively made under the guidance of the teacher are valuable evaluative devices. Children gain increased appreciation of the reasons for testing, gain insight into the selection of key ideas, get practice in analyzing material, and grow in the ability to express themselves with precision. By helping to make tests, children also clarify purposes and see some of the relationships between the program and testing.

Tests designed by children should focus on specific problems in the unit. Each item should be accompanied by the answer and its source. Although the same rules of test construction that the teacher uses should be applied, reasonable expectancies must be set for each group. Children can be guided to see the importance of not copying items from the book, not using "giveaway" terms, and sticking to the topic. Major outcomes should be sharpened thinking, improved precision in expression, and improved self-evaluation and understanding of the topics being studied. The development of perfect test items is not the major purpose of constructing tests. Through group discussion after group-made tests have been given, suggestions and comments may be brought out that will lead to further improvement.

PREPARING ITEMS ON VARIOUS LEVELS

Questions and test items should be formulated on various levels of cognitive and affective response.[1] The following are illustrative of questions and items that can be used with beginning students.

LEVELS OF COGNITION

Knowledge: Which of these pictures shows goods that are produced at home? (Have children select or point to pictures you have selected.)
Make a line under each picture that shows goods. (Provide duplicated test that contains pictures of goods and services.)

Comprehension: Can you tell us the difference between goods and services?
Make a red line under each picture that shows goods and a blue line under each picture that shows services.

Application: How can we find out about goods and services in other families?
Make a line under the pictures that show goods produced by the Eskimo family.

Analysis: How is work divided at home to produce goods and services?
Make a line under the pictures that show mother producing services.

Synthesis: What shall we include in our picture chart to show goods and services?
Select pictures of goods and services from the table and arrange them on the chart.

Evaluation: How can we change our picture chart to show goods and services produced at home?

LEVELS OF AFFECTIVE RESPONSE

Receiving (Attending): What did you notice that was interesting when we visited the dairy farm?

---

[1] Benjamin S. Bloom, ed., *Taxonomy of Educational Objectives: Cognitive Domain* (New York: David McKay Co., Inc., 1956); and David R. Krathwohl, *et al.*, *Taxonomy of Educational Objectives: Affective Domain* (New York: David McKay Co., Inc., 1964).

Draw something that you liked at the dairy farm.

Responding: What was most interesting on the farm?
Draw a picture of what you would like to do on a farm.

Valuing: Can you tell why you would like to live on a farm?
Make a line under the pictures which show things you would like
to do. (Provide test with pictures showing farm and city activities
of children.)

STANDARDIZED TESTS

Standardized tests are available for the evaluation of concepts,
information, word-study skills, and critical thinking. They are
helpful in determining growth over a given period of time, in
planning curriculum revision, in giving group and individual
guidance, in appraising methods and materials, and in conducting
surveys and research purposes. They should not be used as *the*
basis for marking, promotion, rating of teachers, child-to-child
or school-to-school comparisons, or for rating a school system
in terms of national norms; the solution of these problems requires a wider range of data.

Standardized achievement tests should be recognized as only
one part of the total program of evaluation. Reasonable expectancies should be employed for each child and each group on
the basis of mental ability, growth rate, past achievement, and
pertinent background factors. If tests are given early in the year,
they may be used to indicate both individual and group needs,
and thereby to improve planning. Testing should extend over
several grades in order to give a developmental picture. Many
school systems give tests at the beginning of Grades IV, VII,
and IX, in order to facilitate planning in the elementary and
junior and senior high school.

In selecting standardized tests in the social studies, several criteria should be considered in addition to reliability, validity, objectivity, expense, and ease of administration. Questions of prime
importance are:

Is this test related to the social studies topics being considered?

Does this test cover the key learnings of importance to the
children for whom it is intended?

Is the level of difficulty appropriate for the children?

Is this test the best available one for this purpose?

If norms are to be used, are they suitable in terms of local
needs and conditions?

Can the test results be used with other information to assess
children's progress?

Does this test fit into the total pattern of evaluation?

The map shown below is a part of a road map. To help you to find quickly any city or town shown on the map, the names of the cities and towns have been arranged in alphabetical order, beginning near the top. The key to the map is given below it.

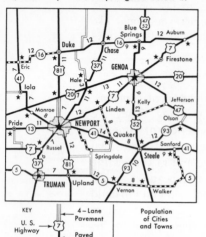

KEY			
U. S. Highway	7	4 – Lane Pavement	Population of Cities and Towns
State Highway	5	Paved Road	○ 0 – 1000
		Graveled Road	⊙ 1000 – 10,000
		Dirt Road	⊕ 10,000 – 25,000
			🏠 25,000 and over

79. What might be the population of Chase?
1) 5,296   3) 23,864
2) 9,231   4) 29,431

80. Assuming all paved highways to be in equally good condition, along which highway could one probably make the best time?
1) U.S. 20   3) U.S. 37
2) U.S. 7   4) U.S. 52

81. How far is it from Blue Springs to Newport by the shortest route?
1) 39 miles   3) 32 miles
2) 34 miles   4) 31 miles

82. What happens to U.S. Highway 52 after it enters Genoa from the south?
1) It ends.
2) It joins U.S. Highway 20.
3) It joins U.S. Highway 7.
4) It joins U.S. Highway 47.

Below is the table of contents of a book called *Playgrounds of America*. Use this table to answer the questions below it.

TABLE OF CONTENTS

37. What chapter would tell us whether Arizona has any national parks?
1) 1   2) 2   3) 3   4) 5

38. What chapter might tell us the rules for building campfires?
1) 4   2) 5   3) 6   4) 7

39. What chapter might tell us how bears are fed?
1) 6   2) 7   3) 8   4) 9

40. We want to find out where the park system gets the money for upkeep. In which chapter should we look?
1) 1   2) 2   3) 8   4) 9

41. If we wanted to know when the first national park was opened, we should look in which chapter?
1) 1   2) 2   3) 3   4) 8

Use the world map below in answering questions 35–39

35 Which letter on the globe locates the world's largest ocean?
1 X   3 Z
2 W   4 Y
35 ○ ○ ○ ○ (1 2 3 4)

36 Which of the following continents is completely shown on this map?
5 Asia   7 North America
6 Europe   8 Africa
36 ○ ○ ○ ○ (5 6 7 8)

37 Which of the following is *not* shown on this map?
1 the South Pole   3 a line of latitude
2 a line of longitude   4 the equator
37 ○ ○ ○ ○ (1 2 3 4)

38 The letter X is used to mark which body of water?
5 a gulf   7 a sea
6 an ocean   8 a tributary
38 ○ ○ ○ ○ (5 6 7 8)

39 In relation to most of the United States, South America is —
1 directly south   3 at the same longitude
2 farther west   4 farther east
39 ○ ○ ○ ○ (1 2 3 4)

DIRECTIONS
*Reading Tables,
Charts and Graphs*

This is a test of how well you can read tables, charts and graphs. Choose the best answer for each question and put a cross through the letter ·in front of the answer you have chosen.

Use the picture graph below in answering questions 16–20.

Number of Appliances Repaired in an Electrical Repair Shop During One Week.

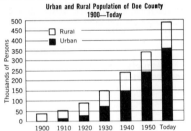

Television sets	
Radios	
Electric mixers	
Washing machines	
Toasters	
Electric irons	
Electric clocks	
Waffle irons	

Each symbol equals one appliance.

Use the bar graph below in answering questions 21–24.

**Urban and Rural Population of Doe County
1900—Today**

Thousands of Persons

☐ Rural
■ Urban

1900 1910 1920 1930 1940 1950 Today

Use the chart below in answering questions 25–29.

Ship's Time in Bells Corresponding to Land Time.

Ship's Time in Bells	LAND TIME					
	Before 12 Noon			After 12 Noon		
1	12:30	4:30	8:30	12:30	4:30	8:30
2	1:00	5:00	9:00	1:00	5:00	9:00
3	1:30	5:30	9:30	1:30	5:30	9:30
4	2:00	6:00	10:00	2:00	6:00	10:00
5	2:30	6:30	10:30	2:30	6:30	10:30
6	3:00	7:00	11:00	3:00	7:00	11:00
7	3:30	7:30	11:30	3:30	7:30	11:30
8	4:00	8:00	12:00	4:00	8:00	12:00

16 This shop repaired the same number of waffle irons as what other appliance?
[a] television sets   [b] electric clocks
[c] washing machines   [d] cannot tell from the graph

17 How did the number of toasters repaired compare with the number of electric mixers repaired?
[e] The same number of each were repaired.
[f] Four times as many toasters were repaired.
[g] Twice as many electric mixers were repaired.
[h] Half as many electric mixers were repaired.

18 How many of the electric appliances shown can be used to receive world news?
[a] 1   [b] 2   [c] 3   [d] none

19 The number of electric clocks repaired was exactly one-half the number of which other appliance repaired?
[e] radios   [f] electric irons
[g] television sets   [h] cannot tell from the graph

20 Which of the electrical appliances shown costs the most to repair?
[a] television set   [b] washing machine
[c] radio   [d] cannot tell from the graph

21 In which year was the urban·population the smallest part of the total population?
[e] 1900   [f] 1910   [g] 1930   [h] none of these

22 During which of the following periods did the total population show the greatest increase in number?
[a] 1900–1910   [b] 1930–1940
[c] 1940–1950   [d] 1950–Today

23 In which of the following years was the total population about twice as large as it was in 1900?
[e] 1920   [f] 1930   [g] 1940   [h] 1950

24 The rural and urban populations were about equal in —
[a] 1900   [b] 1920   [c] 1930   [d] 1940

25 At 11:30 A.M., ship's time would be —
[e] 7 bells   [f] 4 bells   [g] 1 bell   [h] none of these

26 If the ship's bell were to ring "one" just after sunset on a summer evening along the eastern seaboard of the United States, the land time would be —
[a] 8:30 A.M. [b] 12:30 P.M. [c] 4:30 P.M. [d] 8:30 P.M.

27 At which one of the following times would the ship's bell *not* ring "three"?
[e] 1:30 A.M. [f] 9:30 A.M. [g] 2:30 P.M. [h] 9:30 P.M.

28 How many times during a period of 24 hours is the time reported on board ship?
[a] 100   [b] 48   [c] 32   [d] 24

29 How many hours must pass before the ship's bell will again ring the same number of times?
[e] 24   [f] 12   [g] 8   [h] 4

27   SOCIAL STUDIES STUDY SKILLS SCORE _____

Top, left page. Iowa Tests of Basic Skills, Form 2 (Boston: Houghton Mifflin Co.)
Bottom, left page. Stanford Achievement Test: Social Studies: Intermediate Land II (New York: Harcourt, Brace & World, Inc.)

Above. Metropolitan Achievement Tests: Intermediate Battery—Complete: Form B (New York: Harcourt, Brace & World, Inc.)

A recent trend in the construction of standardized tests has been to include items that assess children's ability to apply understandings and to use work-study skills. In addition, attention is given to the measurement of basic concepts, information, and generalizations. On pages 548 and 549 you will find examples of items in recently published tests.

SOURCES OF INFORMATION ON STANDARDIZED TESTS

Many standardized tests are available for use in the social studies. Some of them are included in general achievement tests, and others are available as separate tests. An excellent source of information on recently published tests is *The Sixth Mental Measurements Yearbook*, edited by Oscar K. Buros (Highland Park, N.J.: The Gryphon Press, 1966). Another good source of information on tests currently available is *Tests In Print*, by Oscar K. Buros (Highland Park, N.J.: The Gryphon Press, 1961). The second source also has an index to earlier *Mental Measurements Yearbooks* that have been published. The following list includes social studies tests which are described in greater detail in the above references:

American School Achievement Tests: Part 4, Social Studies and Science. Public School Publishing Company, 345 Calhoun Street, Cincinnati 19, Ohio. For Grades IV–VI and VII–IX, social studies achievement.

California Tests in Social and Related Sciences. California Test Bureau, Del Monte Research Park, Monterey, California. For Grades IV–VIII, information and processes.

Coordinated Scales of Attainment. Educational Test Bureau, Educational Publishers, Inc., Minneapolis, Minnesota. For Grades IV–VIII, history and geography.

Iowa Tests of Basic Skills. Houghton Mifflin Company, 2 Park Street, Boston 7, Massachusetts. For Grades III–IX, work-study skills including map reading.

Metropolitan Achievement Battery, and *Stanford Achievement Tests*. Harcourt, Brace & World, Inc., 750 Third Avenue, New York 17, New York. For Grades V–VI and VII–IX, information and skills.

Sequential Tests of Educational Progress. Educational Testing Service, Princeton, New Jersey. For Grades IV–VI and VII–IX, understandings and skills.

Questions, Activities, Evaluation

1. Consider practical ways in which each of the basic guidelines to effective evaluation (presented in the first section of this chapter) may be used in the social studies. Which do you believe to be the most difficult to apply? Which do you believe need to be given greater emphasis by teachers at the present time?

2. In what ways can you provide for self-evaluation by children in a unit you are planning?

3. Examine a cumulative record currently being used in a school system in your area. What provision is made for the recording of progress in the social studies? What additional provisions, if any, are needed?

4. How can you use observation as a technique of evaluation in a unit you are planning? Discussion? Anecdotal records? Interviews? Logs and diaries? Case studies?

5. Prepare a sample chart, a sample checklist, and a brief questionnaire that you might use in a unit you are planning to teach. Discuss them critically with fellow students or teachers.

6. Prepare several objective-type test items in each form discussed in this chapter. Plan items that you can use in a unit.

7. Examine two or three of the standardized tests listed in this chapter. What outcomes of instruction are they designed to appraise? How might they be used in a complete program of evaluation?

References

Bloom, Benjamin S., ed., *Taxonomy of Educational Objectives: Cognitive Domain*. New York: David McKay Co., Inc., 1956. Sample items on various levels.

Dunfee, Maxine, and Helen Sagl, *Social Studies through Problem Solving*. New York: Holt, Rinehart & Winston, Inc., 1966. Sample items and charts.

Gage, N. L., ed., *The Handbook of Research on Teaching*. Chicago: Rand McNally & Co., 1963. Section on the social studies.

Jarolimek, John, *Social Studies in Elementary Education*. New York: The Macmillan Company, 1967. Principles and techniques.

Krathwohl, David R., Benjamin S. Bloom, and Bertram B. Mesia, *Taxonomy of Educational Objectives: Affective Domain*. New York: David McKay Co., Inc., 1964. Sample items on various levels.

Kurfman, Dana G., and Robert J. Solomon, "Measurement of Growth in Skills," *Skill Development in the Social Studies,* 33rd Yearbook, National Council for the Social Studies, pp. 274–95. Washington, D.C.: National Education Association, 1963. Techniques and sample test items.

Lee, John R., and Jonathon C. McClendon, eds., *Readings on Elementary Social Studies.* Boston: Allyn & Bacon, Inc., 1965. Collection of articles.

Lindeman, Richard H., *Educational Measurement.* Chicago: Scott, Foresman & Company, 1967. Background concepts, principles, and techniques.

Standards for Educational and Psychological Tests and Manuals. Washington, D.C.: American Psychological Association, 1966. Guidelines for planning and assessing tests.

Index

707675